AMERICAN DIARIES IN MANUSCRIPT, 1580–1954
A Descriptive Bibliography

American Diaries in Manuscript, 1580–1954
A Descriptive Bibliography

William Matthews

University of Georgia Press, Athens

Library of Congress Catalog Card Number: 73-76782
International Standard Book Number: 0-8203-0318-6

The University of Georgia Press, Athens 30602

Printed in the United States of America

Contents

Preface

This annotated list of American diaries, nearly all of them unpublished, some published only in part, is a supplement to my *American Diaries* (1945, 1959) which was restricted to published documents. The present list contains over 5,000 name entries and a much larger number of manuscripts and copies of them. It is the harvest of over twenty years of collection, and it is put out now, not because it is in any way complete, but rather because since about 1965 new contributions have become few and the earlier contributors may well be impatient by now, or dead.

The format is basically the same as in the earlier book. However, to permit the more numerous items to be listed in manageable compass, pagination and biographical data about the diarists have been omitted. Each entry therefore gives the name of the writer, the time–span of his diary, a brief characterization of its contents and interest, and a succinct statement (using Library of Congress symbols) of the places where the diary and copies are located. Where no knowledge is available as to the contents of a diary the pregnant initials CNS (contents not stated) are employed. The arrangement is chronological, according to the beginning years of the documents, and within each year the arrangement is alphabetical by author, beginning with anonymous authors who are arranged by order of months of beginning. Undated diaries are gathered together at the end. An author–index is appended, and cross-references are given within the body of the bibliography to other diaries by the same writers.

The list is essentially a cooperative effort. Over the years, my wife and I have examined a score or so of the large collections owned by important university and city libraries. My former assistant, Mrs. Julia Strong (Simmons), scanned about eighty published lists of manuscripts owned by major American libraries. The rest of the list, however, is the contribution of librarians and archivists throughout the country, and I now take pleasure in reiterating publicly my thanks to these for their cooperation, together with apologies for the long delay in bringing their offerings into publication. They are too numerous to identify here by name, but my thanks are none the less sincere for that. My thanks also go to the numerous librarians who reported that their libraries owned no diaries and to various private owners: to the latter also go my apologies, since in revising the list it was decided to omit the privately-owned items for various reasons.

In the early stages of the compilation, all American university, college, city, and historical libraries were applied to for listings. For very understandable reasons, not all of them were able to cooperate. But by one means or another, the holdings of over three hundred and fifty libraries, large and small, have been incorporated in this list. For a variety of reasons, most of them practical, no attempt was made to track down the many new and old diaries that must be in private hands. To two assistants who bore much of the heavy burden of the resultant correspondence, Julia Strong and Robert Gerecke, I once more express my deep gratitude. For invaluable help with the symbols and with checking, I am also deeply indebted to W. Bruce Knapp and to my wife Lois.

As it is here presented, the list is in no way a complete record of all the manuscript diaries in American libraries and it therefore probably represents some areas and some periods less fully than others. Neither can it be claimed that the list has the systematic perfection that the scholar always hopes for in a bibliography. The annotations are uneven: some contributors submitted lengthy analyses, which unfortunately have had to be drastically shortened; some contributed minimal notes; others could not report on the contents. Despite these unevennesses and limitations, however, the work assembles the scholarly devotion of a great many people and, presenting as it does an enormous body of largely unused and unknown material on every aspect of American life, it should prove a useful aid in a great variety of historical and humane studies.

William Matthews

University of California
Los Angeles

Symbols of the Contributing Libraries

The following symbols are used to designate the contributing libraries. The code follows that of the Library of Congress (see *Symbols of American Libraries*, 10th edition, Washington, D.C., 1969). Where no symbol had been assigned by the Library of Congress, one was created. Most of the symbols follow the pattern of the abbreviation for the state first, the abbreviation for the city second, and the abbreviation for the organization last. For example, "NIC" indicates: New York—Ithaca—Cornell University.

A-Ar	Department of Archives and History, Montgomery, Alabama
AzTp	Arizona Pioneers' Historical Society, Tucson, Arizona
BM	British Museum Library, London, W.C.1
BrLPro	Public Records Office, London, E.C. 4
C	California State Library, Sacramento, California
CaMWHi	Manitoba Historical Society, Winnipeg, Canada
CaOOA	Public Archives of Canada, Ottawa, Ontario
CaOOHa	Haldimand Collection, Canadian Archives, Ottawa, Ontario
CaOTHi	Ontario County Historical Society, Toronto 12, Ontario
CaOTP	Toronto Public Library, Toronto, Ontario
CBPac	Pacific School of Religion, Holbrook Memorial Library, Berkeley, California
CCP	Pomona College, Claremont, California
CFM	Monterey-Fresno Diocesan Archives, Fresno, California
CFS	Fresno State College, Fresno, California
CHi	California Historical Society, San Francisco, California
CL	Los Angeles Public Library, Los Angeles, California
CLob	Long Beach Public Library, Long Beach, California
CLSM	Southwest Museum, Los Angeles, California
CLU	University of California, Los Angeles, California
CLU-C	William Andrews Clark Memorial Library, Los Angeles, California
CoU	University of Colorado, Boulder, Colorado
CSaT	San Francisco Theological Seminary, San Anselmo, California
CSbCL	San Bernardino County Free Library, San Bernardino, California
CSd	San Diego Public Library, San Diego, California

CSdHi	San Diego Historical Society, San Diego, California
CSdJHi	Junipero Serra Historical Museum, San Diego, California
CSfC	California State Library, San Francisco, California
CSfCP	Society of California Pioneers, San Francisco, California
CSfU	University of San Francisco, San Francisco, California
CSmatHi	San Mateo Historical Society, San Mateo, California
CSmH	Henry E. Huntington Library, San Marino, California
CSSfm	Sutter's Fort Historical Museum, Sacramento, California
CSt	Stanford University, Stanford, California
CStoPM	San Joaquin Pioneer Museum, Stockton, California
Ct	Connecticut State Library, Hartford, Connecticut
CtCLA	Cornwall Library Association, Cornwall, Connecticut
CtDio	Diocese of Connecticut
CtGuE	Eliot Museum, Guilford, Connecticut
CtHi	Connecticut Historical Society, Hartford, Connecticut
CtLiHi	Litchfield Historical Society, Litchfield, Connecticut
CtMBds	Berkely Divinity School, Middletown, Connecticut
CtMyMM	Marine Museum of the Marine Historical Association, Mystic, Connecticut
CtNhCl	Clark Memorial Library, Woodbridge, New Haven, Connecticut
CtNhHi	New Haven Colony Historical Society, New Haven, Connecticut
CtNl	New London Public Library, New London, Connecticut
CtNlHi	New London County Historical Society, New London, Connecticut
CtY	Yale University, New Haven, Connecticut
CtY-Art	John N. Phillips Art Gallery, Yale University, New Haven, Connecticut
CU	University of California, Berkeley, California
CU-B	Bancroft Library, University of California, Berkeley, California
CVt	Ventura Public Library, Ventura, California
DCU	Catholic University of America, Washington, D.C.
De-Ar	Public Archives Commission, Dover, Delaware
DeHi	Historical Society of Delaware, Wilmington, Delaware
DeU	University of Delaware, Newark, Delaware
DLC	Library of Congress, Washington, D.C.
DNW	National War College, Washington, D.C.
DS	U. S. Department of State Library, Washington, D.C.
FDS	John B. Stetson University, De Land, Florida
FJHi	Florida Historical Society, Jacksonville, Florida
FSaWml	Webb Memorial Library, St. Augustine, Florida
FSlA	St. Leo Abbey Library, St. Leo, Florida
FSM	McClellan Memorial Room, Sarasota, Florida
FSpHi	St. Petersburg Memorial Historical Museum, St. Petersburg, Florida
FTaSCW	Florida State University, Tallahassee, Florida
FU	University of Florida, Gainesville, Florida
G-Ar	Georgia Department of Archives, Atlanta, Georgia
GEU	Emory University, Atlanta, Georgia
GHi	Georgia Historical Society, Savannah, Georgia
GU	University of Georgia, Athens, Georgia
IaCb	Council Bluffs Public Library, Council Bluffs, Iowa
IaCbHi	Pottawattamie County Historical Society, Council Bluffs, Iowa

Ia-HA	Iowa State Department of History and Archives, Des Moines, Iowa
IaKe	Keokuk Public Library, Keokuk, Iowa
IAlbHi	Edwards County Historical Society, Albion, Illinois
Ia-M	Iowa State Medical Library, Des Moines, Iowa
IC	Chicago Public Library, Chicago, Illinois
ICGw	George Williams College Library, Chicago, Illinois
ICHi	Chicago Historical Society, Chicago, Illinois
ICMcCHi	McCormick Historical Association, Chicago, Illinois
ICN	Newberry Library, Chicago, Illinois
IdHi	Idaho Historical Museum, Boise, Idaho
IHi	Illinois State Historical Library, Springfield, Illinois
IHS	Illinois Historical Survey
InEm	Evansville Public Museum, Evansville, Illinois
InGoM	Mennonite Church Archives, Goshen, Indiana
InHi	Indiana Historical Society, Indianapolis, Indiana
InLHi	Tippecanoe County Historical Association, Lafayette, Indiana
InNcHi	Henry County Historical Society, New Castle, Indiana
InNd	University of Notre Dame, South Bend, Indiana
InRE	Earlham College, Richmond, Indiana
InU	Indiana University, Bloomington, Indiana
InU-Li	Lilly Library, Indiana University, Bloomington, Indiana
IRoDC	Diocesan Chancery, Rockford, Illinois
IU	University of Illinois, Urbana, Illinois
KHi	Kansas State Historical Society, Topeka, Kansas
KU	University of Kansas, Lawrence, Kansas
KyHi	Kentucky Historical Society, Frankfort, Kentucky
KyLoF	The Filson Club, Louisville, Kentucky
KyU	University of Kentucky, Lexington, Kentucky
KyU-Ar	University of Kentucky Archives, Lexington, Kentucky
LNHT	Tulane University, New Orleans, Louisiana
LSh	Shreve Memorial Library, Shreveport, Louisiana
LU	Louisiana State University, Baton Rouge, Louisiana
LU-Ar	Louisiana State University, Department of Archives, Baton Rouge, Louisiana
MAr	Arlington Public Library, Arlington, Massachusetts
MArHi	Arlington Historical Society, Arlington, Massachusetts
MB	Boston Public Library, Boston, Massachusetts
MBAd	Adams Manuscript Trust, Boston, Massachusetts
MBAr	Massachusetts Archives, Boston, Massachusetts
MBAt	Boston Atheneum, Boston, Massachusetts
MBBHi	Backus Historical Society, Boston, Massachusetts
MBC	Congregational Library, Boston, Massachusetts
MBD	Massachusetts Episcopal Diocesan Library, Boston, Massachusetts
MBMa	Mayflower Society, Boston, Massachusetts
MBNEH	New England Historical and Genealogical Society, Boston, Massachusetts
MBr	Brookline Public Library, Brookline, Massachusetts
MBrid	Bridgewater Public Library, Bridgewater, Massachusetts
MBSpnea	Society for the Preservation of New England Antiquities, Boston, Massachusetts
MdAA	Hall of Records, Annapolis, Maryland
MdAn	United States Naval Academy Museum, Annapolis, Maryland

MdBDio	Baltimore Catholic Archdiocese, Baltimore, Maryland
MDed	Dedham Public Library, Dedham, Massachusetts
MDedHi	Dedham Historical Society, Dedham, Massachusetts
MDeeP	Pocumtuck Valley Memorial Association, Deerfield, Massachusetts
MdHi	Maryland Historical Society, Baltimore, Maryland
Me	Maine State Library, Augusta, Maine
MeAlP	Parsons Memorial Library, Alfred, Maine
MeB	Bowdoin College, Brunswick, Maine
MeBa	Bangor Public Library, Bangor, Maine
MeBaHi	Bangor Historical Society, Bangor, Maine
MeBP	Penobscot Historical Society, Brunswick, Maine
MeCa	Calais Free Library, Calais, Maine
MeHi	Maine Historical Society, Portland, Maine
MeMonC	Chippewa County Historical Society, Montevideo, Maine
MeP	Portland Public Library, Portland, Maine
MePhl	Paris Hill Library, Paris Hill, Maine
MeSacoY	York Institute, Saco, Maine
MeWC	Colby College, Waterville, Maine
MeWHi	Waterville Historical Society, Waterville, Maine
MFiHi	Fitchburg Historical Society, Fitchburg, Massachusetts
MFm	Framingham Historical Society, Framingham, Massachusetts
MH	Harvard University, Cambridge, Massachusetts
MHa	Haverhill Public Library, Haverhill, Massachusetts
MHaHi	Haverhill Historical Society, Haverhill, Massachusetts
MHi	Massachusetts Historical Society, Boston, Massachusetts
MiD	Detroit Public Library, Detroit, Michigan
MiDbHi	Dearborn Historical Museum, Dearborn, Michigan
MiHi	Michigan State Historical Society, Lansing, Michigan
MiMarqHi	Marquette County Historical Society, Marquette, Michigan
MiMHi	Monroe County Historical Society, Monroe, Michigan
MIpHi	Ipswich Historical Society, Ipswich, Massachusetts
MiU	University of Michigan, Ann Arbor, Michigan
MiU-C	Wm. L. Clements Library, University of Michigan, Ann Arbor, Michigan
MiU-H	Michigan Historical Collection, University of Michigan, Ann Arbor, Michigan
MLa	Lancaster Town Library, Lancaster, Massachusetts
MLexHi	Lexington Historical Society, Lexington, Massachusetts
MLo	Longmeadow Town Library, Longmeadow, Massachusetts
MMe	Medford Public Library, Medford, Massachusetts
MnDu	Duluth Public Library, Duluth, Minnesota
MnDuHi	St. Louis County Historical Society, Duluth, Minnesota
MNeHi	Ould Newberry Historical Society, Newburyport, Massachusetts
MNF	Forbes Library, Northampton, Massachusetts
MnGlHi	Pope County Historical Society, Glenwood, Minnesota
MnHi	Minnesota Historical Society, St. Paul, Minnesota
MnHuHi	McLeod County Historical Society, Hutchinson, Minnesota
MnMAAr	Augsburg Archaeological Society, Augsburg College, Minneapolis, Minnesota
MnManHi	Blue Earth County Historical Society, Mankato, Minnesota
MnMcHi	Morrison County Historical Society, Little Falls, Minnesota
MnMHi	Hennepin County Historical Society, Minneapolis, Minnesota
MnMohCHi	Clay County Historical Society, Moorhead, Minnesota
MnNuHi	Brown County Historical Society, New Ulm, Minnesota

MnRedHi	Goodhue County Historical Society, Red Wing, Minnesota
MnRHi	Olmstead County Historical Society, Rochester, Minnesota
MnSH	Hamline University, St. Paul, Minnesota
MnSSb	Swedish Baptist General Conference of America, St. Paul, Minnesota
MnStclHi	Stearns County Historical Society, St. Cloud, Minnesota
MnU	University of Minnesota, Minneapolis, Minnesota
MnWoHi	Nobles County Historical Society, Worthington, Minnesota
MoSHi	Missouri Historical Society, St. Louis, Missouri
MoSHs	Historical Society of St. Louis, St. Louis, Missouri
MoSU	St. Louis University, St. Louis, Missouri
MoU	University of Missouri, Columbia, Missouri
MPB	Berkshire Atheneum, Pittsfield, Massachusetts
MPlPh	Pilgrim Hall, Plymouth, Massachusetts
MSaE	Essex Institute, Salem, Massachusetts
Ms-Ar	Mississippi Department of Archives, Jackson, Mississippi
MScC	Scituate Center, Scituate, Massachusetts
MSuGL	Goodnow Library, Sudbury, Massachusetts
MTaHi	Old Colony Historical Society, Taunton, Massachusetts
MtHi	Montana State Historical Society, Helena, Montana
MTop	Topsfield Public Library, Topsfield, Massachusetts
MWA	American Antiquarian Society, Worcester, Massachusetts
MWalHi	Waltham Historical Society, Waltham, Massachusetts
MWe	Westfield Public Library, Westfield, Massachusetts
MWeAt	Westfield Atheneum, Westfield, Massachusetts
MWeHi	Western Hampton Historical Society, Westfield, Massachusetts
MWHi	Worcester Historical Society, Worcester, Massachusetts
MWob	Woburn Public Library, Woburn, Massachusetts
N	New York State Library, Albany, New York
NAlU	University of the State of New York, Division of Archives and History, State Education Department, Albany, New York
NbCcHi	Merrick County Historical Society, Central City, Nebraska
NbFrOs	Old Settlers and Historical Association of Dodge City, Fremont, Nebraska
NbHi	Nebraska State Historical Society, Lincoln, Nebraska
NBLiHi	Long Island Historical Society, Brooklyn, New York
NbOP	Presbyterian Theological Seminary, Omaha, Nebraska
NbOUpm	Union Pacific Museum, Omaha, Nebraska
NbU	University of Nebraska, Lincoln, Nebraska
NBu	Buffalo Public Library, Buffalo, New York
NBuC	University of Buffalo, Buffalo, New York
NBuHi	Buffalo Historical Society, Buffalo, New York
NCanHi	Ontario County Historical Society, Canandaigua, New York
Nc-Ar	North Carolina Department of Archives, Raleigh, North Carolina
NcBe	Belmont Abbey College, Belmont, North Carolina
NcD	Duke University, Durham, North Carolina
NcHiC	North Carolina Historical Commission, Raleigh, North Carolina
NCooHi	New York State Historical Association, Cooperstown, New York
NcU	University of North Carolina, Chapel Hill, North Carolina
NcWsM	Archives of the Moravian Church, Southern Province, Winston-Salem, North Carolina
NdHi	North Dakota State Historical Society, Bismarck, North Dakota

NElmHi	Chemung County Historical Society, Elmira, New York
NhD	Dartmouth College, Hanover, New Hampshire
NhHi	New Hampshire Historical Society, Concord, New Hampshire
NHi	New York Historical Society, New York, New York
NIC	Cornell University, Ithaca, New York
NjBt	Blair Academy, Blairstown, New Jersey
NjCmHi	Cape May County Historical Museum, Cape May, New Jersey
NjEliHi	Union County Historical Society, Elizabeth, New Jersey
NjHi	New Jersey Historical Society, Newark, New Jersey
NjNb	New Brunswick Public Library, New Brunswick, New Jersey
NjPatPHi	Passaic County Historical Society, Paterson, New Jersey
NjR	Rutgers University, New Brunswick, New Jersey
NjSpAHi	Atlantic County Historical Society, Somers Point, New Jersey
NjT	Trenton Public Library, Trenton, New Jersey
NjUnHi	Union Township Historical Society, Union, New Jersey
NjViHi	Vineland Historical and Antiquarian Society, Vineland, New Jersey
NKiSh	Senate House Museum, Kingston, New York
NmU	University of New Mexico, Albuquerque, New Mexico
NN	New York Public Library, New York, New York
NNArAr	Archives of the Archdiocese of New York, New York, New York
NNC	Columbia University, New York, New York
NNNGB	New York Genealogical and Biographical Society, New York, New York
NNPM	J. Pierpont Morgan Library, New York, New York
NP	Adriance Memorial Library, Poughkeepsie, New York
NPHi	Dutchess County Historical Society, Poughkeepsie, New York
NPV	Vassar College, Poughkeepsie, New York
NSchHi	Schenectady County Historical Society, Schenectady, New York
NSchoHi	Schoharie County Historical Society, Schoharie, New York
NSchoOsfm	Old Stone Fort Museum, Schoharie, New York
NSchU	Union College, Schenectady, New York
NUtHi	Oneida Historical Society, Utica, New York
NvHi	Nevada State Historical Society, Reno, Nevada
NvU	University of Nevada, Reno, Nevada
NWM	U. S. Military Academy, West Point, New York
NYStJDio	New York Archdiocesan Archives, Yonkers, New York
OCAJA	American Jewish Archives, Cincinnati, Ohio
OClWHi	Western Reserve Historical Society, Cleveland, Ohio
OCoNg	Old Northwest Genealogical Society, Columbus, Ohio
OCUHi	Historical and Philosophical Society of Ohio, University of Cincinnati, Cincinnati, Ohio
OCX	Xavier University, Cincinnati, Ohio
ODa	Dayton Public Library, Dayton, Ohio
OFH	Rutherford B. Hayes Memorial Library, Fremont, Ohio
OHi	Ohio State Archaeological and Historical Society, Columbus, Ohio
OkHi	Oklahoma Historical Society, Oklahoma City, Oklahoma
OkU	Oklahoma University, Norman, Oklahoma
OMC	Marietta College Library, Marietta, Ohio
OMCmm	Campus Martius Museum, Marietta, Ohio
OO	Oberlin College, Oberlin, Ohio
Or	Oregon State Library, Salem, Oregon

OrB	Desckutes County Library, Bend, Oregon
OrFP	Pacific University, Forest Grove, Oregon
OrHi	Oregon Historical Society, Portland, Oregon
OrP	Library Association of Portland, Oregon
OrSaW	Willamette University, Salem, Oregon
OrTilPa	Tillamook County Pioneer Association, Portland, Oregon
OrU	University of Oregon, Eugene, Oregon
OrVMa	Malheur County Pioneer Association, Vale, Oregon
OSHi	Clark County Historical Society, Springfield, Ohio
PAthT	Tioga Point Museum, Athens, Pennsylvania
PBMCA	Archives of the Moravian Church, Northern Province, Bethlehem, Pennsylvania
PCAmB	American Baptist Historical Society, Chester, Pennsylvania
PCarlA	Army War College, Carlisle Barracks, Pennsylvania
PCC	Crozer Theological Seminary, Chester, Pennsylvania
PEL	Lafayette College, Easton, Pennsylvania
PEL-Kpsm	Kirby Political Science Museum, Lafayette College, Easton, Pennsylvania
PHC	Haverford College Library, Haverford, Pennsylvania
PHi	Historical Society of Pennsylvania, Philadelphia, Pennsylvania
PLeHi	Lebanon County Historical Society, Lebanon, Pennsylvania
PLhA	Annie Halenbake Ross Library, Lock Haven, Pennsylvania
PLuL	Lincoln University, Lincoln, Pennsylvania
PMA	Allegheny College, Meadville, Pennsylvania
PPAmS	American Philosophical Society, Philadelphia, Pennsylvania
PPCHi	Church Historical Society, Philadelphia, Pennsylvania
PPG	German Society of Pennsylvania, Philadelphia, Pennsylvania
PPh	Public Library of the Phoenixville School District, Chester County, Pennsylvania
PPHiA	Historical Society of the Philadelphia Annual Conference of the Methodist Episcopal Church, Philadelphia, Pennsylvania
PPi	Carnegie Library, Pittsburgh, Pennsylvania
PPiAcssmh	Allegheny County Soldiers and Sailors Memorial Hall, Pittsburgh, Pennsylvania
PPiPT	Pittsburgh (Xenia) Theological Seminary, Pittsburgh, Pennsylvania
PPL	Library Company of Philadelphia, Philadelphia, Pennsylvania
PPM	Mercantile Library, Philadelphia, Pennsylvania
PPoHi	Historical Society of Schuylkill County, Pottsville, Pennsylvania
PPPRHi	Presbyterian Historical Society, Philadelphia, Pennsylvania
PRHi	Historical Society of Berks County, Reading, Pennsylvania
PSC	Swarthmore College, Philadelphia, Pennsylvania
PSC-Hi	Friends' Historical Library, Swarthmore College, Philadelphia, Pennsylvania
PSew	Sewickley Public Library, Sewickley, Pennsylvania
PV	Villanova College, Philadelphia, Pennsylvania
PVfm	Valley Forge Museum of American History, Valley Forge, Pennsylvania
PWaHi	Greene County Historical Museum, Waynesburg, Pennsylvania
PWbWhgs	Wyoming Historical and Geological Society, Wilkes-Barre, Pennsylvania
PWcHi	Chester County Historical Society, West Chester, Pennsylvania
PWmHi	Lycoming Historical Society, Williamsport, Pennsylvania
PWmP	James V. Brown Library, Williamsport, Pennsylvania
PWW	Washington and Jefferson College, Washington, Pennsylvania
RHi	Rhode Island Historical Society, Providence, Rhode Island

RLcHi	Little Compton Historical Society, Little Compton, Rhode Island
RNHi	Newport Historical Society, Newport, Rhode Island
RPB	John Hay Library, Brown University, Providence, Rhode Island
ScC	Charleston Library Society, Charleston, South Carolina
ScCC	College of Charleston, Charleston, South Carolina
ScHi	South Carolina Historical Society, Charleston, South Carolina
ScU	University of South Carolina, Columbia, South Carolina
TC	Chattanooga Public Library, Chattanooga, Tennessee
THi	Tennessee Historical Society, Nashville, Tennessee
TMG	Goodwyn Institute, Memphis, Tennessee
TNJ-P	George Peabody College for Teachers, Nashville, Tennessee
Tx	Texas State Library, Austin, Texas
TxGR	Rosenberg Library, Galveston, Texas
UHi	Utah State Historical Society, Salt Lake City, Utah
Vi	Virginia State Library, Richmond, Virginia
ViHi	Virginia Historical Society, Richmond, Virginia
ViU	University of Virginia, Charlottesville, Virginia
ViWC	Colonial Williamsburg, Williamsburg, Virginia
ViWI	Institute of Early American History and Culture, Williamsburg, Virginia
VtHi	Vermont Historical Society, Montpelier, Vermont
VtMiS	Sheldon Art and Archaeological Museum, Middlebury, Vermont
WAnHi	Langlade County Historical Society, Antigo, Wisconsin
WaPS	State College of Washington (now WSU), Pullman, Washington
WaS	Seattle Public Library, Seattle, Washington
WaSp	Spokane Public Library, Spokane, Washington
WaU	University of Washington, Seattle, Washington
WaWW	Whitman College, Walla Walla, Washington
WBaHi	Sauk County Historical Society Museum, Baraboo, Wisconsin
WBurHi	Burlington Historical Society, Burlington, Wisconsin
WHi	State Historical Society of Wisconsin, Madison, Wisconsin
WOshM	Oshkosh Public Museum, Oshkosh, Wisconsin
WRacHr	Historical Room, Racine, Wisconsin
WS	Superior Public Library, Superior, Wisconsin
WSheHi	Sheboygan County Historical Society, Sheboygan, Wisconsin
WSHi	Douglas County Historical Museum, Superior, Wisconsin
Wv-Ar	West Virginia Department of Archives and History, Charleston, West Virginia
WWauHi	Waukesha County Historical Society, Waukesha, Wisconsin

1   MAUCAUBIS, Francissi. 1580. CNS. NcBe.

2   FLEETE, Henry. 1631. A voyage to Va. DLC, transcript.

3   LOTHROP, Rev. John. 1634–1653. Happenings in the church; private affairs. CtY.

4   FISKE, Rev. John. 1637–1675. Cases of church discipline within the membership, theological discussions; ecclesiastical councils held in the neighborhood; some baptisms and names of church members. MSaE.

5   SHEPARD, Rev. Thomas. 1640–1644. Record of his religious experiences. NN.

6   KEAYNE, Robert. 1643–1646. Notes of sermons preached by John Wilson. RHi.

7   COXERE, Edward. 1647–1684. Adventures at sea. British Quaker. Published. DLC.

8   BOWNE, John. 1649–1677. Travels in England, America, and West Indies; imprisonment and exile. NN; NHi.

9   WILLOUGHBY, Gov. Francis. 1650–1651. Fire at Charlestown (in cipher). MWA.

10   HIDE, William. 1652?–1716. Sermons; family records; deaths; Newton, Mass. MBNEH. *Same as 51?*

11   WHITING, Rev. Samuel. 1653. Sermons and lectures at Cambridge. MWA.

12   MATHER, Rev. Increase. 1659–1721 (with gaps). Personal insight into his daily life. MWA.

13   COTTON, Rev. Seaborn. 1662–1710. Church meetings; personal items; receipts; marriages, baptisms; family statistics; members of his church; admissions. MBNEH.

14   BATTS, Thomas. 1671. Journal from Va. beyond the Appalachian Mountains. MH.

15   WELCH, George. 1671. Voyage to the West Indies. PPAmS.

16   PENN, William. 1672. Diary of the founder of Pa. during a journey through Kent, Sussex, and Surrey. PHi.

17   CHALKLEY, Thomas. 1675–1724. Journal of a Quaker. PHi.

18   HULL, John. 1675–1676. Military affairs of Mass. Colony; accounts of the government. MB; MBNEH, commonplace-book with notes of sermons.

19   DANKERS, Jasper and Sluyter. 1679–1680. A voyage to N.Y. and a tour of the American colonies. NBLiHi.

20   GILLAM, Benjamin. 1682. A voyage from Boston into Hudson's Bay. CSmH.

21   KNEPP, John. 1683–1684. A voyage in the H.M.S. *Rose*, from the Downs to Boston, and return in the *Thomas and Susan*. DLC, British transcript.

22   WATSON, William. 1684. His voyage with his family from Nottingham, England, to Philadelphia, and to Burlington, West Jersey, where he settled. PHi.

23   HOMES, Rev. William. 1688–1746. Records of births, marriages, and deaths. MBNEH.

24   STRONG, John. 1689–1691. A voyage to the South Seas in the ship *Welfare*. DLC, British transcript.

25   LINDSTROM, Peter. 1691. Account of New Sweden on the Delaware; topography of the territory; society and economic development in the settlements; war with the Dutch (in Swedish). PHi, copy.

26   MATHER, Rev. Cotton. 1692–1717 (with gaps). CNS. MWA.

27 GREENWOOD, Rev. Thomas. 1694–1783. Baptisms, marriages, deaths; records of church business; councils, etc.; after his death kept by Rev. John Greenwood and Rev. Ephraim Hyde. Congregational Church, Seakonk, Mass.

28 HANCOCK, Rev. John. 1694. Sermons. MBNEH.

29 KELPIUS, Johannes. 1694–1708. CNS. PHi, photostat. *See* 4958.

30 GREEN, Joseph. 1696–1714. CNS. MH.

31 TRUE, Capt. Henry. 1696–1719. Military diary and account book by commander of the local forces against the Indians in Salisbury, Mass. NN.

32 SOUTHACK, Capt. Cyprian. 1697–1700; 1717–1718. Diary-letters: sea voyages; Maine, etc. MHi.

33 BULKELEY, Rev. Gershom. 1699. Interleaved almanac: state of his own health; some marriages; mentions Thanksgiving on Nov. 1. DLC.

34 HAWLEY, Joseph. 1699–1710. School affairs; farm and mercantile transactions; many law cases in which he acted as justice; marriages and deaths. MNF, which also has extracts in the Judd mss. from earlier diaries, some as early as 1674. *See* 58.

35 PEÑA, Diego. 1699. An expedition from San Augustino to the bay of Espiritu Santo. DLC, Spanish transcript.

36 STORY, Thomas. 1699–1708. Travels and labors in the Quaker ministry. Nc-Ar.

37 DU RU, Paul, S.J. 1700–1701. Journal in La. ICN.

38 GERRICH, Joseph. 1700. Travel. PMA.

39 ANON. 1701–1779. Pa. journals, with accounts of lands, quit-rents, etc. PHi.

40 STEVENS, Rev. Joseph. 1701–1772. Family and ministerial records; record of church admissions, marriages, baptisms. MBNEH.

41 BUTLER, James D. [1706 and later]. CNS. WHi.

42 LEVERETT, ———. 1707–1723. Meetings of Harvard Corporation; private notes. MH. 1696–1710 (with gaps). Notes of sermons and religious observances. MWA.

43 DUMMER, Jeremiah. 1709–1711. CNS. MH.

44 PRINCE, Rev. Thomas. 1709–1711. Trips to Barbados, London, Madeira; public affairs; smallpox. MHi. 1736–1737. Almanac; farming at Leicester; social. MWa.

45 JAQUES, Stephen. 1710–1796. Accounts; historical happenings; religious musings; additions by later writers. MSaE.

46 PENN, William and Hannah. 1710–1726. CNS. PHi.

47 SIMONDS, ———. 1710. Journey into Nova Scotia. MWob.

48 HESSELIUS, Andrew. 1711–1724. His journey to America. PHi.

49 HILL, Gen. John. 1711. Hovenden's expedition to Canada; Harvard commencement; at anchor in Nantasket Bay; Boston. BrLPro; MHi, transcript.

50 WELLES, Sir Howard. 1711. Official in Boston and Canada. BrLPro.

51 HYDE, William. 1713–1757 (various dates). Deaths and marriages in Newton, Boston, etc.; a Sunday journal with notes about preachers and sermons. MBNEH. *See* 10.

52 MANASSES. Paul. 1714–1718. Accounts; family; births; English with some Indian vocabulary. MBNEH, typescript.

53 WILLIAMS, Rev. Stephen. 1714–1750 (with gaps). Religious activities; chaplain at Louisbourg. MWA; MLo; MHi; DLC.

54 ANON. 1715. At Cape Cod; personal; trips. MHi.

55 HOME, William. 1715–1747. CNS. MeHi.

56 LISLE, Maurice. 1715–1717. Domestic and commercial affairs. PHi.

57 OXLEY, Joseph. 1715–1775. An account of his travels through England, Scotland, Ireland, and the American Colonies (1770–1772) in the service of the Quaker religion; life and religion in Va., the Carolinas, Md., Pa., N.J., N.Y., and New England. PHi.

58 HAWLEY, Joseph. 1716–1735. Accounts; visitors; diary entries. MNF. *See* 34.

59 QUINCY, Col. John. 1716–1758. Notes of legal cases that came before him; lists of marriages and oaths. MHi.

60 TOWNSEND, Rev. Jonathan. 1716–1761 (with gaps). Almanacs; weather; preaching; public events. MDedHi.

61 GERRISH, Rev. Joseph. 1717–1719. Weather, fires, ordinations, marriages, deaths, funerals, baptisms; almanac for 1719. MHi.

62 LITTLE family. 1717–1887. Personal. MeHi.

63 ANON. 1718–1726. Minister's meditations. MWA.

64 DEXTER, Rev. Samuel. 1720–1752. Private and public events. MDedHi.

65 FAYERWEATHER, Mr. ———. 1720. Voyages to Muscongus and St. George; the beginning of the settlement of Thomaston. MeHi, copy.

66 MASCARENE, Capt. Paul. 1720–1725. Kept at Annapolis, where he was commandant; stores, costs, etc. MHi, copy.

67 MOODY, Rev. Joseph. 1720–1724. CNS (in Latin cipher). MeHi.

68 TOURCADE, Dr. Sieur. 1720–1723. Voyage from France to La.; description of La. and Ill. country (in French). ICHi.

69 HOBART, Rev. Nehemiah. 1721–1732. Deaths, marriages, births, miscellaneous. MHi.

70 ROBIE, Dr. Thomas. 1721–1722. Doctor's work and records. MHi.

71 BEALE, Capt. Othniel. 1722. His observations with a dipping needle at Boston. *Pub. Col. Soc. Mass.*, xiv, l36. Published.

72 BUMSTEAD, Jeremiah. 1722–1733 (with gaps). Current news; many names; vital statistics; 1732 and 1733 are interleaved with fuller entries. MWA.

73 D'ARTAGUIETTE, Diron. 1722–1723. CNS. DLC, French transcript.

74 HAMILTON, Alexander. 1722–1723. Capture by the Indians, who took him from the Kennebec River to Canada. BrLPro.

75 PLANT, Rev. Matthias. 1722–1753. Episcopal priest; work for Society for Propagation of Gospel; mission work; marriages. St. Paul's Church, Newburyport, Mass.

76 FAIRBANKS, Capt. Jabez. 1723–1724. Scouting expeditions sent from Lancaster, Groton, and Dunstable. MBAr.

77 HALL, Hugh. 1723. Largely about the sailing of boats. MBNEH.

78 FLYNT, Henry. 1724–1747. Life of the day; personal matters; expenses; affairs of Harvard and of lands and buildings in Groton. MH.

79 GERRISH, Benjamin. 1724–1725. Personal matters; planting his garden; kept in the back of his sea journal. MWA.

80 HULL, Joseph. 1724. Conn. to N.Y,; dinner with governor; a Quaker. MWA.

81 SEWALL, Samuel, Jr. 1724; 1732. Personal. MBNEH.

82 WILLARD, Josiah. 1724–1725. Military scouting and guarding in Mass. MBAr.

83 [MELVIN, Eleazar]. 1725. Account of Lasewell's great fight at Pequaket, in which Melvin took part. MH.

84 WILLARD, Col. Samuel. 1725. Military scouting expeditions in Mass. MBAr.

85 WYMAN, Seth. 1725. Military scouting expedition to Penicook. MBAr.

86 BARBER, Rhoda. 1726–1782. Early pioneers' journey through the wilderness toward the Susquehanna River and the establishment of settlements at Wright's Ferry, Lancaster County; describes the hazardous journey, grandeur of the country, construction of ferries, economic and domestic life of the families, trade with the Indians, etc. PHi.

87 COLLINS, Zaccheus. 1726–1769. Work as blacksmith, maltster, farmer, and selectman; Quaker meetings. MSaE.

88 PIERPONT, Sarah. 1726–1753 (with gaps). Religious life and reflections. MWA, copy.

89 WOODS, Benjamin. 1726–1730. Practically a resumé of the sermons of Rev. Robert Breck, Marlborough, Mass. ICHi.

90 ATKINSON, Theodore. 1727. A voyage to Casco Bay to attend conference with the Indians. DLC.

91 HEATH, Rev. Peleg. 1728–1740. Church activities at Barrington, R.I. Congregational Church, Barrington, R.I.

92 SWIFT, Rev. John. 1728. Religious texts; baptisms; church affairs. MFm.

93 WADSWORTH, Rev. Daniel. 1728–1729. Studying theology at Farmington. CtHi.

94 CLAP, Thomas. 1729–1738. Records by justice of the peace in Scituate and a list of marriages and deaths. MTaHi.

95 FREEMAN, Enoch. 1729–1785 (with gaps). Personal; social life; events; part kept at Harvard. MeP.

96 MORRIS, Susanna. 1729–1754. Journal of a Quaker traveler in the American colonies; describes dangers encountered and shipwreck, Friends' meetings visited in Va., the Carolinas, Md., Pa., N.J., Great Britain, Ireland, and the Netherlands. PHi.

97 ODLIN, Elisha. 1729. Almanac; personal; sermons; earthquakes; Harvard. MWA.

98 ROULLET, Regis du. 1729; 1729–1733. His journey to the Choctaws. DLC, French transcripts. Extracts of diary of journey to the Choctaws. DLC, French transcripts.

99 ANON. 1730. A journey to the Choctaws. DLC, French transcripts.

100 ANON. 1730. At Cambridge, Mass.; Harvard; the Brattles. MWA.

101 BALDWIN, Jonathan. 1730/31–1740. Various wills made, deaths, and the settlement of estates. MWA.

102 DAVENPORT, Jonathan. 1730–1770. Births and deaths; Hallowell, Me., town meetings; construction of roads; employment and dismissal of ministers; pastors' sermons; weather; apprenticeship indenture; taxation and personal dealings. Me.

103 GREENE, Elisha. 1730–1775. Vital records (by a minister?). MBNEH.

104 KING, Daniel. 1730–1767. Main events in his life; deaths in family; a few long entries. MHi.

105 LEWIS, Margaret Lynn. 1730. Life in Scotland and in Va.; pioneer life, social and religious; building of Staunton. NN.

106 ROGERS, Rev. Daniel. 1730–1785. Almanacs; minister's work; visits; social; war news. MBNEH. 1735. Diary. CNS. DLC. *See* 484.

107 SAUNDERS, John. 1730–1755. CNS. Nc-Ar.

108 BRYANT, Walter. [between 1731 and 1742?]. A trip to the White Hills. DLC.

109 EVANS, Joshua. 1731–1798. His journeys in Md., Va., and N. C.; a brief autobiographical sketch. NcU.

110 ANON. 1732. Observations of the Choctaw Indians made on a trip from Mobile to New Orleans (in French). NHi.

111 ANON. 1732–1733. Almanacs; Cambridge, Mass.; personal; deaths. MWA.

112 TILL, Jacob. 1732–1761. Personal, kept in Europe and in America (in German). NcWsM.

113 ORNE, Capt. Timothy. 1733. Ship movements; business. MSaE.

114 ELIOT, Andrew. 1734; 1739. CNS. MH.

115 HALE, Rev. Moses. 1734–1735; 1767; 1769; 1773. Daily events; funerals; local matters; visits, social affairs. MNeHi. *See* 476.

116 WILLIAMS, Rev. William. 1734; 1737. Almanacs; personal; town; pastoral work. WHi.

117 ANON. 1735–1740. The voyage to America by members of the Moravian Church; life in Savannah, etc. (in German). NcWsM.

118 BELCHER, Gov. Jonathan. 1735. From Boston to Deerfield to visit the Housotonnock Indians. MBNEH.

119 INGHAM, Benjamin. 1735–1736. England, voyage to St. Simons Island and Savannah, Ga. Came to Ga. with John Wesley to convert the Indians, and minister to the spiritual needs of the colonists. Diary tells of the journey and his stay in the new colony. Part of the Egmont Papers. GU.

120 MORRIS, Robert Hunter. 1735–1736. Kept in London, where he accompanied his father, Lewis Morris, to protest against the proceedings of Gov. William Cosby; also a second visit to London in 1749. DLC.

121 WARBURTON, Richard. 1735–1736. A tour made in Italy. CSmH.

122 ORNE, Timothy, Jr. 1736–1767 (with gaps). Almanacs; personal; public; church; weather; ship movements. MSaE.

123 ANON. 1737. Poetical, treating such themes as life, God, etc. NHi.

124 PARSONS, Rev. Moses. 1737–1800. Mostly almanacs; pastoral work; farming; family life; social; public affairs; school-teaching; weather. MWA.

125 ROBBINS, Rev. Philemon. 1737–1745. Parochial work and personal religion; family. MH.

126 ANON. 1738–1742. Kept by an officer on board the warship *La Europa,* with an account of the Spanish expedition against Ga. in the summer of 1742. CSmH.

127   GODDARD, Hon. Edward. 1738–1741. Religious experiences and autobiography. MWA.

128   BYRD, William, II. 1739–1741 (in code). Pub. by L. B. Wright. NcU.

129   COOKE, Rev. Samuel. 1739–1783. Parish matters: record of births, deaths, baptisms, and marriages in the 2nd Precinct, Cambridge; notes for sermons. MArHi; MAr.

130   CUSHING, Thomas, Jr. 1739–1742. Various kinds of merchandise sold; lading of ships; adventures; notes, etc. MB.

131   DOLBEARE, Benjamin. 1739; 1777. A trip in England; long descriptions of his experiences in taking the baths in Bath; a trip from Port Royal in Jamaica to Cape Ann. MHi.

132   WALDRON, Col. Thomas Westbrook. 1739. Almanac; farming; trials; weather. MHi.

133   BENNET, Joseph. 1740. A voyage from London to New England. MHi.

134   CABOT, Rev. Marston. 1740–1745. Sabbath day journal of a minister who labored not far from Providence, R.I. MBNEH.

135   CRAIG, Rev. John. 1740–1795. Record of baptisms, recipes, contracts, accounts, agricultural and religious matters. ICMcCHi.

136   ELIOT, Rev. Andrew. 1740–1777 (with gaps). Almanacs; funerals; preachings; earthquakes; comets, etc. MHi.

137   HALL, Rev. David. 1740–1789. Births, marriages, and deaths in Sutton, Mass.; illnesses and epidemics; extraordinary natural phenomena; town affairs; war news; witchcraft; church councils, with many religious meditations. MHi.

138   WATSON, Jeffrey. 1740–1783. Daily events; visits to neighbors and surrounding towns; vital statistics. RHi, typescript.

139   WHEELER, William. 1740–1814. Weather; notes on public affairs; deaths. Ct.

140   CHIRIKOF, Capt. Alexei Ilich. 1741. Voyage to America. DLC, Russian transcripts.

141   GODDARD, Rev. David. 1741. Weather; baptisms; marriages; some personal matters. MWA.

142   HANCOCK, John. 1741. CNS. NNC.

143   HART, Oliver. 1741–1780. Diary of a Baptist minister. ScU, portions in typescript only.

144   ANON. 1742–1772. CNS. PHi.

145   ANON. 1742. The campaign against the Chicachas. DLC, French transcripts.

146   ANON. 1742. A voyage from England: life on board a sailing vessel, daily activities, books read, passengers. PHi.

147   BANGS, Benjamin. 1742/43–1749; 1759–1765. Personal affairs and contemporary events both local and general. MHi.

148   CLEAVELAND, Rev. John. 1742–1776 (with gaps). Conflicts between some of the students and the college authorities at Yale; daily doings; chaplain of a regiment; expedition from Salem to Hartford and Fairfield. Early portions up to 1746 owned by MSaE; copies of later portions owned by DLC. *See* 327, 614.

149   CLEAVELAND, Mrs. Mary. 1742–1762. Two visits from George Whitfield; family and personal matters. MSaE.

150   GODDARD, Ebenezer. 1742–1754. Religious thoughts; some personal matters. ICHi.

151   KHITROV, ———? 1742. Copy of Vitus Bering's journal, by the man who kept the original on the Island of St. Peter. DLC, Russian transcript.

152   METCALF, John. 1742–1791 (with gaps). Surveys in Holliston, Cumberland, etc.; court work; farming notes; family; local news. MHi.

153   PECKHAM, Thomas. 1742–1750. Farming; country life; neighbors; accounts. RNHi.

154   PECKOVER, ———? 1742–1743. Journey to different meetings of the Society of Friends in America. NN.

155   WALLEY, Rev. John. 1742–1751. Pious reflections. MHi, copy.

156   LAWRENCE, John. 1743. Kept during the running of the division line between the provinces of East and West New Jersey; measurements and topographical features relative to the survey. NjR. *See* 427.

157   OCCUM, Samson. 1743–1790. Work among the Montauk and Oneida Indians. Mss. for portions of the years 1748, 1751, 1754 (or 1759), 1757, 1758, 1761, 1764, 1766, 1774, 1775, in the possession of NhD; July 5–Sept. 16, 1787, CtHi; remaining originals in CtNlHi.

158   SOMMER, Peter Nicolas. 1743–1767. Translation of his journal with births, baptisms, marriages, and deaths of members of St. Paul's Evangelical Lutheran Church. NHi; NNNGB.

159   WHEELWRIGHT, Jeremiah. 1743–1782. Public events; revolution; extracts. MHi.

160   WINTHROP, John. 1743–1779. CNS. MH.

161   PLIMPTON, Nathan. 1744. Almanac; meetings; weather. MHi.

162 POTE, Capt. William. 1744–1749. Journal, including his captivity. ICN.

163 ANON. 1745–1748. Captured at sea; imprisonment at Quebec; later in Rhode Island. DLC.

164 ANON. 1745. From Nantasket to siege of Louisbourg. MHi.

165 ANON. 1745–1748. Kept while writer was a prisoner of the French and Spaniards; spent some time in Boston and R.I. DLC.

166 ANON. 1745. Kept by a soldier in the 4th Mass. Regt., at the siege of Louisbourg. CSmH.

167 ANON. 1745. The expedition against Saratoga by French and Indians under Marin. NN, in addition to the original, a 19th-century translation and a transcript.

168 ANON. 1745. Naval expedition to Louisbourg. MHi.

169 ANON. 1745. Siege of Louisbourg. MHi.

170 ANON. 1745. Soldier in Richardson's company; siege of Louisbourg. MHi.

171 BARCLAY, Rev. H. 1745; 1746. A visit to the Mohawks in March, 1745; further material on Indian affairs. NHi.

172 BUCHANAN, John. 1745. A trip to Wood River to sell land; gives names of settlers with whom he lodged and transacted business. WHi.

173 CROOKER, Elijah. 1745–1782. CNS. MeHi.

174 JUDD, Philip. 1745. Military expedition from New London to Cape Breton; sergeant. CtHi.

175 MASON, Jonas. 1745. Almanac; farming; ship movements; Indians; drawings. MBNEH. 1795. Private diary similar to above. MWA.

176 [PEMBERTON, John?] 1745. A journey from Philadelphia to S. C. DLC. See 219, 238.

177 SHIRLEY, William. 1745. Journal of the siege of Louisbourg. CSmH.

178 WINSLOW, Joshua. 1745?–1769? Duties as justice of the peace; probably appointed about 1745 and continued to his death, 1769. MBNEH.

179 WOLCOTT, Roger. 1745. The expedition against Louisbourg. DLC; CtHi.

180 BEAUCHAMPS, de ———. 1746. His voyage from Mobile to the Chactas, by order of Gov. de Vandreuil, to demand satisfaction for the murder of three Frenchmen. DLC, French transcript.

181 BRUCE, David. 1746. Kept by a member of the Moravian Church. PHi.

182 KENDALL?, John. 1746; 1747. Mainly concerned with his spiritual travail. PSC-Hi.

183 LEWIS, Thomas. 1746–1747. Expedition to survey the southwestern boundary of the Fairfax grant of the Northern Neck of Va., from the headwaters of the Rappahannock to the headwaters of the Potomac, commenting on surveying problems and life in the wilderness. ViU.

184 READING, John. 1746/47–1767. Brief entries concerning business, chiefly land, and personal activities. NjR.

185 ROSE, Robert. 1746–1751. Visits to and fro between Albemarle and Essex counties, calling on leading families in the counties between; visiting western Va.; visiting Williamsburg; curing tobacco; colonial Williamsburg. CSmH.

186 WELLMAN, James? 1746–1806. CNS. MBNEH.

187 ANON. 1747–1749. To Grand Pre; French and Indian War; skirmishes. MNeHi.

188 DUNSTER, Rev. Isaiah. 1747. Personal matters; vital statistics; many people mentioned from Eastham, Dartmouth, Cambridge, etc. MSaE.

189 EMERSON, Rev. Joseph. 1747–1775. Personal events during his ministry. MHi.

190 HAWLEY, Maj. Joseph. 1747–1770. Accounts; daily life; almanac; personal. MNF.

191 STEVENS, Capt. Phineas. 1747–1754. Journals in the French and Indian War. NHi. See 210, 239.

192 THOMAS, Dr. John. 1747–1748. Military surgeon at Annapolis. MBNEH.

193 THOMAS, Gen. John, Jr. 1747. Record kept while he was at Annapolis Royal or on board "ye Ordineince Packet." MBNEH.

194 TROTT, Sgt. John. 1747. Scouting on Royal River. MBAr.

195 WASHINGTON, George. 1747–1775; 1781; 1784–1799. Memoirs of 1st president. DLC.

196 WILLIAMS, Dr. Solomon. 1747–1748. Almanacs; at Harvard; teaching in Roxbury, Mass.; personal. WHi.

197 BACKUS, Rev. Isaac. 1748/49–1806 (with gaps). Historical notes of New England Baptist background. MBBHi. See 204, 225.

198 CROGHAN, George. 1748–1751? Mission to the Ohio; Indians; defeat of Col. Washington; mission to Fort Cumberland. PPL. See 350, 362, 420.

199 DUNNING, David. 1748. Scouting and guarding Topsham. MBAr.

200 HUNT, William. 1748–1772. Travels in the Quaker ministry; copies of letters. PHC.

201 LORING, Rev. Isaac. 1748–1765. Events in his ministry; biographical data. MSuGL. 1750–1751. Similar to above. MHi. 1770–1772. Similar to above. CtHi.

202 PARKER, Elisha. 1748–1751. Trips; visits; conversations; letters written in his efforts to collect

accounts, settle mortgages, and the like, dealing with persons chiefly in Middlesex County, N.J. PSC-Hi.

203 ANON. 1749–1750. CNS. DLC.

204 BACKUS, Rev. Issac. 1749–1805. Deaths in Middleboro, Raynham Bridge, Taunton, and Norwich; descriptions of unusual deaths, accidents, murders, storms, earthquakes, and other remarkable events. MBNEH. *See* 197, 225.

205 CUSHING, Rev. Jacob. 1749–1809 (with gaps). His work as a clergyman. DLC.

206 NICHOLSON, Thomas. 1749–1771. Detailed accounts of a trip to England and of his experiences as a preacher. NcU.

207 PENINGTON, Edward. 1749–1751. CNS. PHi.

208 PORTER, Rev. Nehemiah. 1749; 1752–1753. Almanacs; his preaching; deaths. MWHi.

209 REDWOOD, William. 1749–1760; 1782–1787; 1787–1790. CNS. PHi. *See* 526.

210 STEVENS, Capt. Phineas. 1749. A trip to Montreal by way of Albany. DLC. *See* 191, 239.

211 STORER, Ebenezer. 1749–1764. Religious thought and prayer; some family records included. MBNEH.

212 ANON. 1750–1755. A trip made from Suffolk, Va., through various counties, with mention of court proceedings in Granville County, N.C.; goods, debts, names of customers, and expenses of trip. Nc-Ar.

213 ANON. 1750. An account of the expedition against rebellious Indians of Tiburon Island, led by Don Diego Ortiz Parrilla. CtNhCl.

214 CAMMERHOFF, Bishop ———, and Rev. David Zeisbergher. 1750. Their journey from Bethlehem, Pa., to Onondaga, N.Y., and return. PBMCA, original; CaOTHi, copy.

215 CORNWALLIS, Edward. 1750. The expedition to dislodge the French and Indians from Chegnecto; the building of the fort at Mims. NHi.

216 HAZEN, Richard. 1750–175[1]. The surveying of the sea coast from Portsmouth to the St. Croix River. MBNEH.

217 LEAMING, Aaron. 1750–1751; 1761; 1775; 1776. The economic development of Cape May and adjacent territory; land transactions; surveys; early settlers; military organizations; farming; trade in timber and other commodities; acts of New Jersey assemblies; legal and domestic affairs; lists of books. PHi.

218 OGILVIE, John. 1750–1759 (with gaps). Church records; Indian marriages and baptisms. N.

219 PEMBERTON, John. 1750–1795. CNS. (Quaker) PHi. *See* 176, 238.

220 PETERS, Richard. 1750; 1758; 1762. Diary of government official. PHi.

221 SINGER, ———. 1750. From London to Siebenburgen, and return (in German). NcWsM.

222 SPROAT, Rev. James. 1750–1783 (with gaps). Diary written while he was pastor of Congregational Church at Guilford, Conn. and after he succeeded Rev. Gilbert Tennant at Philadelphia. PPPrHi. *See* 249.

223 WALKER, Thomas. 1750. CNS. WHi.

224 WEISER, Conrad. 1750. Journey to Onondtaga. PHi. *See* 232.

225 BACKUS, Rev. Isaac. 1751–1752. His daily doings and those of his friends; mentions some public events and some trips. MBBHi. *See* 197, 204.

226 CABELL, William, Sr. 1751–1798. CNS. Vi-U, microfilm.

227 CARTER, Landon. 1751–1758; 1772–1777. Diary and farm record; notes and observations on agricultural experiments and developments at Sabine Hall and other Carter properties; activities as a justice of the peace; political activities in the House of Burgesses. ViU. *See* 396, 431.

228 CURWEN, Samuel. 1751; 1757; 1759; 1760; 1762. A trip to Philadelphia on horseback; incidents of the journey; a trip to Dunstable. MWA.

229 CUTHBERTSON, John. 1751–1791. CNS. PPiPT.

230 LIVERMORE, Samuel. 1751–1752. Cruise from Boston to Princeton; expenses as senior in college; descriptions. Princeton Univ. 1755. Expedition to Fort Edward; Albany. MBNEH.

231 PRINCE, Paul. 1751; 1753. Almanacs; family affairs. MBNEH.

232 WEISER, Conrad. 1751; 1754. Journey to Albany, with a message from the gov. of Pa. to the Six Nations; to and from Auchwick, while executing a commission for Gov. Hamilton. PPL. *See* 224.

233 WENDELL, Jacob. 1751. Conference with Six Nations Indians at Albany. MBAr.

234 ANDREWS, Joseph. 1752–1787. Personal; farm trips. MHi.

235 BERRY, John. 1752. Personal happenings; weather; deaths. MHa.

236 LANGDON, Ephraim. 1752. Deaths; events at college; weather; books read. RHi.

237 McMILLAN, Rev. John. 1752–1776. Colonial life; adventures as a young man; travel; studies and preachings in various Presbyterian communities. PHi. *See* 540.

238 PEMBERTON, John. 1752–1753. Visits to Friends and Friends' Meetings in Ireland and England. PHi. *See* 176, 219.

239 STEVENS, Capt. Phineas. 1752. Travels in Canada to negotiate the restoration of the captives belonging to the Province of Mass. remaining in the hands of the French and Indians there. DLC. *See* 191, 210.

240 ANON. 1753–1821. Christian Indian congregations, and other papers concerning them (in German). NcWsM.

241 ANON. 1753–1812. The congregation of the Moravian Church at Bethlehem, Pa.; some memoirs included. NcWsM, copy.

242 BARTRAM, William. 1753; 1765–1766; 1773–1777. His travels through the Catskill Mts., the Carolinas, and Ga., and Central and West Florida; observations on plants. PHi.

243 BROWN, Rev. John. 1753–1797. Pastor of Timber Ridge and New Providence Presbyterian churches, Augusta County, Va. PPPrHi.

244 CAMPBELL, John, 4th Earl of Loudoun. 1753–1760. Military. CSmH.

245 KERNSORET, W. de (?). 1753. Explorations. DLC, British transcript.

246 LOW, Anthony. 1753. Voyage from R.I. to Barbados. MH.

247 RODGERS, Daniel. 1753–1777. CNS. MeHi.

248 SMITH, William. 1753–1783. Diary including Revolution, state, and local affairs. NN, microfilm.

249 SPROAT, Rev. James. 1753; 1757; 1778–1780; 1782–1784; 1786. His church activities and visits to settlements throughout Pa. PHi. *See* 222.

250 TRENT, William. 1753. Diary of his carrying a gift of powder and guns to the Six Nations. MH. *See* 404.

251 WHEELWRIGHT, Maj. Nathaniel. 1753–1754. Trip to Montreal, Quebec, to redeem captives from French and Indians. MHi.

252 ANON. 1754–1819. The choir of single brethren of the Moravian Church (in German). NcWsM.

253 ANON. 1754–1756. Different campaigns in the French and Indian War. NN.

254 BROWNE, Mrs. ———. 1754–1757. Kept on the Braddock Expedition. NHi.

255 BUTLER, Gen. Richard. 1754–1788. Revolutionary journals and journals of Indian treaties. WHi. *See* 560.

256 FISKE, Rev. Nathan. 1754–1798. CNS. MWA.

257 GARDNER, Isaac. 1754. Local matters in Brookline, Mass. MBNEH.

258 LIVINGSTON family. 1754–1817. Commercial and legal papers, including import certificates, and journal of Janet (Livingston) Montgomery. CLU.

259 PUTNAM, Rev. Aaron. 1754–1757. Work as preacher. MWA.

260 WHEELOCK, Eleazar. 1754–1756; 1761–1762. Accounts of students at Indian charity school at Lebanon, Conn. NhD. *See* 500.

261 WINSLOW, Rev. Edward. 1754–1755. Sea journal of voyage on the *Earl of Halifax* from Boston to London. NN.

262 YATES, Abraham, Jr. 1754–1758. Journal and copybook. NN.

263 ANON. 1755–1756. From Falltown, Mass., to Albany, etc. DLC.

264 ANON. 1755. Journal of Braddock's expedition by a British soldier. MH.

265 ANON. 1755. Chaplain; to Albany and Lake George. MWA.

266 ADAMS, John. 1755–1777 (with gaps); 1778–1796. His work and doings; a trip abroad; his stay in France and return home; includes another trip to Spain, England, etc. MBAd.

267 ANDREWS, Peter. 1755–1756. Travels and labors in the gospel in England. PHC.

268 BURK, Maj. John. 1755. Camp life; commences at Saratoga; letters. MHi, photostat.

269 CARGILL, James. 1755–1758. Encounters with the Indians in Wiscasset and other places in Me.; scout trips. MBAr.

270 FITCH, Jabez. 1755–1812. Narrative of things he remembered from 1749; his service in the French and Indian wars; an intimate daily record of his life; settlement of northern Vt. MBMa. *See* 566.

271 GERRISH, William. 1755. A scouting expedition from Berwick to Little Falls; a scout journal mostly at Berwick. MBAr.

272 GREEN, John. 1755–1756. Recording daily events; births, marriages, and deaths; military news; texts of Jonathan Mayhew's sermons. RHi.

273 HALE, Robert, Jr. 1755–1762. Important events of the war against the French and Indians; summaries of legislative proceedings and popular feelings. MWA.

274 HAWLEY, Elisha. 1755. The Crown Point expedition. NN.

275 HOWES, Lot. 1755–1773. Mostly accounts; some personal. MBNEH, typescript.

276 LEWIS, Capt. Charles. 1755. CNS. WHi.

277 NICHOLS, Alexander. 1755; 1756. Expedition from Newcastle to St. George's and march to Fort Halifax and Brunswick. MBAr.

278 RICHARDS, Samuel. 1755–1760. Almanacs. MDedHi.

279 SAUTER, Johann Michael. 1755. Travel diary of journey from Bethabara, N.C., to Bethlehem, Pa., and return. NcWsM.

280 SPAULDING, Lt. Leonard. 1755–1779. Diary and account book relating particularly to his experiences in the French and Indian War and while at Fort Frederick. NHi.

281 STACKPOLE, Capt. James. 1755–1821. Diary, with journal of 1790–1821. MeWHi.

282 THOMPSON, Lt. Samuel. 1755–1814. Chief events; local events; weather; sermons; farming; deaths. MWob.

283 WIGHT, Samuel. 1755–1790 (continued by his daughter to 1849). Deaths; weather; sermons. Bellingham, Mass., Town Clerk's Office.

284 WILLARD, Abijah. 1755–1756. Orderly book and journal kept during the expedition to Nova Scotia. CSmH.

285 WOOLMAN, John. 1755–1770. CNS. PHi.

286 ANON. 1756. Indian attack and massacre. MBAr.

287 AMES, Nathaniel, Jr. 1756–1821. Private affairs; current local events; national politics and great events of Europe. MDed.

288 BARROWS, Abner. 1756–1758. The events during the march of Capt. Samuel Thacher's Co. to Albany, Saratoga, Ft. William; where they encamped; number of miles traveled each day; incidents of their camp life. MBMa.

289 CLESSON, Matthew. 1756. Travel on his intended scout from Deerfield, Mass., to Lake Champlain, by way of Otter Creek. DLC.

290 CORS, James. 1756. Journal of the road from No. 4 to Lake Champlain, N.Y. CSmH.

291 COTTON, Rev. John. 1756–1774. A continuation of the diary of his father, Josiah; personal and town affairs. MPlPh.

292 GOODWIN, Samuel. 1756. Scouting expeditions in Me.; part of the time on a sloop near the Kennebec River. MBAr.

293 GRABS, Gottfried. 1756. A journey from Bethlehem, Pa., to Bethabara, N.C. (in German). NcWsM. *See* 843.

294 HAWKS, John. 1756. Journal of the road from No. 4 to Lake Champlain, N.Y. CSmH. *See* 309.

295 MERRITT, Daniel. 1756–1757. Military at Crown Point and Ft. William Henry; company clerk; day-to-day affairs. MeHi.

296 PRESTON, William. 1756. The Sandy Creek Expedition against the Shawnee towns, from Ft. Prince George via Ft. Frederick and Sandy Creek, with Cherokee Indians, ending in mutiny and wholesale desertion. WHi.

297 SHIPPERS, Joseph. 1756–1757. Journal of the building of Ft. Augusta. PHi. *See* 315.

298 STICKNEY, William. 1756–1792 (with gaps). Farming work; family; weather; brief entries. MHi.

299 VAN ETTEN, Capt. John. 1756–1757. Military defense at Ft. Hyndshaw. PHi.

300 ANON. 1757. Indian massacres; Mass. MBAr.

301 ANON. 1757. Kept during the siege and capitulation of Ft. William Henry. PPAmS, contemporary copy.

302 ANON. 1757. The attack on Ft. William Henry. NN.

303 BUFFINGTON, Peter. 1757–1759. Tavern journals. PHi.

304 CHEVALIER, John and Peter. 1757–1761; 1770–1783. CNS. PHi.

305 ENGEL, Lt. A. 1757. Kept while he was stationed at Leckley Township. PHi.

306 FAESCH, Rudolph. 1757. Voyage from Ft. William Henry to Canada. CSmH.

307 FRENCH, Rev. Jonathan. 1757. Company of Mass. troops on the march from Boston to Ft. Edward, N.Y.; author's duties and experiences at that station. MiU-C.

308 FRYE, Col. Joseph. 1757. From the attack on Ft. William Henry until its surrender. DLC, copy.

309 HAWKS, John. 1757–1759 (with gaps). Kept while he commanded the line of forts from Northfield to Hoosac Mountain in Mass. DLC. *See* 294.

310 LIGHTFOOT, Thomas. 1757–1759. Visits to Friends Meetings; homes in which he received hospitality; miles traveled daily. PSC-Hi, typescript.

311 METCALF, Seth. 1757–1758. Military expedition to Ft. Edward; also book covering 1757–1807 with one entry per year. MWHi.

312 PUTNAM, Capt. Israel. 1757. Journal and accounts at Ft. Edward. CtHi. *See* 512, 513.

313 RICHÉ, Thomas. 1757–1761. CNS. PHi.

314 SCOTT, Capt. Moses. 1757–1759. Military investigations; enemy activities. DLC.

315 SHIPPERS, Capt. Joseph. 1757–1758. CNS. PHi. *See* 297.

316 TILLINGHAST, Samuel. 1757–1758. Merchant; personal; marriages, deaths. MBMa, original; RHi, copy.

317 WELLS, Capt. Edmund. 1757. A march from Hartford to Ft. Edward; Indian skirmishes and lists of killed and wounded. NN.

318 WILLIAMS, William. 1757. While member of General Assembly of Conn. CtHi.

319 ANON. 1758. The proceedings of the fleet and army at Ft. Louisbourg. CSmH.

320 ANON. 1758; 1759–1760. Activities at Ft. William Henry; the Louisbourg expedition. MWA.

321 ADAMS, Samuel. 1758–1819. Early life in Killingly, Conn.; teaching; study and practice of medicine in Revolutionary army and in Mass. towns; social life; books; family. NN.

322 BASS, Benjamin. 1758. Expedition against Ft. Frontenac, with lists of officers and men. MH.

323 BIGELOW, Silas. 1758–1761. Personal matters, including minute accounts of the treatment given to his lame leg, various doctors consulted, remedies used, and stockings of various colors worn, etc. MWHi.

324 BRIGGS, David. 1758. At Lake George with Richard Cobb's Co., Col. Timothy Ruggles' Regt. MBAr.

325 BURD, [Col. James?] 1758. A journal kept at Loyal Hannon. PHi.

326 BURR, Asa. 1758. March from Roxbury, through Albany, Ft. Edward to Schenectady. MWA.

327 CLEAVELAND, Rev. John. 1758. The expedition to Ticonderoga. DLC. *See* 148, 614.

328 COMSTOCK, Christopher. 1758–1759. Clerk in Capt. Henry Champion's Co.; sergeant in Ichabod Phelps's 8th Co. in French and Indian War. CtHi.

329 DORR, Moses. 1758. Includes account of erection of Ft. Stanwix. MH.

330 GIST, Thomas. 1758–1759. Journal of man who was taken prisoner by the Wyandot tribe and escaped after about a year of captivity; details of Indian life; treatment of captives, etc. PHi.

331 GLAZIER, Benjamin. 1758. A journal of the French and Indian war; expedition to Lake Champlain and Lake George. MTop.

332 GOODMAN, George. 1758. Journal of the master of ship *Olive Branch*. DLC.

333 HARRIS, Obadiah. 1758. Journal of Ruggles' Regt.: expedition against Ticonderoga. CSmH.

334 HENDERSON, James. 1758–1759. Expedition to Ticonderoga; skirmishes; description of French fort. MBNEH.

335 HENDERSON, William. 1758–1759. Military; personal. NBu; NN, microfilm.

336 HEYWOOD, William. 1758–1760. CNS. NHi.

337 HUSE, Carr. 1758. During the French and Indian War. NHi.

338 NICHOLS, Joseph. 1758–1766. Military journal, the Mass. Provincial Forces during the expedition to Ticonderoga; notes and accounts subsequent thereto. CSmH.

339 POMROY, Benjamin. 1758–1763. Journal of British chaplain. PHi.

340 POST, Christian Frederick. [1758–1759]? Journey from Philadelphia to the Ohio on a message from government of Pa. to the Delaware, Shawnees, and Mingo Indians; contact with Indians. PHi; DLC.

341 SWEAT, Capt. William. 1758. Expedition against Ticonderoga. MSaE, copy.

342 UPTON, Daniel. 1758. Kept with the British troops at Lake George, etc.; gives numbers of British killed, wounded, and missing at Ticonderoga. NN.

343 WILLIAMS, Joseph. 1758–? Beginning at Hatfield, Mass., and ending at Fort Stanwix. MH. 1758. Details of his co., Schenectady, Ft. William, Oneida. MH.

344 ANON. 1759. Military at Crown Point; Saratoga. MWA.

345 ANON. 1759–1792. Diaries from the congregation of the Moravian Church of Bethania, N.C.; especially valuable for the Revolutionary War period. NcWsM.

346 ANON. 1759. Diary kept at Crown Point. MWA.

347 BALCH, Rev. Thomas. 1759. His own doings; installations, exchanges, etc. SWA.

348 CHURCHMAN, George. 1759–1804. Quaker meeting affairs and his travels in the ministry in Pa., N.Y., New England, and Ohio. PHC.

349 CLAGGERT, Wiseman. 1759–1766. Ships; a few indentures and other items; encounters with French privateers (a few entries are in French). MHi.

350 CROGHAN, George. 1759–1763. "Western journal," mainly Indian affairs. PHi. *See* 198, 362, 420.

351 EVERETT, ———? 1759. Departure of the regular troops; scouting parties sent out. RHi.

352 FOBES, Perez. 1759–1760. Kept by a student, Harvard, class of 1762. MH. *See* 432.

353 GARDNER, Daniel. 1759. Deaths and marriages; accidents; much Salem news. MSaE.

354 LANE, Daniel. 1759. Siege of Quebec; death of Wolfe. Office of Secretary of State, Augusta, Me.

355 MAN, Samuel. 1759–1760. British soldier stationed at Ft. Frederick during the French and Indian War. NHi.

356 POOR, Brig.-Gen. Enoch. 1759–1760. Written while he was a private in the co. of Capt. Titcomb at Ft. Frederick; includes a list of all the men in the garrison; records many details. CSmH.

357 WELD, Moses. 1759–1773 (with many gaps). Almanacs; weather; personal; family; burials. MBNEH.

358 BERNARD, Sir Francis. 1760–1768. A surveying trip in the vicinity of Falmouth, Me., and of Mt. Desert; it includes a voyage in 1762 to Mt. Desert and in 1768 on the sloop *Massachusetts* from Boston. MH.

359 BOOTH, Joseph. 1760. Kept while he was in the French and Indian War. CtHi.

360 BRADBURY, Lt. John. 1760–1813. Military orders; duties; journeys; events while he was in the Revolutionary War; names of officers; his marriage, family, and children; births, marriages, and deaths in York, Me.; accounts and quotations. MeHi.

361 CLARK, Rev. William. 1760–1784. Kept as Episcopal minister. MBD.

362 CROGHAN, Capt. George. 1760. His march from Ft. Pitt to Presqu' Isle, and other events. NN. *See* 198, 350, 420.

363 GIBBONS, James. 1760–1769. CNS. PHi. *See* 1218?

364 HUTCHINS, Thomas. 1760. A march from Ft. Pitt to Venango and to Presqu' Isle. PHi; IHS, transcript. *See* 387.

365 JOHNSON, Warren. 1760–1761. Visit to America. N.

366 MacCLINTOCK, Rev. Samuel. 1760. Chaplain in Goffe's regt.; expedition to Conn., Crown Point, etc. NhHi.

367 NIGHTINGALE, Samuel. 1760–1768. Accounts; religious; Presbyterian parsonage lottery. RHi. *See* 377.

368 ROGERS, Maj. Robert. 1760. CNS. NN. *See* 437.

369 SMITH, Rev. Caleb. 1760–1762. Diary of his Presbyterian ministry at Newark Mountains (now Orange), N.J. PPPrHi.

370 VAIL, Lt. Thomas. 1760–1800. Local news of Oyster Point, L.I.; farm work; service with General Amhurst in 1760. MWA, copy.

371 WATERMAN, Asa. 1760. CNS. Ct.

372 WILCOX, Dr. Edmund. 1760–1777. Farm journal. NcU.

373 ANON. 1761. A trip through Holland and Belgium; contains an account of expenses. CSmH.

374 ANON. 1761. The Moravian Indian congregation at a community near Bethlehem, Pa., planned as a village for Christian Indians (in German). NcWsM.

375 CHEEVER, Ezekiel. 1761–1762. War diary. MBNEH, copy.

376 HARNDAN, Capt. Samuel. 1761. Journey to Quebec; ransom of Elinor Noble and of other captives. MBAr.

377 NIGHTINGALE, Samuel, Jr. 1761–1768. Scattered entries relating to remarkable events; sale of lottery tickets. RHi. *See* 367.

378 OWEN, William. 1761–1771. Travels: England, New York, Boston, Philadelphia, France, Nova Scotia, England. NN.

379 RUSSELL, Ezekiel. 1761–1762. Almanacs; ship movements; Salem; weather. MHi.

380 SMALL, Jotham. 1761. CNS. MeHi.

381 ANON. 1762. Kept at siege of Martinique. NN.

382 CAREY, Rev. Thomas. 1762–1806, except 1777. Social and parish affairs in Newburyport, Mass. MBNEH.

383 EYRE, William. 1762. Journey to Pittsburgh by Brig.-Gen. Forbes's route, and return; description of country and towns in the area. MiU-C.

384 FARQUARSON, Alexander. 1762. On British transport, Martinique to Havana. NN.

385 GREEN, Enoch. 1762–1763. Brief entries having to do with sermons, baptisms, in the South. NjR.

386 HAYES, Joseph. 1762; 1770. Personal; accounts; journeys to Hartford. MHi.

387 HUTCHINS, Thomas. 1762. Journal of transactions as government agent with the Indians from Ft. Pitt to Green Bay. MnHi, photostat. *See* 364.

388 LOVEJOY, Nathaniel. 1762–1799 (with gaps). Weather; journeys; family; personal. MWA.

389 MIFFLIN, Benjamin. 1762. Trip by horseback from Philadelphia to Dover, Del., and back; family and business matters. NN. *See* 413.

390 MOODY, Lt. Joshua. 1762. Journal kept on board His Majesty's armed vessel sloop *Masquenonge*, on Lake Champlain. MBNEH.

391 PORTEOUS, John. 1762–1787. Events; weather; traders met; geography; routes; his business activities. MiD. *See* 403.

392 PUGH, Evan. 1762–1801. Activities as Baptist minister and planter. ScU, photostat.

393 ROBBINS, Rev. Ammi Rhamah. 1762. Careful details of his clerical work. CtHi.

394 SMITH, Rev. Hezekiah. 1762–1805. His travels as an itinerant preacher; his services as a chaplain in the Revolutionary army. DLC.

395 BENEZET, Philip. 1763–1764. Account with the sloop *Sally*. PHi.

396 CARTER, Landon. 1763–1778. CNS. ViU. *See* 227, 431.

397 d'ABBADIE. 1763–1764. CNS. DLC. French transcript.

398 DYER, Rev. Eliphalet. 1763; 1765. Journal of a voyage to England; personal notes as delegate to Congress at New York in 1765. Ct.

399 DYERS, ———? 1763–1805. Daily events; family and domestic affairs; financial transactions. PHi.

400 FULLER, Samuel. 1763. The construction of Johnson Hall and other buildings for Sir William Johnson. NSchHi.

401 HAMBURGH, Mr. ———. 1763. Journal while he was traveling about the country; description of the country about Detroit. DLC.

402 LAIDLIE, Dr. Archibald. 1763–1764. Journal in Holland, and including his voyage to N.Y. NHi.

403 PORTEOUS, John. 1763. Pontiac's siege of Detroit. MiD. *See* 391.

404 TRENT, William. 1763. Journal at Ft. Pitt, relating frontier conditions and Indian attacks on white settlements. PHi. *See* 250.

405 TYLER, Royall. 1763. Written at Harvard. VtHi.

406 ANON. 1764–1765. Kept by an officer who traveled in America and the West Indies. DLC, British transcript.

407 CARTER, Robert Wormeley. 1764–1765. Memoranda of winnings and losses at cards. MiU-C. *See* 613.

408 DOD, Rev. Thaddeus. 1764–1770. Daily affairs during his ministry. PWW.

409 FERRIS, Benjamin. 1764–1770. Visits to Friends Meetings, and his impressions of them; introspection on spiritual matters; marriage; birth and death of son; wife's death, his own declining health. PSC-Hi, copy.

410 HASEY, Rev. Isaac. 1764–1809. Local events; weather; preaching and other duties, with many Lebanon, Me., people mentioned. MeHi.

411 HAVEN, Jens. 1764. Journey from Newfoundland to Labrador (in German). NcWsM.

412 KIRKLAND, Samuel. 1764–1765. Life in N.Y. NBuHi, original; NCanHi, copy; CSmH, copy.

413 MIFFLIN, Benjamin. 1764. Journey from Philadelphia to the Cedar Swamps and back. PHi. *See* 389.

414 MORGAN, Dr. John. 1764; 1781–1784. Tour from Rome to London, with details on important persons met, his visit to Voltaire, universities and academies of learning, places, cities, travel and social life in Europe; his professional activities, services rendered, and medical supplies sold to his patients, with data on 18th-century pharmacology, and a list of members of the American Phil. Soc. PHi.

415 STEDMAN, Ebenezer. 1764. Ship movements; weather. MBNEH.

416 ANON. 1765–1766. Through the period of the Stamp Act. DLC, transcript.

417 ANON. 1765–1770. Events in America. DLC.

418 ANON. 1765. Fort Cumberland and Nova Scotia; weather; ship movements; Indians; trips. WHi.

419 CLARK, Henry Payson. 1765–1775; 1785–1805. CNS. MLexHi.

420 CROGHAN, Capt. George. 1765. CNS. Ill. Hist. Survey, transcripts; PHi. 1765. CNS. PPi. *See* 198, 350, 362.

421 FOLLANSBEE, Moody. 1765–1766. Interleaved almanacs; weather with a few other notes. MHi.

422 FOSTER, Hon. Theodore. 1765–1825 (with gaps). Personal and public events; social doings, weddings; law business; war news; trips to Boston, Brookfield, Mt. Vernon, New York, and elsewhere; a list of burials and baptisms in the town of Boston, 1767; also the births in Brookfield. RHi.

423 GODDARD, Rev. William. 1765; 1766; 1770; 1772–1774. Personal matters; many people mentioned; funerals, weddings noted. MWA.

424 HUNT, Dr. Ebenezer. 1765–1767. Studies while he was a student at a medical school in Springfield. MNF.

425 JOHNSON, William Samuel. 1765–1802. His activity, especially away from home. NNC.

426 JONES, Ephraim. 1765. A voyage to Bermuda and return to Marblehead; selectman's journal; activities as a selectman; items about schools and the poor in Portland. MeHi.

427 LAWRENCE, John. 1765–1771. CNS. DLC. *See* 156.

428 PEALE, Charles Willson. 1765–1826. His life's events. PPAmS.

429 ANON. 1766–1918. The Salem congregation of the Moravian Church. NcWsM.

430 BARRELL, William. 1766. Mentions ships sailing. MHi.

431 CARTER, Col. Landon. 1766–1767. CNS. MiU-C. *See* 227, 396.

432 FOBES, Dr. Perez. 1766. CNS. (partly in code). MBNEH. *See* 352.

433 GERRISH, Anna. 1766–1772. CNS. MeHi.

434 GREEN, Joshua. 1766–1774. Personal. MBNEH.

435 JAMES, Abel. 1766–1769. The clearing of swamps, creeks, building of canoes, near Bethlehem at Nazareth, Pa. PHi.

436 JENNINGS, John. 1766–1767. Journal of a trip from Ft. Pitt to Ft. Chartres and New Orleans. PHi; IU.

437 ROGERS, Maj. Robert. 1766–1767. Proceedings with Indians in Michillimackinac area after the war. MWA. *See* 368.

438 WEST, Rev. Samuel. 1766–1790 (with gaps). Almanacs; clerical duties; family; trips; weather. MHi.

439 WOODMASON, Rev. Charles. 1766–1768. His experiences as an itinerant minister in S. C. NHi.

440 BLAKE, Ebenezer. 1767–1786. Commercial services rendered in various ways. Mr. Sherman T. Blake, 429 Sacramento St., San Francisco; to be given to the Public Museum in San Francisco.

441 CLAUS, Daniel. 1767; 1768; 1773. Records of Indian negotiations and journeys of Claus to Canada. CaOOA.

442 CUSHING, Rev. John. 1767. Interleaved almanac; short entries of personal and town matters. MBNEH.

443 FISHER, Samuel Rowland. 1767–1793 (with gaps). Trips to England, Ireland, Charleston, S.C., Va., R.I. PSC-Hi, microfilm.

444 FORWARD, Justus. 1767. CNS. MH.

445 GRANT, Francis. 1767. Trip from N.Y. to Niagara, Quebec, and Lake George for trading with Indians. NN.

446 GRIFFITHS, Thomas. 1767. Visit to the Cherokees. Nc-Ar, microfilm.

447 HUNTINGTON, Rev. Enoch. 1767–1804. CNS. CtHi.

448 MORGAN, George. 1767–1768. Journey from Philadelphia to the Mingo town on the Ohio; a voyage down the Mississippi from Kaskaskia to the Iberville River. PHi.

449 TATE, Joseph. 1767–1778. Local events; recipes; verses; excitements. MBNEH.

450 ADAMS, Dr. Samuel. 1768. A voyage from Nantucket to Belle Isle. NHi.

451 ALLEN, Joseph. 1768; 1786–1791. Daily record of the weather with some shipping news and a little of a political nature; trials held usually at his home in Mass. when he was trial justice. MWA.

452 AVERY, Waightstill. 1768; 1769. In N. C. from Newbern to Missonry; from Chesapeake Bay through various towns in N.C.; mentions the people whom he meets and various court proceedings. WHi.

453 BRADFORD, Col. William and John Kidd. 1768–1776. CNS. PHi. *See* 558.

454 CHADWICK, Joseph. 1768–? Journey through part of Mount Desert. MH.

455 COOPER, Mary. 1768–1775. Life at Oyster Bay, L.I.; focuses on family and religion. NN.

456 LONGFELLOW, Stephen. 1768–1792. Almanacs; farming and family life at Gorham. MeHi.

457 TAIT, Charles. 1768–1835. CNS. A-Ar.

458 WILKINS, John. 1768–1772. Col. in the British Army under Gen. Gage in America; transactions with and presents to the Indians. MiU-C.

459 ANON. 1769. Shopkeeper of Newbury, Mass.; local details; weather. MSaE.

460 GILMAN, Rev. Tristram. 1769–1809 (with gaps). Includes sermons. MeHi.

461 HAVEN, Rev. Jason. 1769–1796. Dedham, Mass.: many deaths, marriages, funerals, visits, exchanges, and the events in his own family. MWA.

462 MIERS, Thomas, and Samuel Fisher. 1769–1795. CNS. PHi.

463 PILMORE, Rev. Joseph. 1769–1774. Related to history of Methodism in America. PPHiA.

464 SERRA, Junípero. 1769. Diary from Loreto to San Diego. ICN. *See* 735.

465 SMITH, Richard. 1769. A tour from Burlington, N.J., to the head of the Susquehannah River, with Richard Wells of Philadelphia, and the surveyors, Joseph Biddle, Jr., William Ridgway, and John Hicks. PPL. *See* 590?

466 TILDEN, D. 1769. Notes on shipping at Boston and Scituate, Mass. NN.

467 WIGHT, Dr. Aaron. 1769. Almanac entries. MHi.

468 ANON. 1770–1854. The congregation of the Moravian Church in Friedland, N.C. NcWsM.

469 ANON. 1770–1926. The congregation of the Moravian Church in Friedberg, N.C. NcWsM.

470 BARRINGER, Gen. Rufus. 1770–1778. CNS. Nc-Ar, typescript.

471 CLARK, Gen. Jonathan. 1770–1811. Weather conditions; his whereabouts from day to day; service as deputy clerk of Spotsylvania Cnty., Va.; Revolutionary War service in Va., S.C., and with the 8th Va. Regt. in the North; farming; social events. KyLoF.

472 CLARKE and NIGHTINGALE. 1770–1795. Arrival and departure of vessels from port of Providence; commercial agreements, etc. RHi.

473 GODDARD, John. 1770–1787. "Expense book" with items of family interest. MBr.

474 [GOERANSON, Rev. Andrew]. 1770. People and places (in Swedish). PPPrHi.

475 GREEN, Jeremiah. 1770; 1771; 1774; 1776; 1778; 1780. Few entries besides the weather; the siege of Boston in 1776. MWA.

476 HALE, Rev. Moses. 1770. Daily events; social affairs; visits, etc.; kept while he was at Harvard. MNeHi. *See* 115.

477 HAZARD, Eben. 1770–1771; 1772–1773; 1777–1778. CNS. PHi.

478 HOLROYD, Joseph T. 1770–1810 (with gaps). Almanacs; ship movements; his tenants. RHi.

479 IREDELL, James, Jr. 1770–1773. Personal diary of his social life; his reading; a smallpox epidemic in eastern N.C. Nc-Ar.

480 LEE, Rev. Joseph. 1770–1783 (with gaps). Religious life and work; weather; fires; farm work. MHi.

481 LIGHTFOOT, Benjamin. 1770–1772. A tour from Reading to Tankhannink Creek, and of surveys of a large tract of land there; topography of the country; Indian relations; frontier life; military posts; means of travel; various adventures. PHi.

482 MATTHEWS, William. 1770. Travels to Friends' meetings along Eastern seaboard. MdHi.

483 PARKER, James. 1770–1829. Almanacs; farming; personal; town meetings; social. MWA.

484 ROGERS, Daniel. 1770. Weather; piety; daily happenings. ICHi. *See* 106.

485 STILES, Ezra. 1770–1790. Local items; accounts of battles; excerpts from intercepted letters; sketches of military movements; notes and comments on public men and events. DLC.

486 WILLIS, Robert. 1770–1789. Travels in England, Scotland, Ireland, and the United States; Friends' meeting-places he visited; people he met; social conditions; transportation facilities; religious sentiments. PHi.

487 ZUBLY, Rev. John Joachim. 1770–1781. Theological matters and personal life; his attendance in the Continental Congress; sheds some light on his political beliefs. GHi.

488 ANON. 1771. Personal; local; member of General Assembly. NN.

489 AVERY, Rev. David. 1771–1805 (with gaps). Chaplain of the Revolution from Bunker Hill to Yorktown; with Washington when he crossed the Delaware, at the battles of Princeton and Trenton and at Valley Forge; events in his pastorates and family history; missionary to the Indians. CtHi has all but 1778, 1787, 1788, 1790, 1792–1804, and parts of 1775 and 1776.

490 BRAYTON, Patience. 1771–1772. Visits to N. C. NcHiC, typescript.

491 BULFINCH, Nathaniel, Jr. 1771. Local items in Lebanon, Conn.; personal doings; affairs of the General Assembly. NN.

492 JOHNSON, Joseph. 1771–1772. Indian's account of his spiritual life and of meetings at Mohegan. NhD. *See* 508.

493 MARCHANT, Henry. 1771–1772. Voyage from Newport, R.I., to London. PPAmS, typescript.

494 PARKE, Thomas. 1771–1772. A journey from Philadelphia to London. PHi.

495 ROSE, Duncan. 1771–1772. Diary; also memorandum book from Sept., 1770–Feb. 15, 1772; many prices given. ViHi.

496 ROTH, John. 1771; [1772]. Journal of a Moravian mission on the Susquehanna River in Pa., and on the Big Beaver River in Pa. (in German). OHi. *See* 542.

497 SOELLE, Rev. George. 1771–1773. Diary of home missionary journeys out of Salem, during which Soelle visited many non-Moravian settlers in N. C. (in German). NcWsM.

498 TIERSCH, Rev. Paul, and Rev. Hans Christian von Schweinitz. 1771. Travel diary of a journey with company, from Bethlehem, Pa., to Bethabara, N.C. (in German). NcWsM.

499 TRUMBULL, Gov. Jonathan. 1771–1774; 1779. Law cases; real estate; religious meditations. MHi.

500 WHEELOCK, Eleazar. 1771–1778. College affairs. NhD. *See* 260.

501 WIGHTMAN, Allen. 1771. A trip from Groton, Conn., to Vt. and return; persons visited; daily events; mentions bundling; contains a later trip to central N. Y. state; contains genealogical information concerning the Wightman family. RHi

502 ANON. 1772. Diary of a Presbyterian minister. ScU.

503 ANON. 1772. Voyage from Providence to New York; deals primarily with smallpox. NHi, photostat.

504 ALLEN, Gen. Ira. 1772. Surveys made of lands in Vt., "It being the first of My Surveying." NN; Secretary of State of Vt.

505 ANDREWS, John. 1772–1775. In the form of letters to his brother-in-law in Philadelphia; descriptions of Boston. MHi.

506 DAVIS, Moses. 1772–1776; 1782–1823. Building of Ft. Edgecomb; description of threatened British attack; other miscellaneous papers. Town Clerk's Office, Edgecomb, Me.

507 EVE, Sallie. 1772–1773. The weather; family matters; excursions to near-by places. NcD.

508 JOHNSON, Joseph. 1772–1773. Teaching Mohegan Indian children at Farmington, Conn.; religion. NN. *See* 492.

509 KENDALL, Rev. Thomas. 1772–1774. Mission to the Caughnawaga Indians. NhD.

510 KING, Richard. 1772–1774. "Justice's Book." MBNEH.

511 MERRIAM, Joseph. 1772–1787 (with gaps). Sundays and holidays; funerals. Charles M. Batcheller, Grafton, Mass. 1775. With Ward's regt.; Cambridge common; battle of Lexington. MB.

512 PUTNAM, Gen. Israel. 1772–1773. To Natchez locating lands for settlement of soldiers of Havannah expedition of 1762. CtHi. *See* 312, 513.

513 PUTNAM, Col. Israel. 1772–1773. Journal of an exploring expedition to the Natchez by order of the Conn. Land Co. DLC, transcript. *See* 312, 512.

514 TAITT, David. 1772. Journal. DLC, British transcript.

515 WADSWORTH, Rev. Benjamin. 1772–1825 (with gaps). Almanacs; daily activities. MHi, transcripts.

516 WICKHAM, William. 1772. Visit to the Crown Point area to inspect his lands there and to investigate charges of mistreatment of settlers by a Capt. Grey; notes of conversations, observations, etc. NjR.

517 WILSON, James. 1772–1774; 1782–1786. Legal cases and personal experiences, chiefly in N. J. and Philadelphia. PPAmS.

518 ANON. 1773–1859. Kept by the congregation of the Moravian church in Hope, N.C. (in German). NcWsM.

519 DUNBAR, Rev. Asa. 1773–1776. Outline of his life. MWA.

520 FISHER, Jabez M. 1773. Tour from Philadelphia to New York, Albany, the Mohawk country, Oswego, Niagara Falls, and down the St. Lawrence River. NUtHi, typescript.

521 HALE, Nathan. 1773–1776. CNS. CtHi.

522 LACEY, John. 1773. Journey to the Indians in western Pa. NHi.

523 McAFEE, James. 1773. An exploring party to Ky.; numerous surveys; topography of the country; table of distances from Pittsburgh to the mouth of the Ohio. WHi.

524 McAFEE, Robert. 1773. Expedition to Ky.; entries of land; table of distances. WHi.

525 NEWELL, Thomas. 1773; 1774. CNS. MH.

526 REDWOOD and BIRKETT. 1773–1775. Journal, ledger, and waste book. PHi. *See* 209.

527 RHODES, Nehemiah. 1773–1775. Almanac; farming; family. RHi.

528 UTLEY, Rev. Richard. 1773; 1775. Home missionary tours in N. C.; visits to many non-Moravian settlers. NcWsM.

529 WELD, Samuel. 1773–1776. Life in Boston and vicinity during the war; battles of Lexington and Bunker Hill. RHi.

530 ZEISBERGER, David. 1773–1777. Gnadenhutten diary (in German). NcWsM, original; OHi, photostat.

531 ANON. [1774–1798?] CNS. WHi.

532 ANON. 1774–1792. Quaker meetings; names of Quaker families; record of personal and domestic events; prices of farm products and commodities; notes on British army in Philadelphia; Capt. Henry Lee. PHi.

533 BARKER, Lt. John. 1774–1776. Military. NN.

534 BISLAND, John, Sr. 1774–1820. Plantation entries, with a son's account aboard the ship *Howard*. LU.

535 CARTER, Robert. 1774–1795. Miscellaneous accounts and a daily record of events. DLC.

536 FITCH, Rev. Elijah. 1774; 1775. Daily record of the weather, with war news and farming notes; places where he preaches and exchanges. 1774 diary, NN; 1775, WHi.

537 HUTCHINSON, Thomas. 1774. CNS. NN.

538 LITTLE, Rev. Daniel. 1774; 1786; 1788. Trips among Indians at Castine, Warren, Penobscot, Gouldsborough, Belfast; conferences. Unitarian Church, Kennebunk, Me., copy.

539 MARSHALL, Christopher. 1774–1793. Events during the Revolution; information on pharmacy. PHi.

540 McMILLAN, Rev. John. 1774–1776. Journal. PWW. *See* 237.

541 PERCY, Rev. William. 1774–1776. Activities in behalf of the religious revival; his travel and preaching in various towns of Pa., N.J., Md., Dela., and his views on the moral influence of the church. PHi.

542 ROTH, Rev. John. 1774. His tour from Friedenhutten through the wilderness to Indian towns and camps in the western part of Pa. (in German script). PHi. *See* 496.

543 SANGER, Abner. 1774–1782. Journal of member of Capt. Wyman's Co. of militia, march to Cambridge, April, 1775. DLC.

544 SEAMANS, Rev. Job. 1774–1820. Baptist ministry; sermons; local affairs. CtNl.

545 WILLIAMS, William. 1774; 1776–1778. CNS. DLC.

546 ANON. [1775–1784]. Diaries kept during the American Revolution by Hessian soldiers. MiU-C.

547 ANON. 1775–1777. By a member of the 47th Regt. of Foot, at Boston in 1775–1776, in Canada in 1776–1777. NN.

548 ANON. 1775–1776. A voyage from England to Boston. NHi.

549 ANON. 1775–1776. The Siege of Quebec; gives a particular account of the writer's part in the defense of Dec. 31, calling it "a glorious day for us, and as complete a little victory as was ever gained." MH.

550 ANON. 1775–1776. Kept in N.Y.; relates general occurrences. DLC.

551 ANON. 1775. Montgomery's Expedition against Canada. NHi.

552 ANON. 1775. French journal kept on board the brig *Washington*. DLC, British transcript.

553 ANON. [1775–?] Revolutionary War diaries by German soldiers (in German). NN.

554 AINSLIE, Thomas. 1775–1776. The most remarkable occurrences in the Province of Quebec from the appearance of the rebels in September, 1775, until their retreat on the sixth of May. MH.

555 ARNOLD, Benedict. 1775. His expedition to Canada. MH.

556 BANCROFT, Capt. Joseph. 1775–1780. CNS. See Drake, *Hist. Middlesex Co.*, II, 229.

557 BOWEN, Ashley. 1775–1777; 1777–1791. Personal; boats; vital statistics; funerals. MWA.

558 BRADFORD, Col. William. 1775. CNS. PHi. *See* 453.

559 BROWN, John. 1775–1778. CNS. DLC.

560 BUTLER, Maj. Gen. Richard. 1775. His travels and negotiations with the Indians. PHi. *See* 255.

561 CALK, William. 1775. Kept on a trip from Prince William Cnty., Va., to Boone's Ft. on the Kentucky River. NcU.

562 CHAPIN, Noah, Jr. 1775. Describes the battle of Bunker Hill, in which he was ensign in Capt. Solomon Willis' Co., in Col. Joseph Spencer's Regt. Ct.

563 CLARK, Elihu, Jr. 1775. Journal by member of Capt. Levi Wells' Co., 2nd Conn. Regt., kept at Roxbury Camp. DLC.

564 CURTIN, Daniel M. 1775–1776. Kept at the siege of Boston and en route to New York, where he was discharged in May, 1776. NjHi.

565 DORR, William. 1775. Military diary with Ward's Co. on Arnold's expedition to Quebec. MHi.

566 FITCH, Lt. Jabez. 1775; 1776. Journals of Lt. in Capt. Jewett's Co., Col. Jedidiah Huntington's 8th Conn. Regt. DLC. *See* 270.

567 FOLLETT, Mrs. Elizabeth Dewey. ca. 1775–1783. CNS. OHi, typescript.

568 FONT, Pedro. 1775–1776. A journey to Monterey and the port of San Francisco, under command of Don Juan Bautista de Anza (in Spanish). DLC, copy. *See* 678.

569 FOOTE, Abigail. 1775; 1776; 1779. Daily life and home duties. CtHi, copy.

570 FOOTE, Elizabeth. 1775. Daily life and home duties of a country girl. CtHi.

571 FOSTER, Judge John. 1775–1778. Diary of the events of the Revolution, written perhaps after the actual happenings. RPB.

572 GARCÉS, Francisco. 1775–1776. A journey through Sonora, Mex., and California. CSmH.

573 GARCÉS, P. 1775–1776. A journey to Monterey and the port of San Francisco (in Spanish). DLC, copy.

574 GODDARD, Capt. ——. 1775. From the journal of the *Duncannon* packet boat. DLC.

575 HAYDEN, William. 1775–1776; 1781. Deaths; accidents, etc. MSaE.

576 HENRY, J. J. 1775. The campaign against Quebec. PHi.

577 JACOBS, Samuel. 1775. His reaction to the American invasion of Canada in 1775. OCAJA.

578 JAMIESON, Capt. Neil. 1775–1778. CNS. DLC.

579 LIVINGSTON, Maj. Henry, Jr. 1775. The Canadian Campaign of the Continental Army. NN.

580 LOGAN, Dr. George. 1775–1779. A trip to England while he was a student at the Univ. of Edinburgh. PHi.

581 NEWELL, Timothy. 1775–1776. A journal kept during the time "yt Boston was shut up." NN.

582 NOYES, Dr. Belcher. 1775; 1782. Almanacs; marriages and deaths in Boston; fires; social life. MWA.

583 OXNARD, Edward. 1775–1786. Diaries of a Tory who took refuge with the fleet of Capt. Mowat and returned to England, when his diary begins; he returned to Falmouth after the war. MeHi.

584 PAGE, John. 1775–1777. A merchant's trip to England. MWob.

585 POLLEY, John. 1775. Battles around Boston, Roxbury, Cambridge. ICHi.

586 POPE, Richard. 1775–1777. Military journal and commonplace-book kept by member of the British 47th Regt. at Boston, Ticonderoga, Saratoga. CSmH.

587 RITZEMA, Col. Rudolphus. 1775–1776. Kept on Montgomery's Expedition against Canada. NHi.

588 ROGERS, Rev. William. 1775. Places where he preached between Baltimore and Providence; expense accounts, etc. RHi.

589 SANDERSON, Ruben. 1775–1815. Experiences in Revolutionary War with Col. Scammell's Light Infantry; contains transcript of congratulatory orders of George Washington on surrender of Yorktown. NNPM.

590 SMITH, Richard. 1775–1776. Private journal of the proceedings of the Continental Congress held at Philadelphia. NN, transcript. *See* 465?

624-668

n. 1776; 1784. Events of the
Rittenhouse and Hutchins
ockin and Quitapahilla

1776. Journal during the
olunteer; begins in camp
Crown Point. MH.
1776. Almanac; family,

n. 1776. With Arnold's
da. DLC, copy.
(Howe). 1776–1780; a

6–1777. Military jour-   di-
nd, New York City,   on   the
                                   ship.
776–1781?] Extracts
e War of the Revolu-   to the

E, Francisco Sylves-   ch in B.
anish). ICN.   pt. Sam-
gust. 1776. Voyage
J-C.

Journal of a ser-   MBSpnea.
on's Philadelphia   76. Journal
                            oyage from

officer, taken in
DLC.
U.S.; comments   s in Gen. An-
                          aign. WHi.
ritish officer in   e Andrew Doria.

t Ft. Stanwix.   ermany to Ameri-

cket Swallow.   ian soldier's journey
                          his embarkation, the
against Bur-   try, and the events
ed Mr. Bur-   ty of record during his
                        York State. N.

d Philadel-   lessian soldier's service
                      the American Revolu-
bach Regt.,   ure from Cassel; descrip-
H.   actions; observations on
         n account of his return to

ston; reg-   averhill and Salem, Mass.;
                    SaE.

9. Alma-   iritish soldier; Boston; Howe.
See 749.
SmH.

78. The   Fragment of a journal kept by
t Valley   bard the ship Queen Charlotte,
rsfield,   ton. ScU, photostat.
songs.   Oliver. 1776–1846. A record of

ALLEN, Daniel. 1776. Work in camp and in
tive service; accounts. CtCLA.

10 BLAKE, Maj. Henry. 1776. A march of Capt.
Hale's command from Winter Hill through Conn.,
N.Y., Ticonderoga, Crown Point, Chambly, and
Sorel back to Castleton, Vt. Mrs. Harriet M. Blake,
19 June St., Worcester, Mass.; to be given to the
NhHi.

611 BLOOMFIELD, Joseph. 1776. Personal and
military activities as captain of a company in the
3rd Regt., New Jersey Continental Line, operating
chiefly in the Mohawk Valley; dealings with Tories
and Indians; description of Indian customs. NjHi,
original; NjR, copy.

612 BROWN, Capt. Moses. 1776–1777. In
Brooklyn, N.Y., at the battles of White Plains and
Trenton; gives a return of the men in his company
who went to Trenton. Augustus Parker, Roxbury,
Mass., owned ms. in 1872; MBNEH, copy.

613 CARTER, Robert Wormeley. 1776. Personal
and business affairs at Sabine Hall, agreements
with overseers, farming on his several plantations,
accounts of winnings and losses at cards, political
meetings, military preparations. ViWC. See 407.

614 CLEVELAND, Rev. John. 1776. A journey
from Conn. to the troops in New York. DLC. See
148, 327.

615 CLITHERALL, Rev. Dr. James. 1776. Kept
on a trip from Charleston, S.C., to Philadelphia,
Pa., by the escort of Mrs. Arthur Middleton and
Mrs. Edward Rutledge. NcU, typescript.

616 COLDEN, Cadwallader, Jr. 1776–1779. During the Revolutionary War. CSmH.

617 CROGHAN, William. 1776–1777. Campaign
in the Jerseys during the Revolution. WHi. See 763,
806, 831, 867.

618 CUSHING, Capt. Charles. 1776. The retreat
from Canada under Gen. Sullivan. DLC.

619 DEWEY, Russell. 1776. March to Saratoga,
Crown Point, Montreal, Quebec; also attacks on
Quebec. MWeAt.

620 ELMER, Ebenezer. ca. 1776–1785. Kept during Revolutionary War. NjHi. See 767.

621 ESCALANTE, Fr., and Dominguez, Fr.
1776–1781. Description of road to newly discovered lands to the north, northwest, and west of New
Mexico. AzTP, typescript.

622 FRANCIS, Col. Ebenezer. 1776. Activities
from the time he set out from Cambridge camp; his
contacts with Gen. Washington and other patriot
officers; the Continental Congress; describes many
New England towns, skirmishes, and ship movements; repeats army gossip and tells of a plot by the
Mayor of New York to seize Gen. Washington.
NIC.

623 GALLUP, Nehemiah. 1776. Capt. John
Morgan's Company's march from Conn. to White
Plains and return. DLC.

624 GOMEZ, ———. 1776–1798. CNS. CU-B.

625 HONEYMAN, Dr. Robert. 1776–1782. Military movements. DLC.

626 "J.R." 1776–1784. Written in old German script by Hessian soldier. MiU-C.

627 JENNISON, Lt. William. 1776–1780. The retreat from Long Island and the battle of White Plains; sea service as marine and privateer. DLC. PHi.

628 LEE, Arthur. 1776–1777. Journal of the American Revolution, covering in part the period of the author's mission to the Court of Spain. DLC.

629 LITTLE, Col. Moses. 1776–1814. CNS. Me-Hi.

630 LOXLEY, Capt. Benjamin. 1776. The Amboy campaign and muster roll for the 1st Artillery Co. of Philadelphia. PHi.

631 LYMAN, Elihu. 1776. Diary of events kept at Headquarters at N.Y. DLC.

632 MALSBURG, Friedrich Wilhelm von der. 1776. By the captain of the Dittfurth Regt., German allied troops in America (in German). DLC.

633 McJUNKIN, Maj. Joseph. [1776–?] Services in the Revolutionary War in S. C. and Ga. WHi.

634 MEDBURY, Lt. John. 1776. Account of British and American activities; arrival of troops from New England; reading of Declaration of Independence. RHi.

635 MILES, Col. Samuel. 1776–? Military; the American Revolution. DLC.

636 MORISON, George. 1776? Expedition to Quebec; the beginning of American Revolution; account of hardships suffered by detachment in passing through wilderness. PHi; MH, copy.

637 MORRIS, Margaret. 1776–1778. Events during the Revolution. MH.

638 NASH, Solomon. 1776–1777. Diary kept while he was a soldier. NHi.

639 NICE, Capt. John. 1776. Diary and notes of military affairs in New York and Long Island. PHi. *See* 728.

640 OSGOOD, Dr. David. 1776–1822. Vital statistics; religious work. MMe.

641 PERRY, Rev. Joseph. 1776–1777. War experiences. GHi.

642 PICKERING, Timothy. 1776–1777; 1781; 1786. CNS. MSaE.

643 PITMAN, Rev. John. 1776–1822. Service with the Pa. militia in N.J.; his ministry. RHi.

644 ROBERTS, Algernon. 1776. Campaign from Philadelphia to Paulus Hook. MH.

645 ROCHAMBEAU, Count. 1776? Military: French forces in American Revolution. DLC.

646 RODNEY, Thomas. 1776–1777. Campaign notes by Del. captain of militia. DLC; NN, transcript. *See* 884, 1087.

647 SELLERS, Natha[...] days; a trip with Messrs[...] to survey the Tulpe[...] springs. PPAmS.

648 SHALLUS, Jacob[...] Canada expedition by a [...] before Quebec; ends nea[...]

649 STANTON, John. [...] weather; war news. MWA[...]

650 STEVENS, Benjami[...] military expedition to Can[...]

651 STORRS, Lucinda [...] 1812–1829. CNS. CtHi.

652 TOWN, Zaccheus. 17[...] nal of service in New Eng[...] Long Island, and N. J. NjR[...]

653 VAIL, Christopher. [...] from a journal kept during th[...] tion. MH. *See* 595.

654 VELEZ de ESCALANT[...] tre de. 1776–1777. CNS (in Sp[...]

655 VON LOOS, Johann Au[...] from England to America. Mi[...]

656 YOUNG, Sgt. 1776–1777[...] geant in Capt. Thomas Fitzsi[...] Inf. company. PHi.

657 ANON. 1777? By a British[...] battle, Philadelphia, July 7, 1777[...]

658 ANON. 1777. A tour in the [...] and reflections. MH, copy.

659 ANON. 1777. Journal of a B[...] Gen. Howe's army. MH.

660 ANON. 1777. By an officer [...] DLC.

661 ANON. 1777. Journal of the p[...] DLC, British transcript.

662 ANON. 1777. The campaign [...] goyne, ending when the writer "atten[...] goyne to Boston." MH.

663 ANON. 1777. Activities arou[...] phia; by a Hessian. MiU-C.

664 ANON. 1777–1781. In the 1st Ans[...] during the American Revolution. CSm[...]

665 ANON. 1777. Military near Bo[...] imental court; Crafts' company. MSaE[...]

666 ADAMS, Rev. Phineas. 1777; 17[...] nacs; deaths; marriages; funerals. MHi.

667 ANDRÉ, John. 1777–1778. CNS. [...]

668 ARMSTRONG, Lt. Samuel. 1777–1[...] capture of Burgoyne and the encampment [...] Forge; marches through Blanford, San[...] etc., to Saratoga; a number of soldiers[...] MBNEH.

669 BACKUS, Elijah. 1777. The war; rumors of battles; counterfeiters; the student housing problem; smallpox; Gen. Benedict Arnold. MoU.

670 BEERS, Nathan. 1777–1782. The army in N.Y. and N.J.; in camp at Providence; most of the time in Conn. and R.I.; mentions André's execution. DLC.

671 [BURKE, Thomas]. 1777. During his attendance at Congress, covering the debates in Feb. at Baltimore and in March at Philadelphia, with regard to retaliation for the treatment of Gen. Charles Lee; Lee's request that a committee of Congress be sent to him at N.Y.; the relative powers of Congress and the individual states; and other general matters. NN; Nc-Ar.

672 COLBRATH, William. 1777. Kept at Ft. Schuyler (Stanwix), N.Y. NN.

673 COWAN, John. 1777. Indian depredations; arrivals and departures; election of Todd and Callaway as representatives from Ky. Cnty. to the Va. legislature; attack on Boonesborough; number of people in fort at Harrodsburg on May 1; Logan's Ft. attacked; arrival of Col. Bowman and his regt. in Ky.; court held at Harrodsburg and officers sworn into commission. WHi, copy.

674 CRAFT, Eleazer. 1777. CNS. MSaE.

675 DU PONCEAU, Pierre Stephen. 1777–1778. Valley Forge maps; account of a trip from Boston to Yorktown to Washington's camp at Valley Forge (in French and Russian chiefly). DeHi.

676 DWINNELL, Solomon. 1777. Revolutionary War diary, with a summary of events. MnHi, typescript.

677 FARNUM, Lt. Benjamin. 1777–1778. The Revolution at Bennington, West Point, and N. Y. state. MHi.

678 FONT, Pedro. 1777. Trip to Monterey via the Colorado River (in Spanish). RPB. *See* 568.

679 GANNETT, Rev. Caleb. 1777–1782. His travels; expenses; many marriages, deaths; court trials; items of college news; prices paid for various articles and other personal matters. MH.

680 GIFFIN, Sgt. Maj. Simon. 1777–1779. CNS. Ct; CtY.

681 GILPIN, Thomas. 1777–1778. His experiences as a political prisoner. NHi. *See* 1233?

682 HARRIS, Samuel, Jr. 1777. Journal while he was in the army; battle of Bemis' Heights and surrender. MH.

683 HILL, Baylor. 1777–1780. Military: the 1st Continental Dragoons. CSmH.

684 HILL, Dr. West. 1777. Surgeon in British Army engaged in American war, expedition to the Chesapeake in 1777. MBNEH.

685 HOWE, Dr. Estes. 1777–1778. Time spent as surgeon with Gates' forces during Saratoga campaign. NN.

686 HOWE, Sir William. 1777. Proceedings of the army under his command; Battle of Brandywine; drawings. MH.

687 KIRKWOOD, Capt. 1777–1782 (with gaps). General orders; marches of Del. Regt.; marches southerly from East Jersey; Carolinas campaign. MH. *See* next item?

688 KIRKWOOD, Robert. 1777–1780. The Del. Regt. DLC.

689 LAURENS, John. 1777–1779 (with gaps). Personal; social events. DLC. *See* 722.

690 LAWRENCE, Jonathan. 1777. CNS. N.

691 LEWIS, John. 1777. CNS. Nc-Ar.

692 LINCOLN, Gen. Benjamin. 1777. Plans of military cooperation with D'Estaing. MPB. *See* 723, 779.

693 LYMAN, Rev. Joseph. 1777. With the Hatfield Co. to Saratoga; Indian raids; news from Ticonderoga; Burgoyne. MBC.

694 MILLER, Maj. Ebenezer. 1777–1799. Weather; farming; household. MHi.

695 MORFI, Padre Juan Augustin. 1777. Kept at the missions of Tex. and N. M. (in Spanish). ICN.

696 PEMBERTON, James. 1777–1778. CNS. PHi.

697 RIDLEY, Matthew. 1777–1782 (with gaps). Diary written in Europe containing "many errors and false suspicions respecting men and things in Paris (particularly Dr. Franklin)." MH.

698 SMITH, Thomas Peters. 1777–1802. Journal in Europe. PPAmS.

699 STEVENS, Enos. 1777–1800. Diary of a Tory. VtHi.

700 SYLVESTER, Barstow. 1777. CNS. MeBP.

701 THORNTON, Dr. William. 1777–1782. CNS. DLC.

702 TURNER, Jacob. 1777–1778. Diary of a N.C. soldier, giving in brief form daily army orders, preparations for marches, comments on court-martials, etc. Nc-Ar.

703 VARNUM, John, Jr. 1777; 1778–1780. Daily life. MBNEH.

704 VON BAURMEISTER, Carl Leopold. 1777. Concerning Hessians' march on Philadelphia. MiU-C.

705 VON RIEDESEL, Friedrich Adolph. 1777. MiU-C.

706 WARREN, Capt. Benjamin. 1777–1778. The Saratoga and Cherry Valley campaigns. MH.

707 ANON. 1778. British garrison at Newport, R.I.; French and British fleets. NN.

708 ANON. 1778–1779. Diary of events of the Revolution as seen by a Tory. PHi.

709　ANON. 1778. Kept while author was in British garrison at Newport. NN.

710　ANON. 1778. CNS. MiU-C.

711　ANON. 1778. In the British garrison of Newport, R.I., describing the arrival and departure of the French and English fleets, and the land operations of the campaign. NN.

712　BELL, Andrew. 1778. CNS. NjHi.

713　BOWMAN, Maj. Joseph. 1778–1779. Expedition against the Indians. WHi.

714　BRIDGE, Deacon Samuel. 1778; 1788; 1791; 1795; 1797; 1798. Interleaved almanacs with few scattered items: weather, deaths, personal doings. MWA.

715　DAVIS, Capt. John. 1778; 1781–1782. Journal of officer who served in the campaign leading to the surrender of Cornwallis at Yorktown. NSch-Hi.

716　D'ESTAING, Comte ———. 1778–1779. CNS. PHi.

717　FELL, Judge John. 1778–1779. Journal while he was a member of the Continental Congress for N.J.; gives an account of the proceedings of Congress. DLC.

718　FISHER, Elijah. 1778–1780. Revolutionary diary. MeHi.

719　GILBERT, Benjamin. 1778–1788. Kept while he was col. in Peter Harnwood's Co., Leonard's Regt.; mostly New York, Hudson River area. NCooHi.

720　HAMILTON, Henry. 1778–1779. CNS. MH, original; MiU-C, photostat.

721　HARMER, Brig. Gen. Josiah. 1778–1780. The Revolution while he served as lt. col. under Gen. Washington. MiU-C. See 857.

722　LAURENS, John. 1778. His visit to R.I. DLC. See 689.

723　LINCOLN, Gen. Benjamin. 1778–1779. Revolutionary War diary. NN. See 692, 779.

724　McCREADY, Robert. 1778. An expedition under Col. Lachlan McIntosh. DLC.

725　McHENRY, Maj. James. 1778. The march from Valley Forge; the reception of an Indian deputation by Gen. Washington; the battle of Monmouth; a visit to the falls of the Passaic; the march to White Plains. NN; MiU-C.

726　MERRIAM, Rev. Matthew. 1778–1797. Religious work; parishioners; their work for him and presents. MBNEH.

727　MÜHLENBERG, Gotthilf Henry Ernst. 1778–1806. CNS (in German). PPAmS.

728　NICE, Capt. John. 1778. Military; at Valley Forge. PHi. See 639.

729　PARKER, James. 1778–1790. Farming and land interests. PSC-Hi, typescript.

730　PORTER, Jonathan. 1778. Service in Wade's regt.; Providence, etc. MSaE.

731　POTTER, Capt. John. 1778–1779. Journal while he served at Peekskill and White Plains as lt. and paymaster of Col. Ezra Wood's regt. of Mass. militia. N, photostat.

732　ROBIE, Samuel. 1778. CNS. NhHi.

733　SAWYER, Ebenezer. 1778–1779. Journal of march of the army from Berwick, Me., to West Point, N.Y. NN.

734　SCOTT, Joseph. 1778–1822. CNS. MH.

735　SERRA, Junípero. 1778–1784. A chronological list of each person confirmed at Carmel Mission; a short account of each trip from mission to mission made by Serra for the purpose of confirming, and the number confirmed at each place. CFM. See 464.

736　STEUBEN, Baron Friedrich Wilhelm von. 1778–1782. Military with Continental Army. NHi. See 819, 967.

737　STONE, John. 1778–1807. Legal cases in Holliston and Essex Cnty., Mass.; marriages. MBNEH.

738　TUCKER, Samuel. 1778. Journal on board the U.S. frigate Boston, bound to Europe on diplomatic service; John Adams was a passenger. MH.

739　TWISS, Dr. Jonathan. 1778. Drummer in Tuttle's company; Boston and Charlestown. Ct, copy.

740　UPDIKE, Daniel. 1778–1779. His studies; social events; British evacuation of Newport; preaching of Jemima Wilkinson. RHi.

741　VON SEITZ, Franz Carl E. 1778. Journey from New York to Halifax. MiU-C.

742　WOODHULL, Rev. John. 1778–1791. Memorandum containing texts of sermons preached by him; members and elders of Freehold, N.J., Presbyterian Church. PPPrHi.

743　ANON. 1779. On the road from Rowan County, N.C., to Leesburg on the Potomac River, Loudoun Cnty., Va.; made by a member of the Stockton or Eddy family, of N.J., escorting a wagon with passengers (and army supplies?) from N.C. to N.J. ViU.

744　ANON. 1779. Journals of officers in the expedition of Major General John Sullivan against the Indians. NHi, original; NCanHi, copy.

745　ANON. 1779. The Moravian mission among the Indians. NcWsM.

746　ANON. 1779. Sullivan's expedition against the Iroquois in N.Y. state. DLC.

747　ANON. 1779–1782. French naval operations in America (in French). DLC.

748　ANON. 1779. Clinton's march from Albany to Tioga; at home in Salisbury. MWA.

749 ADAMS, Rev. Phineas. 1779. Deaths, marriages, funerals, etc. MHi. *See* 666.

750 ARTEAGA, Ignacio. 1779. An exploring expedition to Bucardi Sound and the Northwest Coast as far as Mt. St. Elias, stopping at Cape Mendocino and S.F. on the return. CtY.

751 BALME, Col. Augustin Motten de la. 1779. From Boston to Machias, with Col. Allan, a priest, and another officer; many conversations with people he meets (in French). BM; CaOOHa, copy.

752 BARR, John. 1779-1782. His activities as ensign in the 4th N.Y. Regt. during the Revolution. N, original; DLC, copy.

753 BARTON, William. 1779. By a lieutenant in the Revolutionary War. NjHi.

754 BEATTY, Erkuries. 1779; 1786-1787. Sullivan's Indian Expedition; in western Pa., Ohio, Ind., and Ky.; the collection of money from the government for the regiment in the West. NHi.

755 BEAUREGARD, Elie T. 1779. Trip to the Illinois country. MoSHs.

756 BIDDLE, Owen. 1779-1782. Record of weather and plantings; scientific, medical; political; member of Constitutional Convention. NjR.

757 BLAKE, Thomas. 1779. Sullivan's expedition on the frontier. WHi.

758 BROWNELL, Abner. 1779-1785. Religious experiences during the time he was a follower of Jemima Wilkinson. MWA.

759 BURROWS, Maj. John. 1779. The Sullivan-Clinton campaign. NBuHi.

760 CAMPFIELD, Jabez. 1779. Kept by a surgeon in "Spencers Regiment," attached to Sullivan's Expedition against the Indians. NjHi.

761 CLAP, Daniel. 1779. Journal of Sullivan's expedition. ICN.

762 CLARK, George Rogers. 1779. The recapture of Vincennes. WHi.

763 CROGHAN, William. 1779-1780. March from N.J. to Charleston. WHi. *See* 617, 806, 831, 867.

764 CUTHBERTSON, Rev. John. 1779. Description of missionary work at various frontier settlements. PWW.

765 DEARBORN, Henry. 1779-1781. Army movements about N.Y. and siege of Yorktown. NN.

766 ELIOT, Rev. John. 1779-1782; 1788-1813. Daily weather record with notes largely of his preaching and lectures; sometimes a list of presents received; lists of deaths; marriage fees; his clothing and that of his family; books read. MHi.

767 ELMER, Ebenezer. 1779. Sullivan's expedition. WHi. *See* 620.

768 ERRICKSON, Sgt. Michael. 1779. Journal in Capt. Burrowes's Co., 4th N.J. Regt.; expedition to the Wyoming Valley. DLC.

769 FELTMAN, William. 1779; 1781-1782. Journals of a lt. of the 1st and 10th Regt. of Pa. PHi.

770 FLEMING, William. 1779-1780. His trip to Ky. as commissioner of Va. to settle land titles and public accounts in that country; list of claims; account of moneys received and expended; notes on the topography; natural history and economic condition of the country. WHi. *See* 855.

771 FOSTER, Thomas. 1779-1780. Military journal, account book, and commonplace book, kept by a soldier with the 4th Mass. Regt. CSmH.

772 FRANKLIN, Benjamin. 1779; 1764-1774. A memorandum of letters written and received; record of financial doings, expenses, and disbursements in London. PPAmS. *See* 842.

773 GORE, Lt. Obadiah. 1779. Maj. Gen. Sullivan's march to Genesee River; begins on leaving Wyoming; ends at Conadegago. MH.

774 HAND, Edward. 1779. Sullivan's expedition against the Indians. NN.

775 HAWKINS, John H. 1779-1781. Campaigns in N.E. during the Revolution; troop movements; battles; military and economic conditions; espionage; court-martials. PHi.

776 HENDERSON, Robert. 1779-1823. CNS. PHi.

777 HEYMELL, Carl Philipp. 1779. Journey of the Knyphausen fusiliers on the *Triton*. MiU-C.

778 HUNT?, John. 1779. Experiences while he attended Philadelphia Yearly Meeting of the Religious Society of Friends. PSC-Hi. *See* 1254.

779 LINCOLN, Gen. Benjamin. 1779. Plans of cooperation with D'Estaing. MH. *See* 692, 723.

780 MacARTHUR, Dr. Charles. 1779. Surgeon of the 4th Pa. Regt. of Gen. Sullivan's Western Expedition, from Lake Otsego to Genessee Town, and the return to Wyoming. PPL, copy.

781 McNEILL, Samuel. 1779. On Sullivan's Indian Expedition as quartermaster of Gen. Hand's Brigade. NHi.

782 McQUEEN, Joshua. 1779-1782. Journal of Indian wars and battles with the British; narrow escapes; people killed or captured; hunting experiences; tells of being at Valley Forge and attending church with George Washington. MoU.

783 NORRIS, Maj. James. 1779. Journal of the West expedition, commanded by Maj. Gen. Sullivan; describes the march from Easton, Pa., to Wyoming, Pa., to Kannadasoga and Tioga, N.Y., and return to Easton. WHi; NN; NBuHi.

784 O'CONNOR, M. 1779. The French siege of Savannah, with introduction and commentary by Comte d'Estaing. MiU-C.

785 PARKMAN, Ebenezer, Jr. 1779-1793. Daily life in army; war news; mostly at Morristown; life at Brookfield. MWA.

786 PIERCE, William. 1779. Gen. John Sullivan's aide-de-camp, relating many events of the Western expedition. PPL.

787 REIDHEAD, William. 1779. CNS. MeHi.

788 ROBERTS, Theodore. 1779. Journal on Sullivan's Indian Expedition, with the 5th N.J. Regt. NHi.

789 RUSSELL, Capt. Peter. 1779–1780. Military journal with Clinton to Charleston, S.C.; the siege. CaOTP.

790 SHUTE, Samuel M. 1779. Journal of Sullivan's expedition. WHi.

791 SMITH, Daniel. 1779–1780. CNS. WHi.

792 TREADWELL, Rev. John. 1779. Almanac; brief notes. MSaE.

793 VAUX, Richard. 1779–1780; 1781–1782. CNS. PHi.

794 VON HINRICHS, Johann. 1779–1780. CNS. MiU-C. *See* 823.

795 VON HUYN, Johann Christoph. 1779–1780. Siege of Charleston. MiU-C.

796 WEBB, Nathaniel. 1779. Gen. Sullivan's expedition against the Indians. NElmHi.

797 WINTHROP, Hannah (Fayerweather) Tolman. 1779–1789. CNS. MH.

798 ANON. 1780. Military with Wadsworth's Regt.; Rhode Island. MSaE.

799 ANON. 1780. Kept by a member of the 9th Conn. Regt.; campaign in the Jerseys. DLC.

800 ANON. 1780. Kept by officer in the Jäger Corps. MiU-C.

801 ALLAIRE, Lt. Anthony. 1780. Battle of King's Mountain and other occurrences during campaign of the British in the Carolinas. WHi, copy.

802 ANDERSON, Thomas. 1780–1782. Journal of soldier of the 1st Del. Regt. DLC.

803 BALDWIN, Samuel. 1780. CNS. NjHi.

804 CASTRIES, Armand Charles Augustin de la Croix, Duc de. 1780. Comte de Rochambeau's expedition to America in 1780; an account of the sailing from Brest and the arrival at Newport, as well as minor events at sea. MiU-C.

805 CLOSEN, Baron Jean Christophe Louis Frederic Ignace von. 1780–1783. The campaigns for those years, beginning with the embarkation of Rochambeau's army from Brest (in French). DLC, copy.

806 CROGHAN, William. 1780. CNS. MH. *See* 617, 763, 831, 867.

807 DONELSON, Col. John. 1780. Journal of the boat *Adventure*, which brought the first settlers to the Cumberland settlement. THi.

808 GALE, Edmund. 1780–1781. Military. NHi.

809 GIBBS, Caleb. 1780. CNS. DLC.

810 KEMBLE, Peter. 1780–1785. Weather; farm, garden, and orchard; Revolutionary War. NjR.

811 LYMAN, Daniel. 1780. Kept by Senior Aide to Maj. Gen. Heath and Adj. Gen. of the Eastern Department; received the French army under Rochambeau at Newport. RHi.

812 NELSON, George. 1780–1781; 1790–1802. Accounts of battles, mutiny and dissatisfaction in the Pa. Line of Continental troops; acts of Assembly and of Continental Congress; city affairs; trading conditions; church activities; commercial enterprises. PHi.

813 NEWTON, Daniel. 1780–1781. His trip to Philadelphia with Gen. Artemas Ward, and the events there. NHi.

814 PENNINGTON, William S. 1780–1781. Military accounts of an officer of the 2nd Regt. of Artillery. NjHi.

815 REICHEL, Bishop Johann Friedrich. 1780. Journey from Lititz, Pa., to Wachovia, N.C., and return (in German). NcWsM. *See* 883.

816 SENFF, Christian. 1780. The campaign in S.C. DLC, contemporary copy by Timothy Matlock.

817 SEYMOUR, William. 1780–1783. Journal of a sgt.-maj. in the Del. Regt. during the Southern Expeditions. DLC; 1780 journal in PHi.

818 SHOEMAKER, Rebecca, and her daughters, Anna and Margaret Tawle. 1780–1786. Personal. PHi.

819 STEUBEN, Baron Friedrich Wilhelm von. 1780–1781. Military. MH. *See* 736, 967.

820 STUART and WELSH. 1780–1792. CNS. PHi.

821 VICKROY, Thomas. 1780. A trip from Pa. to Louisville in 1780. OCUHi.

822 VON EWALD, Johann. 1780. Expedition to Charleston. MiU-C.

823 VON HINRICHS, Johann. 1780. Expedition to S.C. MiU-C. *See* 794.

824 WHITE, E. 1780. Journal of the Revolutionary campaigns of 1780, with the words of many war and love songs. MBAt.

825 ANON. 1781–1783. Travel; the Christian Indian congregation captured on the Muskingum, moved to Sandusky, dispersed there, and reestablished on Lake Huron. NcWsM.

826 ANON. 1781–1783. On board the French ship *Hercule*, and campaigns in the West Indies and at Yorktown. NHi.

827 ALLEN, Jacob(?). 1781–1782. Kept while he was a corporal of a company in the 4th Regt. of Militia commanded by John Daggett. MTaHi.

828 ATWATER, Rev. Noah. 1781–1802. Local matters; weather; farming notes; building of houses; bird-watching; beekeeping, etc. MWe.

829 BRINGHURST, Hannah P. 1781. Thoughts and meditations during an illness. PHC; PSC-Hi, copy. 1781–1782. Contemplative journal. PHi.

830 COFFIN, Charles. 1781–1785. Personal; written while he was a student at Harvard (mostly in Latin). MH.

831 CROGHAN, William. 1781. The return to Va. after his capture. WHi. *See* 617, 763, 806, 867.

832 DAVIS, Elias. 1781–1800. Voyages from Baltimore to Boston on the brigs *Hope* and *Augusta*. MH.

833 ELLISON, Robert. 1781–1782. Copies or summaries of letters written to members of his family and other persons. NNC.

834 [LYLE, Hugh?] 1781? CNS. DLC.

835 LYON, Rev. Walter. 1781. His own travels and business; almanac. MWA.

836 MONTEIL, Chevalier de. 1781–1782. Commander of a French naval squadron in the West Indies (in French). MiU-C.

837 PHILLIPS, Abraham. 1781. During service with Gen. Greene. DLC.

838 PRICE, Ezekiel. 1781. CNS. MH. *See* 916.

839 ANON. 1782. Trip back to England by a Hessian soldier. MiU-C.

840 ALLEN, Thomas, Jr. 1782–1800 (with gaps). Largely weather and farm notes. MWA. *See* 932?

841 AVERY, Rev. Joseph. 1782–1800. Funerals in Holden, Mass. MWA.

842 FRANKLIN, Benjamin. 1782. Daily events in Passy, France. DLC. *See* 772.

843 GRABS, Gottfried, and GRUHL, ———. 1782. Travels to Mt. Caucasus. NcWsM. *See* 293.

844 HENKEL, Rev. Paul. 1782–1825. Lutheran missionary activities in western Va., N.C., and Ohio (partly in German). ViU.

845 HOSKINS, Rev. Thomas. 1782–1783; 1784–1785. CNS. DLC.

846 KELSO, William. 1782. Trip down the Ohio and Mississippi Rivers with a cargo of flour. OHi, photostat.

847 MAY, Joseph. 1782–1839. Almanacs; deaths, marriages; family affairs; public events. MHi.

848 TREAT, Capt. Samuel. 1782–1783. At Castle Island; ship arrivals; harbor scene. MH.

849 VON LINDER, Friedrich Carl Ludwig. 1782. Crossing of the Atlantic from Bremerlehe to Halifax. MiU-C.

850 ANON. 1783–1793. Personal; weather; public events; Boston, Charleston, etc. MWA.

851 ANON. 1783. Voyage from Santa Lucia to Cornwall. ViHi.

852 CASE, Rev. Isaac. 1783–1802. Religious, and his family and work. MeWC. *See* 936.

853 CONSTANT, Rev. Silas. 1783–1803. Record of marriages performed. PPPrHi.

854 FITCH, John. 1783–1791. Agreements regarding land, receipts and expenditures; surveyor's notes taken in the Ohio Country; conditions in the Ohio and Allegheny valleys; notes on the climate, etc. DLC. *See* 4932?

855 FLEMING, William. 1783. Second trip to Ky. as commissioner of Va. to settle land titles and public accounts in that country. WHi. *See* 770.

856 FRANCIS, John. 1783–1784. Journey by boat from Philadelphia to Portugal; observations on places and local customs. RHi.

857 HARMER, Brig. Gen. Josiah. 1783–1799. Military and political duties. MiU-C. *See* 721.

858 LEWIS, Joseph. 1783–1795. CNS. NjHi.

859 McCULLY, George. 1783. A tour under Capt. Ephraim Douglass to Detroit with a message from Congress to the Indians. DLC.

860 SEWALL, Henry. 1783. Military. DLC.

861 SHERWOOD, Capt. Justus. 1783. Vermonter's expedition to view Bay of Chaleurs for settlement of loyalists in Lower Canada. Secretary of State's Office, Montpelier, Vt.

862 SHOEMAKER, Samuel. 1783–1785. Diaries written "for the entertainment of [his] wife," during his stay in London as a loyalist refugee. PHi, NHi.

863 SNOWDEN, Rev. Gilbert Tennent. 1783–1785. Daily family affairs, especially touching on his religious life. PPPrHi.

864 TREMPER, Laurence. 1783. Journal of service in N.Y. state with Col Marinus Willett's Regt., "New York Levies." DLC.

865 ANON. 1784–1785. By a student of medicine at the Univ. of Edinburgh; possibility that the diarist is same as Anon. 906. ViHi.

866 ADAMS, Abigail. 1784–1787. Three years spent in Europe; especially the social life, dinners, receptions, etc.; the Marquis de Lafayette and Franklin were frequent guests and appear as familiar friends. Published *Journal* and correspondence, N.Y., 1841.

867 CROGHAN, William. 1784. A trip from Louisville to Nashville, with surveyor's notes by the way. WHi. *See* 617, 763, 806, 831.

868 EVANS, Griffith. 1784; 1795–1796. Trip to Burlington, N.J.; journey to Europe; trip to the West; descriptions of cities visited. MWA. 1784–1785. A trip from Philadelphia to Ft. Stanwix, and thence to Ft. McIntosh to attend treaty negotiations with the Six Nations and the "Western Indians." CSmH.

869 GRAHAM, John. 1784. A trip from Va. to Philadelphia. Nc-Ar.

870 HOLLAND, Park. 1784; 1794; and later. Autobiography to end of Revolution; survey of Passamaquoddy; Shay's Rebellion; Penobscot; day-to-day work. MeBaHi. *See* 1821.

871 [JENKS, John]. 1784-1785. Journal and expense accounts of travels in Eastern states. MH.

872 LIPSCOMB, John. 1784. CNS. THi.

873 RITTENHOUSE, David. 1784-1796. Principally meteorological and astronomical observations. PPAmS.

874 SNOWDEN, Isaac, Jr. 1784-1808. Record of services and sermons at many Philadelphia churches, especially 2nd Presbyterian Church. PPPrHi.

875 SPRAGUE, Thomas. 1784-1850 (part in a later hand). Births and deaths. MWA.

876 WEBSTER, Noah. 1784-1788. Domestic; trips to Southern states and through New England; social life; literary work. NN.

877 YARNALL, Peter. 1784-1796. Visits to Friends' Meetings. PSC-Hi.

878 FILSON, John. 1785-1786. Trips from Pittsburgh to Vincennes to Falls of Ohio; his defeat on the Wabash; Clark's campaign on foot; Hardin and Patton's expedition. WHi. *See* 4931?

879 FRANKLIN, William Temple. 1785. CNS. PPAmS.

880 HUNTER, Robert. 1785-1786. Journal of an English traveler in the United States. CSmH.

881 JACOB MECHLIN estate. 1785-1790. Journal and ledger. PHi.

882 MIDDLETON, Thomas. 1785-1812. Accounts of a plantation; lists of slaves. NcU.

883 REICHEL, Bishop Johann Friedrich. 1785-1786. Journey with wife from Copenhagen to the Cape of Good Hope. NcWsM. *See* 815.

884 RODNEY, Thomas. 1785-1800. Weather; travels; expenses; astronomical observations; dreams; battles of Revolutionary War; career in Continental Congress; political observations of Supreme Court Justice. DeHi. *See* 646, 1087.

885 STEARNS, Hon. Isaac. 1785-1788. Business; farming; religious; travel to New York. MHi.

886 WOOD, Oliver. 1785-1791. His legal cases; marriages. MeHi.

887 [WOODORF, ———]. 1785-1788. A trip through N.Y., N.J., and Pa. PPAmS.

888 ANON. 1786-1859. The choir of single sisters in the Moravian church in Salem, N.C. (in German). NcWsM.

889 ANON. 1786. A passage from N.Y. to Boston, by packet to Providence, with a stop at Newport, then by sleigh through Attleborough and Dedham. DLC.

890 BROWN, Caleb. 1786. Survey of western boundary of Pa. OHi.

891 CUTTING, Nathaniel. 1786-1793; 1790-1792; 1793. Travel: France, England, Boston, Santo Domingo, Algeria. MHi.

892 GIBSON, James. 1786; 1786-1787. College life at Princeton; social life in Philadelphia. PHi.

893 GOULD, Jonathan. 1786-1790. Journals at Providence College (Brown Univ.), and while he preached and taught school. MeHi.

894 JEFFERSON, Thomas. 1786. A tour through the wine-growing districts of France and Italy. CSmH. *See* 979.

895 McCAY, Spruce. 1786. CNS. Nc-Ar.

896 MITCHELL, Nathan. 1786-1790. Local and political; personal; social; weather; Shay's rebellion. MBNEH. *See* next entry.

897 MITCHELL, Nathan. 1786-1791. Sunday observances; morality; deaths. MBNEH.

898 NORTH, William. 1786. Journey across Pa. via Bethlehem and Ft. Pitt to Ohio. NHi.

899 PORTLOCK, Capt. Nathaniel. 1786; 1787; 1788. A voyage to the Northwest coast of America in the ships *King George* and *Queen Charlotte*. MH.

900 SARGENT, Winthrop. 1786; 1790; 1798; 1799; 1820. Trips to Ohio and the Mississippi; gardening; agriculture. MHi. *See* 985.

901 [SMITH, John Rhea]. 1786. Diary of member of class of 1787, College of N.J. DLC, original; NjHi, microfilm.

902 TAYLOR, Francis. 1786-1792; 1794-1799. Family and social life; management of plantation, "Midland"; sale of tobacco in Liverpool; Ky. military lands; current events and elections; slavery; births, deaths, and marriages in Orange County, Va.; cash accounts. Vi, original; KyLoF, microfilm.

903 TRUMBULL, John. 1786. A tour to Paris, Germany, Flanders, etc. DLC.

904 WARDER, Mrs. Ann. 1786-1789. Travel by ship and on land; social customs; Quaker meetings; prominent Philadelphia families. PHi.

905 WHITE, Will. 1786. A trip from Kinston, N.C., to Fayetteville, N.C., describing weather conditions and accommodations. Nc-Ar.

906 ANON. 1787-1788. Kept by a Moravian missionary to the Indians of Cajahaga and Petquotting on Lake Erie. NcWsM.

907 BLODGET, Samuel. 1787–1796. Few family items, chiefly unrelated mathematical and scientific notes. NhHi.

908 CUSHING, John. 1787–1811. Genealogical information taken from the Cushing family bible; events of Freeport, Me.; the launching and sailing of ships; journeys. MeHi.

909 DERING, Henry Packer. 1787–1788. Sales of cargoes of fish and horses in Haiti on a N.Y. schooner. NN.

910 HASWELL, Robert. 1787–1789. A voyage around the world on the ship *Columbia Rediviva* and the sloop *Washington*; a landfall on Cal. coast and Ore. coast; trade with the Indians and contacts with British traders and Spanish explorers. Cu-B. *See* 977.

911 HOLMES. Rev. Abiel. 1787–1794. Weather data kept at Midway in Ga. MBNEH.

912 JOHNSON, Rev. John Barent. 1787–1803. His life at Columbia College and career as a clergyman in Albany and Brooklyn. NNC.

913 [LEDYARD, John]. 1787. Journey toward Eastern Siberia and Kamchatka. NhD.

914 LEWIS, Robert. 1787. A trip from Fredericksburg, Va., to N.Y. DLC, copy.

915 OGDEN, John, Jr. 1787–1792. "A Journal of the Weather and Other Remarkable Events." NjHi.

916 PRICE, Ezekiel. 1787–1788. CNS. MHi. *See* 838.

917 RUTLEDGE, John, Jr. 1787–1788. Travels to Europe. NcD.

918 VAUGHAN, Samuel. 1787. A tour through Pa., Md., and Va. PPAmS, photostat; CtY, original.

919 WOODRUFF, Maj. Joseph. 1787. Diary of U.S. infantry officer. FSaWml.

920 ALDWORTH, Robert R. 1788. European travel journal. PPM.

921 BROWN, Rev. John. 1788. Interleaved almanac; short record of personal matters, deaths, funerals, visits, etc. MLa.

922 JONES, Rebecca. 1788–1789. Journey home after a ministerial visit in England; her activities when she returned to America. PHC.

923 KNOX, Gen. Henry. 1788. Travel from Waldborough, Me., to Portland; land; owners; expenses. MBNEH.

924 LEAR, Susan (Duncan). 1788. An 18-year-old girl traveling from Philadelphia by stage and packet to Providence, R.I., Boston, and vicinity, and return. RHi, microfilm; NjR, typescript.

925 LYONS, Jeremiah. 1788; 1794; 1795. Odd memoranda; weather; property; deaths, etc. NN.

926 MEACHAM, Rev. James. 1788–1794. His travels as a circuit rider for the Roanoke, Hanover, and Portsmouth circuits; meetings held; general church matters. NcD.

927 MOORE, Rev. Jonathan. 1788–1821 (with gaps). Almanacs; brief notes on personal affairs; social events; family; trips with Bishop Seabury, etc. MWA.

928 ROLLINSON, William. 1788–1789. Voyage from Liverpool to N.Y., particularly diversion on ship board. NN; MiU-C.

929 SNOWDEN, Rev. Nathaniel R. 1788–1789; 1791; 1795–1801; 1801–1804; 1836–1839. CNS. PHi.

930 ANON. 1789–1791. Trade notes of journey from Kilkenny to Liverpool, and to Philadelphia and Madeira, and return to Liverpool. NN.

931 ANON. 1789–1800. The congregation of the Moravian Church in Lititz, Pa. (in German). NcWsM.

932 ALLEN, Thomas. 1789–1793 (with gaps). The weather and the sailing of boats. MWA. *See* 840?

933 BARTON, Dr. Benjamin Smith. 1789–1803. His voyage on the *Apollo* from Gravesend, England, to Philadelphia; travels through the states; research in the fields of botany, mineralogy, anthropology, and zoology; his observations on frontier settlements; Indian tribes; the physical condition of the land. PHi; PPAmS, copy.

934 BILLINGS, William. 1789–1790; 1791. A voyage from Philadelphia to Corunna in Spain, and back; a voyage from Philadelphia to Oporto and back; temperature; meteorological readings, etc. PPAmS.

935 BROWN, James. 1789–1790; 1802. Weather; social and political happenings, with mention of many important people of the day. RHi, microfilm.

936 CASE, Rev. Isaac. 1789–1825. His work as a pastor and missionary in Me.; poor condition, hard to read; mentions many families with whom he stopped. MeWC. *See* 852.

937 CLARK, Daniel. 1789–1828. Considerable information about the making of pottery. NhHi.

938 CRESSON, Sarah. 1789–1829. Daily happenings; meetings attended; travels in the ministry; religious meditations, etc. PHC.

939 DOLBEARE, John. 1789–1809. Personal entries; farming notes; deaths and events; public and social affairs. MHi, except Sept. 1, 1799–July 30, 1801.

940 DUNCAN, James. Jr. 1789; 1790; 1792; 1794; 1803; 1804; 1809; 1810. Farming incidents; travels; calls; weather; some civil engineering business; a few vital statistics. MHa.

941 ETTWEIN, Bishop John. 1789. A voyage with Van Vleck and Long from Bethlehem, Pa., to Amsterdam, Holland (in German). NcWsM.

942 HALLEY, John. 1789. Boat trip down the Mississippi from mouth of Ohio River to New Orleans to sell produce; people and places seen. KyLoF.

943 HAY, Henry. 1789–1791. From Detroit to the Miami River. MiD.

944 MACLAY, William. 1789–1791. Journal kept while he was a member of the first U.S. Senate. DLC.

945 MILLER, Ichabod Benton. 1789–1796. Travels; condition of the roads; table of distances; settlement in Ohio; marriage; many early settlers mentioned. WHi, copy.

946 MORRIS, Gouverneur. 1789–1812. CNS. MH.

947 O'BRYEN, Richard. 1789–1791. Political and domestic affairs in the Barbary States; the humiliating conditions imposed upon American and European citizens; the Bey's haughty attitude toward foreign ambassadors and their agents; payment of tribute; ransom exacted for the redemption of prisoners; the cruel treatment of Christian slaves. PHi.

948 PEAKES, Eleazer. 1789–1845. Weather; planting conditions; household matters; church business. MScC.

949 SHELDON, Daniel. 1789–1792. Weather; public events in Litchfield. CtLiHi.

950 ASKIN, John. 1790–1815. CNS. MiD.

951 BUCHHOLZ, C. D. 1790–1802. Personal; kept while he was in Europe and Pa. (in German). NcWsM.

952 DAY, Jonathan. 1790–1791. CNS. MeHi.

953 FORDE, Standish. 1790–1792. A trip from New Madrid, Tenn., to New Orleans. PHi.

954 FRANKLIN, Col. [W.B.]. 1790. CNS. PAthT.

955 GREEN, Calvin. 1790–1844. Records of the 1st Presbyterian Church of Newark; other records. NjHi.

956 HEWARD, Hugh. 1790–1791. Journey from Detroit to the Illinois country. MiD.

957 HOSKINS, John. 1790; 1791; 1792; 1793. Extended narrative of the ship *Columbia Rediviva* on a voyage to northwest coast of America and China; trade and discoveries. CU-B.

958 INGRAM, Joseph. 1790–1792. Kept on a voyage of the brigantine *Hope*, from Boston to the northwest coast of America, including a voyage to China and Hawaiian Islands. CU-B; DLC.

959 JAY, John. 1790–1792. Kept during tours of duty with the U.S. Circuit Courts. NNC.

960 [LENOIR, ———]. (maybe several) [somewhere between 1790 and 1875]. CNS. NcU.

961 NORMAN, Jeremiah. 1790–1801. Diaries of his travels as an itinerant Methodist preacher in Va., S.C., N.C., Washington, D.C., and Baltimore. NcU.

962 OLIVARES, Fray Antonio San Buenaventura, and Fray Isidro de Espinosa. 1790. Diary of priests' expedition to Tex. DLC, Spanish transcript.

963 PENINGTON, ———? 1790–1791. CNS. PHi.

964 PINTARD, John. ca. 1790–1844. CNS. NHi.

965 SOUTHGATE, Robert and Samuel. 1790–1809. Business of a merchant; records of cases tried in the Supreme Court; many other memoranda on a variety of subjects. MeSacoY.

966 SPENCER, Rev. William. 1790. The Williamsburg and Surry circuits; a record of his sermons, their texts, the times and places of their delivery. ViWC.

967 STEUBEN, Baron Friedrich Wilhelm von. 1790–1792. Journal in French, while he resided on his farm in central N.Y., recording his daily activities in connection with farming, running his mill, renting out land, and settling his accounts. NHi, original; N, photostat. *See* 736, 819.

968 WHIPPLE, Hannah. 1790–1795. Religious introspection. NPV.

969 WICKHAM, Dr. Thomas T. 1790. A trip to Easthampton, L.I., with his bride. NHi.

970 WILLETT, Col. Marinus. 1790. His mission to the Creek Indians. NN.

971 ANON. 1791. Almanac; farming in Lancaster, Mass. MWA.

972 ANON. 1791–1794. Pilgrimage of the Moravian Indian congregation of Salem, on Lake Erie, to the Detroit River, to the River Retrenche, and to the River Thames in Upper Canada. NcWsM.

973 ANON. 1791. CNS. ICHi.

974 BREVARD, Joseph. 1791. A tour from Camden, S.C., to N.Y. and Philadelphia, commenting on Charleston, S.C., Va., and N.C. NcU.

975 BROWN, David. 1791. Trips taken by a tailor going from house to house and town to town; mentions many relatives and friends. MWA.

976 CLARKSON, John. 1791–1792. His mission to America concerning the slave trade. NHi.

977 HASWELL, Robert. 1791–1792. Additional information in a 2nd log of Haswell relating to trading on the British Columbia coast. CU-B. *See* 910.

978 HOWLAND, Gilbert. 1791–1805. Logbook; journal kept at sea by author as first mate and master of various vessels. MH.

979 JEFFERSON, Thomas. 1791–1803. Domestic affairs and household expenses. NN. *See* 894.

980 LINCKLAEN, John. 1791–1792. Travels through Pa., N.Y., and Vt. (in French). NN.

981 MANBY, Thomas. 1791–1793. The voyage of H.M.S. *Discovery* and *Chatham* to the northwest coast of America. CtY.

982 ORMOND, William. 1791–1803. Giving an account of his work in various localities of N.C. and Va. NcD.

983 RODNEY, Caesar A. 1791–1793. His courtship of Susan Hunn, whom he calls Amanda; reverse, notes on the Human Mind, 1788–1793, lectures of Rev. Samuel Magan, Univ. of Pa. DeHi. *See* 1475?

984 ST. CLAIR, Gen. Arthur. 1791. Original journal of his expedition. WHi.

985 SARGENT, Winthrop. 1791; 1793–1795; 1801–1802. CNS. OHi, typescript. *See* 900.

986 SEABURY, Bishop Samuel. 1791–1795. Church affairs; a bishop's observations. CtMBds, copy.

987 SOAMES, Benjamin. 1791–1832. Various voyages; destinations not given except for one voyage to Russia. MH.

988 STEPHENSON, Lt. James. 1791. Military. DLC.

989 WALLEY, Thomas. 1791–1795. Almanacs; garden; weather; family. MBAt.

990 WELCH, Rev. James. 1791–1793. Short summation of sermons; difficulties he had experienced with a person in the community. PPPrHi.

991 WHITNEY, Rev. Peter. 1791. Almanac; weather; townspeople. MWHi.

992 ANON. 1792. Gen. Anthony Wayne's expedition. WHi.

993 ANON. 1792. Visit of Indian chief to Nazareth and Bethlehem, Pa. NcWsM.

994 ANON. 1792. Religious meetings and sermons; visits in Columbia County, N.Y. NCooHi.

995 CHAPLIN, Benjamin. 1792. His father's and his own doings; parish matters in Sutton, Mass.; trips; farm matters; some deaths. MWA.

996 FAIRFAX, Ferdinando. 1792. Travels in Va.; taverns; ordinaries; the Va. countryside and roads; visits to distinguished old families, including one to Thomas Jefferson at Monticello. ViU.

997 HART, Nathaniel. 1792. Gen. Anthony Wayne's expedition. WHi. *See* 1038.

998 KENT, James. 1792–1846. Journeys. DLC.

999 [POSEY, Thomas?]. 1792–1800. Journal of an army officer. WHi.

1000 PRICE, James. 1792. A voyage and visit to France. MBNEH.

1001 RUSH, Dr. Benjamin. 1792–1806. Personal; a few letters. NN.

1002 UNDERWOOD, Capt. Thomas Taylor. 1792. With Gen. Wayne in his expedition against the Indians of the Northwest; information about Wayne's camp at Cincinnati and "Hobson's choice." OCUHi, copy; original may be in KyLoF.

1003 VAN DER KEMP, Francis Adrian. 1792. A tour to Oneida Lake. NHi.

1004 WEATHERBURN, John. 1792–1796. Mostly about the weather. MdHi.

1005 ANON. 1793–1845. Personal; weather; general; Taunton, Mass., and vicinity. MTaHi.

1006 ANON. 1793. Campaigns of Maj. Gen. Charles Scott, commander of Kentucky Volunteers on Wayne's campaigns against the Northwestern Indians; followed by an orderly book. KyLoF.

1007 ANON. 1793. A trip by water to Norfolk. DLC.

1008 ANDERSON, Alexander. 1793–1799. On his profession as wood engraver; on anatomical lectures, and on physics lectures. NNC, original; NHi, copy.

1009 BLYTHE, Rev. James. 1793. Private journal including an account of his Southern tour. PPPrHi.

1010 BOND, Edward. 1793; 1809. Trip from N.C. to Pa. and Va.; visit to Ohio and Ind. InHi.

1011 BRAUTZ, Lewis. 1793–1794. A voyage from Baltimore to India. DLC.

1012 BRODEAU, Anna Maria. 1793–1863 (with gaps). Social conditions in Washington; personal; living expenses. DLC.

1013 CURTIS, James. 1793–1830. CNS. MeHi.

1014 HARTSHORNE, William. 1793. Quaker's journey from N.Y. to Mich.; Indian treaty and Indian life. NN and Friends' Seminary; PSC-Hi, typescript.

1015 HAUTERIVE, Comte Alexandre d'. 1793. Journal (in French). NHi.

1016 HECKEWELDER, John. 1793–1857. CNS. PHi. *See* 1095.

1017 HYSLOP, John. 1793. Journey on Connecticut River; earlier life in England. NN.

1018 LEDDEL, William. n.d. [between 1793 and 1801]. NjHi.

1019 LEONARD, Lemuel. 1793–1845. Births, marriages, deaths; weather; personal, general. MTaHi.

1020 LORIMIER, Louis. 1793–1794. CNS. MoSHs.

1021 MACDONELL, John. 1793–1795. Daily entries made at a fur-trading post on the Qu'Apelle River. MnHi, photostat.

1022 McGILLIVRAY, William. 1793. Description of Canadian Northwest; fur-trading methods; relations with Chippewa Indians. MnHi, photostat.

1023 POWEL, Mrs. Elizabeth (Willing). 1793–1822. CNS. PHi.

1024 THORNTON, Mrs. William. 1793–1863 (with gaps). CNS. DLC.

1025 TOULMIN, Harry. 1793–1794. A voyage to North America, with descriptions and statistical information concerning various counties in Va. and Ky. CSmH.

1026 ANON. 1794. Trip from Lancaster County, Pa., to Ohio and Ky. through Cumberland Gap. PPPrHi.

1027 ANON. 1794. Gen. Anthony Wayne's expedition against the Indians; daily entries; gives account of the Battle of Fallen Timbers, etc. InHi.

1028 ANON. [1794]. Kept by a militiaman in the Whiskey Rebellion. PPoHi.

1029 ANDERSON, John, Jr. 1794–1798. Life in New York City. NHi.

1030 ASHMEAD, Capt. Jacob. 1794. Western expedition. PHi.

1031 BACON, David. 1794. His visit to Canandaigua, N.Y., to be present at a treaty with the Indians of the Six Nations; accompanied by John Parrish, William Savery, James Emlen. PHC.

1032 CLARK, Lt. William. 1794. Maj. Gen. Anthony Wayne's campaign against the Shawnee Indians in Ohio. IHS; WHi, typescript.

1033 DICKERSON, Mahlon. 1794–1819. CNS. Vols. 1-2 (through July 1, 1809), NjHi; vol. 3, NjR; vols. 1-2 in microfilm.

1034 DURELL, Daniel M. 1794–1845. CNS. NHi.

1035 EMLEN, Samuel. 1794; 1817–1818. Journey into Md.; living in England with his invalid wife. PHC.

1036 GALES, Joseph. 1794–1795. CNS. Nc-Ar.

1037 HAND, Moses. 1794. A voyage from Birmingham to Liverpool, by canal. NNC.

1038 HART, Nathaniel. 1794. Military journal; service with the Ky. Volunteers on Wayne's campaign against the Indians. KyLoF. See 997.

1039 LITTLE, Edward. 1794–1839. His travels in Maine. MSaE.

1040 LONDON, John. 1794; 1800. On board ship from England to America, with entries on the weather and personal expenses; later chiefly descriptions of places visited and general conditions prevalent in the New World. Nc-Ar.

1041 PAINE, Dr. William. 1794–1826. Medical work; personal and town affairs; social. MWA.

1042 PARRY, Needham. 1794. Trip to Ky. down the Ohio; mentions people and places, descriptions of floating mill. WHi.

1043 PURVIANCE, John Henry. 1794–1796. Comments on American exports (in French); noted persons and Conn. (in English). MdHi.

1044 PUTNAM, David. 1794. Notes kept on board the ship *Magnolia*, on a voyage to London from New York. OHi, typescript.

1045 SCHLEGEL, ———. 1794. Travel diary of a journey from Bethel to Shekomeko, an Indian mission station supervised from Bethlehem, Pa., and return (in German). NcWsM.

1046 SMITH, Capt. Jonas. 1794. During the Whiskey Insurrection campaign. NjHi.

1047 TEN EYK, James. 1794. Expedition to western Pa., during the Whiskey Rebellion. NjR.

1048 TODD, Robert. 1794. Covers march to scene and description of battle of Fallen Timbers; general orders. InHi.

1049 TRUTEAU, Jean Baptiste. 1794–1796. His travels on the Mo. and Ind. rivers, and to the Indians. Séminaire de Québec, original; PPAmS, microfilm.

1050 ANDREWS, Dr. Joseph Gardner. 1795. Kept at Ft. Defiance, Ohio; largely social affairs of himself and his friends; mention of the Indians and the French; meteorological observations. DLC.

1051 BANGS, Edward. 1795–1803. Trials held at his home when he was Trial Justice. MWA.

1052 BARROW, Rev. David. 1795. Exploring trip from his home in Va. to the western country. KyLoF, typescript. *See* 1091.

1053 CRESSON, John Elliott. 1795–1796. Daily happenings in the life of a Philadelphia Quaker. PHi.

1054 CROSSWELL, William. 1795–1833. School notes; purchase of books, clothes, payment of bills, etc. MBNEH.

1055 GODFREY, John W. 1795–1796. From Philadelphia on the brig *Diana* to London; a tour through England, Holland, Brabant, Flanders, and France in the service of an American land company; European cultural and social life; economic conditions. PHi.

1056 GOODERICH, James. 1795–1850. Log books and diaries. CtNhHi.

1057 GREENE, Rowland. 1795–1857. His travels in the ministry; visits to local and yearly meetings; local news; family matters; with autobiographical sketch. PHC.

1058 JONES, Rev. Morgan. 1795. Sea voyage from Philadelphia to Charleston, S.C., and some horseback trips in the vicinity of Charleston; mentions slaves toiling. PCC.

1059 JONES, Nahum. 1795–1806. Schoolteaching at Rindge, N.H., Montgomery, N.Y., and in Mass.; local affairs and history; names of his pupils; Shay's Rebellion. MWA.

1060 KREUZER, Conrad. 1795. Journey from Neuwied on the Rhine to Bethlehem, Pa. (in German). NcWsM.

1061 LAIGHT, [William?]. 1795–1799. 1799–1803; 1816–1819; 1819–1822. Detailed weather reports. NHi.

1062 MONROE, James. 1795–1802. CNS. DLC. *See* 1202.

1063 NEILSON, John. 1795. Two trips from New Brunswick, N.J., to Albany, and return. PSC-Hi. *See* 1114, 1182.

1064 PHELPS, Oliver L. 1795. Journal of trip to Europe. NCanHi.

1065 SCHOFIELD, Oliver W. 1795. Journey with Isaac Martin; entertaining anecdotes. PSC-Hi.

1066 SIMPSON, Samuel. 1795. Plantation affairs and happenings in the community. Nc-Ar.

1067 STUART, Rev. Robert. 1795–1808. Journal of early part of ministry in Ky. PPPrHi.

1068 ANON. 1796. Almanac; at Salem, Mass.; weather; personal; sermons; local events. MSaE.

1069 AUDRAIN, Peter. 1796. Ft. Washington to Detroit, with Gen. Wayne. MiD.

1070 BEMIS, Rev. Stephen. 1796–1798. Reviews of sermons he heard, books he read, etc. MWA.

1071 BETHUNE, Rev. Divie. 1796–1823. Daily devotions: meditations, lengthy prayers, an occasional poem. MiU.

1072 CODMAN, John and Richard. 1796. Business entries; rent of stores, houses; sailing and arrival of ships; a few deaths. MWA.

1073 COFFEE, John. 1796–1887. CNS. A-Ar.

1074 COOPER, James. 1796. Visit to Seneca Indians. PSC-Hi.

1075 CRAFT, James. 1796–1808. Reports on weather conditions, with some notes on current happenings. PHi.

1076 DUGGAN, Thomas. 1796–1800. At post of Michilimackinac; Indian relations. MiU-C.

1077 GLEN, Henry. 1796. Journey from Schenectady to Oswego and Niagara to witness the surrender of Ft. Ontario by the British. NCooHi.

1078 HAIGHT, Charles. 1796–1797. A voyage from Philadelphia to Canton, China, and return. NjR.

1079 HOLLEY, J. M. 1796. CNS. OClWHi.

1080 HUNTER, George. 1796–1809. Travels and explorations of the U.S. from Philadelphia through Ky. and La. PPAmS. *See* 1220.

1081 JUVENAL, Father I. 1796. His experiences at Three Saints Harbor, Pavlovsk, Kenai River, and Ilyamna when Father Juvenal was stabbed to death by the natives. CU-B.

1082 KING, Rufus. 1796–1803. Visits to British public officials. NHi.

1083 NOYES, Rev. Matthew. 1796. Short notes of religious texts, exchanges, etc. MWA.

1084 PIERCE (Peirce), John. 1796. Social and economic conditions of Indians of N.Y. state, Oneidas, Tuscaroras, etc.; proposals made to them by Quakers of help and cooperation in improving their self-sufficiency. PSC-Hi.

1085 PREBLE, Isaac. 1796. A voyage in the schooner *Success* (Isaac Bullock, Master), from Boston, to trade along shore. NHi.

1086 READ, Daniel. 1796–1799. Daily affairs; business; household; finance. CtNhHi.

1087 RODNEY, Thomas. 1796–1797. Cultural and social history of Delaware at the end of the 18th century; daily events; personal affairs; comments on the Revolution. PHi. *See* 646, 884.

1088 VAN CLEAVE, Benjamin. 1796(?)–? CNS. ODa.

1089 WISTAR, Dr. Caspar. 1796–1813. Pertaining principally to yellow fever. PPAmS.

1090 ANON. 1797. Trip from Falls of Ohio (Clarksville), Ind., to St. Louis and return. InHi.

1091 BARROW, Rev. David. 1797. Trip from Va. to Ky. and return. WHi. *See* 1052.

1092 CHABOILLEZ, Charles Jean Baptiste. 1797–1798. A voyage down the Mississippi and through the Lake Superior region. MnHi,photostat.

1093 CROKER, John Wilson. 1797–1850. Political gossip; travel notes in Ireland, Paris, England; visits to George IV. MiU-C.

1094 DUNLAP, William. 1797–1798; 1819–1820; 1833–1834. CNS. CtY.

1095 HECKEWELDER, John and William Henry. 1797. Journey to Indian mission stations on the Muskingum. NcWsM.

1096 MARSHALL, John. 1797–1798. Journal in Paris. DLC, photostat; MHi, contemporary copy.

1097 MEYERS, William. 1797–1798. Voyage to America and back. NN.

1098 MURRAY, William Vans. 1797–1801. Diary notes at The Hague and at Paris. DLC.

1099 ORMAND, Watkins. 1797. CNS. Nc-Ar.

1100 PETERS, John. 1797. Work surveying Magaguadavic River. CaOOA.

1101 SWETT, Mary Howell. 1797–1801. Quaker's account of meetings held and places visited during her travels in England and on the Continent. PHC.

1102 THOMPSON, David. 1797. CNS. MnHi, photostat.

1103 BATES, Tarleton. 1798. Journal of a trip down the Ohio River from Pittsburgh to Cincinnati; detail on condition and size of the settlements along the river, taverns, men encountered. PMA.

1104 BREWER, Thomas. 1798. The weather for 1798, taken three times a day by Fahrenheit thermometer. MBNEH.

1105 BROOKES, William. 1798–1803. Business trip to the U.S.A. NN, microfilm.

1106 CALDWELL, Dr. Charles. 1798–1815. Ledgers and day journals. PHi.

1107 EMERY, John. 1798. Kept on frigate *Constitution's* first voyage. NNC.

1108 FINLEY, Rev. John Evans. 1798. A tour from Kaskaskia to Natchez and Natchidoches, with the names of settlers, geography of the region, mineral deposits, Indian tribes, population of various villages, tables of distances. WHi.

1109 GARRIGUES, Edward. 1798. Quaker activities, meetings, social and domestic events; the yellow fever epidemic in Philadelphia. PHi.

1110 HOWE, Rev. Joseph P. 1798–1816. Marriage records and other brief entries. KyLoF.

1111 HULL, Commodore Isaac. 1798–1800. Sea journal of the first voyage of the frigate *Constitution* by a lt. on board. NHi.

1112 HUMPHREYS, Clement. 1798. CNS. PHi.

1113 KELSO, Dr. Joseph. 1798. Sea diary of surgeon on the *Cleopatra* from Philadelphia bound for Canton. CaOTP.

1114 NEILSON, John. 1798–1832. Farm and garden journal; planting, harvesting, cultivating, slave and hired labor; weather. PSC-Hi. *See* 1063, 1182.

1115 PAINE, Nathaniel. 1798; 1801. Almanacs; weather; public events; news. MWA.

1116 SHARPLESS, Joshua. 1798. A visit to the Seneca Indians of N.Y. state. PHC.

1117 SMITH, Job. 1798–1818. CNS. RHi.

1118 SMITH, Mrs. Samuel Harrison (Margaret Bayard). Between 1798–1845. Personal. DLC.

1119 SPENCER, Nathaniel. 1798; 1813. CNS. OClWHi.

1120 TRUXTON, Commodore Thomas. 1798–1800. Journal aboard the U.S.S. *Constellation*. PHi.

1121 WILLARD, Augustus. 1798–1799. Journal of a voyage to the West Indies. MH.

1122 ZELLER, John. 1798–1813. Travel and military service on the Ohio, in Ky., in Ind., and in the campaign under Gen. Harrison. NBuHi.

1123 ANON. 1799–1805. The Moravian mission among the northern Indians at Gnadenhutten and Muskingum (in German). NcWsM.

1124 ANON. 1799–1800. Christian Indians moving from Fairfield, Pa., to the Muskingum, and thence to Goshen (Hope), Ind. NcWsM.

1125 ANON. 1799. A journal of the brig *Pickering*. DLC.

1126 BAILEY, Robert and Francis. 1799–1856. CNS. PHi.

1127 BEEBE, Lewis. 1799–1800; 1800–1801. A journey from New England to Va., with details on facilities for travel, characteristics of the inhabitants of the states he traversed, their religious sentiments, education, sports, recreations, economic and social conditions, and the political controversies of the period. PHi.

1128 BLEECKER, Elizabeth De Hart (McDonald). 1799–1806. Social life in N.Y.; Burr-Hamilton duel; other public events and celebrities. NN.

1129 EATON, William. 1799–1805 (with gaps). Letter books and journals. CSmH.

1130 GOODWIN, Nathaniel. 1799. Personal life; visits of his friends, etc. MWHi.

1131 JOHNSON, Samuel William. 1799–1800. Travel from Stratford to N.C., and back. CtHi.

1132 KELLOGG, Rev. Elijah. 1799. Brief notes; weather; baptisms; deaths. MWA.

1133 LEAR, Tobias. 1799–1801. An account of Washington's death and funeral; author's appointment as Consul General to Santo Domingo; his subsequent voyage there. MiU-C, photostat.

1134 LOW, Rufus. 1799–1800. Journal of the *Essex*. DLC.

1135 LYON, John. 1799–1814. Botanical journal; travels in Eastern U.S. PPAmS.

1136 MACY, Obed. 1799–1800. Weather; deaths; ship movements; foreign news; fires, etc. MBNEH.

1137 McCLURE, Rev. David. 1799. Trip to Me. and Boston. NhD.

1138 MURRAY, J. R. 1799. Travels in Europe. DLC.

1139 RIPLEY, Sally. 1799–1808. Learning and schoolwork; social; family. MWA.

1140 ROCKY MOUNTAIN FORT JOURNAL. 1799–1800. Kept by a trader in charge of the Rocky Mountain Ft. of the North West Co. recording life at a remote trading post. CU-B.

1141 RUSSELL, [Thomas]. 1799–1802; 1823–1839. Finance; shipping. PHi.

1142 SHAW, John. 1799. A trip in the Mediterranean in the ship *Sophia*, to ports of Algiers, Bizerte, Tunis, Tripoli, etc., presenting details of the hazards of shipping, attempted attack on a French merchant vessel, Oriental customs and life, visits of American consuls to northern Africa, inhuman treatment of an American Negro held captive in Tunis, etc. PHi.

1143 SIMPSON, J. N. 1799. A journey in Va. MnHi.

1144 STEINER, Abraham, and Friedrich Christian Schweinitz. 1799. Travel; their visit to the Cherokees and in the Cumberland settlement in Tenn. NcWsM. *See* 1185, 1209.

1145 STURGIS, William. 1799. Journal kept on board the *Eliza*, while he traded for sea otter on the Northwest coast. CU-B.

1146 ANON. 1800–1833. Historical and artistic events in U.S.A. and elsewhere. NN.

1147 CAMPBELL, Simeon. 1800–1912. CNS. ScU.

1148 DARLINGTON, Dr. William. 1800–1862. Diaries, reminiscences, note books, and letters. NHi. *See* 1177.

1149 ELLIS (Family). 1800–? CNS. NHi.

1150 ELY, Nathaniel. 1800–1806. CNS. MoSHi.

1151 GARDNER, Edmund. 1800–1826. Whaling voyages from Nantucket. MH.

1152 GUEST, Rebecca. 1800–1810. Kept while she was in England, where her husband was head of merchant firm of Guest & Co. MdHi.

1153 KING, Reuben. 1800–1806. Life in Darien, Ga.; mentions some of people there; significant because most early records of community were lost when McIntosh Courthouse burned. GHi.

1154 KOEHLER, John Daniel. 1800. Travel diary of a voyage from Philadelphia, Pa. to Amsterdam, Holland (in German). NcWsM.

1155 TENNENT, Rev. William Mackay. 1800. A visit to eastern shore of Md. by agent of the General Assembly. PPPrHi.

1156 THOMPSON, Samuel. 1800–1810. Events in Setanket, L.I., particularly farming and weather; includes ms. diary of O. Z. Ackerberg. NN.

1157 TOWNSEND, William. 1800–1811. Local affairs in Waltham, Mass.; brief journeys; business. MWalHi.

1158 WADSWORTH, Henry. 1800. Fragments of a journal kept on board the U.S. frigate *Congress*. ICHi.

1159 WILLIAMS, Samuel, and his son, Samuel Wesley. [1800–1880]. Diaries, letters, and surveys. OHi.

1160 ANON. 1801–1837. Cherokee Indian mission of the Moravian Church (in German). NcWsM.

1161 ALEXANDER, Dr. Adam. 1801. Diary of a trip to the North. NcU.

1162 BROWN, Elijah, Jr. 1801. A trip from Philadelphia to the West Indies; legal, commercial, agricultural, and philosophical subjects. PHi.

1163 BYHAN, Gottlieb and wife, and Jacob Wohlfahrt. 1801. Trip to the Cherokees (in German). NcWsM. *See* 1188.

1164 HICKMAN, Benjamin. 1801–1851. CNS. PWcHi.

1165 HOVER, Ezekiel. 1801–1802. A trip from Washington Cnty., Pa., through Canada, Mich., and Ohio. OHi.

1166 KLUGE, John Peter, and Abraham Luckenbach. 1801. Journey from Goshen (Hope), Ind., on the Muskingum to the Indian mission on White River. NcWsM.

1167 LYLE, Rev. John. 1801–1804. Dates and places of preaching; description of services, members. KyHi.

1168 MULFORD, Daniel. 1801–1807. Studies at Yale; activity in theatricals; singing school; social life; declining health; trip from Morristown to New Haven. CtY, original; NjR, microfilm; DLC.

1169 SCHWEINITZ, Rev. Lewis David de. 1801–1812. Stay in Europe where he went from Pa. for his education. NcWsM. *See* 1355, 1732.

1170 SHARPLES, Martha. 1801. Attendance at Philadelphia Yearly Meeting of the Society of Friends and visits in homes while there; quotes from ministering of Elias Hicks. PSC-Hi.

1171 WALKER, James. 1801. His journey from Conway, N.H., to Cincinnati, Ohio, in Sept. 1801. OHi.

1172 WORTHINGTON, Thomas. 1801–1812. Kept by a delegate to the State Constitutional Convention, and U.S. Senator. DLC, original; OHi, microfilm.

1173 ANON. 1802–1837. Information on the character of the Cherokees; the political and economic situation in Ga.; the incidents leading up to the forced removal to the Indian territory, and incidents during the removal. NcWsM.

1174 BAKER, Dobel. 1802–1869. Family experiences; local events. PSC-Hi.

1175 BOSWORTH, Jonathan. 1802. Report on the weather and on vessels entering the port of Bristol. RHi.

1176 CABELL, Joseph Carrington. 1802–1806. His residence in England, Holland, Belgium, Switzerland, France, and Italy, where he studied methods of education in preparation for his long partnership with Jefferson in the founding of the Univ. of Va.; travel expenses; notes on books, art, and architecture; observations on the life of the people, their morals, social customs, political and cultural characteristics. ViU. *See* 1213.

1177 DARLINGTON, Dr. William. [1802–1858]. CNS. PWcHi. *See* 1148.

1178 FISHER, John. 1802–1815. CNS. PHi.

1179 JACKSON, William. 1802–1805. Religious visit to Great Britain and Ireland. PHC.

1180 LITTLE, Nathaniel D. 1802. A trip from Blandford, Mass., to the central part of Ohio and back again, in the interest of the Scioto Company. MiU-C.

1181 MOULTON, Jonathan. [1802–1815]? Includes dates of death of local people. MeHi.

1182 NEILSON, John. 1802–1827. Services, pastoral calls, sermon texts of First Presbyterian Church, New Brunswick, N.J. PSC-Hi. *See* 1063, 1114.

1183 NEVIN, Pim. 1802–1803. Travels from Liverpool, England, to N.Y., Philadelphia, eastern Pa., Baltimore, Washington. PPAms.

1184 REICHEL, Charles G. 1802. Journey from Nazareth, Pa., to Salem, N.C. NcWsM.

1185 STEINER, Abraham. 1802. Travel from Salem, N.C., to Springplace in Cherokee land, and return (in German). NcWsM. *See* 1144, 1209.

1186 THOMPSON, Henry. 1802–1836. Home life; social and political events; weather. MdHi.

1187 VASSAR, Matthew. 1802–1808. References to Vassar College; biographical data, wills, etc. Vassar, original; NN, microfilm.

1188 WOHLFAHRT, Jacob. 1802. Travel; return from the Cherokee land to Salem, N.C. (in German). NcWsM. *See* 1163.

1189 ANDERSON, Richard Clough, Jr. 1803–1826. Kept during student days at William and Mary; service in Ky. House of Representatives, and in Congress, and as U.S. Minister to Colombia. KyLoF, microfilm.

1190 BROWN, Col. Richard. 1803; 1823. A journey on the schooner *Wealthy* from New Orleans to Philadelphia; a boat trip on the Ohio River from Steubenville to Maysville. OHi, copy.

1191 CABELL, Mayo. 1803–1825. Weather records and details of plantation management. ViU.

1192 CLINTON, De Witt. 1803–1828. CNS. NHi.

1193 COOLEY, Rev. Timothy Walter. 1803. A missionary tour through central N.Y. under the auspices of the Hampshire Missionary Society of the Congregational Church, citing for Oneida, Chenango, and Onondaga counties, the size of villages, nature of their population, denominations represented, and names of persons baptized. N. *See* 1277.

1194 DENKE, Christian Frederic. 1803. Journey among the Indians in Ohio. NcWsM.

1195 FISHER, Hannah Rodman. [1803?] Accounts of family illnesses and cures; visit to Westtown Friends Boarding School. PSC-Hi.

1196 HAMILTON and HOOD of Philadelphia. 1803–1838. Journals, ledgers, cashbooks, and letter books. PHi.

1197 HOPKINS, Gerard T. 1803–1804. A tour from Baltimore to Ft. Wayne, in which he traveled as a member of a deputation of the Society of Friends to the Western Indians, for the purpose of instructing them in agriculture; comments on topography, agriculture, economic conditions, and customs and life of the Indians. PHi.

1198 KIRKLAND, Samuel. 1803; 1804. Two periodic reports to the Northern Missionary Society sent by a missionary from the Corporation of Harvard College and formerly from the Society of Scotland to the Oneida nation and others of the Six Nations. NjR.

1199 LEWIS, Meriwether. 1803–1809. Lewis and Clark journal. MoSHs. *See* 1214.

1200 McCOMB, John, Jr. 1803–1808. Discusses the progress of building the City Hall in New York City. NHi.

1201 MERCER, John. 1803. Trip from N.Y. to France. DLC.

1202 MONROE, James. 1803. His negotiations for the purchase of La. DLC. *See* 1062.

1203 MOON, Moses. 1803; 1804; 1811. Journeys to Black River, N.Y.; survey notes on his property. PSC-Hi, photostat.

1204 MOTT, Sarah. 1803–1804. A trip from Philadelphia to Portugal and return, covering an extended stay in Lisbon and a visit to Cintra. NjR, late 19th-century copy.

1205 PREBLE, Edward. 1803–1804. The work of fitting out the *Constitution* at Portsmouth, and an account of the maneuvers and actions in Mediterranean waters. DLC.

1206 [RAVENEL, Stephen]. 1803. Travel; agriculture; personal. ScHi.

1207 RODMAN, Eliza. 1803; 1805; 1807. Going to tea at homes of friends and relatives; shopping; sewing; etc. PSC-Hi.

1208 RUTGERS, Gerard. 1803–1829. Meteorological observations; daily record of weather, temperature, winds. NjR.

1209 STEINER, Abraham. 1803. Travel from Springfield in Cherokee land to Col. Hawkins in the land of the Creeks, his transactions there, and return to Wachovia (in German). NcWsM. *See* 1144, 1185, 1197.

1210 YARNALL, Hannah. 1803. Travel and lodging conditions during trip to Canada. PSC-Hi.

1211 ALLINSON, William. 1804–1805; 1809; 1827–1828. Notes of a tour into Sussex in 1804 with Josiah Reeve of Gershom Craft; notes of a tour to Flemington in 1805 to attend the Circuit Court on the trial for the freedom of a Negro slave, expenses of tour; trip with John Brown in 1809 to visit Indians; meetings held in Philadelphia during 1827–1828. PHC.

1212 BROOKE, Lt. Peter. 1804–1816. A description of the Battle of New Orleans. NHi.

1213 CABELL, Joseph Carrington. 1804. His trip to the Netherlands and England. ViU. *See* 1176.

1214 CLARK, William. 1804–1806. The Lewis and Clark expedition. MoSHi. *See* 1199.

1215 CLIFFORD, [Thomas?] 1804. A trip to Ohio from Philadelphia. PHi.

1216 COUCH, Jesup N. 1804. Journal from Reading in Conn. to Chillicothe, Ohio. OHi.

1217 FLOYD, Sgt. Charles. 1804. The Lewis and Clark expedition. WHi.

1218 GIBBONS, James. 1804. A tour through the western part of Pa. and part of Ohio; topography, immigration, settlements, abundance of game, travel facilities, Quaker families, and their meeting places. PHi. *See* 363?

1219 [HAWARD, Peter?] 1804? A trip from Flemington, N.J., to Pittsburgh, down the Ohio and Cumberland rivers as a deck-hand on a river boat to Nashville, and return home (chiefly on foot) via Lexington, Ky. NjR, typescript.

1220 HUNTER, George. 1804. Journal up the Red and Washita rivers, with William Dunbar, by order of the U.S. govt. PPAmS. *See* 1080.

1221 KELLY, John. 1804–1811; 1812–1820; 1822–1830; 1837–1847. Kept by secretary of NhHi. NhHi.

1222 MORSE, Rev. John. 1804–1805. Daily observations during missionary trip through Greene, Schoharie, and Columbia counties, N.Y.; refers to sermons and towns where he preached, the people's reactions, descriptions of lodgings. NCooHi.

1223 ROBERTS, Edmund. 1804; 1805; 1832–1834. Voyage from Rio de la Plata to London; voyage from London to Madeira, Tall Trees, and Rio de la Plata; journal on board the U.S. ship of war *Peacock*, relating to nautical matters. DLC.

1224 RUFFIN, Thomas. 1804–1805. Diary at Princeton Univ. NcU.

1225 SERGEANT, John. 1804–1805; 1810–1813; 1815–1816; 1818–1820; 1824. Semi-annual report to Society in Scotland for Propagating Christian Knowledge. NhD. *See* 1295, 1554?

1226 STRAGHAN, John. 1804. Travel from "Freepoart," Pa., down the Monongahela, Ohio, and Mississippi rivers to New Orleans, then to N.Y. and return. OHi.

1227 WATTS, Mr. 1804. Courses and remarks on the Windward Coast of South America made during a voyage. MBNEH.

1228 WHITEHOUSE, Joseph. 1804–? Journal of member of the Lewis and Clark expedition. ICN.

1229 ADAMS, Samuel. 1805; 1806; 1809; 1814. Trips from Pa. to and from Knox County, Ind. InHi, copy.

1230 BROWN, William Little. 1805–1814. Home life at Palmyra, Tenn., and Ky.; study at Transylvania Univ.; law study and practice at Clarksville, Tenn.; war service. NN.

1231 COOPE, Rachel. 1805. Description of trip to Indian country by Quaker missionary. PSC-Hi.

1232 FISHER, Miers. 1805–1819. Private life after retirement as lawyer; weather, effects on crops; reference to newspaper reports of events leading up to and during War of 1812. PSC-Hi.

1233 GILPIN, Thomas. 1805; 1809. In the Eastern states, New England, and the West. PHi. *See* 681?

1234 HOOKER, Edward. 1805–1808. Chiefly a self-examination. ScU.

1235 JONES, Sarah W. 1805–1830. CNS. DLC.

1236 MANNERS, David. 1805. Full and well-written, describing farm activity and local life generally. NjR, microfilm.

1237 PIKE, Gen. Zebulon Montgomery. 1805–1806. A military expedition to the Western Territory, "to trace the Mississippi to its head." PHi, original; MnMcHi, typescript. *See* 1257.

1238 POULTNEY, William C. 1805. Journal on board the brig *Washington*. PHi. *See* 1645.

1239 RIGGS, Elisha. 1805. Kept while he was on voyage to England and during visits to English cities. MdHi.

1240 SHOEMAKER, John. 1805–1806; 1808; 1811; 1812–1815. Journey with Richard Mott to Md., Va., Ohio, and Pa.; journey to Canada; journey to N.J.; travels in the ministry in Pa., Md., Va., N.C. PHC.

1241 STEVENSON, Capt. William. 1805. A voyage from Baltimore to Europe and the East Indies in the ship *Erin*. DLC.

1242 STUART, John. 1805–1806. Deals with his work at Rocky Mountain House on the upper Peace River in present Alberta, including gathering food, supplies, and trade with the Indians. CU-B.

1243 ANON. (name not legible). 1806. A trip from high on the Kentucky to New Orleans by flatboat carrying provisions and products for sale at the market. KyHi, photostat.

1244 ANON. 1806–1808. A European trip. NcU.

1245 ANON. 1806–1810. Journal of a cruise in the U.S. brig *Argus*. PHi.

1246 BARTON, Alvin. 1806–1842. School days; personal activities. NCooHi.

1247 CANFIELD, ——. [1806–1819]. CNS. VtHi.

1248 DONNELL, Samuel. 1806. Journey to New Orleans by flatboat; strong moral tone. InHi.

1249 FOTHERGILL, Samuel. 1806; 1808. Trip from Philadelphia to the settlements in Luzerne County; events, descriptions of places, opinions of people; condition of road, inns, etc. PHi.

1250 FRASER, Simon. 1806; 1808. Two journals relating various activities; founding of fur-trading posts in Fraser River country; tracing of the Fraser River determined that it was not connected with the Columbia River. CU-B.

1251 FROBISHER, Joseph. 1806–1810. Chiefly of social activities; sometimes involving personal activities of the fur trade while he was with the Northwest Co. CU-B.

1252 HAVILAND, Eleazar. 1806–1858. Visits to Friends' Meetings; includes indexes of names, places, lists of meetings, and families visited. PSC-Hi, typescript.

1253 HAZARD, Samuel. 1806–1813. CNS. PHi. *See* 1466.

1254 HUNT, John. 1806–1824. A daily account of his religious and civil transactions; attendance at Friends' Meetings and what transpired; daily occurrences among family and friends; his religious views and feelings. PSC-Hi, portions. *See* 788?

1255 MARSHALL, Christopher, Jr. 1806. CNS. PHi.

1256 PHELPS, Anson Greene. 1806–1807; 1816–1853. CNS. NN.

1257 PIKE, Zebulon Montgomery. ca. 1806. Maps, meteorological data, etc. of the West. U.S. National Archives, original; PPAmS, copy. *See* 1237.

1258 POTTER, Robert. 1806–1828. Records of a number of events of the War of 1812 and other historical references. NcU.

1259 POWEL, John Hare. 1806. A sea voyage to Calcutta. PHi.

1260 RAVENEL, Henry, Jr. 1806–1822. Family affairs; contains list of Negroes inherited by his family and their descendants, 1780–1820. GHi.

1261 THOMPSON, Charles C. B. 1806. Journal on the U.S. brig *Franklin*. DLC.

1262 ANON. 1807–1808. A peddler who journeyed through Virginia. VHi.

1263 ADAMS, William L. 1807–? Journal of the barge *Lovely Nan*, Lewis West, master, New Orleans to Louisville, commencing at Natchez. OHi.

1264 BRACKETT, Adino N. 1807–1817. Weather reports, NhHi.

1265 DAVIS, Samuel C. 1807–1809. His last illness; gives the progress of the disease and his thoughts and reflections. PHC.

1266 HURD, Rev. Isaac. 1807–1831. CNS. Nh-Hi.

1267 IRVING, Peter. 1807. Travel in Italy. NN.

1268 JOHNSTON, John. 1807–1808. His activities; weather; accounts and amounts of purchase. OCUHi. *See* 4955.

1269 LEWIS, Thomas D. 1807–1808. On board the *China Packet* on a voyage from Philadelphia to Madras and Calcutta. PHi.

1270 PLUMER, William. 1807–1836. Personal opinions on current events and notes and comments upon matters that came under his observation in his daily reading. DLC.

1271 PRENTICE, Charles. 1807. Journalistic journey from Northbridge, Mass., to Quebec and back, accompanied by Mussey Southwaik, Benjamin Bassett, and Brown Aldrich. CaOTP.

1272 WENTZEL, Willard Ferdinand. 1807. A short trip to the Rocky Mountains from Ft. Simpson in search of the Nahanies. CtY, copy and typescript.

1273 WETHERILL and BUDD. 1807. CNS. PHi.

1274 ANON. 1808–1815. Concerned with local events generally, including social matters, frequent occurrences of drunkenness and other misconduct, weather, and with the operation of the iron furnace; activities of the employees and other associates of the unknown writer. NjR, typescript; original is believed destroyed.

1275 BURR, Aaron. 1808–1812. Personal. CSmH.

1276 CAMPBELL. Robert. 1808–1851. Various experiences from Scotland to the Yukon Valley, including trading, explorations, and adventures among the Indians of the Northwest Coast. CU-B. *See* 1601.

1277 COOLEY, Rev. Timothy. 1808. Missionary tour through the western part of N.Y. state. OCoNg. *See* 1193.

1278 DULLES, Joseph Heatly. 1808–1810. A journey from Charleston, S.C., to New York on the ship *Minerva*, and on the *Princess Augusta* to England; travel conditions; British institutions, debates in Parliament, British-American relations, the Irish question; experiments and progress in science; the British Museum, art galleries, cathedrals. PHi.

1279 GLASS, Anthony. 1808–1809. A voyage from Nackitosh into the interior of La. on the waters of Red River, Trinity, Brassos, Colorado, and the Sabine; the country, customs of the Indians; experiences as a trader; efforts of the Spaniards from San Antonio to influence the Indians against the U.S.; the meteoric iron found in Texas. CtY.

1280 GROSVENOR, Ebenezer. 1808. CNS. NjR.

1281 HINDE, Thomas. 1808; 1825–1826; 1832–1835; 1839–1845. Philosophical and religious reflections; interesting and valuable material on the formative years of the Northwest. WHi.

1282 MONTEITH, Rev. John. 1808–1827. Life and times of a young minister in Mich.; education; ministerial duties; educational, cultural, religious conditions in Mich.; trips to N.Y., N.J., Pa., and Mass. MiU.

1283 PAGE, William. 1808–1812. Family matters; travel and business. PHi.

1284 SELLERS, John, Jr. 1808–1846. CNS. PPAmS.

1285 WILLISTON, Josiah. 1808–1814. Personal. MBNEH.

1286 [BEVIER, Henrietta Cornellia]. 1809. Schoolgirl at Sarah Pierce's School at Litchfield, Conn. NN.

1287 BIRCH, Maj. George. 1809–1825. Army life in the early years of the Republic; a description of the Battle of New Orleans and Indian troubles in the South; a few miscellaneous letters, documents, and drawings. PHi.

1288 FULLER, Maj. John. 1809. A tour from Vt. to the Ohio country; in 1809 and 1810 he was an officer in a rifle regt. on duty in the Miss. Terr. OHi.

1289 FURGERSON, Samuel. 1809–1811. A voyage from Boston to the Northwest coast of America in the brig *Otter*; description of the places visited and the traffic with the Indians. CtY.

1290 GREENE, Anna. 1809–1819. Experiences while she traveled in the ministry. PHC.

1291 HUMPHREYS, Joshua, Sr. 1809. A voyage from Philadelphia to Lisbon. PHi.

1292 HUNT, Mrs. Nancy (Thompson). 1809–1865. CNS. CtHi.

1293 LOGAN, George. 1809–1813. Farm diary. PHi.

1294 ROTCH, Joseph. 1809. Journal of a Southern tour; a description of sitting in House of Representatives and of meeting James and Dolly Madison at White House. PSC-Hi.

1295 SERGEANT, John. 1809–1818. Journal when he was missionary to the Indians at Stockbridge, Mass. NHi. *See* 1225.

1296 THOMSON, Sarah. 1809. A visit with her mother and brother in the family of Judge Ebenezer Tucker, Tuckerton, N.J.; describes various daily social activities, entertainments, etc. NjR, typescript.

1297 VAN SCHAACK, Catherine. 1809. Diary kept at school in Litchfield, Conn. NHi.

1298 BUNTING, Samuel. 1810–1864. Description of living quarters, domestic animals, land and crops, daily occupations; mention of natural phenomena from a single towhee to a comet; some original verses. PSC-Hi.

1299 CHANDLER, Mrs. Nathan S. (Mary Ann Tucker). ca. 1810. Small incidents in daily life. Nh-Hi.

1300 [EDDY, John Harlyhorne]. 1810. A trip from New York to Oswego to examine navigation. NN.

1301 EDDY, Thomas. 1810. CNS. ICN.

1302 ELMER, Lucius Quintius Cincinnatus. 1810–1814. Detail on War of 1812, alarms and events, and activities of the militia and of British ships in the lower Delaware. NjR.

1303 FINLEY, Rev. James Bradley. 1810. Missionary trip to Wyandot Indians in Ohio. OFH.

1304 GAY, Ebenezer. 1810–1837. CNS. NNC.

1305 HALE, Jonathan. 1810. Travel from Conn. to Ohio. OFH, typescript.

1306 LAWTON, Alexander J. 1810–1840. Plantation diary with comments on the weather, crops, and slaves. NcU.

1307 MANGIN, Samuel Henry. 1810. European travel. PPM.

1308 PENROSE, Washington H. 1810–1870. Accounts, ledger. PHi.

1309 SIDELL, William Henry. 1810–1873. Activities of railroad survey party in Isthmus of Panama. CLU.

1310 SMITH, Julia. 1810–1842. CNS. CtHi.

1311 TIDYMAN, Dr. Philip. 1810. Journey from Charleston, S.C., to Canada and return. PHC.

1312 ANON. 1811–1816. Journal by unidentified person covering various voyages, including a voyage from Boston, sojourn in Sandwich Islands, two voyages to Alaska coast, and return from the islands via Canton to New York. CU-B.

1313 ANON. 1811; 1814–1817. Daily happenings and the writer's reaction. NcU.

1314 ANON. 1811. Experimentations with the planting of crops. NSchHi.

1315 ABBOT, Rev. Ephraim. 1811–1812. Journey from Boston to Me. by boat and travels in Maine; also list of distribution of Bibles. MBNEH.

1316 BACON, Mrs. Josiah. 1811–1812. Kept while she traveled with her husband, the quartermaster of the 4th Regt., U.S. Infantry, stationed at Vincennes and Detroit. NHi.

1317 BROWN, Elijah. 1811; 1816; 1820; 1827. Written while he traveled in Europe and the U.S.; describes scenes, natural phenomena, the construction of canals and dams; philosophical and scientific subjects. PHi.

1318 CARR, Lt. Col. Robert. 1811–1823. His participation in the War of 1812; recruiting, army movements, warfare in N.Y. state and Canada, general orders, paymasters' settlements and accounts, etc. PHi.

1319 FORCE, John. 1811–1812. A trip to the Ohio Valley. NjHi.

1320 HEMPSTEAD, Stephen. 1811. Journey from New London to St. Louis. MoSHs.

1321 KELLOGG, Martin. 1811–1813. A journey from Alford, Mass., to Ohio, and return through Pa. OClWHi.

1322 KING, Col. Richard. 1811. Walker's military expedition to Quebec; Boston; storm. BrLPro, original; MHi, transcript.

1323 MALEY, John. 1811–1813. His wanderings in the Red River country to trade with the Indians and look for mineral deposits. CtY.

1324 McLEOD, John. 1811–1814. Account of a fur trader in Red River Valley. MnHi.

1325 RIDGELY, Henry M. 1811–1815. Memoranda of personal expenses, letters written, business and social engagements. De-Ar.

1326 YOUNGS, William. 1811–1814 (with gaps). First at Bethlehem Mills, moved to Coeyman Mills, N.Y.; weather; milling business; shipping on the Hudson River. NCooHi.

1327 ANON. 1812. The writer's hour of rising, food eaten, daily social calls, etc. ViU.

1328 ANON. 1812. Kept by a hospital officer at Pass Christian, Mass. CSmH.

1329 BEGG, William. 1812–1815. Kept on board the H.M.S. *Tenedos*. PHi.

1330 BLACK, Capt. Samuel. 1812. Equipping company, orders, receipts; camp routine; deserters. OSHi.

1331 COCKBURN, Rear Adm. Sir George, K.C.B. 1812–1815. The War of 1812 and the measures taken after the conclusion of peace, regarding the exchange of prisoners and other details. DLC.

1332 DALLIBA, James. [1812–1815?]. War of 1812 on the frontier. WHi.

1333 DUNCAN, Silas. 1812–1813. Kept on board the U.S. frigate *President*. DLC.

1334 DUVALL, ——? 1812–1814. Comments on war and politics; personal items and daily weather observations. MdAA.

1335 FELTUS, W. W. 1812–1814. Journal on board the U.S.S. *Essex*; daily occurrences; sea battles with British warships, chase and capture of pirates, privateers, and merchant vessels; accounts of encounter with savage tribes on the Marquesas Islands in the Pacific. PHi.

1336 FOSTER, James. [1812–1815?]. War of 1812 on the frontier. WHi.

1337 GORHAM, Henry. 1812. Weather. MBNEH.

1338 HANDY, Samuel Clarke. 1812–? Journal of "cruize" on board privateer *Polly* of Salem. MH.

1339 HEALD, Nathan. 1812–1813. CNS. WHi.

1340 HUNT, Caleb. 1812. Trip down the Ohio and Mississippi rivers. MdHi.

1341 JONES, Thomas. 1812–1816. Memorandum and diary with a short description of travels in Ky. DLC.

1342 KEMPER, Rt. Rev. Jackson. [1812–1870]. Diaries, journals, and other documents; his work as bishop, and the institutions with which he was actively connected; a view of conditions in the Northwest for an extended period. WHi.

1343 LUTTIG, Charles. 1812. CNS. MoHi.

1344 McLEOD, John, Sr. 1812–1844. Journal and correspondence of one of the earliest pioneers in the Ore. Terr. OrHi.

1345 MILL, Fries. 1812–1842. CNS. Nc-Ar.

1346 NEWSOM, Nathan. 1812–1813. A journey taken by volunteers from Gallia Cnty. for the purpose of destroying Indians and the invasion of Canada. OHi.

1347 PALMER, Noble. 1812–1815. Activities; detailed accounts of his dreams. NCooHi.

1348 PARSONS, Dr. Usher. 1812–1814. Kept during service with Commodore Perry on Lake Erie; places visited and military events. RHi.

1349 PEARCE, Cromwell. 1812. War diary. PWcHi.

1350 PHILLIPS, Francis. 1812–1815. Journal entries made by clerk aboard the *Raccoon*; sailed from Spithead in Nov. 1812, and returned to Plymouth, England, May 1815; visited Astoria, San Francisco, Monterey, and many South American ports. CU-B.

1351 PHILLIPS, Willard. 1812–1816. Personal journal and miscellaneous Mss. MH.

1352 PROBYN, Edward. 1812–1820. Short notes and many weather reports. NHi.

1353 ROACH, Issac. 1812–1847. Including his participation in the War of 1812 and the military campaign against Canada. PHi.

1354 ROBISON, Capt. John. 1812. Military, Ohio Militia, War of 1812. OHi, typescript.

1355 SCHWEINITZ, Rev. Lewis David de. 1812. Voyage to America; adventurous journey, with wife, from Herrnhut, Germany, to Bethlehem, Pa. (in German). NcWsM. *See* 1169, 1732.

1356 SNELLING, Col. Josiah. [1812–1815?]. Journal of War of 1812 on the frontier. WHi.

1357 STUART, Robert. 1812. Journey from Astoria to N.Y. City; fur trade. NN. *See* next item.

1358 STUART, Robert. 1812–1813. Overland journey from Astoria, Ore., to St. Louis, Mo. CSmH.

1359 THOMPSON, Jonah. 1812. Journals abroad. PHi.

1360 WITHERELL, Judge B.F.H. [1812–1815?]. Journal concerning War of 1812 on the frontier. WHi.

1361 ANON. 1813–1814. CNS. NcD.

1362 ALLEN, Zachariah. 1813–1882 (with gaps). Scholarly notations on current events and a great deal of information on textile mills and management; philosophical observations. RHi.

1363 BROOKS, Charles. 1813–1867. CNS. MiD.

1364 ELLIOT, Amanda (Mrs. Tillinghast). 1813–1821 (with gaps). Life of a young unmarried woman in a small town, living first with one brother and then another; references to the War of 1812. CtGuE.

1365 FERRIS, Benjamin. 1813–1845. Transactions and events at the Barley Mill Property, now Rockbourn; day-to-day life on farm; weather; crops, visitors; errands. PSC-Hi.

1366 FERRISON, Mary. 1813. CNS. OCoNg.

1367 GANO, Rev. Stephen. 1813–1814. Weather, baptisms, births, marriages, deaths; brief notes of travels to Philadelphia and return. RHi. *See* 2033?

1368 GERRY, Elbridge. 1813. Trip by horseback and boat from Cambridge (?) to Pittsburgh and Washington; social life; President Madison; British troops. NN.

1369 HAGERMAN, Lt. Col. Christopher Alexander. 1813–1816. Military journal; attack on Sackett's Harbor; battle of Coysler's farm; aide-de-camp to Gen. Drummond. CaOTP.

1370 HAMTON, Aaron. 1813. Journey from Kingwood, N.J., to Lake Erie, recounting experiences and describing conditions of roads and bridges, taverns, villages, and expenses of moving a family to a new settlement. N.

1371 HARLEY, Hannah Case. 1813–1865. Personal diary by religious fanatic; includes rumor of war in 1858 or 1859. MeWC.

1372 HENRY, Joseph. 1813. Journey from southern Ohio to Detroit. OFH, typescript.

1373 HILL, Samuel. 1813–1814. Journal kept by master of brig on voyage from Boston to Savannah, and to France with cotton; captured by British. NN.

1374 HOWE, Rev. Joseph D. 1813. Two preaching tours through Ky. PPPrHi.

1375 JENNISON, William. 1813–1842. CNS. MWA.

1376 KOCK, Charles. 1813–1878. CNS. Nc-Ar.

1377 McAFEE, Robert Breckinridge. 1813–1814. Company memorandum book and journal of his mounted company in Col. R. M. Johnson's regt.; war activities, battles; weather, etc. OCUHi.

1378 MITCHELL, Elisha. 1813–1816. Chiefly religious reflections. NcU.

1379 PAYNE, John Howard. 1813; 1808–1814 (with gaps); 1821; 1826; 1833; 1838; 1844. CNS. NNC.

1380 RAWLE, Rebecca Warner. 1813. CNS. PHi.

1381 SHINER, Michael. 1813–1865. Events and happenings in Washington. DLC.

1382 VALPEY, Joseph. 1813–1815. Journal continued during imprisonment on Melville Island and in Dartmoor prison. MiD.

1383 ANON. 1814–1847. Plantation diary. NcU.

1384 ANON. 1814. Massacre at Dartmoor Prison; mentions names of several N.H. men. NhHi.

1385 ALLEN, Sally. 1814–1839. Kept at West Greenwich (Conn.?). OHi.

1386 BAINBRIDGE, Joseph. 1814. Kept on U.S. vessel of war *Frolic*. ICHi.

1387 BAYARD, Maria. 1814–1815. Tour of England, Scotland, and France; social and economic conditions, and beauties; includes references to Napoleon. NN.

1388 BOLLING, Leneaus. 1814. Operations on his farm "Chellowe"; expenses; social life, personal and family matters; militia activities around Norfolk. ViU.

1389 CHAMPNEY, William Ingersoll. 1814. Personal diary. MBNEH.

1390 CLAY, Henry. 1814. CNS. DLC.

1391 COCHRANE, Sir Alexander F.S. 1814–1815. Activities along the Southern coast of the United States. NHi.

1392 COPLEY, Alexander. 1814; 1839–1840. CNS. MiU.

1393 ELFRETH, Jacob R. 1814–1870. Personal observations; Quaker meetings; weather in Philadelphia; political events; business matters. PHC. *See* 3445.

1394 FLOWER, George. 1814–1817. Travels in France, interest in agriculture and economics; travels in U.S., N.Y. to the Middle West; visits to Jefferson, governors, etc. ICHi.

1395 GEISINGER, David. 1814. Kept on board the U.S. sloop of war *Wasp*. DLC.

1396 GILMAN, Samuel. 1814. Account of his studies and intellectual pursuits. MH.

1397 MERRELL, William Stanley. 1814–1875. Description of events, personal and public, with history of his drug company. OCUHi.

1398 OSBORNE, Joseph. 1814–1858. Includes an eyewitness account of the bombardment of Ft. McHenry, Md., Sept. 13, 1814. OHi.

1399 PLEASANTS, Thomas Franklin. 1814–1817. Professional activities; daily social events; travel through Southern states; cotton enterprise in New Orleans; military training in the War of 1812, etc. PHi.

1400 TUCKER, Rev. Mark. 1814–1829. Details of his Presbyterian ministry and religious thoughts. RHi.

1401 TYLDEN, Sir John Maxwell. 1814–1815. Military operations behind battle for New Orleans; social and political life in Havana. NN.

1402 ANON. 1815–1838. Farm work and records in almanacs. NN.

1403 ANON. 1815–1816. A member of the United Society of Believers (Shakers) of Pleasant Hill, Mercer Cnty., Ky. Records removals of members from one society to another. KyLoF.

1404 BIGLER, Henry W. 1815–1899. His activities from early life in W.Va.; conversion to Mormonism; pioneering across the Sierra to Salt Lake; gold mining in Cal. and missionary work in Hawaii. CU-B. *See* 2357, 2371.

1405 BROWNE, Samuel J. 1815–1816. A journey from Cincinnati, Ohio, to England. OHi.

1406 BROWNE, Symmes. 1815–1920. Diaries, letters, accounts, many from the Civil War era; Columbus, Cincinnati, and Dayton, Ohio. OHi.

1407 CONDICT, Miss R. W. 1815. CNS. NjHi.

1408 COOPER, John. 1815–1822; 1829–1841. Trips through the county; his mills; the county roads; church affairs; farming activities and his settlement in Cooper; the British evacuation of Eastport. Me.

1409 DAILEY, David. 1815–1817. CNS. PPHiA.

1410 DEMUN, Julius. 1815–1816. CNS. MoSHs.

1411 ELKINTON, Joseph. 1815–1858 (with gaps). Kept by schoolteacher among Seneca Indians in N.Y.; description of relations between U.S. and Indians; personal reflections. PSC-Hi, transcription. *See* 2382, 3175, 4453?

1412 FONDA, Giles. 1815. A trip by a medical student to N.J. N.

1413 GORHAM, John C. 1815–1853. Products and timber shipped on the *Tuscarora*, a local trading schooner. NcD.

1414 HALL, James. 1815. Lt. in 2nd regt. artillery, USA, during expedition of U.S. artillery officers appointed to accompany Decatur against Algiers. OCUHi.

1415 LOGAN, Deborah Norris. 1815–1839. The social life of many prominent Philadelphia families, and political, religious, and cultural developments. PHi.

1416 MICHAEL, David Moritz. 1815. Travel diary from Philadelphia to Ziest, Holland (in German). NcWsM.

1417 MORRIS, Samuel Buckley. 1815–1847. Trip to New England; family news; daily happenings. PHC. *See* 2230?

1418 PAUL, Joseph M. 1815. A journey made by him through central and western Pa. PHi.

1419 PERKINS, Samuel G. 1815–1816. European travels; attribution made by T. W. Higginson as journal is unsigned. MH.

1420 RICHARDSON, William. 1815. Travel from Middle Atlantic through South. KyLoF. 1815. From Boston to New Orleans; from Boston to Western country and down Ohio and Mississippi rivers to New Orleans. MH, typescript.

1421 SQUIRE, Sally. 1815–1816. Religious life (Presbyterian) after son's death. NN.

1422 STRYKER, Peter. 1815–1816. A trip from Belleville, N.J., by a Reformed Church minister, to preach in "Vacant Congregations Westward and Southward"; also a trip from N.Y. to Saratoga and return, visiting vacant congregations. NjR, typescript.

1423 SULLIVAN, Isaac. 1815–1844. Every birth, marriage, or death he heard of in the area of Sussex Cnty., Del.; occasional notes on weather, elections, crimes. De-Ar.

1424 WILSON, H. B. 1815–1816. Occurrences while he was in Europe. PHi.

1425 WOOD, J. 1815. A tour to the Northern states in the summer of 1815 through R.I., Conn., N.Y., N.J., and Pa.; observations and impression of Northern customs, institutions, intellectual life, entertainment, travel conditions, agricultural methods. ViU.

1426 YOUNGS, Isaac. 1815–1823. CNS. DLC.

1427 ANON. 1816–1831. Kept at the Cherokee Indian Mission of the Moravian Church (in German). NcWsM.

1428 ANON. 1816. CNS. PVfM.

1429 BLOCKLEY FARM (almshouse). 1816–1823. Business, professional, and personal account books. PHi.

1430 BOWKER, Richard Rogers. 1816?–1832. Travel journals; Europe, U.S.A., South America, Holy Land, etc. NN. *See* 3286, 4447.

1431 JOYES, Capt. Thomas. 1816–1817. A surveying trip from St. Louis to Ft. Clark near Peoria and then to camp. IHi.

1432 MERCER, Charles Fenton. 1816. CNS. NjHi.

1433 PATRICK, John Menan. 1816–1818. Personal diary while he was a student at Greene Academy, Hookerton, N.C. Nc-Ar.

1434 PEASE, Calvin. 1816–1829. CNS. OClWHi.

1435 READEL, Dr. John Didier. 1816. Kept on voyage from Baltimore to White Rocks in the sloop *Whiskey*. MdHi.

1436 TALLCOT, Hannah (Howland). 1816. Trip to the East while she was a young girl. PSC-Hi.

1437 THACHER, Davis. 1816–1818. His brother's trip from Mass. to N.Y. and Charleston. ScU.

1438 THOMAS, Maurice. 1816–1817. Weather; events in the colony of Shakers; farming operations; travels and removals of members from one family or society to another; clothing received. Ky-LoF.

1439 WRIGHT, Nathaniel. 1816–1818; 1820–1825. Reflections, feelings, and occurrences; social life and customs of Va. NhD.

1440 ANON. 1817. Short journey in Fox Islands, Penobscot Bay, Me. NN.

1441 ADAMS, Philo. 1817; 1831. Two journeys; one from Middlebury, Vt., to Ohio; one from Lake Erie to Green Bay. ICHi.

1442 BEALE, Edward. 1817–1818. Beale's and Honor Green's questionable romance, with occasional references to his man, Horace, and the treatment of Negroes in Charleston (S.C.?) (in code). NcD.

1443 BOWER, Alexander, Sr. and Jr. 1817–1846. Local, political, and social events in Ulysses, N.Y., and the development of a farm. NIC.

1444 BREVARD, Thomas. 1817–1846. Minutes of the meetings of the Union Library Society of Lebanon, Tenn.; and other notes. NcU.

1445 FARRAGUT, David G. 1817. Journal kept on board the U.S. ship *Washington*. MdAN. *See* 4146.

1446 GUEST, Mary Ann. 1817. Journey from New Brunswick to Cincinnati. NjNb.

1447 HANDY, Charles O. 1817. Journal of the mission to Algiers. PHi.

1448 HICKS, Elias. 1817; 1828. A first-hand record of the so-called liberal ideas held and impressively preached by the individual whose name was the label attached to one of the two Quaker groups resulting from the Separation of 1828, into the Orthodox and "Hicksite" Friends. PSC-Hi.

1449 LANGSLOW, Richard. 1817. Round trip from New London, Conn., to Niagara Falls. NCoo-Hi, typescript.

1450 LONG, Stephen H. 1817; 1823. Expeditions of 1817 and 1823. MnHi.

1451 MURRAY, Mary. 1817; 1819; 1825. Summer trips to Conn., to Rockaway, through N.Y. state and along the Erie Canal, and to Saratoga. NHi.

1452 NEWTON, Lucy. 1817. Journey from Union, Ohio, to Mecanicksburgh and from there to Anderson Township, Hamilton Cnty., Ohio. OHi.

1453 RANDOLPH, John. 1817? CNS. ViHi. *See* 1474?

1454 RASER, William. 1817–1818. Life in Paris and tours through France. NN.

1455 ROBINSON, Jeremy. 1817–1823. Travels, Buenos Aires, Concepcion, Valparaiso, Lima, and several of the islands in the Pacific. DLC.

1456 SCANLAND, John. 1817. His trip through the "Western states and territories" during the winter and spring; observations on scenic beauty, bird and plant life, types of soil, methods of cultivation, crops, houses, manners, and social customs. ViU.

1457 STATHEM, David E. 1817–1819; 1825; and 1836. CNS. OHi, typescripts of 1817–1819 and 1836 volumes.

1458 WILSON, William B. 1817–1871. Domestic affairs; farming; weather; Quaker meetings. PHi.

1459 ANON. (somewhere between 1818 and 1831). Some diary notations, chiefly on treatment of sick persons, yellow fever, etc. NcU.

1460 ANON. 1818–1819. Log and journal of the U.S.S. *Ontario*, on a passage from Valparaiso to Lima. DLC.

1461 ANON. 1818–1819. The travels of two Englishmen on the continent. MiU-C.

1462 BELL, Richard. 1818–1827. His voyage to America and his residence in Del. PHi.

1463 CHURCHILL, George. 1818–1841. Farming in Madison Cnty., Ill.; state and local politics by an opponent of slavery. IHi.

1464 FOTHERGILL, Elizabeth. 1818. The visit of seven Seneca Indians to York, England. NHi.

1465 GARDINER, Luke. 1818–1819. Sea journal, Atlantic coast. MiD.

1466 HAZARD, Samuel. 1818. Medical. PHi. *See* 1253.

1467 HOWLAND, Mrs. John Hicks. 1818–1822. Trips from N.Y. city to Pa., New England, and through N.Y. state. NHi.

1468 LEIGHTON, Gen. Samuel. 1818–1848. Routine affairs of his later life and local happenings. MeHi; MeAIP, copy.

1469 MARECHAL, Most Rev. Ambrose. 1818–1830. Personal accounts of archbishop of Baltimore. InNd.

1470 McDONALD, Truman Crawford. 1818. Voyage in brig *Good-Intent* from Sandwich Islands to East Indies. MH.

1471 McGUIRE, Dr. R. F. 1818–1852. Monthly reports of weather; health of inhabitants of Monroe, La.; local personal items. LU, typescript; LSh, original.

1472 PERKINS, Samuel H. 1818–1832. His travel in Mattamuskett, N.C., in 1818; legal apprenticeship and admittance to the Philadelphia bar; professional struggles; social and religious life of the city. PHi.

1473 RANDOLPH, Edward. 1818. Kept by an officer in the Seminole War in Georgia and Florida. NcU.

1474 RANDOLPH, John. 1818–1819. Introspective reflections; his movements day by day; meteorological record. DLC. *See* 1453?

1475 RODNEY, Caesar Augustus. 1818. Kept in Buenos Aires as U.S. minister. MH. *See* 983?

1476 SWAN, Caroline Knox. 1818. CNS. MeHi.

1477 TALLCOT, Phebe. 1818. Journey by a young girl to the Eastern states. PSC-Hi.

1478 WEBB, Daniel Cannon. 1818–1850. Combination plantation journal and personal diary; some travels, one to Graniteville, some to Eastern cities; Gen. Lafayette's visit, 1825; nullification agitation of 1831; fire of 1838. ScHi.

1479 WOODHOUSE, Commodore Samuel. 1818. Notes of a tour in Brazil. PHi. *See* 2631, 3393.

1480 WORTHINGTON, W. G. D. 1818–1821; 1825–1842. Kept at Washington, D.C., and during a stay in Chile; his tour to Mo.; miscellaneous. DLC.

1481 ANON. 1819–1829. Kept at Mt. Vernon. DLC.

1482 BALDWIN, William. 1819. The expedition to the Rocky Mts. commanded by S. H. Long, 1819–1820. NNC.

1483 BECK, Lewis Caleb. 1819–1850. Kept by a scientist during trips between Albany and St. Louis and periods of residence in the latter area, with descriptions of events, towns, natural features, etc. NjR, microfilm and copy.

1484 BONN, Jacob. 1819–1823. By a resident of the Hope neighborhood near Salem, N.C. NcWsM.

1485 DOBBER, Daniel. 1819–1844. Daily events (in German). PHi.

1486 FAIRMAN, Sarah Amelia. 1819–1821. Social life of the area, daily activities, parties, games, summer jaunts, visits to sugar bush. NCooHi.

1487 GRISWOLD, Rt. Rev. Alexander Viets. 1819–1821. Notes of Episcopal bishop. MBD.

1488 KING, Richard Hugg. 1819–1823. Notes on sawmill, gristmill, and plantation affairs; striking for its records of deaths among slaves in 1819. Nc-Ar.

1489 KIRKPATRICK (Littleton) papers. 1819. Certificate of election to Congress, commissions, etc.; letters received by his wife, Sophia (Astley) Kirkpatrick; trip to Canada. NjR.

1490 [LOGAN, Charles F.?] 1819–1822; 1822–1824. Loganville mill journals. PHi. *See* 1508.

1491 LONG, Maj. ———. 1819–1820. His explorations up the Platte Valley from the Missouri to the Rocky Mts. NbFrOs.

1492 [LOWELL, John Amory]. [1819–?] CNS. MH. *See* 2694.

1493 McLEAN, John M. 1819–1844. Service with the Hudson's Bay Co. in Canada. NBuHi.

1494 PEALE, Titian Ramsay. 1819. Assistant naturalist on the expedition of Maj. Stephen H. Long; journey by steamboat from Pittsburgh down the Ohio and Mississippi rivers and up the Missouri. DLC.

1495 SHALER, William. 1819; 1827–1828. Journals of the U.S. consulate at Tunis, and of the U.S. consulate at Algiers. PHi.

1496 WOOSTER, "Great-grandmother." 1819–1825. Religious diary, probably in Ohio. OHi.

1497 ANON. 1820. Trip through Pa. describing scenery, people, towns, roads. NN.

1498 BELL, J. R. 1820. CNS. CSt.

1499 BOURNE, Edward Emerson. 1820–1823. CNS. MiD.

1500 FARNSWORTH, Benjamin Stow. 1820–1842. Early days in New England; small general store and its purchase; travel in the East; financial distress. MiD.

1501 FOUKE, Isaac. 1820. CNS. Wv-Ar.

1502 HARBRIDGE, George. 1820–1825. A voyage from Gravesend to Hudson's Bay and inland to the Red River Colony. CtY.

1503 HARVEY, Isaac. 1820–1856. Events in Philadelphia, weather, etc. PHi.

1504 HASKELL, Nehemiah. 1820–1821. A voyage on the schooner *Eagle* from Boston to Hawaii. CU-B.

1505 JAMES, Edwin. 1820–1827. Journal by the second botanist and geologist of the expedition to the Rocky Mts. commanded by S. H. Long, 1819–1820. NNC.

1506 KEARNY, Gen. Stephen W. 1820; 1824. Trips by keel boats from Council Bluffs to St. Peters, and St. Louis to Council Bluffs. MoSHi. *See* 2287.

1507 LAVALLETTE, Elie A. F. 1820–1822. Lavallette's voyages from Rio de Janeiro around Cape Horn to Lima, Peru; Valparaiso, Chile; Panama; along the Southwest coast of Mexico; and back to San Blas; comments on currents, winds, barometer readings, the ice islands around Cape Horn in winter, periodical rains at San Blas, etc. NcD.

1508 LOGAN, Charles F. 1820–1823; 1823–1825. CNS. PHi. *See* 1490.

1509　MUNN, Silas. 1820–1870. Comments on his parentage, family, illnesses, occupation, butchering, farming, boarders, weather, politics, orations, anti-masonic meetings, prices of produce and lawsuits. ViU.

1510　PIERREPONT, Hezechiah Zeers. 1820–1823. Visits to author's farms in upper N.Y. NN.

1511　PIERREPONT, William Constable. 1820–1850. Information about the land business, the settlers, and agricultural conditions. NIC.

1512　SHARPLESS, Phebe. 1820–1828. Notes how she has passed the day, in order to keep watch on her spiritual life; introspective. PSC-Hi.

1513　SKINNER, Tristim Lowther. 1820–1862. Plantation diary containing comments on the weather, crops, and slaves. NcU.

1514　TROWBRIDGE, Charles Christopher. 1820. Journal of the exploring expedition of Gov. Cass. MiD; MnHi, microfilm.

1515　VAILL, William F. 1820. A missionary's journey to and work with the Osage Indians; he was sent by the United Foreign Missionary Society. Ok-Hi.

1516　YARNALL, Edith S. 1820–1823. Notes on legislature and banks; accounts of money spent on Philadelphia shopping trip; altercation over a fence; receipts for potent yeast, red dye, and other items. DeHi.

1517　ANON. 1821. Journal of a Muncy immigrant farmer. PWmP and PWmHi.

1518　BROWN, John. 1821–1865. Experiences of a lawyer and plantation owner in Arkansas. OkU.

1519　COLLINS, John. 1821–1823. CNS. PPHiA.

1520　CREMER, John. 1821–1822. A voyage from N.Y. to the Pacific on the U.S. *Franklin*; Cremer was drowned March 20, 1822. CU-B.

1521　DULANY, Mary. 1821; 1863–1864. Campaigns and battles of the Civil War and their effect on the civilian population. ViU.

1522　EVANS, James W. 1821–1850. Incomplete record of an overland journey from Ft. Smith, Ark., across the Plains. CU-B.

1523　GRIMES, Capt. Eliah. 1821–1822. Kept by him aboard the *Eagle* on a trading voyage to Cal. from Sandwich Islands. CU-B.

1524　HAMERSLEY, Lt. Thomas S. 1821–1824. Kept on board the U.S. ship *Franklin*, in the Pacific Ocean. DLC.

1525　HEDGES, John. 1821–1865. Weather observations, accounts, etc. DeHi.

1526　HILL, Laura (Porter). 1821–1828. Her religious life. NCooHi.

1527　MURRAY, Hannah. 1821. Summer visits to Genesee and to Philadelphia. NHi.

1528　NASH, William. 1821–1841. Personal accounts; daily activities; community news, marriages, deaths; sales; and treatments for various diseases. MoU.

1529　PICKERING, William. 1821. Voyage and overland trip as far as the west side of the Appalachians made by a governor appointed by Lincoln after serving in the Ill. legislature. IAlbHi.

1530　PRALL, David M. 1821. Trip from New York City to Niagara. NHi.

1531　RUSH, Richard. 1821. CNS. DLC.

1532　SIPPLE, Mr. and Mrs. 1821. Trip from Delaware to Ballston Spa. NHi.

1533　TALIAFERRO, Lawrence. 1821–1839 (short gaps). Indians, Indian oratory and councils; traders, explorers, missionaries, treaties, Indian payments; British intrigue in the Northwest; trading posts and fur sale. MnHi.

1534　TURNER, Anne A. 1821–1837. Religious introspection and family matters. NcD.

1535　WILTBERGER, Christian, Jr. 1821. A voyage to Liberia· in the brig *Nautilus* with a shipload of African colonists; missionary labors there; much concerning the American Colonization Society. DLC.

1536　WINSLOW, Isaac. 1821. A voyage from Boston to Halifax. DLC. *See* 1597.

1537　ANON. 1822–1880. St. Philip's Negro mission of the Moravian Church. NcWsM.

1538　ANON. 1822–1859. Diary in Edinburgh and Canfield, Ohio. OClWHi.

1539　ANON. 1822. Diary of European travel of the Arnold or Appleton family of Boston or Savannah. NcU. *See* 1540, 1714, 2089, 2120, 3218, 3858, 4001, 4005.

1540　ANON. 1822. Financial records and personal diary; probably of Arnold or Appleton family. NcU. *See* 1539, etc.

1541　ANON. 1822. A European tour; probably written by Mr. Crane who was in Europe at this time with Dr. Wm. Waring of Savannah; among Dr. Waring's papers. GHi.

1542　BROWNSON, Orestes. 1822–1825. Personal. InNd.

1543　CAREY, Edward L. 1822–1839. CNS. PHi.

1544　GILPIN, Henry D. 1822–1859. CNS. PHi. *See* 2923.

1545　GRAHAM, George. 1822. Trip from Stoystown, Pa., down the Ohio valley and Mississippi River to New Orleans. OCUHi.

1546　GRAY, M. R. 1822–1831. Weather; social gatherings; inventories of chinaware, comments on local events; sale of slaves; recipes for plum pudding, biscuits, etc.; bread accounts; family matters. ViU.

1547 HALL, Rev. Richard, Sr. 1822–1823. A voyage from N.H. to New Orleans and return overland. MnHi.

1548 HALL, Richard D. 1822–1823. Work performed for American Bible Society. PPPrHi.

1549 HAMBLETON, Samuel. 1822–1823. Kept while he was on a cruise as purser in U.S. Navy; contains descriptions of South America. MdHi.

1550 HEACOCK, Joel. 1822–1853. Farm work and family comings and goings. PSC-Hi.

1551 HUDSON, John S. 1822. Journal in the form of two periodic reports sent to the Northern Missionary Society of the Saginaw Mission Family at Ft. Gratiot; religious work, education of the Indians; observations and experiences generally. NjR.

1552 MARSTON, Henry W. 1822–1832; 1855–1884. Struggle to maintain his plantation; absentee plantation ownership; business of Clinton and Port Hudson Railroad Co. and Silliman Female Collegiate Institute; local news; politics. LU.

1553 SCHOOLCRAFT, Henry Rowe. 1822. Journal of Indian affairs kept at the agency of Sault Ste. Marie. DLC. See 1591.

1554 SERGEANT, John. 1822. CNS. MoSHi. See 1225?

1555 STONE, Edward Martin. 1822–1831. A trip from Ind. to Pa.; social life at Blairsville, Pa.; a trip to Mass.; social and religious life in Boston. MnHi, microfilm.

1556 WADDEL, Rev. Moses. 1822–1829. Diary kept while he was President of the Univ. of Ga. DLC.

1557 WALKER, ———? 1822. Journey from Genessee, N.Y., to Wellington, Mass. NN.

1558 WHITE, Carrie M. 1822–1884. CNS. WaU.

1559 ALLAN, John. 1823. CNS. ViU.

1560 AMBLER, John Jaquelin. 1823–1826. His "grand tour" of Europe, supplemented by notes on his life at "Glen Ambler" for several years after his return. ViU. See 1715.

1561 BIDDLE, Cmdr. James. 1823–1824. Journal on the U.S. Frigate Congress. PHi.

1562 FORSYTH, John. 1823. Voyage in the ship Othello from Bordeaux to N.Y. DLC.

1563 HAYDEN, Richard. 1823–1870 (with gaps). Shipping, milling, and surveying in the vicinity of Robbinston, Me., as well as a brief account of the inauguration of John Q. Adams and many matters of more local interest. MeCa.

1564 JANNEY, Ann Shoemaker. 1823. Sea voyage to West Indies for sake of husband's health; perils of life on a sailing vessel; scenes and manner of living in the Indies. PSC-Hi.

1565 JOHNS, James. [ca. 1823–1873]. CNS. Vt-Hi.

1566 JOHNSON, Jothan T. 1823–1825. Religious. NHi.

1567 MORRIS, Henry. 1823. Expense account and journal (in Spanish) of a trip to Spain. PHi.

1568 RAVENSCROFT, Rt. Rev. John Stark. 1823–1828. Diary of Protestant Episcopal bishop of North Carolina. NHi.

1569 SMITH, Benjamin R. 1823. Journey from Providence to Cincinnati by way of New York, Philadelphia, and Pittsburgh; by boat and stage from Providence to Philadelphia; by wagon from Philadelphia to Pittsburgh and by keelboat from Pittsburgh to Cincinnati; also family genealogical data. InU-Li.

1570 STOWELL, Rev. David. 1823–1848 (with gaps). Mementos of Congregational minister. Nh-Hi.

1571 WHITLOCK, William C. 1823. A journey made from Virginia to Union County, Ill. OHi, copy.

1572 ANON. 1824–1887. CNS. OHi.

1573 ANON. 1824–1829. Ky. travel. WHi.

1574 ALLINSON, Samuel. 1824–1883. Temperance, anti-slavery, prison reform activities of a Quaker philanthropist in N.J.; farming. NjR.

1575 BERNARD, Rev. Overton. 1824; 1858–1863. Personal; descriptions of church work and the Civil War. NcU.

1576 BETHUNE, Joanna Graham (Mrs. D. Bethune). 1824–1849. Daily devotions and meditations; weekly remarks of sermons heard. MiU.

1577 BLACK, Samuel. 1824. Abstracts from his journal made by J. B. Tyrrell, 1894, of an exploration up the Finlay River. CU-B.

1578 BRODIE, John Pringle. 1824–1832. Kept in Mexico and Cal. ICN.

1579 BUNKER, Alexander D. 1824–1827. A whaling voyage to the South Seas and Pacific Ocean on the Ontario. MHi.

1580 CRANE, Elizabeth (Mulford). 1824–1828. Regular entries describing farming, church, domestic, and social activities, family events, visits. NjR.

1581 DAVIDSON, William B. 1824–1825; 1827. Activities in law college; daily local events; politics; tours through Pa.; travel by coach and canal; a reception for Lafayette on his visit to Philadelphia. PHi.

1582 DREW, George W. 1824. Journal between Eastport, Me., and New Brunswick ports. MiD.

1583 FOULKE, Joseph. 1824; 1835; 1837; 1851. Visit to the Friends' Meetings of Concord, Mass., the Western Quarterly meetings, and Yearly Meetings of Ohio, Ind., Baltimore, Philadelphia, and Nottingham. PSC-Hi.

1584 HAYES, Chloe Smith. 1824–1845. About family and friends, local events, and religious thoughts. OFH.

1585 HOUSTON, William H. and George W. [1824–1868?]. Economic, social, agricultural, political, military. ICMcCHi.

1586 JOHNSTON, George. 1824–1827. Trading with the Indians for the American Fur Company. DLC.

1587 LAWTON, William. 1824–1861. A visit to Conn. MBNEH.

1588 McCORMICK, Stephen. 1824–1835. Plow manufacture; economic, social, agricultural. ICMcCHi.

1589 [ROCHE, John]. 1824. A trip from Maysville, Ky., to Boston, visiting points of interest in the various cities as well as Williams, Amherst, Harvard, Brown, and Yale colleges. WHi, copy.

1590 SALTER, William. [between 1824 and 1903]. CNS. Ia-HA.

1591 SCHOOLCRAFT, Henry Rowe. 1824; 1837. A small journal of Indian affairs begun at Mackinaw. DLC. *See* 1553.

1592 SCHULLING, S. 1824–1825. Summer trips through Pa., N.Y., and New England. PHi.

1593 SMITH, Gulielma. 1824–1825. Journey to New England and persons visited. PSC-Hi.

1594 STEVENSON, Martha Ann Curtis. 1824–1825. CNS. MBSpnea.

1595 TAYLOR, Robert. 1824–1825. Voyage from Saybrook, Conn., to Guadalupe; covers trading, shipwork. NN. *See* 2206, 2305.

1596 WICKES, Simon A. 1824–1834. Kept by a student in Conn.; later opened a medical practice in Philadelphia. MdHi.

1597 WINSLOW, Isaac. 1824. Travels by stagecoach and boat from Boston to Charleston, S.C., via Richmond, Va., and Raleigh and Wilmington, N.C. NcD. *See* 1536.

1598 WORK, John. 1824–1834. Personal adventures of a trader employed by the Hudson's Bay Co., including long overland journeys to Mo. and other places. CU-B.

1599 ATKINSON, Gen. Henry. 1825. Trip up Missouri River. MoHi. *See* 1658?

1600 BROBSON, William P. 1825–1828. Weather; finances; philosophical observations on misfortunes of friends; mentions Daniel Webster and his speeches; local Del. and Washington, D.C. comments. DeHi.

1601 CAMPBELL, Robert. 1825–1835. Kept in 1870 by William Fayel about Col. Campbell's experiences in the Rocky Mt. fur trade from 1825–1835. CU-B. *See* 1276.

1602 CLARK, James F. 1825–1861. Prices, daily work, weather, etc. and journals of trips into other sections of the state. NcHiC.

1603 DAVIS, Joseph. 1825. Survey from Fort Osage to Santa Fe. MoSHs.

1604 GILDANT, Horace Nelson. 1825. Trip through England and Ireland. MoSU.

1605 MAURY, Matthew Fontaine. [between 1825 and 1874]. CNS. DLC.

1606 McLAUGHLIN, John. 1825–1856. Relations with American trappers and settlers; land claim in Ore. CU-B.

1607 OGDEN, Peter Skene. 1825–1827. Journal while he was on the Snake Expedition. OrTilPa.

1608 OTIS, Harriet. 1825. Trip to Niagara. MH.

1609 RUSSELL, William Henry. 1825. Narrative of a trip by steamboat and stage from Chesapeake Bay area? to N.Y. city through Baltimore, Philadelphia, N.J.; stays in Philadelphia and N.Y. NjR.

1610 SNOWDEN, James R. 1825; 1864–1865. Information on the Civil War, civic, and legal matters. PHi.

1611 STOKES, Thomas. 1825–1831. Events among family and friends; Friends' Meetings. NjR.

1612 STORRS, H. R. 1825–1830. Personal. NBu-Hi.

1613 TODD, John Payne. 1825–1830. Private diary of son of Dolly Madison. PPPrHi. *See* 2207?

1614 WILLSON, George. 1825. A voyage from Buenos Aires to Philadelphia on board the brig *Hippomenes*. NHi.

1615 WOLFE, James. 1825–1828. Journal of a voyage of discovery in the Pacific and Bering Strait on board H.M.S. *Blossom*. CtY.

1616 ANON. 1826. CNS. NbOP.

1617 GORDON, John Milton. 1826–1827. His work for S. S. Union among children of Philadelphia; an account of his failing health and spiritual struggle. PPPrHi.

1618 HEDGES, Reuben F. 1826–1827. CNS. Wv-Ar.

1619 HENSHAW, Mary Catherine. 1826–1827. A tour from Middlebury, Vt., via the Great Lakes to Green Bay. CSmH.

1620 HOBART, Samuel B. 1826–1827. Voyages of brig *Massachusetts* between Boston and New Orleans. MH.

1621 HORNER, Dr. G. R. B. [1826–1892]. Journals and diaries from his graduation to his death, of value to medical, naval, topographical, meteorological, and archaeological students; include distant voyages on naval vessels and U.S. Navy service in the Civil War. ViU.

1622 LANDIS, Rev. Robert Wharton. 1826–1882. Daily activities including outlines of sermons preached. PPPrHi.

1623 PITCHER, Zina. 1826. An expedition along the west end of Lake Superior accompanied by Brush, Parke, Schoolcraft, McKenny, and King, searching for copper, studying Indian customs and geography. MiD.

1624 RODGERS, Harrison G. 1826–1827. Journey to the Pacific Coast. MoSHs.

1625 THURBER, Albert K. 1826–1875. Concerning early life in R. I.; his journey to Utah and conversion; mining; his return to Utah at Spanish Fork; his pioneering in central Utah. CU-B.

1626 VAIL, Alfred. 1826–1829; 1850–1858. CNS. NjHi.

1627 BAIRD, Henry I. 1827–1841. CNS. PHi.

1628 BARTON, Charles Crillon. 1827–1831. Logs and journals written during his cruise on U.S.S. *Hornet* to the West Indies, and off the coast of Brazil, on the U.S.S. *Vandalia* and U.S.S. *Hudson*. PHi.

1629 BILL, John. 1827–1828. Tour through Canada and central and southern United States. NHi.

1630 BROUSE, Rev. John Andrew. 1827–1858. His work as a Methodist pastor and circuit rider in Ind. MnHi.

1631 CONNER, Juliana Margaret. 1827. Journey from her home at Charleston, S.C., to her husband's home in Mecklenburg Cnty., N.C., via Columbia and Charlotte; other travels; social notes. NcU; NcHiC.

1632 DALLAM, Francis J. 1827. Trip to Saratoga Springs. MdHi.

1633 DAVIS, Alexander Jackson. 1827–1853. Work and social life in N.Y.; books and pictures, buildings he designed, etc. NN.

1634 GALLOP, Alexander. 1827–1829. On board the U.S. frigate *Brandywine* and on the schooner *Dolphin*. NHi; DLC.

1635 GRANGER, John A. 1827. A tour from Detroit to Saut de Saint Marie [sic], Lake Superior, Mackinac, and Green Bay. MiU.

1636 HOLLAND, Frederick West. 1827–1828. Personal life at Harvard. MH.

1637 HUDSON'S BAY CO. 1827–1830. Probably kept by James McMillan from time he left Ft. Vancouver, 1827 to 1828; then kept by Archibald McDonald; describes founding of fort and daily affairs. CU-B. *See* 1822.

1638 JONES, J. M. 1827. Tour from Savannah, Ga., through Pa., N.Y., Upper Canada, New England, and back to Savannah. MiD.

1639 KEENEY, Salmon. 1827. Journey to Michigan in search of land to bring family to. Monroe Cnty. MiHi, copy.

1640 MASON, Samuel. 1827–1835. His farming and domestic interests. PHi.

1641 MAURY, Ann. 1827–1832. Trips on Atlantic packet boats and through N.Y., Pa., and the Southern states. ViU.

1642 MOORE, Nathaniel S. 1827–1837. Life as student at Clinton Academy, L.I., and at Yale; trip to Ireland. NN.

1643 PARKER, James. 1827–1828. Cruise in the Mediterranean on board the U.S. sloop of war *The Warren*. NjR.

1644 PLUMMER, John Thomas. 1827. A trip from Richmond to Yale Medical School; includes some medical notes. InRE.

1645 POULTNEY, William C. 1827. Trip to Europe on the *Montyuma*. PHi. *See* 1238.

1646 SARGENT, John Osborne. 1827. CNS. MH.

1647 SHEPARD, Burritt. 1827–1830. Journal kept by a midshipman on board the U.S.S. *Lexington*, cruising in the Mediterranean. NjR.

1648 SMITH, Hamilton. 1827–1829. Diary by a college student. InU-Li.

1649 STEVENS, Jedediah Dwight. 1827–1830. A record of the activities of a Presbyterian missionary in Wis. NdHi. *See* 1688.

1650 THOMAS, John Peyre. 1827–1856. Weather and occurrences. ScU.

1651 VAIL, William Penn. 1827. A trip from N.Y. city to Genito (Powhatan), Va., and return. NjR.

1652 WARD, John D. 1827–1830. A trip to England and the Continent, for information relative to his iron works at Vergennes, Vt. NNC.

1653 WELLES, Gideon. 1827–1855; 1861–1869. CNS. DLC.

1654 ANON. 1828. Visit to some of the meetings of the Society of Friends. PSC-Hi.

1655 ANON. 1828–1832. Plantation account book and diary; record of cotton production of each slave and other valuable data on plantation life and practices. Ms-Ar.

1656 ANON. 1828–1829. Kept in N.J. by Catholic priest (in Italian). NjEliHi.

1657 ANON. 1828. Journey from Tisheville, R.I., to Beechwood, Pa.; N.Y. city sights. NN.

1658 ATKINSON, Henry. 1828. Kept on a Yellowstone expedition. MoSHs. *See* 1599?

1659 CRAFT, C. 1828. CNS. MBAt.

1660 EDWARDS, Weldon N. 1828–1835. Chiefly farming and treatment of diseases among livestock. Nc-Ar.

1661 ERMATINGER, Francis. 1828. An expedition against the Clallam Indians of Southern Puget Sound. CU-B.

1662 HERNDON, William L. 1828–1850. CNS. NHi.

1663 HONE, Philip. 1828–1851. N.Y. city events. NHi.

1664 KNOX, Aletta V. 1828–1831. Student life at Van Doren's Collegiate Institute, Brooklyn Heights, N.Y., and vacation visits at her home farm, Raritan, N.J. NjR.

1665 LOVEJOY, Julia Louisa. 1828–1864. CNS. KHi.

1666 McNEMAR, Richard. 1828–1830. CNS. DLC.

1667 MUNSELL, Joel. 1828–1830; 1832–1834. CNS. NHi.

1668 PHELPS, William Dane. 1828–1832. Logbooks, journals, account books, etc., personal journals including trips. MH.

1669 ROOT, Mrs. Rebecca (Fish). 1828–1851. Written in various places 1828–1833; after 1833, in Rochester, N.Y. MiD.

1670 SELDEN, George L. 1828–1830. Journal on board the U.S.S. *Fairfield*, Foxhall A. Parker, cmdr. DLC.

1671 SELLERS, Ann. 1828; 1830. CNS. PPAmS.

1672 VAN BRUNT, Cornelius. 1828–1830. Kept on farm near Brooklyn, N.Y.; family, religious, and farm matters. NN.

1673 WILLARD family. 1828. A journal of the Newington School. PHi.

1674 ANON. 1829–1873. Diaries and albums of young women at select schools, and of their families; these journals throw light on the social history of the last century. NIC.

1675 ANON. 1829. Kept at the Sunday School of the Moravian Church. NcWsM.

1676 ARMIJO, Antonio. 1829–1830. A trading and exploratory journey from New Mexico to Cal., and back. CU-B.

1677 BAKER, Rev. Asmon Cleander. 1829–1833. CNS. NhHi.

1678 BANCROFT, Dr. Amos. 1829. A trip from Groton, Mass., to Ohio. OHi.

1679 BARTLETT, Charles. 1829–1890. Farm life in Lake Cnty., Ill. ICHi.

1680 BOORAEM, Henry. 1829. Mediterranean and Caribbean naval cruises. NjR.

1681 BROWNELL, Rt. Rev. 1829–1834. His missionary tours as Episcopal bishop. CtDio.

1682 GALLUP, Simeon M. 1829–1833; 1835; 1839. Kept by a schoolboy and young man starting in business. NHi.

1683 HARRISON, Jesse Burton. 1829–1830. Travels in Germany and Italy during a period of study at Göttingen; visits to Weimar, Jena, Leipzig, Dresden, Munich, Venice, Ferrara, etc.; and interview with Goethe. ViU.

1684 NEWELL, Robert. 1829–1842. A "memorandum" of his travels as associate of Sublette, Jackson, and Jedediah Smith in the fur trade; western explorations. OrU.

1685 PENINGTON, Henry. 1829. Legal. PHi.

1686 PERCIVAL, James Gates. 1829–[1839?]. CNS. MH.

1687 SHARKEY, John. 1829. Travel down the Ohio River from Pt. Pleasant, Va. to Trinity at the mouth of the Ohio; travel on the *Herald* to Louisville. KyLoF.

1688 STEVENS, Jedediah D. 1829–1830; 1837–1876. A tour to determine for the Presbyterian Board of Missions the feasibility of establishing missions near Ft. Snelling or in the valley of the St. Croix River. MnHi. *See* 1649.

1689 VOGLER, John, and Vaneman Zevely. 1829. Travel from Salem, N.C., to the Cherokee mission in Ga. NcWsM.

1690 WILLIAMS, Annabelle. 1829. Journal of a trip from Philadelphia to Cleveland. PHi.

1691 WRIGHT, William. 1829–1898; 1836–1918. With the papers of William Wright are John Wright's (his brother) diaries about service in the Civil War; campaign in Mo., Tenn., and Miss.; in many skirmishes against Nathan B. Forrest. CU-B.

1692 ANON. 1830. Journey southward with John Foulke; met with the governor of Del. and the President of U.S. PSC-Hi.

1693 BELL, Sir William. 1830–1833. Notes on Barbados, slavery, Gibraltar. MiU-C.

1694 BROWN, Ebenezer Lakin. 1830. Trip to Mich. from Vt. via Erie Canal and Great Lakes; scenery, coast, conditions of travel. MiU.

1695 CHAVALIER (Chevalier), Rev. Nicholas. 1830–1865. Activities and interests of student in Princeton Theological Seminary and minister of Presbyterian Church at Christiansburg, Va., and principal of Female Seminary, Holly Springs, Mass. PPPrHi.

1696 COLES, Tucker. 1830–1856. Farm diary. ViU.

1697 COOK, Charles. 1830. A journey from Boston to Washington. DLC.

1698 DARRACH, Dr. William. 1830–1838; 1832–1837. Notes on pharmacology and his professional activities; his interest in Presbyterian church affairs, prayer meetings, religious revival, and doctrinal controversies. PHi.

1699 DICKINS, Francis A. 1830–1833. Various trips in connection with Revolutionary War claims. NcU. *See* 3440.

1700 EDDY, Lucy H. 1830; 1835; 1851. Household and social activities; trips; religious affairs of the Society of Friends in N.Y. and N.J. NjR.

1701 EGGLESTON, Dick Hardaway. 1830. Diary of Learmont Plantation near Woodville, Miss. LU.

1702 GUERRERO, Vicente. 1830. Plans for a compilation of a history of the Indies. MiU-C.

1703 HACKLEY, William R. 1830–1863. CNS. FU.

1704 HAMILTON, Thomas. 1830–1831. Trip from Liverpool to N.Y.; through Atlantic states, down the Ohio and Mississippi rivers to New Orleans, through Southern states; comments on slavery and general conditions. NN.

1705 HILL, Col. John. 1830. Plantation diary; crops, weather, etc. NcU.

1706 HOWELL, Charles. 1830–1832. Whaling voyage. DeU.

1707 JACKSON, Henry and Martha. 1830–1831; 1833–1834. CNS. NcU.

1708 KENRICK, Francis Patrick. 1830–1863. CNS. PV.

1709 LYONS, Edward. 1830–1856. CNS. PHi.

1710 RAVENEL, Dr. Henry. 1830–1832. Diary and crop book; list of Negroes born 1809–1829. GHi.

1711 TAYLOR, Judge Lester. 1830. Travel journal with descriptions of land and towns. OHi, typescript.

1712 ANON. 1831. By a young American sightseer in France, Belgium, and London. NN.

1713 AFFLECK, Thomas. 1831–1832. His education and early interest in agriculture and agricultural improvements; in 1832 he came to the U.S. from Scotland. LU.

1714 ALLEN, Eliza Harriet (Arnold). 1831; 1837; 1841. A trip from Providence to Savannah, Ga.; sojourn on brother's plantation and plantation life; daily life in Providence. RHi. *See* 1539, etc.

1715 AMBLER, John J. 1831. CNS. ViU. *See* 1560.

1716 BLAIR, John George. 1831. A trip to N.Y. and Philadelphia. CSmH.

1717 CHURCHILL, Edwin. 1831–1835. Sea voyages, Portland, Me., and the West Indies. MiD.

1718 DAVIS, Prof. Calvin Olin. 1831. Trip abroad; descriptions of Spain, Pompeii, Italy, Greece, Turkey, and Egypt; observations on people, customs, housing, etc. MiU.

1719 DUBOIS, John L. 1831–1834. Kept on cruise around the world aboard the U.S. frigate *Potomac*. MdHi.

1720 GRIFFITH, Richard. 1831–1834. CNS. PHi.

1721 HABERSHAM, Robert. 1831–1832. Discusses books, literature, and poetry; social life in Savannah. GHi.

1722 HUBARD, Susan W. 1831. CNS. NcU.

1723 MARTIN, Rev. Arma R. 1831. CNS. NHi.

1724 MAY, William. 1831–1833. Kept while he was on cruise around the world in U.S. frigate *Potomac*. MdHi.

1725 McLAUGHLIN, J. T. 1831–1832. U.S. navy man recovering from duelling wounds at Port Mahon. NN.

1726 MOORE, Marion Louise. 1831. CNS. OClWHi.

1727 PARKER, James Lawrence. 1831–1833. Kept while he was a midshipman on a Pacific cruise of the U.S. frigate *Potomac*. NHi.

1728 PETTENGILL, Daniel M. 1831–1833. Complete account of work done by blacksmith and difficulties in obtaining pay; also trip to Enfield, N.H., with statements of expenses. NCooHi.

1729 POLK, William. 1831–1871. CNS. NcU.

1730 PORTER, Jeremiah. 1831–1848. Arrival in Mackinac from East; life in the wilderness, Indians, food; bitter anti-Catholicism. ICHi.

1731 PRICE, John. 1831–1847. Farm economy, sowing, harvesting, prices, and building. PHi.

1732 SCHWEINITZ, Rev. Lewis David de, and Früauf, Eugene Alexander. 1831. Journey from Bethlehem, Pa., to Goshen (Hope), Ind., and Gnadenhutten and Sharon, Ohio. NcWsM. *See* 1169, 1353.

1733 SHANE, Dr. C. G. 1831–1832. Trip on schooner *Crawford* taking 21 emigrants to Liberia from Ky. PPPrHi.

1734 SILL, Joseph. 1831–1854. Books, plays, art, lectures, travel; religion; political leaders and issues; U.S. bank affairs; railroad and canal. PHi.

1735 STEWART, Alvan. 1831. Trip to England. NHi.

1736 STRANG, James Jesse. 1831–1836. CNS. MiD.

1737 TAYLOR, Daniel Carrington. 1831–1832. His tours through Europe. NHi.

1738 TODD, William. 1831–1858. Family history; community life, neighbors; agriculture; climate, etc. KyHi.

1739 WILDER, Oshea. 1831. Journey from Buffalo, N.Y., via boat to Detroit and nearby areas; freight rates, countryside, towns. MiU.

1740 WILSON, Sophia S. 1831. Journey from Charleston, S.C., to Sulphur Springs in Va., with description of the various springs. DLC.

1741 ANON. 1832. Journal of a trip from Flemington, N.J., to Boston, via N.Y., Albany, Saratoga, Bennington, etc. NjR, original and typescript.

1742 ANON. 1832–1833. Incomplete; arriving from Boston in New Bedford, writer relates experiences on whaler *John Howland*. MH.

1743 ANON. 1832–1834. Private and business matters. PPPrHi.

1744 BAYLIES, Hon. Francis. 1832. His life while he was chargé d'affaires in Buenos Aires. MTaHi.

1745 BERLANDIER, Jean Louis. 1832–1835. Astronomical observations in Tex. and Mexico by member of commission to survey northern boundary of Mexico. MiU-C.

1746 BIRCHARD, Sardis. 1832–1833; 1842–1843; 1852. Travel diaries of trips through Southern states, to Barbados and Caribbean Islands; and business trips from Fremont, Ohio, to N.Y. OFH.

1747 BOUTWELL, William T. 1832–1837. Schoolcraft's expedition to source of Mississippi River and Boutwell's term as missionary at Leech Lake Indian Mission of the Chippewas. MnHi, copy.

1748 BRADFORD, Charles Frederic. 1832–1839. Latitudes and longitudes during a series of voyages on brig *John Gelpen*, from Baltimore to China and between China and west coast of South America. MH.

1749 BRADFORD, Phebe George. 1832–1839. Teas, church attendance, social calls; weather, gardening; comments on local events and people; books she has read. DeHi.

1750 BRADLEY, Cyrus Parker. 1832–1837. Literary interests. NHi.

1751 BYRNES, Daniel. 1832–1840; 1846–1850. Weather, eclipses; deaths of friends; Quakers and Hicksites; meteoric phenomena; Mexican War; steam locomotive (partly in shorthand). DeHi.

1752 CAPLEY, Alexander. 1832. Trip from Dayton to St. Joseph River region in Mich. MiU.

1753 CARR, Lt. George Kirwan. 1832. Tour in Quebec; Niagara to N.Y. and Atlantic states and New England; discusses manners. NN.

1754 CHOWELL, Ralph. 1832–1833. Observations in line of duty by member of frontier commission of Mexico. MiU-C.

1755 COFFIN, Miss E. 1832–1833. CNS. MeHi.

1756 DICKEY, Rev. John Miller. 1832–1856. Meetings, visits, etc. and other journals, n.d. PLuL.

1757 GRAY, Milly R. (Mrs. William Fairfax Gray). 1832–1840. Family life in Fredericksburg; the journey of the Gray family by boat to Tex. and

their life in Houston, where they were intimates of officials in the government of the Texas Republic. TxGR.

1758 GREGORY, Rev. John. 1832–1872. Lists of towns in which he served as pastor; marriages performed and funerals attended. FSpHi.

1759 GRIMBALL, John Berkeley. 1832–1884. Plantation records; family and social and political affairs in Charleston, S.C.; life during the Civil War and Reconstruction. ScCC, typescript.

1760 HAROLD, John. 1832–1833. Trip from England to N.Y., and life in the city. NHi.

1761 HIXSON, Richard W. 1832–1836. Voyage to Pacific Ocean in the ship *Maria* of Nantucket, and visit to Pacific Islands. MH.

1762 HOUGHTON, Douglass. 1832. CNS. MnHi, typescript.

1763 HUNT, Randall. 1832. Travel diary, Charleston, S.C., to New Haven, Conn.; ideas and reflections on love, literature, religion as much as scenes, events, and people. ScHi.

1764 HYDE, Orson. 1832. A tour with Samuel H. Smith through Ohio, N.Y., and New England. CU-B.

1765 JOHNSTON, Albert Sidney. 1832. Troop and Indian activities in the Black Hawk War. LU, typescript.

1766 MASON, Rachel. 1832–1834. Daily happenings; thoughts and reflections; copies of letters written by her to her family. PHC.

1767 MONROE, Rev. Thomas H.W. 1832. Journal kept during cholera plague. MdHi.

1768 MYERS, Frederick. 1832–1834. Garrison life at Ft. Dearborn, Ft. Brady; comments on the country; cholera; record of vessels sailing for Lake Michigan ports; recollections of Battle of Lake Erie. ICHi.

1769 OSBORN, Charles. 1832–1840; 1808–1850. Journal kept in England and Europe during his visits to all the Quarterly Meetings of the Society of Friends; diary of similar travels in the U.S. OHi.

1770 PERRY, Benjamin F. 1832–1863. Personal, social, and political activities as governor of S.C. NcU.

1771 SAWYER, Asaph. 1832. Letter-diary to wife in Me.; Panama, Mexico, Cal.; natives, gold-seekers, and disappointments. NN.

1772 SOMES, Benjamin. 1832–1833; 1835. Voyages on board *Malay* and *Neponset*; other voyages. MH.

1773 STOCKTON, Francis B. 1832–1834. Trip to South America and the Orient; many statistics. ICHi.

1774 SWAIN, David L. 1832–1840. Weather conditions; books he has read; deaths in the community; experiences as a circuit rider; observations on farming; work on the Dismal Swamp Canal. NcAr.

1775 WRIGHT, Henry Clarke. 1832; 1835; 1845; 1847; 1848. CNS. MH. *See* 3855.

1776 ANON. 1833–1870. Occurrences at Ft. Nisqually and dependencies in Washington Territory. CSmH.

1777 ANON. 1833–1859. Occurrences at Nisqually House, Washington Territory. WaU, original; DLC, photostat.

1778 ANON. 1833–1842. Diary of sermons preached, texts, etc. DLC.

1779 ANON. 1833–1834. Kept by student in Massachusetts. NN.

1780 ANON. 1833. Journal of a young Irishman who made a sightseeing tour, which took him from Boston to Philadelphia, Baltimore, Norfolk, Richmond, Washington, New York, up the Hudson to Buffalo, into Canada, returning via New England to N.Y., and back to London. CSmH.

1781 ANON. 1833. About Sussex Cnty., Del. De-Hi.

1782 BARROW, Bennet H. 1833–1846. Plantation affairs, parties, activities and health of slaves; weather and crop conditions; a hunter and sportsman who makes many references to hunting dogs and race horses. LU-Ar, typescript.

1783 BICKNELL, George Augustus. 1833–1836. Law student's diary; daily life; reading law in N.Y. law office. InHi. *See* 1882, 4070?

1784 BULLARD, J. S. 1833–1834. Journal on board ship *Henry Clay*, and on brig *Oriental*. MBAt.

1785 BULLOCK, James. 1833–1869. Farm accounts and comments on crops, weather, deaths, and marriages. NcU.

1786 BYERS, Joseph Perkins. [between 1833–1849]. By supervisor of penal institutions in Ohio, Ind., Pa., N.Y., and N.J. OHi.

1787 CALKIN, Milo. 1833–1842. A whaling voyage. CSmH.

1788 COREY, Mrs. A. E. 1833–1835. CNS. NjHi.

1789 DAVIDSON, Margaret Miller. 1833. Trip from Canada to Plattsburg, N.Y., and Saratoga Springs and New York. NjR.

1790 ELY, Rev. Edmund F. 1833–1854 (with gaps). Diaries of a missionary of the American Board of Commissioners for Foreign Missions to the Chippewa Indians in Minn. and on the southern shore of Lake Superior; topography, fur trade, Indian life, and missions of the region. MnDuHi, original; MnHi, typescript.

1791 EVANS, ———. 1833. Journal of a trip from Philadelphia to Boston, via N.Y. and Providence by steamboat, stage coach, and railroad. MiU-C.

1792 GODDARD, Abner S. 1833. A trip from Pa. to Ill. MnHi.

1793 HOFFMAN, David. 1833–1834. Travel in England with family; English social life and manners; tours through France, Switzerland, Western Germany, and Belgium. NN.

1794 KELLOGG, Miner Kilbourne. 1833–1837. Trip to Ky.; through Ohio, to Philadelphia and New York; art details; personal events of his travels; description of country; Shakers; various places in Ohio; weather. OCUHi.

1795 KIDDER, Daniel Parish. 1833–1882. Diary of a Methodist minister and educator in N.Y. and N.J.; member of the Methodist mission to Brazil; extensive travel. NjR.

1796 LEWIS, W. D. 1833–1846. Weather; social life; freighting business and shipping; banking, national and local, Girard Bank of Philadelphia; accounts of building new house, interest, loans, mortgages. DeHi.

1797 McCUE, John Marshall. 1833–1835; 1837–1838. Experiences of a college boy at Washington College in Va. and immediately after college. KyU.

1798 MILLER, Hiram. 1833. Trip to Schenectady via Albany and return; canal boats and towns. NN.

1799 RULON, Moses, Jr. 1833. Difficulties of travel over stony, muddy roads. PSC-Hi, photostat.

1800 SCRIPPS, William Arminger. 1833. Trip to visit relatives in the U.S.; begins at Buffalo, from there to Detroit with Black Hawk as a fellow passenger; describes the journey across Mich. and Ill. to Rushville and conditions in Ill. then. IHS, transcript.

1801 SHELDON, Henry L. 1833–1907. CNS. Vt-MiS.

1802 SMITH, Arvilla Almira. 1833–1845. Personal diary; religion; her family; trip to Mich. MiU.

1803 SMITH, Orrin F. 1833. Description of trip from Pa. to Ill. MnHi.

1804 STEVENS, Mrs. Henry H. (Catherine Clarkson). 1833; 1835. Short descriptions of two pleasure trips from N.Y. city, one through N.Y. state and the other to Va. NHi, original; NjR, typescript.

1805 TOLMIE, William F. 1833. Details of his life as head of Ft. Nisqually with additional extracts from June, 1834. CU-B.

1806 VASSAR, Matthew, Jr. 1833–1881. CNS. NP.

1807 WALKER, Mary (Richardson). 1833–1837. Life in Me. CSmH.

1808 WILLIAMS, John. 1833. Personal diary, with copies of letters and personal accounts. NcU.

1809 WILLIAMS, John, and William A. 1833–1852. Account books; short diary entries; letter books. NcU.

1810 ABBOTT, Caroline (Belcher). 1834–1853. CNS. NNC.

1811 BRINKLE, Rev. S. C. 1834–1844. CNS. PHi.

1812 BURROUGHS, William. 1834–1836. Presbyterian minister's work; chiefly river trip to and from New Orleans. NjR.

1813 CARY, Wilson Miles. 1834–1857 (with gaps). CNS. VHi. *See* 3163, 3427, 4735.

1814 CRANZ, Dr. Johann D. F. 1834–1848. CNS (in German). OHi.

1815 FISHER, Sydney George. 1834–1870. Philadelphia social life and the political problems of the times, with unusually intimate sidelights of the lives of Philadelphia's prominent citizens, and life at his Md. farm. PHi.

1816 HAND, Richard Charles. 1834. Trip through N.Y. state to Philadelphia by secretary for the American Board of Commissioners for Foreign Missions. NHi.

1817 HARDEN, Edward. 1834–1849 (with gaps). Plantations, crops, livestock, and the overseer; law practice; dealings with the Cherokee Indians, visits of the Indians and his arguing the Indian Injunction case; weather conditions; billiard playing; his children. NcD.

1818 HARRISON, Carter Henry. 1834–1835. Weather observations; crop records; Episcopal Church activities; and local political and social events. ViU.

1819 HAYES, Rutherford B. 1834; 1838–1885; 1886–1893. Personal; family friends; education; religion; politics. OFH, original; OHi, copy.

1820 HIGGINSON, Waldo. 1834–1858. CNS. MH.

1821 HOLLAND, Park. n.d. [1834?] His exploring trips in the Me. woods; written from his notes. MeBaHi. *See* 870.

1822 HUDSON'S BAY CO. 1834–1837. Journal of the company describing the founding of the fort on McLoughlin Bay and other matters. CU-B. *See* 1637.

1823 KIRKPATRICK, Jane (Bayard). 1834. Diary; also letter received from S[amuel] B[ayard], Princeton, Nov. 20, 1829. NjR.

1824 LAPHAM, Increase Allen. 1834–1875. CNS. OHi.

1825 LARPENTEUR, Charles. 1834–1837; 1864–1872. CNS. MnHi, microfilm.

1826 MEEK, Alexander Beaufort. 1834; 1836. Descriptions of feminine charms; short autobiographical sketch; many descriptions of church services; references to members of the Ala. legislature; comments on his study. NcD.

1827 MORELAND, William F. 1834–1850; 1861–1867. Journey from Macon Cnty. by way of New Orleans to Tex.; plantation diary. LU, microfilm.

1828 PAULI, Rev. Charles Augustus. 1834–1850. CNS. PRHi.

1829 PIERREPONT, Henry Evelyn. 1834–1848; 1850–1851. His work as executor of Hezekiah Pierrepont's estate, including annual visits to lands in upper N.Y. NN.

1830 PLUMMER, Hiram. 1834–1835. CNS. MHa, typescript.

1831 POPE, William. 1834–1843. Ornithologist's description of Canadian life; includes a journey to Philadelphia, Baltimore, and Washington. CaOTP.

1832 RANNEY, Darwin Harlow. 1834–1836. Religious reflections of a student at Middlebury, Vt., and Baptist minister at Westport, N.Y. 1835–1836; lists sermons preached. NCooHi.

1833 RHODES, Willis, and Company. 1834–1836. CNS. PHi.

1834 RODNEY, Thomas M. 1834. Occurrences on sea trip to Mexico. DeHi.

1835 SCOTT, Robert W. 1834–1859. Farm day book with accounts and diary entries. KyLoF.

1836 SHEPARD, Cyrus. 1834–1835. His trip across the plains with the Wyeth Expedition and his life and labors among the Indians of Oregon Terr. CtY.

1837 SLEIGHT, Morris. 1834–1835. Trip through Mid-West; descriptions of Chicago and other Ill. towns; various modes of travel. ICHi.

1838 TAPLEY, Warren. 1834. Sunday travel. MH.

1839 TEN EYK, Margaret. 1834–1844. Brief entries concerned with visits, finances, sewing and quilting work. NjR.

1840 WADE, Dr. Walter. 1834–1854. Practice of medicine and management of plantation; accounts of the plantation and patients; "Rates of charges for Professional Services." Ms-Ar, typescript.

1841 WAKEMAN, Burr. 1834–1843. Daybook and journal. NHi.

1842 WHEELER, Dr. Samuel Jordan. 1834–1879. Diary and medical daybook. Nc-Ar. *See* 3987.

1843 WILLIAMS, Eleazer. 1834–1836; 1866–1874. By "the lost Dauphin," who was connected with the migration of the N. Y. Indians to Wis. (in the Oneida language). WHi.

1844 ANON. 1835–1837. Personal reactions to plantation life and expression of personal discontent with the South; amusements; visits to neighbors. LU-Ar.

1845 AITON, John Felix. 1835. Passage to Canada from Scotland. MnHi.

1846 ANDREWS, Mrs. Abby (Fisher). 1835–? Relating chiefly to Mrs. Andrews' Sunday school class at the Hollis St. Church, Boston; later entries, particularly poems. MH.

1847 BRONSON, Arthur. 1835. Winter in Fla.; illness. NN.

1848 CATHRALL, Charles E. 1835. Account of a visit to Florence, Italy. PHi.

1849 CHAMBERLAIN, Thomas. 1835–1860. Journey from Portsmouth, England, to New York; journey to Quebec and Philadelphia and return to England; life and work of printer; marriage and family in New York. NN.

1850 CHANDLER, William. 1835–1836. Cruise from Norfolk, Va., to West Indies and Pensacola. NN.

1851 DOUGLAS, Sir James. 1835; 1853; 1858; 1860. Among miscellaneous letters and notes of his official duties, several diaries kept in these years have been extracted. CU-B.

1852 EARLE, Dr. Pliny. 1835–1891. CNS. MWA.

1853 ELY, Catherine Goulais. 1835–1838. Family life and environment and the mission school at Fond du Lac, Minn. MnDuHi, typescript.

1854 EVANS, David. 1835–1898. Daily happenings in his home; Quaker meetings and Chester Cnty. affairs; trip to Ohio; formation of Abolition society; Malvern, Pa., civic affairs. PHC.

1855 FORREST, Edwin. 1835. CNS. MH.

1856 GORDON, John M. 1835–1842; 1867–1869. Early years in Baltimore; trip to Mich. and residence in Va. MdHi.

1857 HARRIS, Caroline G. 1835–1844. Daily events. MHa.

1858 JAMES, Samuel. 1835–1852. Includes a day-by-day account of a journey across the plains. WaU.

1859 JOHNSON, William T. 1835–1851. Private lives of prominent persons; descriptions of events of a social nature, duels, theatrical performances, hunts, and horse races. LU.

1860 JOHNSTON, Robert. 1835–1839. His residence at Newport. PHi.

1861 JONES, John Davis. 1835–1875. Self and family; happenings on his trip west; family register; church news; weather accounts; obituaries. OCUHi.

1862 McCALL, Duncan G. 1835–1851; 1852–1854. Plantation journal and diary of a Mississippi cotton planter; accounts, records, lists of supplies; personal items. NcD.

1863 McDOWELL, Benjamin. 1835–1841. The severe winter of 1835–1836 and farming operations. PSC-Hi.

1864 PARK, Thomas B. 1835–1841. A voyage in the *California* from Boston to Santa Barbara, via Cape Horn, and after; agent of Bryant, Sturgis Co. CSmH.

1865 PARKER, Samuel. 1835. Trip to Oregon. OrHi, copy. *See* 2235.

1866 PATTERSON, Gen. Robert. 1835. A trip from Philadelphia to Iowa, Wis., Ky., Tenn., and other states; historical landmarks visited; stopping places; means of travel; social events. PHi.

1867 POND, Gideon. [between 1835–1877.] CNS. MnMHi.

1868 SHERWOOD, Rev. Elisha Barber. 1835–1898. Private journal and family records. PPPrHi.

1869 SMITH, Rev. George N. 1835–1879. Diary of Indian missionary in Mich. DLC. *See* 2140.

1870 STRONG, George Templeton. 1835–1875. Life in N.Y. city; programs, clippings. NNC, original; NN, microfilm.

1871 TICKNOR, Anna (Eliot). 1835–1837. European travels. NhD.

1872 WALKER, James. 1835–1839. Diary of a student at Washington College, Lexington, Va. ViU.

1873 WHITE, David L. 1835–1842. CNS. FDS.

1874 WILSON, Margaret. 1835–1837. CNS. MsAr, copy.

1875 ANON. 1836–1858. Journals and diary notes of travel. PHi.

1876 ANON. 1836–1838. A journey from Providence, R.I., to Trenton, N.J., Philadelphia, Reading, Pottsville, and Pittsburgh, Pa., Cincinnati, Louisville, and Pittsburgh again. PWW, typescript.

1877 ANON. 1836. By a young physician. PHi.

1878 ANON. 1836. Journey by boat, train, and canal from N. Y. city to Pittsburgh, Cincinnati, Louisville, Dubuque; notes on Indian life, Gov. Dodge, and employment in Dubuque. NN.

1879 ATHERTON, Faxon D. 1836–1839. Trading trips and activities up and down the Cal. coast, including many visits to the early Cal. missions. CU-B.

1880 BACHE, Alexander Dallas. 1836–1838. Notes on educational institutions he visited and observations on foreign affairs. DLC.

1881 BARRON, Commodore James. 1836–1839. Journal of events, U.S. Navy Yard, Philadelphia. NcU.

1882 BICKNELL, George Augustus. 1836. A trip through the Middle West. InU-Li. *See* 1783, 4070.

1883 BINNEY, Horace. 1836–1837. A trip to Europe. PHi.

1884 BRIDGE, H. 1836. Trip by boat and stage from New Orleans to Columbia, Pa., via Louisville, Maysville, and Cincinnati; description of towns, social life, and customs. IHi.

1885 BROWN, Rev. Dr. Allen H. 1836–1907. Weather conditions; means of travel; places visited; people contacted and work accomplished each day. NjSpAHi.

1886 BUXTON, Hannah Prince. 1836–1845. Weather and personal affairs. MeHi.

1887 CHANDLER, Sarah. 1836. Her family's journey from Louisa Cnty., Va., to Cooper Cnty., Mo. MoU.

1888 CONANT, Augustus H. 1836–1853. Farmer's daybook, Des Plaines River, Cook Cnty., Ill. ICHi.

1889 CORSS, Ann Hoyt. 1836–1851. CNS. PLhA.

1890 CROES, John. 1836–(1839); 1845. Episcopal activities, trips, personal business of the rector of Christ Episcopal Church, New Brunswick. NjR.

1891 DAVIDSON, James D. 1836. Kept during travels in Ohio, Ind., Ky., and down the Ohio and Mississippi rivers to New Orleans, from La. through Ala. and Ga., up the coast by boat to Norfolk, and across to Lexington. ICMcCHi.

1892 DE SELLEM, Rev. John L. 1836–1837. A trip by a flatboatman from Pittsburgh to Memphis; contains a description of Cincinnati. OHi.

1893 DICKSON, William. 1836. A trip from Cherry Valley, N.Y., west through central N. Y. and northern Ohio to Defiance. NCooHi. *See* 1928?

1894 DUYCKINCK, Evert Augustus. 1836–1875 (with gaps). CNS. NN.

1895 EMERSON, Rev. Daniel H. 1836–1861. Lists of marriages, baptisms, and funerals. PHi.

1896 GINRITE, Isaac G. 1836–1838. CNS. FTaSCW.

1897 GRAY, William H. 1836–1837. Daily mission events; conversion of Indians; religious affairs. OrHi.

1898 HAMMOND, James Henry. 1836–1838; 1841–1850. His travels in America and abroad, and later diaries. DLC.

1899 HENTZ, Mrs. Caroline Lee. 1836–1860. CNS. NcU.

1900 HOPPIN, William Jones. 1836; 1837. European tour. MH. *See* 4220, 4386.

1901 HURLBUT, Mrs. Mary Crawford (Hattrick). 1836–1847. Domestic matters and concerns of the Congregational Church. MiD.

1902 KAPLE, Bela J. 1836–1844. Farming. NCooHi.

1903 MASON, Charles. 1836–1855. Political, economic, and social life of the first half of the 19th century. N, typescript; DLC, typescript.

1904 MAXWELL, Dr. James Darwin. 1836–1844. Trip to Philadelphia and attendance at Jefferson Medical College; accounts of expenditures, formulas for prescriptions, etc. InU.

1905 McHENRY, James Howard. 1836–1878. CNS. MdHi.

1906 MIDDLETON, Arthur. 1836–1837. Daily "Notes on the (Carlist) Spanish Revolution" kept by the American chargé d'affaires in Madrid. NcD.

1907 PATERSON, William. 1836. Along with several poems and an essay, accounts of his boredom, philosophical ideas, dislike of foreigners, and a few details of family and personal activity. NjR.

1908 PEIRCE, Henry A. 1836–1837. Voyages from Sandwich Islands to China; from China to N.Y. city; from Boston to Sandwich Islands. MH.

1909 PERRY, Rev. David I. 1836–1841. Record of pastor of Presbyterian Church of Bloomington, McLean Cnty., Ill.; also list of subscribers to his yearly salary. PPPrHi.

1910 POTTER, William Henry. 1836–1837. Study at Colchester, Conn. NN.

1911 PUTNAM, Henry. 1836–1839. Diary and account book of town clerk. NHi.

1912 RONALDS, Mary Lorillard. 1836–1837. Tour of Italy; sightseeing, art, archaeology, theater, opera. NN.

1913 SMITH, Hatfield. 1836–1841. Concerned with his interest in a gristmill at Raritan Landing; merchandising of grain and mill products; river and weather conditions; ship traffic on the canal. NjR.

1914 SPALDING, Mrs. Henry Harmon. 1836–1840. CNS. OrHi. 1836. Journey across the continent. WaWW.

1915 STEWART, Clark B. 1836–1885. Journal kept by soldier, planter, and minister. ScU.

1916 VOLK, James S. 1836–1879. About his youth in Germany; emigration to N.Y.; to Cal. via Panama; mining in Cal. and Ore.; events in San Francisco. NN.

1917 WHITMAN, Dr. and Mrs. Marcus. [1836?] Journey from the Rockies to Ft. Vancouver. CSaT.

1918 WOODCOCK, Thomas S. 1836. Trip from N. Y. city to Niagara Falls. NN.

1919 WRIGHT, W. W. 1836–1850. Trip from N.Y. to Wis.; incidents in the first 10 years of life in a Wis. frontier town. WOshM, typescript.

1920 ANON. 1837–1848. Reports of the Cherokee Indian Mission of the Moravian Church. NcWsM.

1921 ANON. 1837–1838. A cruise on board the U.S.S. *Ontario*. NHi.

1922 ANON. 1837. Trip from Richmond to Niagara Falls; contents include travel, Indians, religion, towns. NN.

1923 ALSTON, John. 1837–1847. Accounts of visiting Quaker ministers, religious reflections, etc. PSC-Hi.

1924 CAMPBELL, Gov. David. 1837–1857. Political (Gov. of Va.) but mostly personal. Copy at NcD.

1925 CANBY, William. 1837–1839. Student diary telling of affairs at Haverford College. PHC.

1926 CARMICHAEL, Mary Eliza Eve. 1837–1845. Personal. NcU.

1927 DELANO, Asa. 1837–1855. Farm activities and family events. NCooHi.

1928 DICKSON, William. 1837–1852. The weather and store and farm activities. NcU. *See* 1893?

1929 EDMISTON, Evan. 1837–1840. Kept at Granville College (now Denison Univ.), Granville, Licking Cnty., Ohio, and Columbus, Ohio. OHi.

1930 EDWARDS, Philip L. 1837–1839. His journey from Ore. to Cal. and return to purchase cattle for Ore. company. CU-B.

1931 EMORY, Gen. Thomas. 1837. Member of three-man commission sent by gov. of Md. to England and Holland to float public improvement securities; interested in railroads, canals, and agricultural methods. MdAA, microfilm.

1932 EVANS, Daniel. 1837–1844. CNS. MiD.

1933 EVANS, Josiah. 1837–1838. Daily happenings at his home on a farm in Chester Cnty.; affairs in Quaker meetings; formation of an abolition society; a journey to Ohio. PHC.

1934 GARRIOCH, Peter. 1837; 1843–1847. Visits to missions at Lac qui Parle and Lake Harriet; fur trading in Dakota Terr.; a trip from Mississippi to the Red River. CaMWHi, original; MnHi, photostat. *See* 2161.

1935 HIGGINSON, Thomas Wentworth. 1837–1864. CNS. MH.

1936 HORT, Mary. 1837–1861. Comments on religion and various ministers. ScU.

1937 HUNT, Horace. 1837–1838. CNS. NjHi.

1938 JOHNSON, George. 1837–1840. Journals and papers on the Erie Canal enlargement. N.

1939 [KOLLOCK, ———]? 1837–1861. Plantation accounts and diaries of Coffee Bluff Plantation, Rosedew Plantation, and Ossabaw Island Plantation. NcU.

1940 LENOIR, William Avery. 1837–1838; 1845–1852. Trips; surveying; farms; social life. NcD.

1941 [MATHEWS, Mme. Lucia Elizabeth (Bartolozzi) Vestris]. 1837. Private diary with references to many friends and to productions at Olympic theater. MH.

1942 MAXCY, Virgil. 1837. Voyage from N.Y. to Liverpool in the packet ship *Virginia*. DLC.

1943 MORAGNE, Mary Elizabeth. 1837–1842. Descendants of a French Huguenot family of Abbeville District; large portions published in *The Neglected Thread*. ScU.

1944 MOTE, Marcus. 1837. CNS. InRE.

1945 OSTRANDER, John D. 1837–1870. CNS. NKiSh.

1946 PARVIN, Theodore Sutton. 1837. Describes year he taught as superintendent of 4th district in Cincinnati and studied law at the same time. OCuHi.

1947 PETERS, Mary Lorrain. 1837–1839. Schoolgirl's diary kept in New Haven, N. Y., and Philadelphia. NHi.

1948 SMITH, Joshua Toulmin. 1837–1838. Journal in America. MiD.

1949 TERRELL, Adam Thompson. 1837–1839. St. Louis to Belleville; account of E. P. Lovejoy at St. Louis and his death; Alton riots. MH.

1950 WALKER, Mary (Richardson). 1837–1848. CNS. CSmH. *See* 1807, 1996.

1951 WEIR, Julia (Sweet). 1837–1839. Social events; visits to art galleries and artists' studios in Europe. RHi.

1952 WILSON, Israel. 1837–1838; 1844. Account of a trip to Ohio and of a trip to Saratoga Springs, N.Y. InU-Li.

1953 ANON. 1838–1842. The Wilkes South Sea expedition, kept on board the U.S.S. *Vincennes*. DLC.

1954 ANON. 1838. A trip from Natchez, Miss., to Tex. NcD.

1955 ANON. 1838. A cruise of the U.S. frigate *Constellation*. NHi.

1956 BENNETT, Thomas T. 1838–1845. Tours by musician with a traveling circus. MH.

1957 BRECKENRIDGE, William D. 1838–1841. Daily happenings on Wilkes Expedition to the South Pacific and later explorations in Ore. and Cal. MdHi. *See* 2046.

1958 BURNETT, Peter H. 1838; 1843; 1849. Describes Mormon war and Joseph Smith in Missouri, 1838; went to Ore., 1843; gold rush in Cal.; elected first gov. of Cal. CU-B.

1959 CARTER, J. B. 1838–1888. Trip from N. Y. in 1838 to Chicago on which he took a stock of goods to open a store; the trip necessitated 12 changes of transportation. MnDuHi, typescript; ICHi, typescript; MnHi, typescript; NjEliHi, typescript.

1960 CHAPMAN, James Marsh. 1838–1844. Family and social activity; N. Y. visits; law; religion; politics. NjR.

1961 CHENERY, Albion P. 1838–1911 or 1912. Traveling in and from Ind.; joined New England Trading and Mining Assoc. bound for Cal.; sailed from Boston to Cal.; voyage, mining, Indians in Cal.; record of important events, births. OrHi.

1962 DAVIS, Gherardi. 1838–1841; 1904; 1908. Education in Germany and at Columbia Univ.; study and practice of law and politics; trip to Germany and Italy; trip to France. NN.

1963 DOUGHERTY, Rev. Peter. 1838–1839. Journey from N. Y. city to Mackinac Island and Grand Traverse Bay, a return trip to N. Y. for supplies, and his trip back to the island. MiU. See 2054.

1964 DUER, Hannah Maria Denning (Mrs. William A.). 1838–1862. CNS. NNC.

1965 EELLS, Mrs. Myra Fairbanks. 1838. Kept "while passing through the U.S. and over the Rocky Mountains"; describes journey and mission, and comments on religious matters. OrHi.

1966 EMMONS, George Foster. 1838–1842. Kept while he was attached to the South Sea Surveying and Exploring Expedition under the command of Charles Wilkes, on the U.S. sloop of war *Peacock* and, after the wreck of the *Peacock*, on the *Vincennes*. CtY. See 4115?

1967 FEBIGER, John C. 1838–1843. Journal kept by a midshipman on frigate *Macedonian*, ship *Concord*, and brig *Chipola*. NHi.

1968 FERRIS, David. 1838–1849; 1866–1908 (with gaps). Weather; plantings, harvesting; family events; visit to Whittier's birthplace and Amesbury home; references to social reform concerns. PSC-Hi.

1969 GARNETT, Grace Fenton. 1838–1839 (with gaps). Daily schedule; travels; health. ViU.

1970 GIDDINGS, Joshua Reed. 1838–1839; 1849. The second session of the twenty-fifth Congress of the U.S.; CNS for later date. OHi.

1971 GROVE, Jacob. 1838. Daybook and journal. PHi.

1972 HARRINGTON, John. 1838–1857. Social life; politics; plans to move to Minn. from Ohio. MnHi.

1973 HILL, Jediah. 1838. Journey from Hamilton Cnty., Ohio, to N. J. OHi, typescript.

1974 HOCKER, Isaiah. 1838–1866. CNS. PHi.

1975 HOLMES, Dr. Silas. 1838–1842. A cruise in the U.S. ship *Peacock* and brigs *Porpoise* and *Oregon*, on the exploring expedition under Wilkes; events of the voyage, the countries visited, customs of the natives. CtY.

1976 JENKS, M. H. 1838. A tour to Ind. InHi.

1977 [KNOWLES, Sallie?]. 1838. The building of the Annapolis and Elk Ridge RR. PHi. See 2228.

1978 LUMPKIN, Wilson. 1838–1863. Athens, Ga. Partly a diary, partly reminiscences, with lists of births and deaths of family and of slaves; accounts of plantings. GU.

1979 LYTLE, Robert. 1838. A trip from Alexandria to various points in Ohio. OClWHi, typescript.

1980 McLEES, John. 1838–1864. Life as a student at the Columbia Theological Seminary and experiences as pastor of various Presbyterian churches. ScU.

1981 MELLUS, Francis. 1838–1847. Voyages to and along Cal. CSmH.

1982 MEYERS, William H. 1838–1839. Sea journey from Philadelphia to Cuba and Bahamas and return; social life; ship life; places. NN. See 2107.

1983 O'BRION, Thomas Wilson. 1838–1874. Detailed description of houses in Portland that O'Brion built; personal matters. MeHi, copy.

1984 PEALE, T. R. 1838–1839; 1841. Travels from Philadelphia to Brazil; thence to Tahiti; subsequent travels to Ore. and S. F. CU-B.

1985 PLEASONTON, Gen. August. 1838; 1841; 1844. Diary of the "Buckshot War"; military activities in Harrisburg; abolitionists and Negro riots in Philadelphia; the Me. boundary controversy; incidents in the Canadian insurrection; Nicholas Biddle and the Bank of the U. S.; presidential elections; destruction of the steamer *Erie*; personal and social interests. PHi.

1986 PRATT, William Moody. 1838–1891. Events of local and national interest; observations on his ministry; a record of his reading. KyU-Ar. See next item.

1987 PRATT, Rev. William M. 1838–1891. Events in church life of a Baptist minister. KyU, original; InHi, typescript.

1988 RHINELANDER, Philip. 1838–1839. Journey from N. Y. to Liverpool; touring in British Isles, France, Italy. NN.

1989 RIDDICK, Edward L. 1838–1864. CNS. NcAr.

1990 RÜDE, Herman. 1838. Trip to the Cherokee Indian Terr. (in German). NcWsM. See next item.

1991 SCHMIDT, Vogler, and Rüde. 1838. Travel diary from the Cherokee land to the Indian Terr. NcWsM.

1992 SHUTE, Robert C. 1838. A trip from Camden, Preble Cnty., Ohio, to Barnesville, Belmont Cnty., Ohio. OHi.

1993 SPALDING, Henry Harmon. 1838–1842; 1843. Personal. OrHi. See 3268.

1994 TAYLOR, William. 1838–1842. Daily activities and operations of a sugar and cotton plantation. LU. See 5003.

1995 UNDERWOOD, Joseph A. 1838–1840. Journal on the U.S.S. *Relief* and *Vincennes* during the exploring expedition under Wilkes. CtY.

1996 WALKER, Rev. Elkanah and Mrs. (Mary Richardson). 1838–1852. Letters and diaries. WaSp, typescript; WaU, typescript; WaPS, typescript. MSS. OrHi and CSmH. See 1807, 1950.

1997 WALKER, Samuel Swan. 1838–1839. Journey from Cincinnati, Ohio, to the Northeastern states. OHi.

1998 WALKER, Timothy. 1838?–1852. Law notes; personal affairs; current events; thoughts and ideas; special mention of death of Henry Clay, for whom he was pallbearer. OCuHi.

1999 WHITTLE, John. 1838–1841. Personal experiences on the Wilkes' expedition to the Pacific. ViU.

2000 WILLIAMS, Rev. John W. M. 1838–1839; 1842–1843; 1845–1855; 1867. Includes European trip. NcU.

2001 WOOD, Norman Knox. 1838. Sea journal; N. Y. to Liverpool via New Orleans, and then to Portland, Me. Illustrated. MH.

2002 ANON. 1839. An Oregon journey. WHi.

2003 ANON. 1839–1840. A cruise on the U.S. schooner *Grampus*. NHi.

2004 ANON. 1839–1840. Personal. NcU.

2005 BALLARD, Addison M. 1839–1853. Personal; weather; prices of food, clothing, livestock. KyHi. *See* 2045.

2006 BOSTWICK, Alanson. 1839; 1841. Journey from home to Chicago and return; also an account of journey from N. Y. to Springfield, Ill. IHS, typescript; MnHi, typescript.

2007 BRODHEAD, John Romeyn. 1839. Voyage from Liverpool to N. Y. NjR.

2008 CALDWELL, John Day. 1839–1842. Business; political, social, and philanthropic life of Cincinnati; personal data; description of trips including one to Mexico; notes on current situations. OCuHi.

2009 CARMICHAEL, Oswell K. 1839. A European trip. NcU.

2010 CATLIN, Julius. 1839–1888. CNS. CtHi.

2011 CONVERSE, Miss ———. 1839–1869. CNS. OClWHi.

2012 COOK, George Hammell. 1839; 1841–1846. Geological tours with students from Rensselaer Polytechnic Institute to Mass. and Lake Champlain. PSC-Hi. *See* 2093, 2155.

2013 CORBETT, Marion. 1839–1840. Trip to America, with descriptions of life in Washington and N. Y. city. NHi.

2014 COUPER, James Hamilton. 1839–1854. Plantation journal for Hopeton Plantation, Glynn Cnty., Ga. NcU.

2015 DAY, Mahlon. 1839–1840. A voyage to the West Indies. NHi.

2016 ELD, Henry. 1839. Kept during the Wilkes' expedition. CtNhHi. *See* 2094.

2017 FOOTE, R. Adm. Andrew Hull. 1839–1842. Incidents at Honolulu and the Sandwich Islands; his thoughts, feelings, and prayers. DLC. *See* 2503.

2018 FRANCHÈRE, Gabriel. 1839. His voyage of inspection to the fisheries of upper Lake Superior. MnHi.

2019 GANO, Stephen. 1839. His reading and his behavior; daily life. OCuHi. *See* 1367?

2020 GREY, Lt. Col. Charles. 1839. Travels in Quebec and in N.Y., Philadelphia, Washington, and Connecticut. CaOTP, typescript.

2021 HAMPTON, Oliver. 1839–1840. CNS. MiU.

2022 HUNTER, W. C. 1839. Occurrences at Canton during the cessation of trade. MBAt.

2023 INGALLS, Theodore. 1839–1848. CNS. MiD.

2024 JOHNSON, John P. 1839–1842. Religious. NhHi.

2025 KNOWLES, David E. 1839–184?. "Journey to the Cherokes" [*sic*]. PSC-Hi.

2026 LIDDELL, St. John R. 1839–1844; 1867–1868. Weather; work done on the plantation; health of the slaves; water stages of the Mississippi and Black rivers; visitors to the plantation. LU.

2027 LUSHER, Robert M. 1839–1840; 1856–1857; 1862–1864; 1872; 1875–1890. Personal and business activities of state superintendent of education and agent for the Peabody School Fund. LU.

2028 MOORE, Henry S. 1839–1857. Details about New Orleans, 1839–1840; three sea trips between that city and N.Y., 1839–1842; the furniture business, with some reflections on the Panic of 1857. NjR.

2029 PAGE, Anne F. 1839. Trip through France and Italy; describes cities visited, historical monuments, manners, and customs. PHi.

2030 SKEWES, Samuel. 1839–1870. Agricultural. WHi.

2031 SMITH, Sidney. 1839. A trip across the plains with the "Peoria Party" from Independence, Mo., to the Willamette Valley. OrFP.

2032 SPRAGNE, Lt. John T. 1839. Kept in Fla., with pencil drawings and maps. DLC.

2033 STEWARD, Thomas L. 1839–1903. Pocket diary relating to Lt. Steward's Civil War experiences; correspondence; war reminiscences. CLU.

2034 SUTTER, John A. 1839–1848. The Sutter diaries from 1839–1848. CU-B. *See* 2246.

2035 VAN SCHAICK, Augustus Platt. 1839. Geological tour with students of Rensselaer Polytechnic Institute into western Mass. and the edge of Vt.; contains notes on geological lectures at Rensselaer by Prof. Amos Eaton. NjR.

2036 VERMILYE, Mrs. Elizabeth Breese Rockwood. 1839–1850. Activities of husband, Rev. Thomas E. Vermilye. MH.

2037 WALLER, Alvin F. 1839; 1844; 1845. Personal notes; trip from Oregon City to the mouth of the Columbia, thence to Wascopam. OrHi.

2038 WHEELER, Emily L. 1839. A round trip between Stratford, Conn., and Saratoga Springs, N.Y., including stays at the Springs. NCooHi.

2039 WILLSON, Chloe Aurelia Clark. 1839. CNS. OrSaW.

2040 WILSON, Dr. James W. 1839. A trip from New Berlin, Pa., to Lower Sandusky (now Fremont), Ohio. OFH.

2041 WILSON, Milton. 1839–1879. Lumber accounts; poetry; family record. OHi.

2042 ANON. 1840. Journey from England to Prince Edward Island; ship life and Prince Edward Island scenes. NN.

2043 ANON. 1840–1841. Apparently kept by a Presbyterian minister, "M.L.F."; contains religious musings on his wife's death. NcD.

2044 ANON. 1840–1846. Chiefly religious reflections. MiU.

2045 BALLARD, Addison M. 1840. A trip from Henry Cnty., Ky., to Spotsylvania Cnty., Va.; total miles, with stops named; return trip; itemized expenses of both trips. KyHi. *See* 2005.

2046 BRECKENRIDGE, William Dunlop. 1840–1841. The Wilkes' Exploring Expedition to Cal. CSmH. *See* 1957.

2047 BRUCE, Mrs. James Coles. 1840. A trip to N. Y. ViU.

2048 BURGUM, Emma and John. 1840? CNS. NhHi.

2049 BURGWYN, Henry King. 1840–1848. CNS. Nc-Ar.

2050 CASE, William. 1840–1855. CNS. OClWHi.

2051 COLLINS, Richard Henry. 1840. Reflections of a youth in an academy and at Centre College, Danville, Ky., including essays and speeches which he made. KyU.

2052 COMFORT, Ellwood. 1840. Accounts and description of a trip from Mich. to the East. MiU. *See* 2377.

2053 CORYELL, Tunnison. 1840. CNS. RPB and PWmHi.

2054 DOUGHERTY, Rev. Peter. 1840–1842. A trip from N. Y. to Mackinac. MiU. *See* 1963.

2055 DUBOIS, ———. 1840–1843. Trip from N Y. to Mobile, New Orleans, Wheeling, Niagara, Buffalo, Rochester, etc.; expenses; scenes. NN.

2056 FAWCETT, Joseph. 1840. A trip from Wheeling, Va., down the Ohio and Mississippi to New Orleans, and from New Orleans by sail to Boston. ViU.

2057 FRANK, Michael. 1840–1890. CNS. WHi.

2058 FRIES, Francis Levin. 1840–1842. The progress in building and operating the Fries Woolen Mill, and records of farm work. Nc-Ar, typescript.

2059 GAY, Sydney Howard. 1840–1841. Personal. NNC.

2060 HARDENBERGH, Ann Maria. 1840–1841. Containing short compositions as a regular school exercise at Raritan Seminary. NjR.

2061 HENLEY, John Wesley. 1840–1900. CNS. OHi.

2062 HICKS, Benoni. 1840–1843. A trip through N.Y. state and Pa. NHi.

2063 HONE, Robert S. 1840–1842. CNS. NHi.

2064 HUDSON, Boyd R. 1840–1842. CNS. NCooHi.

2065 JONES, John T. 1840. Kept by a law student at Yale College. NcU.

2066 JONES, Wilfred Goldsborough. 1840–1867. Education at Columbia and Harvard; legal training; law practice in N.Y. city; social scene in N.Y.; travels to Cal. and Hawaii, etc.; public affairs. NN.

2067 LAWLER, Davis Bevan. 1840–1841. Trip to Europe, giving details and weather reports. OCUHi. *See* 4963.

2068 LOGAN, Sir William Edward. 1840–1841. Geologist's travels in eastern Canada, Pa., N. Y., Boston. CaOTP.

2069 MORRIS, Albert F. 1840. A personal record of the "Grahm affair" in Cal. written by one of the victims. CU-B.

2070 MORRIS, Mrs. Eliza. [between 1840 and 1846]. Daily activities, recreation; family affairs; the weather and similar data. MoU.

2071 NELSON, Francis K. 1840–1845. Farm diary kept at "Belvoir," Albemarle Cnty., Va. ViU.

2072 OTEY, Rt. Rev. James. 1840; 1842; 1844; 1846–1849; 1852; 1854; 1857; 1859–1862. Diary of brief entries on parochial visits of episcopal bishop in Tenn., letters written and received, confirmations performed, and journeys made. NcU.

2073 PHILLIPS, George S. 1840–1881. Correspondence and journals of itinerant Methodist preacher and members of his family. CSmH.

2074 RANSDELL, John H. 1840–1865. Politics and the Civil War in La. ViU, microfilm.

2075 RICE, Charles. 1840. Diary of professional theatrical performer. MH.

2076 SEWALL, Edmund Quincy. 1840–1844. Diary of Harvard student, class of 1844. MH.

2077 SIMPSON, Edward. 1840–1843. Kept while he was on cruises aboard the *Potomac, Constitution,* and *Congress.* MdHi.

2078 SMITH, Edmund. 1840–1859. CNS. CtHi.

2079 SULLIVAN, Levi. 1840–1865. Lists births, deaths, and marriages of family and neighbors. De-Ar, typescript.

2080 THOMPSON, Joseph. 1840–1841. Two trips from Readington, N.J., to Batavia, N.Y., with short accounts of Rochester, Seneca Lake, etc. CU-B. *See* 2307?

2081 TOWNSEND, Isaiah. 1840–1841. Voyage from N. Y. to Liverpool; tour through England, France, Italy. NN.

2082 TROVATTEN, Ole. 1840–? An account of a trip from Norway to Wis. and of life in the Norwegian settlements (in Norwegian). MnHi.

2083 VALLANDIGHAM, John L. H. 1840–1845. Journal at Jefferson College, Canonsburg, Pa., Lisbon, Ohio, etc. OHi.

2084 WATKINS, Emily. 1840–1863. Life in N.Y.; domestic. NN.

2085 WESTBROOK, Frederick E. 1840–1843. Kept in N. Y. city; law practice; social, business, and public affairs; retrospections. NN.

2086 WILKINSON, Asbury. 1840–1853. Daily entries; services and activities of M.E. churches in southern Ind.; comments on personalities. InHi.

2087 ZINN, Peter. 1840–1842. Studying law and doing work for various newspapers; amusements; current events; expense account. OCUHi.

2088 ALEXANDER, William. 1841. Journey to Beresford Hall, late seat of Charles Colton, Esq., London. MH.

2089 APPLETON, Mary Ellen. 1841–1869. CNS. NcU. *See* 1539, etc.

2090 BLAIR, James L. 1841–1842. Journal of a cruise in the U.S. ship *Vincennes*, from Honolulu to Manila Bay, Mangsee Islands, Singapore, Table Bay, James Town, and St. Helena on a U.S. exploring expedition. CtY.

2091 BOND, Mrs. Sarah (Wight). 1841–1844. CNS. MH.

2092 CLARK, C. J. 1841–1874. Notes taken by C. J. Clark of Selma, Ala., a medical student in Louisville, Ky. and later a practicing surgeon in the Confederate Army. NcD.

2093 COOK, George Hammell. 1841–1846. Geological study trips each July or Aug. by faculty member of Rensselaer Polytechnic Institute and his students to Northampton, Mass., and back or northerly along the west side of Lake Champlain. NjR. *See* 2012, 2155.

2094 ELD, Henry Jr. 1841. An overland expedition from Vancouver, Wash., to San Francisco, as part of a U.S. exploring expedition under Wilkes; an expedition to survey Gray's Harbor and Shoalwater Bay. CtY. *See* 2016.

2095 ESTE, David Kirkpatrick. 1841–1873 (with gaps). Personal data; family history; weather; business details; religious and philosophical remarks. OCUHi.

2096 EWING, Thomas. 1841. CNS. DLC.

2097 FRANCIS, Samuel Dexter. 1841–1862. Life in Vt.; travels in the Mid-West; his stay in Ill. and the daily record of his trip across the plains and life in Ore. CtY, original plus typescript.

2098 GILMER, Jeremy F. 1841. Personal. NcU.

2099 GROVER, George W. 1841–1842. Kept during the Texas-Santa Fe expedition. TxGR.

2100 GULICK, John Thomas. 1841–1862. Experiences and events in Cal. and the Hawaiian Islands. CU.

2101 JACKSON, Mitchell Young. 1841–1873. Farmer's diaries of life in Ind. and Minn.; trips to Minn. MnHi.

2102 JENKINS, Dr. John Carmichael. 1841–1855. Records the results of his agricultural and horticultural experiments; plantation routine; financial transactions; social and literary activities; travels; purchases of slaves and health of his slaves. LU, typescript.

2103 JOHN, James. 1841. Trip to Cal.; Indians; game; terrain. OrHi.

2104 KNOX, John Pray. 1841–1882. Religious. NjR.

2105 LENOIR, Walter Waightstill. 1841?–. Started while he was a student at U.N.C., and concerned also with the death of his wife and with his career as an attorney. NcD.

2106 MARTIN, John F. 1841–1844. Voyage in a whale-ship *Lucy Ann*, of Wilmington, Del. ICHi.

2107 MEYERS, William H. 1841. Cruise on the U.S.S. *Cyane* from Portsmouth, Va., around Cape Horn, stopping at various South American ports on the East and West coasts and various ports of Cal. and the Pacific Northwest. CU-B. *See* 1982.

2108 MILTON, Emerson J. 1841–1842. His trip from Haverhill, Mass., to Accomac Co., Va.; his year of teaching at Machipongo Academy near Pungoteague, Va.; and his return trip. NcD.

2109 MONROE, James M. 1841–1845. His conversion and work for the Mormon church in northern N.Y., and his tutoring the children of Joseph Smith and Brigham Young. CtY.

2110 MULLINS, Will S. 1841–1845. The curriculum at U.N.C., dining places, companions, entertainment, and other features of college life. NcU.

2111 POLLARD, Calvin. 1841–1842. Concerns his work as architect. NHi.

2112 POWEL, Samuel. 1841. Kept while he was in Europe. PHi.

2113 SALAZAR, Damasio. 1841. Diary of the operations against the Texans. CSmH.

2114 STANDAGE, Henry. 1841–1846. Military. CSdHi, typescript. *See* 2303.

2115 STRATTON, Pauline H. [1841–1887?] Daily incidents in the lives of the Stratton family and their slaves; friends and acquaintances; births, deaths, and marriages of the Stratton children; Mr. Stratton's long illness prior to his death; the Civil War in Mo. MoU, typescript.

2116 THAYER, Rev. Charles E. 1841–1908. Records of a Presbyterian minister of Minn., Wis., and Ohio. MnHi.

2117 VAN DUZER, J. H. 1841. Journey to England. NIC.

2118 WILLIAMS, Jeremiah D. 1841–1842; 1878–1896. Personal; weather; church; family; events and professors at Univ. of Mich.; local politics, trip to Washington; inauguration and funeral of President Harrison. MiU.

2119 WISTAR, Thomas. 1841–1876. Journal; copies of letters by and to Wistar; early reminiscences interpolated; miles traveled; matters relating to Indian affairs; genealogical information; verses. PHC.

2120 ANON. 1842. Personal and financial records of the Arnold or Appleton family. NcU. *See* 1539, etc.

2121 BAYLEY, Most Rev. James Roosevelt. 1842–1850. Kept by the Catholic Archbishop of Baltimore. MBDio. *See* 4110, 4279.

2122 CAPELL, Eli J. 1842–1850; 1867. The activity on Pleasant Hill Plantation, Amite Cnty., Miss.; assignments of slaves; condition of crops; war events and the effect of war upon plantation life. LU-Ar.

2123 CHANDLER, Samuel. 1842–1844. Remarks on board the bark *Champion* by the bark's cooper; sailed from Westport, Mass. MH.

2124 GRANT, Dr. Gabriel. 1842–1844. Schoolboy diaries. NHi.

2125 HALLER, Granville Owen. 1842; 1850. CNS. WaU. *See* 2925, 2997, 3055, 3116, 3908, 4494.

2126 JENKINS, George B. 1842–1893. CNS. WHi.

2127 KING, John Lyle. 1842–1874. Social life; law practice. InHi.

2128 LANCEY, Thomas. ca. 1842–1849. The conquest of Cal. CLU.

2129 McCLELLAN, George B. [1842–1885]? Notebooks and private journals. DLC. *See* 2294, 2935.

2130 McCOLLAM, Ellen E. 1842–1851. Family life; domestic activities; general plantation matters; social life; national, state, and local politics; visits of prominent men; household accounts. LU. *See* 4970.

2131 MEADE, Mrs. Louisa W. 1842–1853. Accounts and day book. ViHi.

2132 MOORE, C. W. 1842–1871 (with gaps). Business; travels in U. S. and Europe. NN.

2133 PALFREY, William T. 1842–1868. Operation of the Palfrey plantation, St. Martin and St. Mary parishes. LU-Ar.

2134 PAXTON, Mrs. Eliza Bailey. 1842. A journey from Washington County, Pa., to Richland County, Ohio; speaks of abolition talk in Ohio, and describes Cadiz, Wooster, Mansfield, etc. OHi.

2135 PHELPS, Jedidiah. 1842. CNS. MiD.

2136 PREBLE, George Henry. 1842. A canoe expedition into the Everglades. MeHi.

2137 PREUSS, Charles. 1842–1849. Kept on John C. Fremont's Western expeditions; printed and translated from German by E. G. and E. Gudde's *Exploring with Fremont* (Norman, Okla., 1958). CU-B.

2138 RANDOLPH, Bennington Fitz. 1842. Law business and personal activities. NjR.

2139 RICE, Justin. 1842. Negotiations with Chippewa Indians at La Pointe, Wis., for extinction of their title to lands in that vicinity. MiD.

2140 SMITH, Rev. George Nelson. 1842–1845. Activities as Presbyterian minister and missionary; family matters. MiU. *See* 1869.

2141 SMITH, William. 1842–1851. CNS. NHi.

2142 UPHAM, Dr. Albert Gookin. 1842–1845. European experiences. NhHi.

2143 WARD, Samuel Dexter. 1842. Journal of a tour to N. Y. and other places in the summer. NHi.

2144 WHEELER, John E. 1842–1880. CNS. Tx, typescripts.

2145 WISE, George D. 1842–1848. Daily memoranda and comments on various cities. MdHi.

2146 ANON. 1843. Journal aboard the schooner *Cadboro*. OrHi.

2147 ANON. 1843–1871. Family journal kept by order of the Deaconesses of the East House; important events; improvements; moves; changes; admissions; decease and departure of members; journeys; domestic concerns; work; produce for sale; accommodations. KyLoF.

2148 ANON. 1843–1884. Kept by order of the Deacon of the East House; an account of family work; concerns and accommodations; produce for sale; articles purchased and brethren's shoes. KyLoF.

2149 [ALLEN, A. T.] 1843–1844. Diary of a young Northern schoolmaster with comments on Henry A. Wise. NcD.

2150 BLACKFORD, William M. 1843–1845. His diplomatic mission to New Granada, Columbia. ViU.

2151 BRADLEY, Joseph P. 1843–1891. CNS. Nj-Hi.

2152 BREWER, Mrs. Jemima (Bliss). 1843–1854. CNS. CtHi.

2153 BUCK, I. E. 1843; 1845. A trip from Delaware, Ohio, to Cincinnati, to see the laying of the cornerstone of the Mt. Ida Observatory; a trip to Upper Sandusky, Ohio. OHi.

2154 BULL, Commodore James H. 1843–1844. A trip through Mexico and lower and upper Cal. with data on economic and social conditions, the influence of the Catholic Church and Jesuits among the Indians, missions, pearl fisheries, travel, topography of the country, and incidents of the trip. PHi.

2155 COOK, George Hammell. 1843–1846. Travel to Boston and Philadelphia; conversations with leading scientists; the equipment and operations of their laboratories; Boston factories; Pa. coal mines. PSC-Hi. See 2012, 2093.

2156 CRAWFORD, Richard R. 1843–1844. CNS. DLC.

2157 DAVIS, John. 1843–1845. A journey to Ill. to examine the Ill. canal and estimate the probable cost of completing its construction; a trip to Europe. MH.

2158 DOWNER, Prof. John R. 1843–1877. Kept at Denison Univ., Granville, Ohio; also covers Zanesville and Xenia, Ohio. OHi.

2159 DUFFIELD, Divie Bethune. 1843–1892. CNS. MiD.

2160 FREMONT, John Charles. 1843? Astronomical observations while a member of Jean N. Nicollet's expedition for exploring Minn. Terr.; also touching on his trip to the Pacific Coast in 1843 while he was with the U.S. Geographical Engineers. CLSM.

2161 GARRIOCH, Peter. 1843–1847. Diary of a fur trader in Dakota, Minn., and at Ft. Garry. Nd-Hi. See 1934.

2162 GOODALL, Charles. 1843–1846. A whaling voyage to the Pacific on the ship *Milo*. CSmH. See 2507.

2163 HUNT, Timothy D. 1843. Describes the voyage of Rev. and Mrs. Hunt on the brig *Globe* from Boston to Hawaii via Cape Horn and Tahiti; natives and missionary activities. CU-B. See 4949.

2164 HUNTINGTON, Oliver B. 1843–1900. His experiences from 1835 with Mormons in Ohio, Mo., and Ill.; his life and journeys in Salt Lake City; southeastern Utah; other places; later life at Springville as farmer, beekeeper, and schoolteacher. CU-B.

2165 JOHNSON, Anna G. 1843–1844. A tour through Pa. and N.Y.; other personal entries. PHi.

2166 MUELLER, Ferdinand. 1843. CNS. Tx, typescript.

2167 NEWBY, William T. 1843; 1861–1864. Journal of overland trip, Mo. to Oregon City; day-by-day account of small businessman. OrU.

2168 PALMER, Thomas. 1843–1853. CNS. NSchU, original; NSchHi, typescript.

2169 READING, Pierson B. 1843. His Mo. to Cal. journey. CSfCP. See 4990.

2170 ROBBINS, Thomas S. 1843–1846. Kept by a ship master from Nantucket, operating vessels on the Cal. coast from San Diego to Monterey. CU-B.

2171 RUFFIN, Edmund. 1843. Agricultural survey of S. C. NcU. See 2202, 3138.

2172 SHARPE, James M. 1843–1848. His travels and trading in the Mid-West; includes descriptions of Nauvoo and Joseph Smith. CtY.

2173 SHAW, A. C. R. 1843. Trip from Ill. to Mo. OrHi.

2174 STRATTON, Rev. Joseph Buck. 1843–1903. Records calls made, travels, yellow fever epidemics, weddings performed, funerals conducted, baptisms, prayer meetings, and services conducted. LU-Ar.

2175 TOLER, William Pinckney, U.S.N. 1843–1848. Journals of two voyages to the Pacific Coast and the conquest of Cal., with drawings and diagrams. CL.

2176 WALSH, Rev. John Johnston. 1843–1844. Voyage in Indian Ocean from the equator up Bay of Bengal to Calcutta. PPPrHi.

2177 WEBB, Dr. Henry Y. 1843–1858. Kept as a student at U.N.C. and as a physician at Eutaw, Ala. NcU.

2178 WHISTLER, Anna Matilda McNeill. 1843–1844; 1845–1848. Painter's mother; family affairs and papers; travels. NN.

2179 ANON. 1844. Apparently written by a teen-age boy (possibly ——— Pierson) who lived near Westfield, N.J.; accounts of his reading and studies; religion. NjR.

2180 ANON. 1844. Tour in South Wales and Monmouth; scenery and customs. NN.

2181 ANON. 1844. CNS. NcU.

2182 ANON. 1844. A tour through Europe. DLC.

2183 ANON. 1844–1870. Entries on church and family affairs, politics, and the Civil War. NcU. (Under seal until 1975).

2184 ADDAMS, John H. 1844. Trip from Kriedersville, Pa., to Cedarville, Ill., by horse and buggy, train, and lake steamer; a wedding trip to northern Ill. to buy a farm; lake steamer taken from Buffalo to Chicago via Cleveland, Detroit, and Milwaukee; concludes with the purchase of a saw mill and grist mill. PSC.

2185 BLANCHARD, Elizabeth (Howell). 1844. Trip from Greenville, Ill., to Long Island. IHi.

2186 BOOTH, Nathaniel. 1844–1854. CNS. NKi-Sh.

2187 CANBY, Samuel. 1844–1875. Weather; Civil War clippings; assassination of Lincoln; du Pont explosions; impeachment of Andrew Johnson; Wilmington earthquake, 1871; Chicago fire, 1871. DeHi.

2188 CARR, Dr. Vannep. 1844. CNS. NCooHi.

2189 CLYMAN, James. 1844–1846. An overland trip from Independence, Mo., to Ore. and Cal. and return. CSmH.

2190 COOPER, Jeremiah. 1844–1854. Copybook, verses on Henry Clay, and accounts of produce. OHi.

2191 COWAN, John. 1844. Personal. NcD.

2192 FREDERICK, James Daniel. 1844–1899. Athens, Univ. of Ga., Marshallville, Ga. Parts of diary written while a student at Univ. of Ga., contains some literary society minutes. Later diaries deal with farming in middle Ga. before and after the Civil War. No entries for war years. Some accounts, notes, and clippings. GU.

2193 GAUSE, Eli. 1844. Trip to attend Quaker meeting in Baltimore. InHi.

2194 HATHAWAY, Miss ———. 1844–1847. CNS. MiD.

2195 HOLT, Edwin Michael. 1844–1854. The weather; personal matters; varied economic activities. NcD, typescript.

2196 KIDDER, Harriette (Smith). 1844–1859; 1863; 1868; 1871–1874; 1885; 1891–1902. Some extended retrospective narrative, family sketches, reminiscences of life in N. Y. city, Newark, Madison, and Evanston, Ill., of the wife of a Methodist minister; American and European travels. NjR.

2197 KING, Johnson W. 1844. Business transactions; farming; legal business; duties as postmaster in Murphy, N.C. NcD.

2198 MERRILL, Charles Benjamin. 1844–1847. Student at Bowdoin; vacations in Portland; work; sport; religion. NN.

2199 PEALE, Mary Jane Patterson. 1844. Daily events. PPAmS.

2200 PUTNAM, Israel Ward. 1844–1845. Journal of a trip to Hamilton College (now Colgate University), N.Y., from Belpre, Ohio, and account of student life. OHi.

2201 REEVE, Job W. 1844–1848. A voyage to the Indian and Pacific oceans in the whale ship *Awashonks* of Falmouth, Mass. NjViHi.

2202 RUFFIN, Edmund. 1844–1855. Farm operations. Vi. *See* 2171, 3138.

2203 SPALDING, William Witter. 1844–1848. Journey from Iowa, up the Mississippi, to Lake Superior region in search of minerals; comments on Indians, travel, and weather conditions, copper mining. MiU.

2204 STATES, John A. 1844–1849. Whaling on ship *Eugene* in Pacific Ocean. CtMyMM.

2205 STICKNEY, Annette Bradley. 1844. A visit to Me.; copy made by John Elliot Bowman in 1927. MeBaHi.

2206 TAYLOR, Robert. 1844. Trip from N. Y. city to Montreal by steamboat and canal boat; scenery, etc. NN. *See* 1595, 2305.

2207 TODD, John Payne. 1844–1848. Letter book and diary on the management of his property and legal matters. DLC. *See* 1613?

2208 VAN BIBBER, Isaac. 1844. Kept while he was touring Md. to collect money to build an Episcopal Church in Westminster. MdHi.

2209 ANON. 1845; 1861. Kept by students at Blair Academy, N.J. NjBt.

2210 ADAMS, Dennis Patterson. 1845–1846. Trip from Marietta, Ohio, to Boston on a sailing vessel built at Harmar, Ohio, and return overland. OHi, typescript.

2211 BAILY, Joshua Longstreth. 1845–1856. Activities; personal notes; meetings attended; daily record of the weather, etc. PHC.

2212 BELT, Capt. William J. 1845. Kept on board vessel. MdHi.

2213 BOYD, James McHenry. 1845–1847. Voyages to South America and Europe. MdHi.

2214 BROWN, William R. 1845–1846. Pioneer farming activities such as making soap, threshing, and storing vegetables. MnHi.

2215 CHAPLIN, Thomas B. 1845; 1860–1886. CNS. ScHi.

2216 CHASE, Percy. 1845–1855. Voyages on clipper ships; collected from newspapers, logbooks, files of shipping offices, personal diaries. MH.

2217 COLLINS, Rev. Judson Dwight. 1845–1851. Religious activities in Mich.; teaching at Albion College; comprehensive remarks on trip to China—scenery, people, customs, religion, missionary activities. MiU.

2218 COOKE, Ebenezer. 1845–1862. Remarks on board the *Fairy* and on schooner *Belle Isle* and schooner *Seychelle*; journal of whaling voyage on *E. H. Hatfield* in the north Atlantic. MH.

2219 DAWLEY, Allen W. 1845–1925. Farming activities; prices of produce; dates of plowing and threshing; wages of employees; information about various phases of community life. MnHi.

2220 DREW, Mr. and Mrs. James. 1845–1846. Trip from Glasgow, Scotland, to Wis. NHi.

2221 GAULDIN, Martin A. 1845. A journey from Marshall, Mo., to Austin, Tex.; the people along the way, the timber and water resources, and fertility of the country. MoU, typescript.

2222 GRANT, Elijah P. 1845. CNS. IHi.

2223 HARRITT, Jesse. 1845. Trip to Oregon. Or-Hi.

2224 HEATH, Rev. Uriah. 1845–1852. The M.E. preaching circuits in Ohio, chiefly Zanesville, Springfield, Worthington, Columbus, and Marietta. OHi.

2225 HENTZ, Dr. Charles A. 1845–1850; 1852–1860. Personal. NcU.

2226 HOBART, Rev. Chauncey. 1845–1846. Kept by a Methodist circuit rider in Wis. and Ill. MnHi.

2227 JONES, Horatio Gates, Jr. 1845. Written on a trip West—Ill., Ind., Ohio. PCC.

2228 KNOWLES, Sallie. 1845–1850. CNS. PHi. *See* 1977.

2229 LELAND, Charles Godfrey. 1845; 1847; 1856. Travel. PHi.

2230 MORRIS, Samuel B. 1845; 1849–1851. Trip from Flat Rock Bridge to Towanda; farm and domestic expense accounts. PHi. *See* 1417?

2231 NEW HELVETIA. 1845–1848. A record of events at New Helvetia continued, in turn, by J. Bidwell, W. Swasey, and J. Sutter. CU-B.

2232 NICHOL, Walter. 1845–1849. Comments on business, the weather, and family affairs. NcU. *See* next entry?

2233 NICKOL, Walter. 1845–1849. CNS. Nc-Ar.

2234 OWEN, John D. 1845–1852. Comment on Owen's medical calls, farming operations, and the weather; brief description of a trip to New Orleans. NcD.

2235 PARKER, Samuel. 1845. Trip to Oregon via Meek's cut-off. OHi, copy. *See* 1865.

2236 PITMAN, Frederick. 1845–1884 (with gaps). CNS. NN.

2237 POLK, James K. 1845–1849. Personal diary kept as U.S. president. DLC.

2238 PRAY, George. 1845. About his baptism in the Huron River. Ann Arbor 1st Baptist Church Records, MiU.

2239 RAVENEL, Thomas Porcher. 1845–1903. Gives good picture of family life on plantation; entries dealing with Civil War and reconstruction era. GHi.

2240 REGAL, Abel. 1845. School work at Gregory's Commercial College, Detroit, and social activities at home in Berea, Ohio. MiU.

2241 RUSH, Madison. 1845–1848. A cruise in the *Columbus* from N. Y. to China and return, with descriptions of various ports of China, the Sandwich Islands, Valparaiso, Callao, and Monterey. DLC.

2242 SHAW, William J. 1845–1892. Includes his accounts and notes pertaining to business in S.F. and Sacramento. CLU.

2243 SMITH, Joseph Belknap. 1845–1850; 1861; 1863–1864; 1864–1865; 1866–1867. Journeys; speculations; mining and milling operations. NcD.

2244 STILLWELL, Albert G. 1845–1850. Local events; church and social affairs; happenings in the town. RHi.

2245 STUMP, David. 1845. Journal from Mo. to Ore. Or.

2246 SUTTER, Capt John Augustus. 1845–1848. Original diary at "New Helvetia." CSSfm and CSf-CP. *See* 2034, 2231.

2247 TODD, Mrs. W. 1845–1847; 1853–1854. CNS. NHi.

2248 TOWER, L. F. 1845–1846. Local events; prominent visitors; weather; steamer arrivals; Protestant ministers and their activities; celebrations and holidays. LU.

2249 WADDELL, James Pleasants. 1845–1847. Athens, Ga. Daily life of a professor of Ancient Languages at the Univ. of Ga. Weather and temperature for years covered. GU.

2250 WINNER, Septimus. 1845–1902. CNS. PHi.

2251 ANON. 1846. Diary of a visit to Columbia. ScU.

2252 ANON. 1846. Kept at San Antonio pertaining to the Mexican War. NHi.

2253 ANON. 1846. A trip in Argentina up the Paraná River from near its mouth to the junction with the River Feliciano. CSmH.

2254 ANON. 1846–1847. Daily life on a small farm. NcU.

2255 ANON. 1846–1867. Proceedings of a church meeting; family meetings; union meetings and one public meeting; accounts of funerals; descriptions of rites; some account of their doctrines. KyLoF.

2256 ANDERSON, Alexander C. 1846; 1847. An exploration to open a route from Ft. Alexander to Ft. Langley; a second journal of an expedition from Kamloops to Langley, via the Thompson and Fraser rivers. CU-B.

2257 BACKUS, Electus. 1846–1848. Journal of the Mexican War. MiD.

2258 BAKER, Everard Green. 1846–1853. Personal; medicinal recipes; family genealogy. NcU. *See* 2436.

2259 BLISS, Robert S. 1846–1847. Diary in U.S. Army, Co. B. CSdHi.

2260 BROWNING, James C. 1846–1847. Kept during the Mexican War. Ms-Ar.

2261 BURNS, Archibald W. 1846–1847. Visit to Mexico during the Mexican War; references are made to Maj. Gen. Winfield Scott, Gen. Zachary Taylor, army headquarters at Camargo, and the battle at Monterey. NcD.

2262 BUTLER, Francis Eugene. 1846–1862. Observations on the 1849 cholera epidemic in N. Y., the Mexican War, political events, religious affairs; excerpts from the diary of a forebear, Joseph Pease of Suffield, Conn.; a visit to the White Mountains. NjR.

2263 CARRIGER, Nicholas. 1846. An overland journey from Mo. to Cal. including arduous crossing of Sierra Nevada. CU-B.

2264 CATLIN, Dr. Hiram Wesley. 1846–1850. Kept in the 2nd Ind. Inf. during the Mexican War. MnHi.

2265 CHANEY, Josiah B. 1846–1851; 1858–1909. Journeys between Dover, N.H., and Moline, Ill., from Aledo, Ill., to Minn.; life in the Twin Cities. MnHi.

2266 COOK, P. St. George. 1846. CNS. CSdHi.

2267 COUTS, Cave J. 1846–1849. A march from Mexico to Cal., 1848, as a lt., 1st U.S. Dragoons, under Maj. L. P. Grahm, and an expedition from San Diego to the Colorado River, 1849. CU-B.

2268 CRAWFORD, Martha (Foster). 1846–1881. Kept as a young woman in Ala., 1846–1851, and later a Baptist missionary to China; reactions to China; political conditions in America. NcD.

2269 DANIEL, William H. 1846–1847. Military in Mexican War. KyLoF.

2270 DAVIS, John. 1846–1848. Religious. MdHi.

2271 ELMER, Elijah. 1846–1847. Military. CSd-Hi, copy.

2272 ERWIN, William. 1846–1856. Plantation accounts and comments on the weather, crops, and slaves. NcU.

2273 GIBSON, Lt. George R. 1846. March from Ft. Leavenworth under General Kearny to Santa Fe, for occupation of N. M. MoHi. *See* 2329, 2386.

2274 GILLESPIE, Mother Angela (Maria Eliza). 1846. Personal. InNd, original and typescript.

2275 GILMAN, William Henry. 1846–1858 (with gaps). Voyages and cruises on *Merrimac*, etc. to So. America; social life. NN.

2276 HARPER, George W. F. 1846–1921 (with gaps). Business affairs and private life, including his service in the 58th N. C. Inf., C.S.A. NcU.

2277 HARRIS, Francis L. 1846–1864. Sea journals and letters; voyages in bark *President*, on U.S.S. *Massachusetts*, and in Arctic Ocean; rules and regulations for U.S.S. *Daylight*. Author was volunteer in Isaac I. Hayes expedition. MH.

2278 HARRISON, Christopher. 1846–1847. Weather observations with occasional personal comments. MdAA.

2279 HAYDEN, George W. 1846–1848. Kept while he was a member of Stevenson's Regt. in Cal. CU-B.

2280 HAYES, Sophia Birckard. 1846–1866. About family, friends, and events, including thoughts on religious subjects. OFH.

2281 HOLBROOK, E. 1846–1863. CNS. CSmH.

2282 HOLLINGSWORTH, John McHenry. 1846. A member of the "Stevenson Regiment" sent to Cal. by boat in 1846 and remaining through the pre-gold years. CHi, original; CSt, copy.

2283 HUGHES, Most Rev. John. 1846–1856. Almost daily account of his activities as archbishop of N.Y. NNArAr.

2284 JAGGER, D. 1846; 1849; 1850. A voyage on the Great Lakes; an overland journey from Ohio to Cal.; scattered entries of experiences in Calif. CU-B.

2285 JONES, Nathaniel V. 1846–1847. Kept on a march with the Mormon Battalion from Ft. Leavenworth to Santa Fe and San Diego and return in escort of Gen. S. W. Kearny. CU-B.

2286 JORDAN, Francis. 1846–1877. CNS. PHi.

2287 KEARNY, Gen Stephen W. 1846–1847. Expedition to N. M. and Cal. MoHi. *See* 1506.

2288 KIEFER, Dr. Hermann. 1846. Travel diary. MiU.

2289 KREITZER, John. 1846–1848. Journal, eye witness account of the Mexican War. PHi.

2290 LAFETRA, Elizabeth Rylee. 1846–1854. Descriptions by a young Quaker of daily social activity and visits with relatives. NjR.

2291 LEINHARD, Heinrich. 1846. On the emigrant trail. CU-B, typescript.

2292 MAGRUDER, Eliza L. 1846–1857. Crops; social events and other amusements; types of literature read; treatment of the Negroes and their unrest; religious life including texts of sermons and names of ministers, yellow fever epidemics. LU.

2293 MATHERS, James. 1846. A journey from middle crossing of the Platte river to Mission San José, Cal. CU-B.

2294 McCLELLAN, George B. 1846–1853. Private journal containing many notes and sketches of fortifications, etc., taken in Mexico. DLC. *See* 2129, 2935.

2295 McKINSTRY, George M. 1846. Written while he was crossing the plains. CU-B. *See* 3313?

2296 NEVILLE, Harvey. 1846–1847. Mexican War diary. ICHi.

2297 NICHOLAS, Henry M. 1846–1860. Kept by a teacher and preacher in Mass. and Minn. MnHi.

2298 PENDERGAST, Solomon. 1846–1869. Social and economic life in N.H.; a trip to Minn.; life in Hutchinson, Minn. MnHi, microfilm.

2299 PRINGLE, Virgil Kellog. 1846. Travel from Hickory Grove, Warren County, Mo., to Salem, Ore. Terr.; reports conditions and miles traveled daily. InU-Li; OrFP, copy. *See* 2945.

2300 RANTLETT, Charles A. 1846–1862. Various voyages to and from San Francisco. CSmH.

2301 ROGERS, James Lloyd. 1846. Kept on voyage to the Orient in the *Stephen Lurman*. MdHi.

2302 SMITH, Capt. Franklin. 1846–1847; 1855. Detailed information on Mexico, the war, participation of Mississippians. Ms-Ar.

2303 STANDAGE, Henry. 1846–1847. Overland journey to Cal. with the Mormon Battalion. CSmH. *See* 2114.

2304 SWEENY, Brig.-Gen. Thomas William. 1846–[56]? Personal correspondence, diaries, etc., of young officer in Mexican War, later stationed at Ft. Yuma and member of Sioux Expedition. CSmH.

2305 TAYLOR, Robert. 1846–1847. Autobiography and diary of cooper in N. Y. city; includes material on his public offices. NN. *See* 1595, 2206.

2306 TAYLOR, W. E. 1846. Written while he was crossing the plains. CSSfm.

2307 THOMPSON, Joseph. 1846–1847; 1849–1883; 1885. Written by a surveyor and conveyancer, farmer, teacher, orphans court judge of Hunterdon and Somerset Counties, N.J. NjR. *See* 2080?

2308 TWIGGS, John D. 1846. A trip to London describing the voyage and the sights of London. NcU.

2309 VINCENT, Joshua S. 1846–1847. 1st Sgt. in Co. 1. CSdHi, copy.

2310 WILBUR, Rev. J.H. 1846–1848. Journal of his voyage on the *Whiton*, other travels, and his affairs in Cal., Portland, and the Willamette Valley. OrSaW.

2311 WINCHELL, Alexander. 1846–1891. Student days at Wesleyan Univ.; N. Y. city, Washington, D.C.; slavery; records of scientific observations; journey from Ala. to New Orleans and up the Mississippi and Ohio rivers by boat (1853); comments on university events and people; geological trips in U.S.; trip to Europe (1873–1874); family affairs. MiU; MnHi.

2312 ANON. 1847–1852. Kept by Mormons; CNS. NbFrOs.

2313 ANON. 1847–1849. Record of activities as Presbyterian Elder; observations on responsibilities and privileges of the office. PPPrHi.

2314 ACKLEY, ———. [between 1847–1875]. CNS. UHi.

2315 ANDREWS, Christopher Columbus. 1847–1922. His career in N.H., Mass., Washington, D.C., Kan., Minn., and Sweden. MnHi.

2316 BAKER, Dr. Simmons Jones. 1847. Recollections of the family. Nc-Ar.

2317 BARROW, Col. David C. 1847–1849; 1851–1852; 1856–1858; 1863; 1876; 1879. Oglethorpe Cnty., Ga.; Athens, Ga. Plantation diaries, accounts, work done, family affairs on a large Ga. plantation. Good material on plantation life. GU.

2318 BRYANT, Julia Sands. 1847. Kept in school notebook. NNC. *See* 3159, 4071.

2319 BUFFUM, Joseph C. 1847–1855. Kept in N. H. before the gold rush; reflects the growing interest in the far West; continues on an overland trip to Independence, Mo.; thence to Cal. and a return trip via Nicaragua. CU-B.

2320 BURD, Sarah. 1847–1849. CNS. PHi.

2321 BURTON, Gen. Robert T. [1847–1875]. CNS. UHi.

2322 CAMPBELL, William B. 1847. Capture of Vera Cruz in Mexican War. NcD.

2323 COX, Leander M. 1847–1848. A campaign to Mexico; account of the march, camp life, and conditions, diseases, etc., and return home. KyHi.

2324 CRAVENS, F. 1847. Recording the receipt of degree of LL.B. from Transylvania Univ.; the recruiting of a company of U. S. Dragoons in Adair County; presentation of horses by citizens of Adair Cnty. to Capt. E. B. Gaither and Lt. Wagley; visit to former home at Burkesville; trial of George Wagley for killing F. M. Ewing; engagement and marriage. KyLoF.

2325 DAKIN, James H. 1847–1850. The choice of the site of the capitol of La., plans for the building, selection and cost of materials, progress of construction, and a trip made to Washington and Pittsburgh in the interest of the project. LU-Ar.

2326 DARST, Paul. 1847; 1866. Overland journey from Ft. Laramie to Ore. in 1847; detailed expense account of overland trip to Cal. from Ore., 1866. OrU.

2327 DUNLAP, Dr. John N. 1847. The Mexican War; the climate; health; traveling conditions; his associates; other items of interest, particularly of a medical nature. MoU, typescript.

2328 FERGUSON, Philip C. 1847–1864. Mexican War, etc. MoSHs.

2329 GIBSON, Lt. George R. 1847. Return trip from Chihuahua to Santa Fe with a caravan of Chihuahua traders. MoHi. *See* 2273, 2386.

2330 GRAHAM, Rev. Walter Scott Finney. 1847–1854. Record of marriages, baptisms, etc. DeU.

2331 GREENING, John. 1847–1849. An ocean voyage from England to the U. S. and experiences in Dane County, Wis. MnHi, typescript.

2332 GRIFFIN, John S. 1847. A journey as surgeon with "Kearney's Dragoons" from Santa Fe to Cal. CU-B.

2333 HAGAN, Dr. Robert. 1847–1848. A U.S. surgeon with Scott in Mexico. Tx.

2334 HASTINGS, Loren B. 1847. Traveling from La Harpe, Ill., to Portland, Ore. Terr. CtY, typescript.

2335 HERNDON, Dr. Brodie Strachan. 1847–1886. His medical practice before and after the Civil War; experience as a surgeon in the Confederate service; a visit to relatives in Scotland. ViU.

2336 HOWARD, Maj. Gen. Oliver Otis. 1847–1855. Kept at Bowdoin and West Point. MeB.

2337 JOHNSON, W. S. 1847–1848. A trip from Mobile, Ala., to Mexico; experiences in Mexican War; return to Columbia. ScU.

2338 JONES, E. M. 1847. School events and social life. RHi.

2339 JUDAH, Henry M. 1847. Military journal of the Mexican campaign with the 4th U.S. Inf. DLC.

2340 LATROBE, John H. B. 1847. Ocean voyage to Europe. MdHi.

2341 LESTER, Dr. Thomas Bryan. 1847–1848. Trips from Ft. Leavenworth, Kan., to Santa Fe, N.M.; references to the Sacs and other Indian tribes encountered, to the large herds of buffalo, and to Gen. Sterling Price. MoU.

2342 LUKENS, Esther. 1847. A trip to western Pa., Philadelphia, and Wilmington, Del. OHi.

2343 MANSFIELD, Mrs. Margaret (Worthington). 1847–1852. Personal and family matters; marriage and family deaths. OCUHi.

2344 MATHERS, John Hutchison. 1847–1848. Daily activities and thoughts when he was a college student at Jefferson College. PWW.

2345 McCAULEY, Adm. Edward Yorke. 1847; 1853–1854. Kept on the west coast of Africa and in Japanese waters with Commodore Perry. DLC; NHi.

2346 McCOY, Lt. Thomas Franklin. 1847. Mexican War journal, with 11th Pa. Inf.; camp life; guard duty; drilling; rumors; marching; skirmishes; many men dying from sickness; movement of troops; strategy; plans. NNC, typescript.

2347 MINOR, William J. and R. A. 1847–1870. Business and personal entries interspersed; medical information including prescriptions; log books of slave care; doctors' bills, etc. LU.

2348 PETTIJOHN, Isaac. 1847–1848. An overland journey from Mo. to Ore. and the return journey to Mo. CU-B.

2349 PIERCE, Franklin. 1847. Diary of U.S. President during the Mexican War. CSmH; DLC.

2350 PLATT, Rev. Isaac Watts. 1847–1858. Work and difficulties of pastor of Presbyterian Church at West Farms, N.Y. NN, typescript.

2351 PULLAN, James. 1847–1859. Business transactions. OHi.

2352 ROBERTS, George Barber. 1847–1848. About operation of Cowlitz Farm for Hudson's Bay Co. OrHi.

2353 ROSECRANS, Bishop Sylvester H. 1847–1852. Personal. InNd.

2354 SAUNDERS, Mary. 1847. Journey from Iowa to Ore. covering the "Whitman massacre" of which she was a survivor. CU-B.

2355 SESSIONS, Peregrine. [between 1847–1875]. CNS. UHi.

2356 SHAW, Cornelius G. 1847–1848. Fishing; weather; prospecting and mining at Isle Royale, Mich. MiU.

2357 SMITH, Azariah, and Henry Bigler. 1847–1848. Diary of Cal. pioneers. CSfCP.

2358 SMITH, Levi Lathrop. 1847–1848. Records the visits of his partner and neighbors in Ore.; the progress of his farm work; his health and attacks of "falling sickness"; and his thoughts, which were often melancholy. CtY.

2359 STANTON, James H. 1847–1849. Diaries of Springboro, Warren Cnty., Ohio; visits to the meetings of the Society of Friends in N.C. and Ohio. OHi.

2360 THOMPSON, ———. [between 1847–1875]. CNS. UHi.

2361 VAIL, Rebecca (Warden). 1847. Daily activities of a young Quaker including frequent visits with friends and relatives, largely or entirely Quakers, of Green Brook, Rahway, etc. NjR.

2362 VAN WYCK, Lawrence. 1847–1857. Kept while he was working on railway construction in N.Y. state; fellow workmen; social opinions; slavery. NN.

2363 VOORHEES, Peter A. 1847–1883. Weather; farming; visits; church; funerals; various personal activities. NjR.

2364 WOODRUFF, Wilford. 1847. Abstract of Woodruff's journal en route to Utah (it differs however from the actual diary record). CU-B.

2365 WRIGHT, Gordon J. 1847–1860's. Including account books and scrapbook. OHi.

2366 ANON. 1848–1852. The congregation of the Moravian church in Woodstock Mills, Fla. (in German and English). NcWsM.

2367 ANON. 1848; 1852–1854. The Cherokee Indian Mission of the Moravian Church (in German and English). NcWsM.

2368 ANON. 1848–1866. Religious. OHi.

2369 ANDERSON, William Wright. 1848. Overland from St. Joseph, Mo., to Oregon City. InU-Li, copy.

2370 ATKINS, Benjamin Elberfield. 1848–1909. CNS. Nc-Ar.

2371 BIGLER, Henry William. 1848; 1856–1876. A Mormon in Cal. and the discovery of gold. CU-B. *See* 1404, 2357.

2372 BLACKFORD, Dr. Launcelot M. 1848–1913. Personal. NcU.

2373 BLOOR, Alfred Janson. 1848–1867. About N. Y. city life. NHi.

2374 BOND, Edward Pearson. 1848–1862 (with gaps). CNS. MH.

2375 CHAMBERS, Dr. Rowland. 1848–1863. Trips to Panama; work there and in Yazoo Cnty., Miss., and in La.; charges for dental work; account from the inside of the Union siege of Vicksburg. LU.

2376 CLEAVER, Benjamin. 1848. Overland journal; begins in eastern Ore. Or, microfilm.

2377 COMFORT, Ellwood. 1848. A journey on horseback from Tecumseh, Mich., to Philadelphia. MiU. *See* 2052.

2378 CURRAN, Rev. Charles W. 1848–1853. Diary of Methodist minister in southern Ind. InHi, microfilm.

2379 DALLAS, George Mifflin. 1848–1849. Last few months of Polk's administration; Senate politics; tariff controversy; territorial expansion; gold discovery in Cal. PHi.

2380 DAVIS, Stephen C. 1848–1854. A voyage from Dunstable, Mass., to Cal. via Panama. CSmH.

2381 EASTIN, Thomas N. 1848. Travel with company from Henderson, Ky., en route to gold mines of Cal. via Independence, Mo., and the Santa Fe Trail; passed through Fts. Kearney, Laramie, and Bridger; Salt Lake City; Bear River; Goose Creek; and the Valley of a Thousand Springs; description of scenery; contacts with other emigrants and with Indians; ravages of cholera; hardships. KyLoF.

2382 ELKINTON, Joseph Scotton. 1848–1905. Visits to the Seneca Indians of N.Y. state; New England, and Nova Scotia; Doukhobors in Canada; visits to prisons and miners. PSC-Hi, transcription. *See* 1411, 3175, 4453?

2383 FINLEY, Rev. Jonathan P. 1848–1887. Personal diary as student, preacher, and teacher. PPPr-Hi.

2384 FORBES, Cleveland. 1848–? A voyage from N.Y. to San Francisco via the Straits of Magellan on the S.S. *California*. CSmH.

2385 GAGE, George. 1848–1849. Kept during his youth. OHi.

2386 GIBSON, Lt. George R. 1848. Return trip from Santa Fe to Ft. Leavenworth with the U. S. mail. MoHi. *See* 2273, 2329.

2387 GILE, Judith (Sargent). 1848–1886. Family and local events; deaths, marriages, etc. NjR.

2388 [GORHAM, Jason Martin]. 1848–1849. Harvard student, class of 1851. MH.

2389 HOLBROOK, A. M. 1848–1849. CNS. Nj-Hi.

2390 HUGHES, Henry. 1848–1853. CNS. Ms-Ar.

2391 KERN, Benjamin, Edward M., and Richard H. 1848–1851. Exploration expeditions with Fremont and others. CSmH. *See* next entry.

2392 KERN, Edward M. 1848. First part of Fremont's fourth expedition. CSmH.

2393 LEE, James Kendall. 1848–1849. Kept while he was a student at Princeton. ViHi.

2394 LEWIS, Henry. 1848. Canoe voyage from the Falls of St. Anthony to St. Louis; the removal of the Winnebago Indians to Long Prairie by the government is mentioned. MnHi, typescript.

2395 LORTON, William B. 1848–1850. Travels in N.Y., Canada, and the Mid-West, then overland via the Mormon Trail to Salt Lake and the southern route to Los Angeles; was with various parties associated with Death Valley. CU-B.

2396 LOVE, Alfred H. 1848–1913. Personal and business activities as well as his interest in social reform; the pacifist movement, temperance, and prison reform. PSC.

2397 MANDEVILLE, Rebecca. 1848. Home and social life of Natchez. LU.

2398 MERCER, William Newton. 1848–1874. Business records giving a day-to-day account of Mercer's financial transactions, and accounts of personal activities. LU.

2399 MONETTE, James. 1848–1863. Farming operations and plantation accounts; personal matters. LU, typescript.

2400 MORRIS, Elliston P. 1848–1849. CNS. PHi.

2401 MORRIS, Samuel. 1848–1904. Journal, ledger, daybooks, accounts, cashbooks. PHi.

2402 PARKER, Isaac. 1848. Journey on Mississippi and Ohio rivers with some expense accounts; clippings on political subjects pasted on last pages. InHi.

2403 PORTER, Dr. Lemuel C. 1848–1862. Weather conditions; notes on crops; organization of Sons of Temperance; medical, political comments. KyLoF.

2404 PRATT, Orville C. 1848. An overland journey from Ft. Leavenworth to Los Angeles; describes in detail events of the journey, the country, encounters with Indians. CtY.

2405 RAYNOR, James. 1848–1849. CNS. OrHi.

2406 REED, A. M. 1848–1899. CNS. FSaWml.

2407 ROLLINS, Irvin W. 1848–1879. Farm life in southern Minn. MnHi, microfilm.

2408 ROLLINS, John. 1848. A trip from Me. to Minn. by way of the Great Lakes to Milwaukee, overland to Galena, and northward along the Mississippi and St. Croix rivers. MnHi.

2409 ROOS, Carl. 1848–1871; 1881; 1889; and n.d. Including diary kept while he was in the Union army (in Swedish). MnRedHi.

2410 SEYMOUR, George Edward. 1848–1849. Detailed daily accounts of lessons, escapades, teachers, and fellow pupils of a lively student at the Poughkeepsie Collegiate School, "College Hill School"; Hudson River steamboats; cholera; transcribes letters from his parents. NCooHi.

2411 SMITH, J. V. C. 1848; 1849; 1851; 1852. CNS. MBNEH.

2412 STEVENS, Isaac Ingalls. 1848. Mexican War diary. WaU.

2413 THOMPSON, John Bodine. 1848–1879. Extended account of religious feelings which led to the ministry. NjR. *See* 2958.

2414 WALKER, Lewis. 1848–1864. CNS. PHi.

2415 WILLCOX, Cyprian Porter. 1848; 1852–1854. N. Y., France, Rome, Madrid, Geneva, Berlin, Dresden. 1848 diary contains much re Revolution of 1848 in France, reactions and affairs in other countries, Louis Napoleon, President Polk. 1852–1854 diaries concern European travels of a young man. GU.

2416 WINTHROP, Theodor. 1848–1860. CNS. NN.

2417 ANON. 1849–1851. A voyage from Aberdeen, Miss., to San Francisco and the gold regions. CSmH.

2418 ANON. 1849–1853. Journal of the *Lewis*, New England whaler, on a voyage to the Pacific. DLC.

2419 ANON. 1849–1850. The voyage of the brig *Metropolis* of Beverly bound to San Francisco, Cal. OrHi.

2420 ANON. 1849–1850. Voyage to Cal. by way of Cape Horn in brig *William Penn*. MH.

2421 ANON. 1849–1850. Voyage from N. Y. to San Francisco in the bark *Harriet Newell*. CSmH.

2422 ANON. 1849. Voyage of the bark *Sylph* from Panama to San Francisco, with list of passengers. CSmH.

2423 ANON. 1849. A voyage from N. Y. to San Francisco via Cape Horn on the ship *Robert Bowne*. CSmH.

2424 ANON. 1849. A voyage to and from Cal. CSmH.

2425 ABBE, Alinson. 1849–1850. A voyage from Boston to San Francisco via Cape Horn. CSmH.

2426 ABRAMS, William P. 1849–1851. Daily record of journey from New Orleans to Chagres on the brig *Pedraza*; from Panama to San Francisco on the brig *Copiapo*; experiences in Cal. including "Stanislaus diggings." CU-B.

2427 ALLEN, W. T. 1849–1853. Trips from Leominster, Mass., to surrounding areas. NN. *See* 2812.

2428 ANTRIM, B. Jay. 1849–? Travels in Mexico. DLC.

2429 ARMSTRONG, J. E. 1849. An overland trip from Hebbardsville (Athens Cnty.), Ohio to Cal. OHi.

2430 AUSTIN, Henry. 1849. Diary of a journey across the plains under J. G. Bruff, via the Jasper cutoff, and arrival at Sutter's Fork Farm, Cal. CU-B.

2431 BACHELDER, Dr. Amos. 1849. A trip overland by way of Lassen's cutoff. CHi, typescript.

2432 BACKUS, Gurdon. 1849–1851. A journey from Burlington, Vt., to St. Louis, Mo., and across the plains to Sacramento; his stay in Cal. CtY.

2433 BADGER, Charles L. 1849–1850. Voyage from Boston to San Francisco in brig *Triumph* commanded by Hiram Burt; log kept on "Seamans' Journal" printed forms. MH.

2434 BADMAN, Philip. 1849. A journey from Warren, Pa., to Cal.; describes the country, birds, flowers, and wagon trains. CtY.

2435 BAILEY, George F. 1849; 1864. A trip to Cal. from Ohio; diary of Civil War service in Co. G, 132nd Regt., Ohio Volunteer Inf. OHi.

2436 BAKER, Everard Green. 1849–1876. Plantation, farm accounts. NcU. *See* 2258.

2437 BAKER, George H. 1849. Boston to Cal. journey. CSfCP.

2438 BAKER, Isaac W. 1849–1852. A record of voyage around the Horn on bark *San Francisco*; experiences in mines; return voyage. CU-B.

2439 BALDRIDGE, Alex H. 1849–1853. Kept by a medical student at Madison, Ind., Louisville, Ky., and Cincinnati, Ohio. OHi.

2440 BARKER, Pierce W. 1849–1850. On the ship *Nestor* from Salem, Mass., to San Francisco. WaU.

2441 BEAN, Hiram P. 1849–1851. A voyage around the Horn. CSmH.

2442 BECK, Robert. 1849–1850. A journey from Baltimore via New Orleans to Vera Cruz, Mexico; across Mexico, sailing from Mazatlan to San Francisco. CU-B.

2443 BEECHING, Robert. 1849. Trip from N.Y. on the bark *Norumbega* to Galveston and thence overland through Tex., Mexico, Ariz., and southern Cal. to San Diego. CSmH.

2444 BEESLEY, Maurice. 1849. Journey over Humboldt-Truckee-Donner route to Cal. NvU, copy.

2445 BELL, John W. 1849. Voyage from N. Y. city to San Francisco around the Horn; ship life and perils; gold mining. NN.

2446 BENSON, John E. 1849. From St. Joseph to Sacramento, overland journey. NbHi, typescript. *See* next item.

2447 BENSON, John H. 1849. A journey from St. Joseph, Mo., across the plains to Sacramento, Cal. CU-B. *See* above.

2448 BLIGHT, Atherton. 1849–1856. Trips through Egypt, Turkey, Palestine, and other Mediterranean countries; notes on the Crimean War and state of affairs in Germany. PHi.

2449 BOGGS, John. 1849. Written while he was crossing the plains. CU-B, photostat.

2450 BOND, Robert. 1849. A journey from Newark or Ohio to Great Salt Lake City. CtY.

2451 BOOTH, Anne. 1849. A voyage around Cape Horn, putting in at Valparaiso and arrival at San Francisco, including seven weeks at anchor in the Bay and life in San Francisco. CU-B.

2452 BOULDIN, Capt. James E. 1849–1850. CNS. CSt.

2453 BOWLES, Isaac. 1849. A voyage on the ship *Mount Vernon* from Mass. to San Francisco. CU-B.

2454 BOWMAN? 1849. A trip to Chicago by way of the Lakes. NIC.

2455 BRANDT, Marie Ester. 1849–1868. Life in a small town community and college, social and family life of period. InHi.

2456 BRISBANE, William. 1849. A trip from Ft. Leavenworth to Santa Fe. CSmH.

2457 BROWN, Edward Monroe. 1849–1851. Trip around Cape Horn; a year's mining activity on the Mokelumne River. CSmatHi.

2458 BROWN?, William H. 1849–1895. Professional (legal) and private life; memoranda; business; expenditures; weather. MiU.

2459 BRUFF, J. Goldsborough. 1849–1850. Overland trip to Cal. by way of Oregon and Lassen trails. CSmH. *See* 4907.

2460 BUCKINGHAM, Charles Electus. 1849. Voyage from N. Y. to Chagres on the *Empire City*, the Isthmus crossing, and voyage to San Francisco on the *Panama*. CSmH.

2461 BURBANK, Augustus Ripley. 1849–1898. Overland journey to Cal.; life in Cal.; early history of Portland, Ore. OrU.

2462 BURRALL, George. 1849. A journey from Mich. overland; ends at Little Sandy on the Salt Lake road. CU-B.

2463 CAMERON, J. B. 1849. CNS. CSt.

2464 CAPLES, Mrs. James. 1849. Overland to Cal. CSfC, typescript.

2465 CARDER, James B. 1849. Daily record on board the ship *Hopewell* from R.I. via Cape Horn to San Francisco. CU-B

2466 CARSON, William M. 1849. Incomplete record of a voyage around Cape Horn from Baltimore to Cal. CU-B.

2467 CARTER, Theodore G. 1849; 1869; 1883; 1887–1911. Kept in part while he was a boy in N.Y.; other parts while engaged in fire insurance and real estate business at St. Peter, Minn. MnHi.

2468 CASTLEMAN, P. 1849–1851. A journey from Ky. to Cal., with scattered entries of experiences in the northern mines and the Sacramento valley. CU-B.

2469 CHAFEE, Zechariah. 1849. Journal on board ship *Andely Clark* from Newport, R.I., around the Horn to San Francisco. CtY.

2470 CHALMERS, Robert. 1849. Trip across the plains by way of Hasting's cutoff. CSfC.

2471 CHAMBERLIN, William E. 1849. An overland journey from Iowa, via Ft. Hall, and thence to Sacramento, Cal. CU-B.

2472 CLAFLIN, Lee. 1849–1869 (with gaps). Sabbath journal. OFH.

2473 CLAIBORNE, Dr. James W. 1849. Travel journal; voyage around Cape Horn to Cal. ViHi.

2474 CLARK, Addison S. 1849; 1850; 1852; 1854; 1855. N. Y. to Cal. around Cape Horn; passengers; conflict with ship's captain; return trip, 1852, to Panama Isthmus to N.Y.; list of Cal.-bound ships in Rio. NjR.

2475 CLARK, Amos. 1849–1854. Member of the party of founders of the community of Marquette, Mich. MiMarqHi.

2476 COGSWELL, Moses Pearson. 1849. Trip via Cape Horn in the ship *Sweden* from Boston to San Francisco in quest of gold; daily life on shipboard; observations on weather, stars, natural life. NhHi.

2477 CORNELISORN, John Henry. 1849–1850. Voyage from N.Y. to San Francisco around the Horn; scenery; ship life; prices; San Francisco scene and economy. NN.

2478 CORTLAND, Gertrude Whittier. 1849–1867. CNS. MH.

2479 COSAD, David. 1849–1850. A trip to Cal. by the overland route and life in the gold fields. CU-B.

2480 COUCH, Capt. John. 1849. Voyage of brig *Chenamus* from Newburyport to Oahu; bark *Toulon* from Oahu to Hong Kong and Manila; ship *Minstrel* from Manila to Boston; bark *Madonna* from N.Y. to San Francisco and Columbia River. Illustrations. OrHi.

2481 COWELL, William G. 1849–1856. Trip from Quebec to Head of Lakes. MnDuHi, typescript. 1849–1857. Mining interest. WSHi. 1849–1857. Primarily about copper mining at Head of the Great Lakes. WsHi, typescript.

2482 COX, Cornelius C. 1849–1850. An overland trip from Tex. to Stockton, Cal., by way of El Paso, Yuma, Warner's Ranch, Los Angeles, Santa Barbara, etc. CSmH.

2483 DANIELL, Josiah. 1849–1851. Clarke Cnty. Ga. Typescript of excerpts from an almanac diary, weather, activities, neighbors and family news, some births and deaths. Original was burned. GU.

2484 DARWIN, Charles Benjamin. 1849–1850. A trip across the plains from Council Bluffs, Iowa, to San Francisco, via Salt Lake, then back through Mexico. CSmH.

2485 DEANE, Benjamin H. 1849–1851. Journey aboard the packet *Arkansas* from N.Y. around Cape Horn to San Francisco, and subsequent experiences in the gold fields. CU-B.

2486 DECKER, Peter. 1849–1871. Overland journey to Cal., 1849; mining experiences in Yuba River area, 1850–1851; a trip east by sea and return 1853; various mountain trips, 1854–1855; journey from Portland, Ore., to Marysville, 1857, and various other trips in Cal. CU-B.

2487 DE COSTA, William H. 1849. Passage of the ship *Duxbury* to San Francisco, via Cape Horn, with the *Petrel* and the *Shark*. CSmH.

2488 DELANO, Alonzo. 1849–1851. An overland journey from St. Joseph to Cal. and life in the mines. CtY.

2489 DEMAREST, David D. 1849–1850. A trip in the bark *Norumbega* to Galveston, Tex., thence overland to Cal.; including experiences in the mines. CU-B.

2490 DeWOLF, Capt. David. 1849. Written while he was crossing the plains from Independence, Mo., to Cal., by way of Ft. Laramie. CSmH, typescript.

2491 DOUGAL, William H. 1849–1850. A voyage on the bark *Galindo* from N. Y. to Cal.; his return; original sketches. CU-B.

2492 DOYLE, Simon. 1849–1852; 1854–1856. Overland journey from Rushville, Ill., to the Feather River valley, and his stay in the mines; from Rushville to Petaluma, Cal.; record of the weather, and return from San Francisco by the Isthmus of Panama. CtY.

2493 DWINELLE, John W. 1849. Record of a journey from N.Y. to Chagres on the S.S. *Empire City*; voyage to San Francisco on the S.S. *California*; establishment as a lawyer in San Francisco. CU-B.

2494 ECCLESTON, Robert. 1849–1856. Diaries with drawings throughout of a journey to Cal. by water via Galveston, Tex., and overland through the Tucson cutoff; subsequent volumes record his experiences in the mines, Yosemite Indian uprising, and trips on sheep-buying ventures. CU-B.

2495 EDDY, Samuel. 1849–1859. 1861–1865. Religious concerns and church activity; visits and a few short trips; life in San Francisco, 1850–1852; a trip to the Sandwich Islands; contemporary politics and current events in N.Y. and the Civil War; a trip to Cuba in 1856, returning by boat up the Mississippi and Ohio rivers. NjR.

2496 ELKINTON, George. 1849–1850. Voyage from Philadelphia to the West Indies; descriptions of crops on Barbados plantations. PSC-Hi.

2497 EVANS, Burrell W. 1849. A journey from Oregon, Mo., to Sacramento with a company of gold seekers. CU-B.

2498 EVANS, George W. B. 1849–1850. Defiance Gold Hunters' Expedition to Cal. CSmH.

2499 EVERTS, F. D. 1849. A journal on and of the route to Cal. from Kingsbury, Ind.; the events of the journey and the sickness and hardships encountered. CtY.

2500 FARWELL, John V. 1849–1853. Religious moralizing; wonders of nature; some current events. ICHi.

2501 FLAGG, Hiram B. 1849. His Boston to San Francisco voyage. CSfCP.

2502 FLAGG, Josiah Foster. 1849. CNS. PHi.

2503 FOOTE, R. Adm. Andrew Hull. 1849–1851. The cruise of the U.S. brig *Perry* to the African coast, in pursuit of slave ships, with accounts of sea chases, and notes on Liberia and St. Helena. DLC. *See* 2017.

2504 FOSTER, Isaac. 1849–1850. The route to Alta, Cal.; mining on the American River; voyage from San Francisco to N.Y. CSmH; CVt.

2505 FOWLER, Stephen L. 1849–1852. A voyage to Cal. on the vessel *Brooklyn*; experiences in the northern mines; work on the Bodega ranch; life in Sonoma County. CU-B.

2506 GAY, Charles. 1849. Voyage to Cal. MH.

2507 GOODALL, Charles. 1849. A voyage around Cape Horn to San Francisco; experiences in the gold fields. CU-B. *See* 2162.

2508 GOODRICH, Adelmorn H. 1849–1850. A voyage on the steamer *Philadelphia*, across the Isthmus, and thence to San Francisco, includes personal experiences from 1840–1849. CU-B.

2509 GOULD, Charles. 1849. An overland journey from Boston to Cal. InU-Li.

2510 GOULD, Walter B. 1849. Passage on bark *Maria* from Boston to San Francisco. NHi.

2511 GRAY, Charles G. 1849. Overland passage from Independence, Mo., to San Francisco by way of Lassen's cutoff. CSmH.

2512 GREEN, James S. 1849–1850. Voyage from N. Y. to San Francisco. MH.

2513 HAINES, Asa. 1849–1865. Jayhawkers' route from Knoxville, Ill., to Rancho San Francisquito, Cal. and return via Panama. CSmH.

2514 HALE, Israel and Titus. 1849. A journey from Mo. to Cal. CSfCP.

2515 HALE, Richard Lunt. 1849? Log of a forty-niner; journal of voyage from Newburyport to San Francisco. MH.

2516 HALL, O. J. 1849. Diary of a forty-niner, extracted from his daily journal from Nauvoo to Weaverville. CSfC, typescript.

2517 HAMELIN, Joseph P., Jr. 1849–1857 (with gaps). Overland journey from Lexington to Los Angeles, and up the coast to Sacramento; journey from Leavenworth City to Ft. Laramie; year at Laramie as agent for Majors, Russell Co.; return to Leavenworth. CtY.

2518 HARDIN, Robert Stephens. 1849 and 1852. CNS. CSt.

2519 HARRIS, Benjamin Butler. 1849. A journey from Panolo County, Tex., to the gold mines, by way of Chihuahua and Sonora; reminiscences of early days in Cal. CSmH.

2520 HAUN, Catherine Margaret. 1849. A woman's trip across the plains. CSmH.

2521 HAWKS, J. D. 1849. Panama to San Francisco journey, via Lower Cal. and San Diego. CSf-CP.

2522 HAYES, Benjamin. 1849–1850. An overland journey on the Gila route to Cal. CU-B.

2523 HAYNES, Asa. 1849. Overland diary by a member of the Jayhawkers. CSmH.

2524 HERBERT, William H. 1849. A voyage from Boston to San Francisco, via Cape Horn, on the ship Elvira. CSmH.

2525 HILLIARD, Mrs. Isaac H. 1849–1850. Activities on a plantation near Vicksburg; experiences with a runaway slave; scenes witnessed while on a steamboat trip to New Orleans. LU; LSh.

2526 HIXSON, Jasper Morris. 1849. Trip from Liberty, Mo., to Cal. with wagons and mules. CHi, copy.

2527 HOVEY, John. 1849–1851. Journal of a voyage to San Francisco via the Horn; occurences in the mines. CSmH.

2528 HOWELL, Elijah P. 1849. Written on the emigrant trail by way of Lassen's cutoff. CU-B, typescript.

2529 HUGHES, Ann (Williams). 1849–1852. Daily farm chores and a few social activities. NCooHi.

2530 HUTCHINGS, James M. 1849. An overland journey from New Orleans to the Carson River. CU-B.

2531 HUTCHINSON, Dr. David. 1849. Includes medical observations. Ia-M.

2532 HUTCHINSON, Robert. 1849–1850. A voyage around the Horn in the bark Belgrade from Cherryfield, Me., to Cal. CSmH; NN, typescript.

2533 JACOBS, Enoch. 1849–1850. A voyage to Cal. via the Horn. CSmH.

2534 JEWETT, George E. 1849–1850. Written on the emigrant trail by way of Lassen's cutoff. CU-B, typescript.

2535 JOHNSON, Joseph H. 1849–1851. An overland journey to Cal. via the Oregon Trail. CSmH.

2536 JORDAN, David. 1849. An overland journey from Ft. Smith, along the southern route to Los Angeles; thence to the gold fields in northern Cal. CU-B.

2537 JOSSELYN, Amos P. 1849. Written while he was crossing the plains by way of Lassen's cutoff. CSfC.

2538 JUDGE, Timothy. 1849–1850. A journey from Salt Lake City to Cal.; experiences in the mining regions of Pleasant Valley and El Dorado Cnty.; a list of those who died en route. CU-B.

2539 KENT, George F. 1849–1850. A gold-hunting expedition to upper Cal.; from Boston to San Francisco and the diggings, via Cape Horn. CSmH.

2540 KETTELLE, William G. 1849. A voyage from Boston to San Francisco around Cape Horn in the ship Pharsalia. NNC.

2541 KIMBALL, ———. 1849–1863. Farming conditions; crop prices; social and church affairs; military movements, etc., in the lower Shenandoah valley. ViU.

2542 KING, A. D. 1849–1850. From Ark. to Cal., N. M., Rio Grande, Ariz., Los Angeles, Santa Cruz. NN.

2543 KINGSLEY, Nelson. 1849–1851. A voyage from New Haven to San Francisco on the bark Anna Reynolds, with additional entries for experiences in the mines, and departure for home. CU-B.

2544 KIRKPATRICK, Charles A. 1849–1850. Begins upon leaving Grafton, Ill., and continues while on the overland route to Cal.; a summary of experiences in Cal. CU-B.

2545 LASELLE, Stanislaus. 1849. An overland journey by way of Ft. Smith, Ark., to Santa Fe, N.M., and the Spanish Trail. CSmH.

2546 LEWIS, John F. 1849; 1852–1854. An overland journey from St. Joseph to Deer Creek, Cal.; on his farm near Glasgow, Mo., after his return from Cal. CtY.

2547 LINDSEY, Tipton. 1849. Kept while crossing plains as a member of the South Bend Cal. Joint Stock Mining and Operating Co. CU-B.

2548 LONG, Charles L'Hommedieu. 1849. An overland journey from Cincinnati to Cal. CtY.

2549 LORD, Isaac S. P. 1849–1851. Overland trip to Cal. by way of the Oregon Trail; life in the mines; return journey by way of the Isthmus of Panama to New Orleans, by Mississippi river boat to Peru, Ill., and to Aurora, Ill. CSmH.

2550 LOVE, Alexander. 1849–1852. An overland journey from Leesburg, Pa., to the Cal. mines; experiences in Cal., and the journey home by Panama. CtY.

2551 MAIN, Charles. 1849–1851. A voyage from Boston to Cal. on the ship *Leonore*; experiences in the mines and San Francisco; some drawings and descriptions of the scenery. CU-B.

2552 MANN, Henry R. 1849. Written on the emigrant trail, last half only, west from Deer Creek on the North Platte. CU, copy.

2553 MARKLE, John A. 1849. Travel of a gold digger to Cal. CU-B, photostat.

2554 MASON, Col. Leonard. 1849–1851. N. Y. to San Francisco on the bark *Belvedere*; descriptions of San Francisco and other towns, and of the various mining regions, with daily tabulation of expenses and of gold dust mined. CtY.

2555 MAY, Richard. 1849–1850. Sketches of a migrating family en route to and at San Francisco. CU-B.

2556 McCABE, ———. 1849–ca. 1882. Notes on actors, minstrels, theaters, plays, operas, circuses, concerts, readings, fire brigade, and military benefits in San Francisco. CSfC.

2557 McCARTY, John. 1849. A sea voyage to Cal. NjHi.

2558 McDOUGAL, Jane. 1849. Voyage from San Francisco to Indianapolis on S.S. *California* via the Isthmus. CSmH.

2559 MORSE, E. W. 1849–1850. A voyage from Boston to Cal. by way of the Horn on the ship *Leonore*. CSmH.

2560 MULFORD, Thomas. 1849. A description of his N. Y. to San Francisco voyage on the bark *Keoka*. CSfCP.

2561 MUNRO, George A. 1849–1850. Voyage round the Horn from Rio to San Francisco and a year's residence in Cal. mining and return by Panama. AzTP.

2562 NEVINS, Julius M. 1849. An overland journey from Wis., across the plains to Cal. CU-B.

2563 NUSBAUMER, Louis. 1849–1850. A trip to the gold fields of Cal.; from his diary, translated from the German and typed by his daughter, Bertha Nusbaumer Whitmore, 1933. CU-B, typescript.

2564 ORVIS, Andrew M. 1849–1850. An overland trip from Lake Maria, Marquette County, Wis., to Cal., and life in the mines. CtY.

2565 OVERTON, Elias P. 1849. A voyage on the bark *Keoka*, from N.Y. to San Francisco. CU-B.

2566 PARKE, Charles R. 1849–1851. A trip across the plains from Ill. to Cal. by way of Ft. Laramie and Donner Pass; mining on the Feather River. CSmH.

2567 PEARSON, Octavius C. 1849. Written while he was crossing the plains by the southern route. CU-B.

2568 PEASE, David. 1849–1850. An overland journey from Ill. by way of St. Joseph to Oregon Trail; added notes on Astoria and vicinity. CU-B.

2569 PERKINS, Elisha Douglas. 1849–1850. Sketches of a trip from Marietta, Ohio, to the valley of the Sacramento, by way of the Oregon Trail. CSmH.

2570 PIERCE, Hiram D. 1849–1851. A voyage on the steamer *Falcon* to Chagres; experiences in the Cal. mines, esp. Rensselaer Cnty. Exploring Co.; and return by way of Nicaragua. CU-B.

2571 PLUMB, Edward Lee. 1849. A voyage from N. Y. to Rio de Janeiro, and to San Francisco by way of Cape Horn. DLC.

2572 POND, Ananias Rogers. 1849–1852. Describing a trip to the Feather River "diggings"; life at the mines; farming in Solano Cnty. CSmH. *See* 2879.

2573 POWELL, H. M. T. 1849. Detailed diary of an overland journey from St. Louis, Mo., along the southern route to Cal.; return via Panama to New Orleans. CU-B.

2574 POWNALL, Joseph. 1849–1854. Letter book and journal of overland trip. CSmH.

2575 PRINDLE, Samuel L. 1849–1850. A trip across Nicaragua with an account of a passage to Panama on the brig *Esmeralda*; thence to San Francisco on the S.S. *Panama*; mining experiences on the Mokelumne River. CU-B.

2576 PRITCHARD, James Avary. 1849–1850. Trip from Petersburgh, Ky., through Mo., en route to the gold fields of Cal.; daily experiences; landscape descriptions; people encountered; prairie chickens; activities in the gold fields. MoU.

2577 PRITCHET, John. 1849–1851. An overland journey from Wayne Cnty., Ind., to Cal.; his return home via the Isthmus and New Orleans. CU-B.

2578 RAMSEY, Alexander. 1849–1854; 1860–1862; 1863; 1864. Prices of food and clothing and details of his real estate transactions. MnHi.

2579 RANDALL, Dr. Andrew. 1849. Written while he was crossing the plains, Cincinnati, Ohio, to Santa Fe. CSfC.

2580 RANDALL, William Edgar. 1849–1850. A voyage from Boston to San Francisco on the ship *Hannibal*. CU-B.

2581 REGAL, Eli. 1849–1854. Establishing churches in new communities; speeches in Mich., Ohio, Iowa, Wis.; financial records; records of Baptist church duties and costs of journeys. MiU.

2582 REID, Thomas. 1849. A voyage from Boston to San Francisco, via Cape Horn. CU-B.

2583 RICHARDS, Samuel K. 1849–1854. Surveying and construction of Madison, Indianapolis, and Lafayette Railroad (now part of the Big Four-New York Central). InLHi.

2584 RICKS, Caspar S. 1849. A journey from Santa Fe, along the southern route, ending before the party reached Los Angeles. CU-B.

2585 ROBINSON, R. B. 1849. Overland journey to Cal. CLob.

2586 ROWLAND, William. 1849. Journal of a voyage from N. Y. to Cal. by bark *Isabel*, by a member of the New Brunswick, N.J., and Cal. Mining and Trading Co. expedition. NjR.

2587 ROYAL, James Henry Bascom. 1849–1853; 1855. Early sectarian education in Ore. by a teacher at the Umpqua Academy. OrU, photostat.

2588 SAXON, William M. 1849. A voyage from N. Y. to San Francisco in the ship *Brooklyn*, via Cape Horn. CSmH.

2589 SCARR, Mrs. F. J. 1849–1850. A voyage from Cleveland to San Francisco. OClWHi.

2590 SCHAEFFER, Luther Melanchthon. 1849–1852. Journal on the *Flavius* from N. Y. to San Francisco; the winter of 1850 in San Francisco; experiences in the mines. CtY.

2591 SCHNECWEISS, Franz Sales Maximillian Ignatz Aloise. 1849–1855. Kept by him as an Austrian soldier, refugee, and American resident; reminiscences, family biographies, etc. NjR.

2592 SEAMAN, W. Valentine. 1849. A voyage on board the bark *Susan* from N. Y. to San Francisco around Cape Horn via Rio de Janeiro; includes record of the meetings of the Aurelian Assoc. CtY.

2593 SEARLS, Niles. 1849. An overland journey from St. Louis, Mo., to Cal. in wagon train; list of members who died on the journey. CU-B.

2594 SHEARER, ———. 1849. A journey with the Grinwell family and H. Stickney, from Salt Lake City via Hastings' and Lassen's cutoffs; thence along the southern route to the Mohave river. CU-B.

2595 SHERMAN, George. 1849–1853. A voyage from N. Y. to San Francisco, via the Isthmus, and on to Astoria, Ore. CSmH.

2596 SHILLABER, Benjamin Penhallow. 1849–1851 (with gaps). Various accounts; an essay; verse. NNC.

2597 SHOMBRE, Henry J. 1849. An overland journey to Cal. KHi.

2598 SMITH, Anna Maria. 1849. Religious outlook; love affair; other personal reflections. NjR.

2599 SMITH, John Wilson. 1849–1857. Work in the patent office in Washington until 1849; meeting with President Taylor; descriptions of Washington of that time. RHi.

2600 SMITH, Rev. Whitefoord. 1849; 1853–1863. Brief notes relative generally to Methodist pastoral activities. NcD.

2601 SNOW, Joseph Chester. 1849–1851. A voyage from Boston to San Francisco; experiences in the southern mines. CU-B.

2602 SPADER, James Voorhees. 1849. Voyage from N. Y. to Cal.; stock certificates of the New Brunswick and California Mining and Trading Company of which he was secretary. NjR.

2603 STAPLES, David. 1849. An overland journey from Mass. to Cal., via the South Pass route. CU-B.

2604 STARR, Franklin. 1849. An overland journey from Alton, Ill., to the gold fields in Cal. CU-B.

2605 STEUBEN, William N. 1849. An overland journey from Neb., across the plains to the gold fields in Cal. CU-B.

2606 STONE, John M. 1849. Cape Horn voyage in the S.S. *Robert Bowne*, with a list of the passengers and crew. CSmH.

2607 STORER, Daniel M. 1849–1905. A trip from Me. to Ill.; life in Stillwater and Shakopee; activities as carpenter, storekeeper, fiddler, and investor. MnHi, microfilm.

2608 STOWELL, Levi. 1849. A trip across the Isthmus. CSt.

2609 STUART, Levi B. 1849–1851. A voyage from Bridgewater on the bark *Anna Reynolds* to Cal. via the Horn, and the return on the *Talma*; ends en route to Panama. CtY.

2610 STURDIVANT, Henry. 1849. A voyage to Cal. via the Isthmus of Panama. CSmH.

2611 SWAIN, H. 1849. A voyage on the bark *Belvedere*, with a company of seventy-four gold seekers from N. Y. to San Francisco. CU-B.

2612 SWAIN, William. 1849. An overland trip from Youngstown, N.Y., to Feather River Valley, Cal. CtY.

2613 SWAN, James G. 1849–1850. A voyage from Mass., including miscellaneous accounts as teacher, journalist, and lawyer. CU-B. *See* 3327?

2614 TATE, Col. James. 1849. A trip to Cal. MoU.

2615 TAYLOR, Augustus FitzRandolph. 1849. A voyage from N.Y. to Cal, by bark *Isabel*, by a member of the New Brunswick, N.J., and California Mining and Trading Company expedition. NjR.

2616 TAYLOR, John. 1849. A voyage on the vessel *Orpheus* from N. Y. to San Francisco. CU-B.

2617 TAYLOR, Joseph Wright. 1849–1862. Travels in Europe, etc. PHC.

2618 TAYLOR, Sereno. 1849; 1851–1852; 1854–1858; 1862–1863. Weather; school affairs; religious matters and personal observations. LU-Ar.

2619 TAYLOR, William P. 1849–1855. Account book and diary. PHi.

2620 THOMPSON, George W. 1849–1850. Voyage around the Horn to Cal.; interesting account of San Francisco; return east by Panama because of illness. AzTP.

2621 THURMAN, David. 1849–1851. Daily record in the life of a plain man living in northern Ga.; current prices of food, merchandise, etc. TC, typescript.

2622 TIFFANY, P. C. 1849–1851. A journey from Mount Pleasant, Iowa; overland to Cal.; experiences at the mines; the voyage home by the Isthmus. CtY.

2623 WEED, L. M. 1849–1850. A journey to Cal., by steamer to Galveston, Tex., and overland to Los Angeles and the mines by the southern route; mines and weather. CtY.

2624 WILLIAMS, Albert. 1849. Notebook of a voyage to San Francisco on the ship *Crescent City*. CSmH.

2625 WILLIAMS, Charles H. 1849–1850. A voyage to San Francisco in the ship *Pacific* via Cape Horn. CSmH.

2626 WILLIAMS, F. 1849–1850. Kept on a voyage to Cal. on the bark *Domingo*; experiences in the mines and in San Francisco. CU-B.

2627 WILLIAMSON, Robert S. 1849. His experiences with the U.S. topological engineers recording exploring trips in the northern Sierras, chiefly along the Lassen cutoff for a possible railroad route. CU-B.

2628 WILLIS, Edward J. 1849. Travel from Independence, Mo., to Cal., across the Plains. CtY.

2629 WINCHELL, Horace. 1849–1850. A trip to Cal. by schooner around the Horn, giving an account of a stay at Valparaiso; conditions in Cal. during the gold rush; the return trip. MnHi.

2630 WOOD, Joseph Warren. 1849–1853. Overland trip. CSmH.

2631 [WOODHOUSE, Commodore Samuel?] 1849. Expedition under Capt. L. Sitgreaves and Lt. I. C. Woodruff, to establish a boundary between the Creek and Cherokee Indians. PHi. *See* 1479, 3393?

2632 WOODS, James. 1849–1882. Including voyage around the Horn. CSmH.

2633 WOODWARD, E. M. 1849–1850. Kept by an unsuccessful gold miner, including his return voyage via the Isthmus of Panama. CU-B.

2634 YOUNG, Sheldon. 1849–1850. Diary of the Jayhawkers' journey from Joliet, Ill., to Rancho San Francisquito, Cal. CSmH.

2635 ANON. 1850–1873; 1881–1886. The congregation of the Moravian Church in Philadelphia. NcWsM.

2636 ANON. 1850. A trip from Utica, N.Y., to San Francisco via Isthmus. CSmH.

2637 ALLEN, Joseph N. 1850–1851; 1870. Record of a voyage to Nicaragua and return to N. Y. on the S.S. *Prometheus*; part time in company with Cornelius Vanderbilt; diary of a trip to Cal. in 1870 with visits to Yosemite, Lake County, Grass Valley, and Donner Lake. CU-B.

2638 AMES, Peramus Green. 1850–1864. Journal of overland trip and account book. CSmH.

2639 BABER, George Francis Burleigh. 1850–1853. Journal of cruises on U.S. ships *John Adams*, 1850–1851; *Dale*, 1851–1852; *Germantown*, 1852–1853. List of officers of *John Adams;* day-by-day account of cruises in detail. GU.

2640 BARNARD, Daniel Dewey. 1850–1853. Kept by ambassador to Prussia. N.

2641 BARRINGTON, Alexander R. 1850. Voyage from Panama to San Francisco on bark *Paoli*; northern mines; return to Panama on steamer *Antelope*; includes a trip from Sacramento to Nevada City. CSmH.

2642 BARTHOLOMEW, Jacob. 1850. Travel overland from St. Joseph, Mo., to a point on Humboldt River in present state of Nev.; notes on route; prices. InU.

2643 BARTON, George Washington. 1850. Voyage from N. Y. to San Francisco in the *Elsinore*, under Capt. Thomas S. Conden. PHi.

2644 BEALE, Jane B. 1850–1862. Including a detailed description of the capture of Fredericksburg and the 1862 campaign in northern Va. ViU.

2645 BERCKMAN, Prosper. 1850. "Voyage en Amérique." New York, Philadelphia, Charleston, S. C., Augusta, Ga., Rome, Ga., tours Ga., describes towns, Tallulah and Toccoa Falls, plantations he visits; goes back to Philadelphia, Baltimore, New Orleans, and out to the middle west and back to the East. In French. GU.

2646 BISHOP, Leander H. 1850. Diary of a gold miner in Placer Cnty., Cal. CU-B.

2647 BLOOD, James A. 1850. On the overland trail from Peoria, Ill., to Sacramento, Cal. CSfC, typescript.

2648 BLOOM, Henry A. 1850. Written on Overland Trail by way of Hastings' cutoff. CSfC, typescript.

2649 BOURNE, Ezra. 1850–1852. His overland journey from Oxford, Ohio, through Mo. and across the plains to Cal.; includes many of his experiences in the gold fields. CU-B.

2650 BROWNING, Orville Hickman. 1850–1881. Ill. and national politics; social and business affairs. IHi.

2651 BURROWS, Silas Enoch. 1850–1851. Travels in France, England, Spain, Germany, and So. America. CtMyMM.

2652 CAMPBELL, James. 1850–1852. A journey to Cal.; mining in Nevada City; farming in Santa Clara; return to N.Y. via Panama. CU-B.

2653 CHAPMAN, A. H. 1850. A trip to Cal. gold mines by way of the Oregon Trail. MnHi.

2654 CHAPMAN, W. W. 1850. Overland journey and account book. CSmH.

2655 CLARK, Joseph S. 1850–1851. Written in N. Y. NNC.

2656 COGWIN, N. A. 1850. Written on emigrant trail. CSfC.

2657　COOL, P. 1850–1852. Experiences in the mines and in San Francisco. CU-B. *See* 2764?

2658　CRANDALL, Ethan. 1850–? An overland trip from Ill. to Cal. MiHuHi.

2659　CROWELL, Dr. John. 1850–1851. CNS. MHa.

2660　CULBERTSON, Thaddeus A. 1850. A trip by steamer and overland from St. Louis; stops made; purchase of additional equipment; scenery; buffalo hunts; visits with trappers and traders; ride through prairie fire; travels with Indians. CUL.

2661　CUNNINGHAM, George A. 1850–1875. Detailed weather record; local items and those of surrounding towns; world events. MFiHi.

2662　DAGGY, Elias. 1850. An expedition from Green Castle, Ind., to Cal. MnHi, microfilm.

2663　DOWELL, Benjamin Franklin. 1850. Trip by ox team from St. Joseph, Mo., to Cal.; the route and daily mileage; records the deaths in his company; conditions as to grazing, game, water, supplies, etc.; continued in Ore.; Indian War. CtY; CU-B. *See* 3048.

2664　DRAPER, ———. 1850–1851. A journey through Palestine, Egypt, etc. MH.

2665　EDGERLY, Rev. David Leighton. 1850–1891. Ministry in numerous towns near New Durham, N.H. NhHi.

2666　ELLSWORTH, Stukely. 1850. Travel through N. Y., Conn., R. I., and Mass. InU-Li.

2667　FERRELL, Thomas J. 1850–1853. The cruise of the U.S. ship *Germantown* on the coast of Africa. NNC.

2668　FRUSH, William H. 1850. Journey across the plains to Ore., with observations on the country passed through; details of the route; information and advice to emigrants on the overland trail. CtY.

2669　GAINES, Archibald K. 1850–1858. The voyage of Gov. John P. Gaines and his family from N.Y. to San Francisco on the U.S. store ship *Supply*, and from San Francisco to Astoria, Ore. Terr., on the sloop of war *Falmouth*; with a summary of their life in Ore., his father's career as governor, and death. CtY; OrHi, copy.

2670　GAYLORD, Orange. 1850–1851; 1853. Journey from Ill. to Cal.; voyage to Ore. from San Francisco; return to Ill. via Panama and N. Y., and overland journey to Ore. OrU, typescript.

2671　GODDARD, E. 1850? CNS. NhHi.

2672　GORGAS, Solomon A. 1850–1851. From St. Joseph, Mo., to Placerville, Cal., and return by way of the Isthmus. CSmH.

2673　GROW, S. L. 1850. The overland march from Clinton, Wis., to Ft. Laramie, and the formation of the Beloit Company. CtY.

2674　GWYN, Hugh A. 1850–1851. By a young man; family life at his home; and his experiences at an unnamed college. NcU.

2675　HARDY, Francis A. 1850. Journal from Piqua, Ohio, to Auburn, Cal. CtY.

2676　HELMAN, Abel D. 1850; 1851; 1858–1859; 1883–1892. Voyage to Cal. and to Ore.; trip from Ore. to Ohio and return; weather data; journal of "Mountain Rangers," Ore. Militia. OrU, typescript and photostat.

2677　HILL, John Birney. 1850. Overland journey from St. Joseph to Cal.; comments on the soil and vegetation; accessibility of water, fuel, and forage; the weather. CtY.

2678　HINDS, Rev. T. W. 1850. Written on the emigrant trail. CU-B, typescript.

2679　HOADLEY, Milo. 1850–1852. Journal and field note books, probably in San Francisco. CSmH.

2680　JACKSON, Isaac P. 1850–1857. CNS. PHi.

2681　JAY, Mahalah Pearson. 1850. CNS. InRE.

2682　JOHNSON, R. Adm. Phillip C. 1850–1859. His navy service. WaS.

2683　KEARNY, Philip. 1850–1851. Overland trip from San Francisco to Vancouver, and return. OrU, photostat.

2684　KILGORE, William H. 1850. A journey from Iowa to Placerville and in the mines. CU-B.

2685　KIRKPATRICK, T. W. 1850–1871. CNS. FDS.

2686　KRILL, Abram. 1850. An overland journey from Independence, Mo., to Weaverville, Cal. CtY.

2687　KRISE, Mrs. Rebecca. 1850? CNS. MdHi.

2688　LANE, S. A. 1850. Written while he was crossing the plains. CU-B, photostat.

2689　LEONARD, H. C. 1850–1851. Weather conditions and the arrival and departure of vessels. NN and OrHi.

2690　LITTLETON, Micajah. 1850. On the emigrant trail from Independence, Mo., to Cal. CSfC; CHi, copy.

2691　LOCKE, Samuel. 1850. Life and hardships of mining in Cal. and on return home via Panama. NN.

2692　LONDONER, Wolfe. 1850–1860. A voyage around Cape Horn, 1850; life in San Francisco; interim in N.Y. and St. Louis; thence to Colo. in 1860. CU-B.

2693　LOVELAND, Cyrus Clark. 1850. Crossing the plains. CSfC.

2694　[LOWELL, John Amory]. 1850–1852. Trip abroad. MH. *See* 1492.

2695　LUELLING, Seth. 1850–1853. Overland journey to Ore.; information on early fruit culture in Ore.; several ballads and songs. OrU, typescript. 1850–1875. Miscellaneous daily accounts of weather. OrHi.

2696　MACLAY, Charles. 1850–1851. CNS. CSmH.

2697 MAYNARD, David Swinson. 1850. An overland journey from Cincinnati via the Platte and Snake rivers and the Oregon Trail, to Ore. and Puget Sound. CSmH.

2698 McBRIDE, W. S. 1850. A trip overland from Goshen, Ind., to Salt Lake City. CSmH.

2699 McFARLAN, John R. 1850. Voyage to Cal. via the Horn. CSmH.

2700 McKINSTRY, Byron N. 1850–1852. A journey from Ill. to Cal.; experiences in the mines and return to Mass. via Panama. CU-B.

2701 MERRIMON, Augustus Summerfield. 1850–1851; 1853. Personal. NcU.

2702 MILLINGTON, D. 1850–1851. Experiences in the Cal. mines. CU-B.

2703 MORRIS, Anna Maria Jackson De Camp. 1850–1858. Trip West over the Santa Fe Trail in 1850 to Santa Fe; life in N. M. ViU.

2704 NEWCOMB, Silas. 1850–1851. Overland trip from Darien, Wis., to Placerville, Cal., via St. Joseph, Mo., Salt Lake City, and Hastings' cutoff; then to San Francisco and by boat to Ore. CtY; CSmH, facsimile.

2705 NEWSON, George. 1850. CNS. WBaHi.

2706 NOYES, George F. 1850–1855. A journey on the S.S. *Chagres* from N.Y. to San Francisco via the Isthmus, including experiences in Cal. and a trip to Egypt. CU-B.

2707 OWENS, Isaac. 1850–1851. Diary of overland trip. CSmH. *See* 4978.

2708 PARRISH, Susan (Thompson). 1850. Westward from Muscatine, Iowa, to Cal., by way of Santa Fe and the Spanish Trail. CSmH.

2709 PAYNE, William Harold. 1850–1904. CNS. TNJ-P.

2710 PETERS, Henry Hunter. 1850. Trip from Cal. to Ore., from Vancouver to Salem and back to Astoria; descriptions of Portland, Oregon City, Clackamas, and Salem. OrHi, copy. 1850–1871. Trips from N.Y. city to San Francisco and Ore.; farm diary. NN.

2711 PETTIGREW, James Johnston. 1850–1851. Political. NcU.

2712 PITTS, R. H. 1850–1862. CNS. NcU. *See* 3379.

2713 QUESENBERRY, William Minor. ca. 1850. CNS. NcD.

2714 REDINGTON, Edward S. 1850. Kept on a trip from Cold Springs, Wis., to Cal. MnHi, microfilm.

2715 ROEDER, Henry. 1850–1877. Diaries and letters to and from Mrs. Henry Roeder (Ethel Austin Roeder). WaU, typescript. *See* 3264.

2716 ROTHWELL, William Renfro. 1850. An overland trip from Mo. to Cal. CtY.

2717 SANGER, Lewis. 1850. A voyage from Boston to San Francisco via Cape Horn. CSmH.

2718 SCHOLFIELD, Nathan. 1850. Journal of the Klamath Exploring Expedition. Or.

2719 SCOTT, Abigail Jane (later Mrs. Ben C. Duniway). 1850. Journal from Illinois to Ore. Or.

2720 SHAFFER, Dr. ——. 1850–1912. Names of patients; weather conditions; medicine prescribed; activities as an entomologist; home life and activities; experiences as a newspaper correspondent (in English and Latin). IaKe.

2721 SHARP, Rev. John. 1850. Penciled notes about trip across plains. CSfC.

2722 SHIELDS, James G. 1850. Trip from St. Joseph to Sacramento; details of the route, camping places, and incidents on the way. CtY.

2723 SHINN, John R. 1850. Kept while he was crossing the plains to Cal. CU-B.

2724 SHOEMAKER, Dr. Nathan. 1850–1863. Spiritual introspection by a physician. PSC-Hi.

2725 SHUMWAY, Robert Garrick. 1850. Voyage from San Francisco to Panama en route to N.Y. on board the bark *Clarissa*, "the longest passage known," with boredom, inconvenience, and some shipboard sickness. NjR.

2726 SMITH, Charles W. 1850. Written while he was crossing the plains from Weston, Mo., to Weber Creek, Cal. CHi.

2727 SMITH, George W. 1850. Journey from Bowling Green, Ohio, to Cal. and experiences in Cal. gold mines. MH.

2728 SMITH, Joseph R. 1850. Trip taken through Tex. in 1850. OkU.

2729 STANDISH, Zachariah. 1850? Private memorandum book, mainly family record. MBNEH.

2730 STAUDER, John A. 1850. A trip from La Grange, Mo., to the gold fields of Cal., describing the route taken, miles traveled, the condition of grass, water, and wood, weather conditions, prices of articles purchased, rivers crossed, other wagon trains met, and the number of graves and Indians encountered. MoU.

2731 STEELE, Andrew. 1850–1851. A voyage from N. Y. to Port Lavaca, Tex.; an overland journey to Mazatlan; a voyage to San Francisco; his experiences in Marysville, Cal. CU-B.

2732 STEVENS, William Arnold. 1850–1859. Largely concerned with religion and the Baptist Church; diary by student at Baptist Theological Seminary, etc. InHi. *See* 3834.

2733 STIMSON, Fancher. 1850. Overland trip to Cal. by way of the Platte River and South Pass. CSmH.

2734 STINE, Henry Atkinson. 1850. Overland trip from St. Louis to Sacramento. CSfC, transcript.

2735 STOCKTON, N. 1850. A prospector and miner in the Cal. gold fields. CU-B.

2736 STOCKTON, N. H. 1850. A trip from the states to Cal. CU-B, typescript.

2737 SULLIVAN, Dr. Amos H. n.d. [between 1850 and 1939]. CNS. MoU.

2738 THOMPSON, William P. 1850; 1852. Overland journey from St. Joseph to Sacramento, and his return journey from Nevada City to the East by the Isthmus and New Orleans. CtY.

2739 THORNTON, John Wingate. 1850–1876. Mentions George Folsom, J. S. Pike, Henry Dearborn, Henry Giles, Prof. Thomas C. Upham, and other eminent men associated with Me.; family photographs pasted on the leaves and information of a genealogical character. MBAt.

2740 TOMPKINS, Edward Alexander. 1850. Expedition to Cal. via St. Louis, Independence, Salt Lake, Humboldt River, Carson's Valley, and Fremont's south pass of the Sierra Nevada. CSmH. CHi, copy.

2741 VROOM, Peter Dumont. 1850–1872. CNS. MiD.

2742 WADE, Thomas H. 1850–1852. CNS. LNHT.

2743 WARD, Rev. Henry Dana. 1850–1857. Kept by rector of St. Judes P. E. Church, N. Y. city; church sources; social and public events; opinions on slavery. NN.

2744 WATSON, Robert. 1850. A trip up the Mississippi River from Galena to St. Paul. MnHi.

2745 WATTS, John W. 1850. Written while he was crossing the plains. CHi.

2746 WHEELER, George Nelson. 1850–1851. A trip from Hudson, Ohio, to Marysville, Cal., via the Ore. and the Cal. trail; life in the gold diggings near Auburn. CSmH.

2747 WHITING, C. E. 1850–1852. A journey from Huntsville, Ala., to Cal. by way of the Isthmus; life in the mines. CSmH, microfilm.

2748 WHITMAN, Abial. 1850. An overland journey from Rochester, Wis., to Georgetown, Cal., and a brief stay in the mines. CtY.

2749 WOLCOTT, Lucian M. 1850–1851. Journal of overland trip. CSmH.

2750 ZIEBER, Albert. 1850. Overland journey from Peoria, Ill., to South Pass. OrU.

2751 ZIEBER, Eugenia (later Mrs. Asabel Bush). 1850–1851. Journal from Ill. to Ore.; record of religious experience. Or.

2752 ANON. 1851. Trip to Europe: England, France, Switzerland, Germany, etc. NN.

2753 ANON. 1851–1868. Kept by members of the United Society of Believers; events in the Shaker colony; first operation of the printing press; resumption of public meetings; resumption of the use of imported tea and coffee. KyLoF.

2754 ANON. 1851–1884. Kept by members of the United Society of Believers; farming operations with notes on events in the colony. KyLoF.

2755 ANON. 1851. Returning East from the gold fields of Cal. MoU.

2756 AKEHURST, Amelia Jane (Jennie). 1851; 1855–1871. New Hartford, Conn; Covington, Ga; New Haven, Conn; Oxford, Ga; Atlanta, Ga. Minute description of day to day life of a family of moderate means; school teacher and music teacher; married a printer. Prices of commodities, what they ate, wore, did. GU.

2757 ANDERSON, ———? 1851. Kept while he mined in El Dorado Cnty., Cal. CU-B.

2758 ARMSTRONG, William G. 1851–1888. Political, social, and cultural affairs in the U.S. PHi.

2759 BEESON, Welborn. 1851–1852; 1853–1856. Describes rural life in Ill. and Ore. OrU, typescript.

2760 BOWEN, James E. 1851. Crossing the plains from Wis. to the gold mining area in Cal. CU-B.

2761 BYERS, Dr. Albert Gallatin. 1851–1890. CNS. OHi.

2762 CLARK, Adaline C. (Mrs. H. S. Davis). 1851; 1854–1858; 1860–1861; 1865–1868; 1871; 1874–1886; 1891–1892; 1894–1898; 1900–1911. Everyday events. IHi.

2763 COFFIN, Alexander Hamilton. 1851–1862. CNS. NPHi. See 4408.

2764 COOL, Peter Y. 1851–1852. Mining and Methodism in and near Amador Cnty., Cal. CSmH. See 2657?

2765 COPLEY, Jane Helen (Hathaway). 1851–1857. Household duties; a few costs listed. MiU. See 2913.

2766 COTTEN, Charles B. 1851–1852. A business trip through Middle Atlantic, Mid-West, and the South, visiting principally the county seats and describing the country, the cities and towns, the natural resources, industries, agricultural products, the people and customs, etc. InU-Li.

2767 CRANSTONE, Susan M. 1851–1859. Overland journals from St. Joseph, Mo., to Ore. CU-B.

2768 CROSWELL, Charles M. 1851. Daily events. MiU.

2769 DALY, Charles Patrick. 1851. N. Y. judge's stay in England: London sights and personalities. NN. See 3887, 4339, 4476, 4920.

2770 DAVIS, Hannah. 1851–1859. Written from the ages of 12 to 19 years. OHi.

2771 DICKSON, Rev. Cyrus. 1851–1853. Daily affairs; local events during his ministry. PWW.

2772 EPPES, Richard, IV. 1851–1854; 1858–1861; 1865–1896. CNS. ViU.

2773 FAUCETT, George. 1851–1862. Family life, quarrels, etc. InHi, microfilm.

2774 FOOTE, H. B. 1851–1855. Mined from San Francisco to Ore.; farm and family life. AzTP.

2775 FORBY, George. 1851–1879. A voyage to Cal. via the Isthmus. CSmH.

2776 FOSTER, Thomas. 1851. CNS. MnHi.

2777 [FREASE], Mrs. Celia Pumpelly (Ricker). 1851–1852. Spent winter in New Orleans with her cousin, Leontine Ricker; mostly feminine chats about family, friends, activities. OCUHi.

2778 GORDON, Robert. 1851; 1853; 1857. CNS. Ms-Ar.

2779 HADLEY, Emilia A. 1851. Trip from Galesburg, Ill., to Oregon City. OrU, typescript.

2780 HAMPTON, Sarah Ann. 1851. Kept while she was an Earlham College student. InRE.

2781 JENNINGS, Oliver. 1851. An overland trip from Oregon City to Vancouver and by the Columbia River and Blue Mountains to Ft. Boise, Ft. Hall, and Great Salt Lake City. CtY.

2782 JOHNSON, J. L. 1851. At the age of 16 as he crossed the plains from Mo. to Ore. OrFP. *See* next item?

2783 JOHNSON, John Lawrence. 1851. The overland journey from Mt. Pleasant, Iowa, to Ore. CtY; Or, microfilm. *See* previous item?

2784 JOHNSON, Mrs. Walter Rogers. 1851. A trip to Europe with her husband, when he was commissioner to the International Exhibition at the Crystal Palace in London; descriptions; sightseeing trips in London and Hamburg; a stay in Wales. DLC.

2785 LAY, Julia Anna Hartness. 1851–1878. Family; religious, social, and public events; holidays. NN.

2786 LEWIS, John N. 1851–1855. An overland journey from Ind., via Mo., thence to Oregon City. CU-B.

2787 LOCKE, Elbridge G. 1851–1853. Experiences in Concord, N.H., 1851; a voyage on the vessel *Georgia* to the Isthmus, and on to San Francisco on the steamer *California*; thence to Knights Ferry to mine; his return to San Francisco. CU-B.

2788 MEEK, Samuel Mills. 1851–1855. His travels from Tuscaloosa via Columbus, to the Choctaw Agency, Oktibbeha Cnty., Miss., where he taught school; includes descriptions of weddings, accounts of political rallies at Starkville, Miss., a debating society, his reading of current literature, camp meetings, Masons, and frequent comments concerning girls. NcD.

2789 MERCER, George A. 1851–1860; 1862–1865. Hunting and war diary. NcU.

2790 MORAN, Benjamin. 1851; 1857–1875. Service in London at the American legation and in Portugal as minister. DLC.

2791 MYERS, A. 1851. A trip to the Skiskowit mine and other copper mines near Lake Superior. PHi.

2792 OWEN, John. 1851–1865. CNS. MtHi. *See* 4048.

2793 PASSMORE (Pasmore), Pennock. 1851–1852. Traveling by horse and carriage; description of log meeting house; New Garden Boarding School. PSC-Hi.

2794 PEASE, Rufus F. 1851–1857 (gaps). Journal of a voyage in the ship *Pacific* of Fair Haven; remarks on board the bark *Robert Morison* of New Bedford. MH.

2795 PIKE, Robert, Jr. 1851–1858. CNS. MnHi.

2796 RANK, William. 1851–1881. Agriculture; local politics; social events, Pa. PLeHi.

2797 RASLOTT, William. 1851. His journey from England to America. WRacHr.

2798 ROGERS, William H. 1851–1857. Relating principally to school work. InU-Li.

2799 RUCKER, Dr. Thomas Holloway. 1851. Acrostic and portion of diary. InHi.

2800 RUFFIN, Edmund, Jr. 1851–1862; 1866–1873. Plantations in Va. NcU.

2801 SCHULTE, J. 1851. A trip from San Francisco to the Feather River mines and return (in both German and English). CU-B.

2802 SHARPLESS, Phebe Ann. 1851; 1853–1855. Descriptions of Pa. farm and social life; comments on books and lectures; description of trip to N. Y. and the Crystal Palace Exhibition. CtY-Art.

2803 SHELDON, Henry B. 1851–1854. A Methodist minister; begins at Ohio Univ.; trip to Cal. via the Isthmus, 1852; experiences on circuit in Cal. CU-B.

2804 SMITH, Mary Caroline. 1851; 1852. Voyage from Philadelphia to China and stay at Shanghai. OHi.

2805 TLILTHLOW, ———? 1851–1859. CNS. WaU, original; DLC, photostat.

2806 WALDRON, Daniel G. 1851. A voyage from N. H. to Chagres on the S.S. *Ohio*, via the Isthmus. CU-B.

2807 WHITNEY, Mrs. Helen Barstow. 1851. CNS. WWauHi.

2808 ZIEBER, John S. 1851. Travel from Peoria, Ill., to Linn City, Ore. Terr.; describes conditions and prices of supplies. InU-Li.

2809 ANON. 1852–1863. A trip around Cape Horn to Ore. OrFP.

2810 ANON. 1852. Written while the writer crossed the plains; discovered between walls of firehouse on B Street, Virginia City, Nev. CU-B, copy.

2811 ADAMS, Mrs. Cecilia Emily McMillan. 1852. Journey from Mo. to Ore. OrHi.

2812 ALLEN, W. T. 1852. Trip from Leominster, Mass., to Savannah, New Orleans, Niagara, Albany, N. Y. city, Boston. NN. *See* 2427.

2813 ANABLE, Henry. 1852–1854. An overland journey from Wis., across the plains to the gold fields in Cal. CU-B.

2814 ANDREWS, D. B. 1852. An overland journey from Ind. to Cal. CtY.

2815 ASHLEY, Algeline (Jackson). 1852–1853. Crossing the plains by way of Salt Lake City. CSmH; CSd.

2816 BAILEY, Mary Stuart. 1852. Written while she crossed the plains, Ohio to Stockton, Cal. CSmH.

2817 BAKER, William B. 1852. Written while he crossed the plains. CSfC, typescript.

2818 BARBER, Peter J. 1852. A journey to Cal. via the Isthmus of Panama. CU-B.

2819 BARTLETT, John Russell. 1852. Crossing the desert from San Diego to Camp Yuma, on the Colorado River. CSmH.

2820 BASKERVILLE, William. 1852–1853; 1861–1864. A journey from the Rio Grande to Cal. by the southern route and back by Tejón Pass and Mohave Desert toward Albuquerque; scattered entries about the weather, crops, and farming conditions; a journey from Peralta, via Albuquerque, Las Vegas, Pawnee Rock, Council Grove, to Warrensburg, Mo. CtY, typescript.

2821 BEACH, Charles H. 1852. Trip from Whitehall, N.Y., to Cincinnati by boat and train; surveys ten miles of road through White River valley; names of party and pay; hotels, houses, countryside. InHi.

2822 BERESFORD, J. H. 1852. An overland trip to Cal. from Independence, Mo. OHi.

2823 BISHOP, Edward. 1852–1865. Athens, Ga.; garden and farm diary; also contains memoranda, recipes, accounts. GU.

2824 BLAKELY, Sara A. (later Mrs. James W. Hubbard). 1852–1854. CNS. ICHi.

2825 BOGERT, William. 1852–1893. Religious; personal experiences and observations; social and welfare problems; current affairs, e.g., Civil War. NjR.

2826 BOINEST, Thaddeus Street. 1852–1870. His work as farmer, official of Newberry College, and Lutheran minister. ScU.

2827 BOOTH, Joseph W. 1852–1853. Mining operations in the "Northern Mines"; Methodist church; wild life; digger Indians, etc. CU-B.

2828 BRADLEY, Henry. 1852. An overland trip to Cal. from Elkhorn, Wis., to the headwaters of the Humboldt River; describes the country, road conditions, camp sites, flowers and wildlife, Mormons and others. CtY.

2829 BREWSTER, Charles G. 1852–1859. His work for the Boston and New York Central Railroad, the Illinois Central; his claim in Sibley Cnty., Minn., and steamboat travel on the Minnesota and Mississippi rivers. MnHi, microfilm.

2830 BROWN, Charles Lafayette. 1852–1860. Kept while he was in Cal. MiD.

2831 BUDD, Daniel H. 1852–1856. Trip to Cal. and sojourn there. MH.

2832 BURROUGHS, George H. 1852–1853. Study in schools in Jackson, Tenn., and Bloomfield, N.J. NjR.

2833 CHADWICK, Samuel. 1852. Trip from Marshall, Wis., to Cal.; travel events and conditions; also memoranda and portion of diary kept in N. Y. state. NN.

2834 CLARK, John Hawkins. 1852. Written while he crossed the plains. CSfC, copy.

2835 CLARK, Perkins Kirkland. 1852. Partially written in shorthand by a pastor of the Congregational church in Chester Village, Mass.; visit to Saratoga. NjR.

2836 CLARKE, James A. 1852–1854. Journey from N. Y. to Cal. on the steamer *Sierra Nevada* to Chagres, and the steamer *New Orleans* to San Francisco; notes on quartz mining in Nevada Cnty.; account of a trip east on the steamer *Uncle Sam* as far as Grey Town, Nicaragua. CSmH.

2837 CORNELL, George. 1852. A voyage from N. Y. to Cal. via the Isthmus. CtY.

2838 CORNING, Robert Nesmith. 1852–1862; 1863–1865. Political activities; N.H. militia; appointed postmaster at Concord, N.H., by Pres. Lincoln. NhHi.

2839 CRANE, Addison Moses. 1852. A trip from Lafayette, Ind., to Volcano, Cal., via Ft. Laramie, Salt Lake City, and the Humboldt River. CSmH.

2840 CUSTER, Elizabeth Bacon. 1852–? CNS. CtY.

2841 DALLAM, Richard. 1852–1864. Journey over the trail from Tex.; Cal. and Ore.; weather; miles covered; details of the trail and camps; places visited; people met; the Vigilante excitement in San Francisco. CtY.

2842 DANIEL, William T. 1852–1885. Tobacco market; plowing methods; farming; family and daily and social life. ViU.

2843 DODSON, John F. 1852. Overland journey from Moline, Ill., to Cal. MtHi, typescript.

2844 DOYLE, Chloe A. (Terry) (Mrs. Reuben Doyle). 1852. CNS. WaU, typescript.

2845 DREW, Edward B. 1852–1892. His life from arrival in Winona Cnty., Minn., as a member of a townsite company; farming operations; prices and wages; weather; schools; railroads; other topics. MnHi.

2846 EGBERT, Eliza Ann McAuley. 1852. A journey across the plains. CSSfm, typescript.

2847 FISHER, James Samuel. 1852–1853. Overland trip to Cal. in search of gold; return trip by sea; brief, factual comments on mining and events of journey. MiU, typescript.

2848 FRIZZELL, Lodesa. 1852. CNS. NN.

2849 FUNK, John F. 1852–1920. Various trips in the interest of church work, especially relating to settlement of Russian Mennonites in America during the 1870's. InGoM.

2850 GALE, Samuel C. 1852–1877. Life as a student at Yale, as a school teacher, and as a lawyer in Minneapolis. MnHi, microfilm.

2851 GARDNER, Caturah. 1852–1853. CNS. NP.

2852 GORDON, Rebecca. 1852. Kept while author was 9 years old. MdHi.

2853 GREEN, Jay. 1852. Crossing the plains, St. Louis to Hangtown; also his will. CStoPM.

2854 GWYN, James. 1852–1884. Personal and plantation diaries. NcU.

2855 HAMPTON, William H. 1852–1859. An overland journey from St. Joseph, Mo.; across the plains to the Cal. gold fields; includes his mining experiences and his return voyage home. CU-B.

2856 HANNA, Esther Belle. 1852. A journey from Pittsburgh, Pa., to Oregon City. CU-B, WaPS.

2857 HAYDEN, Charles W. 1852–1853. Trip across the plains from Wis. to Ore. CtY.

2858 HAYDEN, Jacob S. 1852. Trip across the plains. Wv-Ar, copy.

2859 HILLYER, George S. 1852. Trip from Granville, Ohio, to Cal. by way of N.Y. and Nicaragua. KHi.

2860 HODGE, George. 1852–1853. Trip from Dallas to Ft. Owen. MtHi.

2861 KAHLER, William. 1852. Journey overland from McConnellsville, Ohio, to a point on the Ore. road beyond the turnoff for Shasta. CtY.

2862 KEEN, Richard. 1852. Journey overland to Cal. from Logan, Ind.; the return voyage via Panama to N.Y. CSfC, copy.

2863 KING, Mitchell. 1852–1854; 1853–1856; 1855–1858. Personal, family, social, and business activities and expenditures pertaining to his life in Charleston, S.C., and in summer at Argyle, his home at Flat Rock, N.C. NcU.

2864 LAFAYETTE, John. 1852–1869. CNS. Tx, photostats.

2865 LAIRD, Moses F. 1852–1855. Autobiographical, plus his trip across the plains as well as his subsequent experiences in the gold mines and in the saddling business. CtY.

2866 LAKE, William B. 1852–1899. Trip via Panama to Cal., 1853, Jefferson Lake with his father; in a saw mill near Sacramento; events there 1850's and 1860's; experiences in Aurora, Nev., and life in San Francisco. CU-B.

2867 LAND, Handel. 1852. A trip from New Orleans on the S.S. *Sierra Nevada*; a crossing of the Isthmus of Panama, and thence to San Francisco. CU-B.

2868 LANE, John L. 1852–1867. A journey to Cal. overland to Mazatlan; thence by ship to San Francisco; his gold prospecting and return home overland from southern Cal. CU-B.

2869 LE DUC, William G. 1852; 1853; 1860. CNS. MnHi.

2870 LEWIS, William David, Jr. 1852–1853. Travel to Italy, France, British Isles. PSC-Hi.

2871 MAPLE, Eli B. 1852. Account of experiences crossing plains from Iowa and pioneering in Washington Territory. CU-B.

2872 MATHER, Joseph. 1852–1859. Day-by-day activities of a sugar plantation, noting the weather, work done at various times of the year, condition of crops, and health of slaves and stock. LU.

2873 MAXFIELD, W. S. 1852–1856. Whaling voyage on board ship *Niger*. MH.

2874 McCULLOUGH, Isaac. 1852–1855. Diary kept in Cal. during gold rush. MH.

2875 McQUEEN, Angus. 1852; 1873–1874. CNS. CSt.

2876 MOORE, Henry Miles. 1852–1880. Family and social life; theater and other entertainments; the weather; court cases; expenses; church activities; other local and world events. CtY.

2877 MUSTARD, David Lewis. 1852–1853. CNS. DeU.

2878 PENDLETON, Ralph Cross Johnson. 1852. Voyage around the Horn from N.Y. to San Francisco in the clipper ship *Ino*. CSmH.

2879 POND, Ananias R. 1852–1862. Kept in the Vaca Valley; events during the flood of 1862. CSmH. *See* 2572.

2880 RICHARDSON, Caroline. 1852. Written while she crossed the plains. CU-B.

2881 ROSE, Mrs. Rachel C. 1852. Written on the plains. CSfC.

2882 RUDD, Lydia A. 1852. An overland journey from the Missouri River to Burlington, Ore. InU-Li.

2883 SAWYER, Mrs. Francis H. 1852. Overland to Cal. (notes from a journal written while she crossed the plains). CU-B, typescript.

2884 SHARP, Robert L. 1852. A trip to Cal. from Sugar Grove, Fairfield Cnty., Ohio. OHi.

2885 SNODGRASS, R. H. P. 1852. The trip from Piqua, Ohio, to Sacramento across the plains. CtY.

2886 STABLER, Edward, Jr. 1852–1853. CNS. MdHi.

2887 STILL, William. 1852–1857. Data on contraband, escaped slaves, the underground railway, efforts to improve the condition of Negroes, etc. PHi.

2888 TOWNSEND, David. 1852–1853. CNS. PWcHi.

2889 VAN SCHAICK, Holmes D. 1852–1854. An overland journey. ICN.

2890 WAILES, Benjamin Leonard Covington. 1852–1862. Detailed accounts of his farming operations and the collection of fossils. NcD.

2891 WASHINGTON, George. 1852–1853. A trip from Waukesha to Cal. and back. WWauHi.

2892 WEST, David J. 1852–1912. Life in Ill.; voyage to Cal. via the Isthmus; odd jobs; his return to Ill.; life in Ill.; his return to Cal. via the Isthmus; life in San Francisco and Antioch, Cal.; a trip to Chicago after the fire and his return to San Francisco. CU-B.

2893 WILLETS, Rubin. 1852. CNS. NjCmHi.

2894 WILLIAMS, Rev. Moses A. 1852–1897. Important diary of resident Presbyterian minister and circuit rider; good details of life in western Ore. from Jacksonville to Portland; useful for baptismal and marriage records and church history. OrU.

2895 WOODRUFF, S. W. 1852. A trip across the plains to Ore. WaU, typescript.

2896 WOOLSEY, Melancthon Brooks. 1852–1874. Kept on various naval vessels and during shore leaves. MiD.

2897 YEATON, John G. 1852. A voyage to Cal. on the vessel *North American*; experiences in Cal., chiefly Sacramento; mining and saw mills. CU-B.

2898 ANON. 1853–1864. Kept by a member of the United Society of Believers (Shakers); work of members of the society; deaths; events of local interest; the setting up of a printing press; references to Negroes; the impact of the Civil War on the society and the community; movements of John Hunt Morgan's raiders; weather reports. KyLoF.

2899 ANON. 1853. A young woman's trip west: N. Y. to Ore.; beauties of the journey; privations; wrangling among emigrants. ICHi.

2900 ANON. 1853. Brief descriptions by a young man of his personal and social life, and his occupation as a maker of shovel handles; a few later (1862) records of fruit trees and other plants, two short diary entries in cipher, 1864. NjR.

2901 AITKIN, James Stuart. 1853–1854. Kept by him while a student at Rutgers College. NjR.

2902 ALLEN DIARIES. 1853–1859. Kept by Oliver Allen, 49'er and Marin Cnty. pioneer, and his son, Charles D. Allen. CU-B.

2903 AYER, Monroe. 1853–1857. CNS. MHa.

2904 BENT, Silas. 1853. Kept by a lt. on board the U.S. steam frigate *Mississippi*, with the U.S. naval expedition to Japan under Commodore Perry; accompanied by two scrapbooks relating to his interests in polar exploration. NjR.

2905 BLANCHARD, Nathan W. 1853–1863. Kept chiefly while he lived in Placer Cnty., Cal., at Independence Hill, Iowa Hill, Wisconsin Hill, Roach Hill, Dutch Flat, etc. CSmH.

2906 BRADWAY, Dr. Joseph R. 1853. On overland trail in 1853. CSfC, copy.

2907 BRAINARD, Clementine H. 1853–1855. Her first few years in Columbia, Cal., to which she came as a bride. CU-B.

2908 BURY, Richard Augustus. 1853. Boat trip from Detroit to Lake Huron, Mackinac Island, and Eagle River; comments on copper mining. MiU.

2909 CHANDLER, William Eaton. 1853–1854; 1880–1917. CNS. NhHi. *See* 2981.

2910 CLEAVER, Joseph. 1853–1854. CNS. DeU.

2911 COMSTOCK, Noah D. [1853?–1854?] Journey from Ash Hollow, Neb., to the mines in Sierra County, Cal., and a year in the mines. CtY.

2912 COOK, Seley M. 1853–1855. Journal of religious meetings and classes in Ore. InU.

2913 COPLEY, Jane Helen (Hathaway). 1853–1859. CNS. MiU. *See* 2765.

2914 DEALY, Dennis F. 1853–1857; 1858–1860; 1887. CNS. PHi.

2915 [DINWIDDIE, David or John]. 1853. An overland trip from Ind. to Ore. Or, typescript.

2916 ELY, Charles A., and his wife, Louise C. (Foot). 1853–1876. Includes a voyage to the Orient. OHi.

2917 EVANS, Elwood. 1853. The Northern Pacific Railroad Exploration and Survey. CtY.

2918 FLETCHER, Asa. 1853. Journey by rail and steamboat from Ind. to New England and return. InHi.

2919 FORBES, R. N. 1853–1858. CNS. Nc-Ar.

2920 FORBES, Solomon. 1853–1857. Overland trip to Cal. to prospect for gold; return by sea; weather; description of country; events of journey. MiU.

2921 GARFIELD, James Abram. 1853–1855. CNS. OHi.

2922 GILBERT, William W. 1853. An overland trip from Milwaukee, Wis., to Placerville, Cal. MnHi, typescript.

2923 GILPIN, Henry D. 1853–1854. A tour through Europe. PHi. *See* 1544.

2924 GRAHAM, Calvin Heron. 1853. CNS. KHi, typescript.

2925 HALLER, Granville Owen. 1853–1860. Memorandum book kept at Ft. Dalles, Ore. Terr. WaU. *See* 2125, 2997, 3055, 3116, 3908, 4494.

2926 HEALD, Daniel G. 1853–1881. Scattered entries San Francisco, 1853; voyage to Me., via Panama and return to San Francisco, 1868; daily record of life, 1871, 1876–1877, etc. CU-B.

2927 HICKMAN, Peter L. 1853. Written on the emigrant trail. CSfC.

2928 HITE, Abraham. 1853. A trip across the plains. CSfC, typescript.

2929 HOFFMAN, William. 1853. Travels from Covington, Ind., to Jacksonville, Ore. OrU.

2930 HOTH, H. 1853–1857. A portion written while he crossed the plains via Salt Lake City to Los Angeles. CU-B, facsimile.

2931 JONES, Talbot, Jr. 1853. Personal and business affairs; weather; information on other people; cases and fees collected. OCUHi.

2932 KENT, Henry Sewall. 1853–1854. The voyage from San Francisco to N.Y., via Panama. CSmH.

2933 LEWIS, John R. C. 1853–1855. Perry's expedition from N.Y. to Japan; places passed and visited. NN.

2934 LEWIS, Mary Alice. 1853–1854. Reading; needlework; practicing piano and singing; lessons or exercises in French, Italian, and English; various household and social activity. PSC-Hi.

2935 McCLELLAN, George B. 1853. An exploring expedition eastward from the Pacific coast. DLC; MnHi, photostat. See 2129, 2294.

2936 McCLURE, Andrew S. 1853. An overland trip from Kan. to the Willamette Valley, Ore. OrU, typescript.

2937 McPHERSON, Samuel Davidson. 1853–1857. Activities and thoughts while he was a student at Jefferson College and during his first year of teaching at Oakland College. PWW.

2938 MEADE, Richard Worsam, 3rd. 1853–1854. Kept as a midshipman. NHi. See 4480.

2939 MELLON, Sam W. 1853. Kept on a round trip on horseback from Jasper through northeast Tex.; describes many Tex. towns and the condition of the country through which he passed. TxGR.

2940 MOORE, George W. 1853–1877. Farm records; farm and personal accounts; general store daybook (practice accounts?); account of brig *Cohansey*, carrying freight and passengers between Philadelphia and Mobile, New Orleans, Gibraltar, etc.; Cumberland Cnty., N.J. NjR.

2941 MOORE, Joseph. 1853–1865. Kept at Earlham College. InRE.

2942 MULBERRY PLANTATION JOURNALS. 1853–1889. Plantation accounts; neighborhood events and public affairs. ScHi.

2943 OWEN, Benjamin Franklin. 1853. Trip overland from Mo. to Ore., and Cal. OrU, typescript.

2944 PARRY, George T. 1853–1886 (with gaps). Daily events; family affairs; professional and business activities. PHi.

2945 PRINGLE, Virgil Kellog. 1853–1856. Weather and daily happenings on the farm. OrFP. *See* 2299.

2946 RICHARD, John Casper. 1853. Overland trip from Bellevue, Ohio, to Cal.; entries end 165 miles beyond Salt Lake City. InU-Li.

2947 ROWE, William. 1853. Personal reminiscences of an overland trip from Rochester, Wis., to Cal. CSmH.

2948 SANFORD, Mary Fetter Hite. 1853. A trip across the plains. CSfC, typescript.

2949 SCAMMON, Charles M. 1853; 1863. Journal account of two whaling voyages. CU-B.

2950 SEALE, H. M. 1853–1857. Day-by-day account of plantation business. LU.

2951 SMITH, Rev. George Gilman. 1853–1906. CNS. GEU.

2952 SMITH, John. 1853. Overland journey from Pittsburgh, Ind., to Ore. CSmH.

2953 SMITH, William P. 1853–1855. Life at the U.S. Military Academy including living conditions, amusements, health treatment, curriculum, and discipline. LU.

2954 SOWERS, John. 1853; 1860. CNS. OClWHi.

2955 STACKPOLE, Julia Ann. 1853–1918. CNS. MeWHi.

2956 STANLEY, David Sloane. 1853–1854. A march from Ft. Smith, Ark., to San Diego, Cal., on an exploring expedition. CSmH.

2957 TEN EYCK, John. 1853–1877. Full entries describing all aspects of a farmer's life. NjR.

2958 THOMPSON, John Bodine. 1853. A trip from Flemington, N.J., to Batavia, N.Y., and vicinity; a two-week visit there among relatives; includes his brief stop at New Hampton as an agent soliciting subscriptions for the *Christian Diadem* and distributing tracts. CU-B. *See* 2413.

2959 THOMPSON, W. G. 1853. A trip across the plains to Ore. OrVMa.

2960 TOLAND, Harford. 1853–1854. Diary kept while he attended Mr. Robbins' School in Springfield, Ohio. OHi.

2961 WALSWORTH, H. G. (a woman). 1853. Trip to San Francisco from Mass. by boat to Panama, muleback across the Isthmus and ending with arrival at San Francisco on boat. AzTP.

2962 WARD, Mrs. Harriet Sherrill. 1853. Trip across the plains from Wis. to Cal. CU-B, typescript.

2963 WHARTON, Thomas K. 1853–1859; 1862. Journey from New Orleans to Boston; work on New Orleans customhouse and a Methodist church; yellow fever epidemics of 1853–1854; public improvements of New Orleans; federal occupation. LU. *See* 3086?

2964 WHIPPLE, Rt. Rev. Henry B. 1853; 1857; 1865–1900. Personal. MnHi.

2965 WILLIAMS, Joseph. 1853. Written on the trail from Ohio to Ark. to Cal. CU-B, typescript.

2966 WILLIAMS, Samuel Wesley. 1853–1859 (with gaps). College life at Ohio Wesleyan, Delaware, Ohio, and McKendrice College, Lebanon, Ill., where he was on the faculty; work as editorial assistant on *Ladies' Repository*. InU.

2967 WILLIAMS, V. A. 1853. Overland trip from Iowa to southern Ore. OrU.

2968 ZILHART, William. 1853. An overland journey from Mo. to Santa Rosa, Cal. CU-B.

2969 ANON. 1854–1856. Daily incidents kept by the clerk of the American Fur Co. at Ft. Benton, Mont. MtHi, typescript.

2970 ANON. 1854–1855. An account of a lumberman's experiences on the Rum River after the crew had left. MnHi.

2971 ANON. 1854. Kept by a passenger on board the ship *America* from Melbourne, Australia, to San Francisco. CSmH.

2972 AINSWORTH, Mrs. F. L. 1854–1856. Trip from Jones Cnty., Iowa, to Ore., and experiences in the gold mines in southern Ore.; trip to Cal., returning East by way of the Isthmus. Or, typescript.

2973 ALLEN, Mrs. Chestina Bowkes. 1854–1858. Life in Pottawatomie Cnty., Kan. KHi.

2974 ANDERSON, Harrod Clopton. 1854–1888 (except years 1863 and 1884). Political and religious convictions; home medical remedies; farming operations; commodity prices; weather conditions. LU.

2975 BALLINGER, William Pitt. 1854–1887 (with gaps). Personal but also references to his law practice as well as much comment on public events, questions of the day, local and state matters. Tx-GR.

2976 BISHOP, James. 1854–1889. Journal of European trip, chiefly in Germany and Switzerland but also in France and England; accounts of St. James M.E. Church (New Brunswick, N.J.) fund drives; letters concerning wreck of the *Ville du Havre*, 1873; stock certificates of Trenton & New Brunswick and Spruce-Run turnpikes. NjR.

2977 BOWEN, Ben. 1854–1859. Mining experiences in Amador Cnty., Cal., including observations on his associates, notable events (social, political, and criminal), and his travels to San Francisco and Sacramento. CU-B.

2978 BOYER, John. 1854. Weather conditions; personal expenses; purchases; repairs; investments. PHi.

2979 BURRELL, Mary (Mrs. Wesley Tonner). 1854. A journey overland from Council Bluffs to Green Valley, Cal. CtY.

2980 CHANDLER, W. P. 1854–1856. Kept during his consulate at Tunis. DLC.

2981 CHANDLER, Mrs. William Eaton (Lucy Hale). 1854–1869 (with gaps). Social life in N.Y. and life in Madrid, Spain, as seen by an ambassador's daughter. NhHi. *See* 2909.

2982 CLARK, Thomas, II. 1854–1865. Record of his surveying, with descriptions of the locality. WS; WSHi.

2983 CLEVELAND, Charles M. 1854–1858. School days at Gross Ile; membership in the Adrian Voluntary Fire Dept.; marriage; some important national events of 1858. MiU. *See* 3430, 4378.

2984 COMLY, Emmor. 1854; 1871–1876. Visits to Friends meetings in N.J.; daily events and family. PSC-Hi.

2985 CONDIT, Rev. Philip. 1854. An overland journey from Council Bluffs, Iowa, to Ore. OrU, photostat.

2986 CONDIT, Sylvanus. 1854. Parallels diary of Philip Condit. OrU, photostat.

2987 COTTRELL, Rev. Joseph B. 1854–1892. Personal. NcU, typescript.

2988 CRAPO, Henry Howland. 1854–1869. Trips from New Bedford, Mass., to Mich., from Mich. to Cincinnati; itemized costs; lumbering; acquaintances. MiU. *See* 4144.

2989 DAVIS, William W. H. 1854–1855. Journey to a meeting at Abiquin with Gov. Meriwether and the Ute Indians under Kit Carson; includes further journey and negotiations with Navaho Indians. CU-B.

2990 EBEY, Winfield Scott. 1854–1858; 1861–1863. Crossing the plains; Port Townsend, Wash. Terr.; Whidby's Island, Wash. Terr. WaU.

2991 FERRIS, Anna M. 1854–1856. Dinners attended; meetings; visits; church; speakers; visits to the poor; social life in general. DeHi. *See* 3177.

2992 FRIEZE, Prof. Henry Simmons. 1854. Personal. MiU. *See* 3053, 4288.

2993 GOODELL, Anna Maria. 1854. Crossing the plains. WaU.

2994 GROVER, James M. 1854–1905. A voyage from N.Y. to Cal. via Nicaragua on the steamers *Prometheus* and *Pacific*; notes on family and early life; Cal. associates; mining ventures; vigilance committees, etc. CU-B.

2995 GUMMERE, Samuel James. 1854. Traveling in England, France, Switzerland. PHC.

2996 HALL, Gustavus F. 1854. A trip from Charleston, Mass., to San Francisco, Cal. OHi.

2997 HALLER, Granville Owen. 1854. Journal of the campaign against the Snake Indians about Boise River, Ore. Terr. WaU. *See* 2125, 2925, 3055, 3116, 3908, 4494.

2998 HARDIN, Mary B. (Mrs. Charles H.). 1854–1860 (with gaps). CNS. MoU.

2999 HUNT, Daniel H. 1854–1859. Travels in New England; a sea voyage to S. C.; travels in Minn. MnHi, typescript.

3000 IRWIN, J. Warner. 1854. CNS. PHi.

3001 KANE, ———? 1854–1855. Journal of arctic explorer. CSt.

3002 KIRBY, Henry. 1854. Difficulty in operating railroad cars; incident involving an individual's opposition to the Clinton and Port Hudson Railroad; record of bills paid; letters written or received; a trip to Tex. by way of New Orleans. LU.

3003 KIRBY-SMITH, Edmund. 1854–1855; 1858. CNS. NcU.

3004 KITCHELL, William. 1854. Life as a student of metallurgy at Freiburg; visits to Berlin, including a meeting with Alexander von Humboldt; return voyage to America; observations on German life and customs. NjR.

3005 LANSDALE, Richard Hyatt. 1854–1855. Personal. CtY.

3006 MARCH, Clement. 1854–1869. Except 1865 and 1868. NmU.

3007 McCOWEN, George. 1854–1861. A journey across the plains, from Ind. to Grass Valley, Cal., by way of Ft. Laramie and Klamath Lake, Ore. CSmH.

3008 McIVER, Sarah Witherspoon Ervin. 1854–1889. Family activities and management of the plantation. ScU.

3009 MOSHER, William Collins. 1854. Overland journey. CSmH.

3010 MYRICK, Elizabeth T. Rankin. 1854. Written while she crossed the plains. CU, copy.

3011 NEWCOMB, George W. 1854. Business matters; descriptions of the Mid-West; time-consuming and difficult travel in Ill. ICHi.

3012 PALMER, Joel. 1854; 1856; 1860–1861. Travel and description; treaty negotiations with Indians; removal of Indians to reservation; operating pack train to gold mines in British Columbia. InU.

3013 PARRISH, Edward Evans. 1854–1855. CNS. OrHi.

3014 PARSONS, Theron. 1854–1892. Diary with voyage to Cal. via the Isthmus in 1868. CSmH.

3015 PERKHAM, Phila M. 1854. Includes lists of household expenses for 1862. NIC.

3016 PETERSON, Andrew. 1854–1898. Diary and account book (in Swedish). MnHi.

3017 QUINN, James H. 1854. Journal of the Spy Company in the expeditions against the Indians in N. M. CSmH.

3018 ROEDER, Elizabeth Austin (Mrs. Henry Roeder). 1854. Crossing the plains. WaU.

3019 STEELE, Thomas. 1854–1856. Weather; crops; farm records; accounts. NcU.

3020 STEVENS, George Edward. 1854. Kept while still in school; relates to school and family life. InU-Li.

3021 STUART, James. 1854–1857. Experiences in Cal. and during the journeys northward to Ore. boundary in 1854 and 1855, and eastward in 1857 across the plains to northern Utah. CtY. *See* 3541.

3022 TAYLOR, Elizabeth Gurney. 1854–1886. Daily routine; people; school work; family; church; etc. MiU.

3023 TEN BROECK, Peter G. Stuyvesant. 1854. A voyage from N.Y. to San Francisco via the Isthmus of Panama. CSmH.

3024 UPFOLD, Rt. Rev. George. 1854–1872. Diary destined for Episcopal National Cathedral, D.C. InHi, microfilm.

3025 VAN BUREN, Angelica Singleton. 1854–1855. Trip to Europe accompanied by her family. ScU.

3026 VAN LOAN, Walton. 1854; 1856; 1858. Kept by a clerk for a San Francisco stationer and bookseller; including a trip home to N.Y. via the Isthmus. CU-B.

3027 VAN WART, Irving. 1854–1855. Kept in N.Y. city and Craigsville, N.Y., by grand-nephew of Washington Irving; school work; sports and life with brother; family life. NN.

3028 WELLES, Rt. Rev. Edward R. 1854–1856. Trip from Waterloo, N.Y. to Vicksburg, Miss.; also the two years he was in charge of a select girls' school in Vicksburg. Ms-Ar, typescript.

3029 WHITE, Daniel. 1854–1859. Overland trip to Cal. CSmH.

3030 WILLIAMS, James Harrison. 1854–1878. CNS. ViU.

3031 WING, S. A. 1854–1868. Accounts. MnRHi.

3032 ANON. [between 1855 and 1926]. CNS. MnHi.

3033 ANON. 1855. CNS. WSheHi.

3034 ANDRUSS, William Benajah. 1855–1856. Everyday doings of a small businessman in a rural community (Amboy, Ill.). ICHi.

3035 AVERELL, Jane Russell. 1855. Social life of the period; visits, etc. (part in French). NCooHi.

3036 AYERS, Alexander Miller. 1855; 1864; 1865. CNS. GEU, copy.

3037 BARAGA, Friedrich. 1855–1860. Excerpts of Minn. interest in the presbytery of St. Ignatius Church, Houghton, Mich. (in German). MnHi.

3038 BEEKMAN, Kate. 1855. Trip through France, Switzerland, Sweden, Norway (in French). NN.

3039 BROWN, Henry Billings. 1855; 1858–1875. Early life in New England; college days at Yale; legal career in Detroit before appointment to U.S. Supreme Court. MiD.

3040 BROWN, Reese P. 1855. Accounts, recipes. KHi.

3041 BURGWYN, John Fanning. 1855–1856. CNS. Nc-Ar.

3042 CHAMBERS, James H. 1855–1859. Journal at Ft. Sarpy on the Yellowstone; later at Ft. Union. MtHi.

3043 CHASE, Salmon Portland. 1855–1872. Political trends; economic situations; social history. PHi. *See* 3165, 3428.

3044 CROWELL, Caroline. 1855–1856. CNS. MHa.

3045 CUMMINS, John R. 1855–1916. Prices, crops, and agricultural methods. MnHi.

3046 DODGE, Gen. Grenville Mellen. 1855?–? CNS. IaCb.

3047 DONNELLY, Ignatius. 1855–1900. Personal life; politics in Minn.; national politics; travel and private business. MnHi.

3048 DOWELL, Benjamin Franklin. 1855; 1856. Deals with troubles in supplying army with food and ammunition by mule train during Rogue River wars in Ore. OrU. *See* 2663.

3049 FELT, Charles Dwight. 1855. Includes cash accounts. WsHi; WS, copy.

3050 FORKER, William R. 1855. CNS. CSt.

3051 FRANCIS, Anna Mercer LaRoche. 1855–1869. Comment on the political scene in Philadelphia during the Civil War. NNC.

3052 FREEMAN, George W. 1855–? CNS. KHi, typescript.

3053 FRIEZE, Prof. Henry Simmons. 1855–1856. Activities while he lived in Providence, R.I.; descriptions of travel in Europe, including customs, religion, architecture, art, and teaching methods; his studies at the Univ. of Berlin. MiU, typescript. *See* 2992, 4288.

3054 FURBER, Mrs. Lucy. 1855. Social and family life in Me. MnHi.

3055 HALLER, Granville Owen. 1855. Principal daily events and occurrences during the Winnass expedition in the Snake River Indian country, the day after the arrival of the headquarters of the expedition at the camp at the mouth of Boise River, Ore. Terr. WaU. *See* 2125, 2925, 2997, 3116, 3908, 4494.

3056 HARRINGTON, Lewis. 1855–1856. A trip to Minn. from Dalton, Ohio; surveying in various parts of Minn., and pioneer life in McLeod Cnty. MnHi.

3057 HATCH, Edwin A. C. 1855–1856; 1863–1864. Kept by Indian agent among the Blackfoot Indians, and on the Red River. MnHi.

3058 HAWLEY, Augustine B. 1855–1856. Studying medicine in Europe. MnHi, typescript.

3059 HAYES, W. R. 1855. Diary of a government quartermaster, including his activities in and around Salt Lake City and his observations of Brigham Young and Mormons; overland journey to southern Cal. CU-B.

3060 HEMBREE, W. C. 1855–1856. During the Yakima war. OrP, typescript.

3061 HICKS, G. P. 1855–1874. A trip from La Chute, Lower Canada, to St. Paul, Traverse des Sioux, and Ft. Ridgely. MnHi, typescript.

3062 HOWELL, George W. 1855–1857; 1860; 1865–1866; 1876. Farming at Littleton; social and neighborhood activities; life as student and teacher at the State Normal School, Trenton, N.J.; work as civil engineer for the Morris & Essex Railroad and for the Somerset County Bridge. NjR.

3063 HUNTER, David Eckley. 1855–1857. Personal. InU-Li.

3064 INGRAHAM, George B. C. 1855–1866. Journal while he was in Honolulu and trip to San Francisco. CSmH.

3065 JOHNSON, Philip C., Jr. 1855–1856. Personal. CSdJHi.

3066 LEVER, Charles. 1855. Journal aboard the U.S.S. *Release* on the voyage of relief to rescue Dr. Kane's Arctic exploring expedition. DLC.

3067 MERCER, K. B. 1855–1856. Kept by a member of Co. A, 1st Regt. of Ore. Mounted Vols., during the Yakima War. CtY.

3068 MILLER, J. C. 1855. Items on early Topeka. KHi.

3069 MOORE, David A. 1855–1858. Kept as a mission clerk at Salmon River, Mo.; includes the eventual abandonment of the mission under Indian attack. CU-B.

3070 NAPTON, John. 1855–1858. CNS. NjT.

3071 NILSSON, F. O. ca. 1855–1865. CNS. MnSSb.

3072 NIXON, Orville A. 1855. A trip from Centerville, Tenn., to Bent's Fort, Colo. and return. CSmH.

3073 OSBORN, Sullivan. 1855–1859. Written during his mining days in Auburn Ravine, Cal. CSmH.

3074 PEAKE, E. Steel. 1855–1905. An Episcopal clergyman stationed as a missionary among the Chippewa Indians. MnHi.

3075 PECK, John Mason. 1855–1856. Journal of Baptist minister and author. IHS.

3076 PETTIT, Ethan. 1855–1881. Journals of Mormon pioneer; life as a farmer at Hot Springs Lake, occasionally noting significant occurrences in Utah history. CU-B, microfilm.

3077 SETON, Rt. Rev. Robert. 1855–1899. Personal. InNd. *See* 4709?

3078 SHAW, George F. 1855. Diary of a day laborer in San Francisco. CU-B.

3079 SIMMONS, Rev. William. 1855–1869. Diaries in Springfield, Piqua, Xenia, Hillsboro, and Zanesville, Ohio. OHi.

3080 SIMONIN, Amedée H. 1855–1856. Diary in French describing the farm lands and products around Austin, Tex. DLC; IHS, microfilm.

3081 SMITH, Robert Barclay. 1855–1900. Vivid, personal account of local affairs in Va. and Ind. and international affairs. InNcHi.

3082 STEWART, James R. 1855–1860. Pioneer settler of Burlingame, Osage Cnty., Kan. KHi.

3083 STRAUGHN, Mrs. Nell Miller. 1855; 1872; 1880; 1885. CNS. OHi.

3084 TALLEY, Wesley. 1855–1860; 1864–1870. Detailed and religious; tells of powder mill explosion, balloon ascension, camp meetings; comments on opening of Wilmington schools with one male teacher—females being hired at a cheaper rate. De-Hi.

3085 TODD, John Blair Smith. 1855. A field diary of Gen. Harvey's expedition from Ft. Leavenworth to the Black Hills with sketches of the route, and descriptions of herds of buffalo and the scenery of the Black Hills. MnHi.

3086 WHARTON, Thomas Kelab. 1855–1862. Personal; social; church and religious life; includes architectural work and drawings. NN. See 2963?

3087 WIGHT, Henrietta Calmes. 1855–1857. Visiting relatives in Va.; sewing games, etc. ICHi.

3088 WINCHELL, Newton H. 1855–1872. Social life at Lakeville, Conn.; college life at the Univ. of Mich.; a geological excursion along Lake Huron, and the schools he taught in Dutchess Cnty., N.Y., and at Port Huron, Kalamazoo, and Adrian, Mich. MnHi.

3089 WOOLRIDGE, William. 1855–1858. Personal; comments on a smallpox epidemic. NcD.

3090 YAGER, F. L. J. 1855–1858. CNS. CSbCL.

3091 ANON. 1856–1861. Remarks on board the bark *Lafayette* of New Bedford. MH.

3092 ANON. 1856–1857. A trip from England on the S.S. *Anglo-Saxon* to Quebec, by boat to Chicago, overland to Mississippi River, by boat to New Orleans and Havana. IHi.

3093 ANON. 1856–1908. CNS. Nc-Ar.

3094 ANON. 1856. Account of round trip from Princeton, W. Va., to Asheville, N.C., to place journalist's daughter in Holston Conference Female College. OFH.

3095 ANON. 1856. CNS. NcU.

3096 ADAMS, Susan. 1856. Daily routine of Minn. housewife. MnHi.

3097 BARRY, William. 1856. Notes concerning the Chicago Historical Society. ICHi.

3098 BATCHELOR, Albert A. 1856?–1930? Explains plantation life and operation; student life at schools in La., Ky., and Miss.; early years of the Civil War; study of medicine; opinions on rechartering territory. LU.

3099 BATEMAN, [Mary]. 1856. Personal observations of plantation social life. LU, typescript; NcU, original.

3100 BENTON, A. L. 1856. CNS. NNC.

3101 BERMINGHAM, Twiss. 1856. Mormon trek, Dublin, Ireland, toward Salt Lake City; hardship and defeat. ICHi, typescript; NN, typescript.

3102 BERNARD, Jesse. 1856–1891. Personal; descriptions of church work and the Civil War. NcU.

3103 BUCK, Marcus Blakemore. 1856–1870. Agricultural routine; troop movements and war conditions in the lower Shenandoah valley. ViU.

3104 CARPENTER, Helen McCowen. 1856–[1857?]. Written while she was crossing the plains; rewritten by herself from original in 1911. CSmH, typescript; CSfC, typescript.

3105 CASE, Hamet H. 1856–1860. Overland journey, including diary, June–Sept., 1859, while en route from Ft. Laramie to Walla Walla. CU-B.

3106 COPLEY, Napoleon Eugene. 1856–1857. Trip in covered wagon from Little Prairie Ronde, Mich., to site of what is now Emporia, Kan.; process of building cabin; climate; travel conditions; settlers' cabins. MiU.

3107 CRAWFORD, S. W. 1856. Trip from El Paso Del Norte to the City of Mexico; description of route, inhabitants and occupations, battle grounds of Mexican War, Chihuahua. AzTP.

3108 DAVIDGE, William. 1856; 1860–1867; 1869; 1870; 1873; 1875–1877; 1880. CNS. MH.

3109 DEERING, John Henry. 1856 and 1858. Living in Bath, Me.; pioneer settler of Palmyra, Douglas Cnty., Kan. Terr. KHi.

3110 DICKINSON, Albert. 1856. Chiefly weather reports for Chicago. ICHi.

3111 DUNSTAN, Caroline A. 1856–1870. Household; family life; social and public events; Civil War news, etc. NN.

3112 EBERHART, Uriah. 1856; 1861–1862. CNS. ICMcCHi.

3113 FISHBURN, Prof. Junius M. 1856. Traveling in Europe; descriptions of travel in Germany, Italy, Greece, and France; religion; conditions of the land, art, architecture, etc. MiU.

3114 FRIDLEY, Henry C. 1856–1912. Agricultural and general economic conditions in Minn.; journeys to Washington, D.C., New Orleans, and Cal. MnHi.

3115 HALL, Rev. Richard, Jr. 1856–1872. Preaching tours in Minn.; giving information on the population of towns and the growth of churches. MnHi.

3116 HALLER, Granville Owen. 1856. Journal of the third expedition into the Yakima country. WaU. *See* 2125, 2925, 2997, 3055, 3908, 4494.

3117 HARRIS, John S. 1856–1901. Kept by a farmer at LaCrescent, Minn.; mentions the Minn. Horticultural Society, state and cnty. fairs. MnHi, microfilm.

3118 HELSABECK, Rev. S. J. 1856–1910. Personal activities and duties relative to his work as minister of the Methodist Church. NcU.

3119 HEYWORTH, J. O. 1856–1857. From Europe to Chicago; description of the new steamer *Adriatic*; sights of N.Y.; business in Chicago; data concerning Illinois Central Railway. ICHi.

3120 HOLMES, George Frederick. 1856–1864; 1864–1865; 1872; 1873; 1874; 1881; 1885; 1887; 1891. Agricultural journal; the Civil War; reading and teaching; politics (part in Latin). NcD.

3121 KING, Horatio. 1856. CNS. MePhl.

3122 KINZER, William L. (or T.). 1856–1860. Part kept at Dickinson College, Pa. ViHi. *See* 3480.

3123 LARISON, Mary Jane (Sergeant). 1856–1857. Student diary kept at New Jersey State Normal School, Trenton. NjR, abridged typescript.

3124 LARPENTEUR, Francis B. 1856–1861. Farming near St. Paul, Minn. MnHi.

3125 LAWRENCE, E., and Henry Clay Warmoth. 1856–1863; 1880–1927. Plantation journals; the hurricanes and crevasses of 1856 and 1860 and the condition of Negroes after being enticed from the plantations by the Federal troops; plantation activities at Magnolia Plantation. NcU. *See* 3553.

3126 MALLETT, Peter. 1856–1861; 1865–1881; 1883; 1898. CNS. NcU.

3127 MEARS, Charles. 1856. Lake shipping; lumber trade; conditions under which men were hired; fur trade; current events. ICHi. 1856; 1859. Daily occurrences and business deals. MiU.

3128 MENDENHALL, Richard J. 1856–1861. Description of Minn. customs, land surveying, and holidays. MnHi.

3129 [MILLER, C?]. 1856. Trip from Wis. to Vt.; removal to Wis.; real estate transactions. NN.

3130 MOORE, Clement Clarke. 1856–1863. The weather and temperature and his benefactions. NNC.

3131 MORRIS, Prof. George Sylvester. 1856–1861. Personal. MiU. *See* 4094, 4537.

3132 NEARING, Mary. 1856–1864. Life as a teacher in Pompey and Lafayette, N.Y. NIC.

3133 PEET, James. 1856–1865. Diaries of his work as Methodist minister in Minn., Wis., Mich.

MnHi, typescript; WSHi, typescript; MnDuHi, typescript.

3134 POND[?], Elihu Bartlit. 1856–1898 (with gaps). Activities as editor of the *Michigan Argus*; local happenings; family; military, political, economic aspects of Civil War. MiU.

3135 POTTER, E. W. 1856. CNS. NSchHi.

3136 PUTNAM, Samuel M. 1856–1857. Diary and surveying notes of a trip from Little Falls to Otter Tail Lake in 1856 and a journey to the Red River in 1857. MnHi.

3137 REBELE, Charles. 1856–1864. CNS. MdHi.

3138 RUFFIN, Edmund. 1856–1865. Information and criticism of the Confederate government; a minute account of the war, illustrating the extreme anti-union point of view. DLC. *See* 2171, 2202.

3139 SATTERTHWAITE, Daniel. 1856. Daily account of student's life at the Univ. of Mich.; religious activities; farming during vacation; current events; student reaction to Sumner-Brooks affair. MiU.

3140 SMITH, Benjamin Hayes. 1856–1863. Student days at Haverford College; experiences in the Union Army during the Civil War. PHC.

3141 SPYKER, Leonidas Pendleton. 1856–1860. Plantation diary at Hard Times Plantation and New Hope Plantation. LU.

3142 SWAYZE, Jason C. 1856. CNS. KHi.

3143 TURNER, Joseph Thomas. 1856. Minutes kept by orderly sergeant Joseph (or Junius) Thomas Turner, company I Northern Battalion, Wash. Territorial Vols.; partial list of members belonging to the company; diary of the journey of the company from Ft. Ebey up the Snohomish River. WaU.

3144 TUTTLE, Philemon M. 1856–1881. Kept by a farmer near High Forest, Minn. MnHi.

3145 UNDERHILL, Robert. 1856. Passage from N.Y. to San Francisco on the ship *Sweepstakes*. NHi.

3146 VASSER, Rebecca. 1856–1862. Introspective meditations by a deeply religious person, including some comment on the "Yankee" invasion of northern Ala. NcD.

3147 VEDDER, Charles Stuart. 1856. Diaries of a French Protestant Church minister in Charleston. ScU.

3148 YARNALL, Anna. 1856–1885. Daily events and news of family and friends. PHC.

3149 ANON. 1857. Kept on a fishing boat cruising near Nantucket: events, fishing, manners. NN.

3150 ALMY, John Jay. 1857–1860. Kept during his command of U.S. ships protecting American shipping, Nicaragua, Tampico, blockading in Civil War. NN.

3151 ATWOOD, Angus K. 1857–1869. Kept by a ship's captain, native of Barrington, Vt., sailing cargo vessels variously from Halifax or N.Y., chiefly to West Indies ports; deals largely with the periods at sea or brief stops in foreign ports, with comments on reading, morality, his lonesomeness, etc. NjR.

3152 BACON, L. S. 1857. CNS. KHi.

3153 BAILEY, Lawrence D. 1857. His journey to Kan. from N.H. and events in Douglas Cnty., Kan. KHi.

3154 BALCH, Nathaniel Aldrich. 1857–1883 (intermittently). Legal notes; expense accounts; business memoranda; a record of the cost of moving and rebuilding a house in 1867. MiU.

3155 BANDEL, Eugene. 1857. Written on the trail from Ft. Leavenworth to Ft. Scott. CSfC, typescript.

3156 BEADLE, Erastus F. 1857. Round trip journey from Buffalo to Omaha; incidents of travels; political sentiments of day; migration to new territory; life in Neb.; financial panic of 1857. LU.

3157 BENNERS, Henry B. 1857–1879. Important happenings of the day. PHi.

3158 BROWN, Benjamin. 1857; 1860. Overland trip from Mich. to Ore. in 1860, and subsequent life in northeastern Ore. OrU, typescript.

3159 BRYANT, Julia Sands. 1857–1858. A visit to Europe. NNC. *See* 2318, 4071.

3160 BULLENE, Lathrop. 1857. Journey from Richmond to Lawrence, Kan. Terr. KU.

3161 BURR, Frederick H. 1857–1858. Kept in the Bitterroot Country and during his journeys from Ft. Owen to Salt Lake and return to the gold diggings. CtY.

3162 BUTLER, William W. 1857; 1874; 1876. Prices of commodities, labor, etc.; apparently in grocery business. InHi.

3163 CARY, Wilson Miles. 1857–1911. CNS. ViU. *See* 1813, 3427, 4735.

3164 CASS, Lewis. 1857. A trip through the Mediterranean. MiU-C.

3165 CHASE, Salmon Portland. 1857; 1865. Personal and political interest. NhHi. *See* 3043, 3428.

3166 CLARK, Micajah A. 1857. Journal of travels between Miss. and S. C. ScU.

3167 CLARK, William. 1857. Trip across plains. MH, typescript.

3168 CLARK, William Adolphus. 1857–[1875]. Theatrical interest; photographs, letters, and clippings are inserted in the original ms. MH. *See* 4918.

3169 CRUDUP, E. A. 1857–1872. Plantation diaries, containing accounts of expenses incident to keeping slaves; local news; accounts of crop conditions. NcD.

3170 CUMMINS, Henry. 1857–1863. A daily record of his studies, work, and social life; discusses local events and his keen interest in science and spiritualism. CtY.

3171 CUTLER, William Parker. 1857. Financial difficulties and other business of the Marietta and Cincinnati Railroad Co. (now part of the Baltimore & Ohio). NjR.

3172 DAVIDSON, Greenlee. 1857. A visit to Northwestern states. ICMcCHi.

3173 DENSMORE, Benjamin. 1857. Overland trip from St. Paul to Ottertail Lake. MnHi.

3174 DOZIER, Richard. 1857; 1874–1876. Personal notes and law practice accounts. NcU.

3175 ELKINTON, Joseph. 1857. Visit, in company with Wm. Evans, to the Meetings of the Society of Friends belonging to Indiana Yearly Meeting; homes visited; meetings attended. PSC-Hi. *See* 1411, 2382, 4453?

3176 EWING, Mrs. Catherine Fay. 1857–1861. CNS. OHi.

3177 FERRIS, Anna M. 1857–1890. Describes beauties of nature; gives impressions of books read; political events; social events. PSC-Hi. *See* 2991.

3178 FRIEND, Andrew. 1857–1880. Employment in sawmills and gristmills in Minn., with brief references to the Sioux outbreak of 1862. MnHi, typescript.

3179 HAGEMAN, John. 1857. Journey through Ohio, Ind., Ill., Iowa, and Mo. as solicitor for religious magazine; describes attendance at Sunday schools and church meetings, at religious services in a prison, and in an insane asylum, his leadership at temperance meetings, sermons heard, speeches delivered, and comments on religious activities and attitudes of the persons he met. LU.

3180 HAIGHT, Henry Huntley. 1857. A hunting trip in Sonora and Mendocino Counties, Cal. CSmH.

3181 HALLETT, Samuel. 1857–1858. Business; economic, political, and social accounts. NIC, microfilm.

3182 HART, William A. 1857–1914 (with gaps). Personal. OFH.

3183 IVES, Robert Hale. 1857–1875. Business and family affairs; politics. RHi.

3184 JUSTIS, Horace Howard. 1857–1859. Diary of a law student, apparently from Cincinnati, Ohio, later a country schoolmaster in Miss.; comments on the customs of the Southern people, the "young" ladies dipping snuff, the indolence of the slaves, and his travels. NcD.

3185 KAUTZ, Gen. August Valentine. 1857–1895. CNS. DLC.

3186 KLIPPART, John Hancock. 1857–1865. CNS. OHi. *See* 4036, 4037.

3187 LE DUC, James M. 1857. CNS. MnHi.

3188 LEWIS, Exum. 1857. A trip to Europe. NcU.

3189 LINCKLAEN, Mr. and Mrs. Ledyard. 1857. A trip to Cuba and the Southern states. NHi.

3190 McGOVERN, Patrick Francis, and Charles Sauters. 1857. Work, treatment, punishment, food, clothing, illness, birth, death, and general welfare of the slaves and livestock; daily records of the amount of cotton picked; visits of owner. Ms-Ar.

3191 MILLER, Howard. 1857–1867; 1878–1888. Weather conditions; farming operations; births, marriages, deaths; attendance at St. Paul's Episcopal Church; building of library wing at "Clover Hill"; his election as captain of the Home Guards; movements of troops and events of the Civil War; freeing of slaves; building of school house. KyLoF.

3192 MUNSON, Myron Andrews. 1857–1873. CNS. MH. See 4323.

3193 NESBIT, Robert. 1857–1858. Duty as agent of the American Bible Society for the northern part of Brazil; area, people, customs, Nesbit's distributing of tracts and Bibles. NjR.

3194 NICHOLS. Henry K. 1857. Journal of the construction of Ft. Kearney, South Pass, and Honey Lake Wagon Road. CtY.

3195 NICHOLSON, Thomas A. 1857–1860. A cruise of a medical officer of the U.S. Navy (evidently a dentist) on the U.S.S. *Powhatan*; describes ports and people. NcD.

3196 POMEROY, Edward Noyes. 1857–1858. A sea voyage from Portland, Me., to England, and return via Grenada and Puerto Rico; includes "ideas" and poems. NNC.

3197 POTTER, W. C. 1857–1858. Personal. NElmHi.

3198 PUTNAM, R. 1857–1860. Kept by a soldier in the southwest, in Mexico, and along the border. CU-B.

3199 PUTNAM, R. P. 1857. Written while he was crossing the plains to Cal. by the southern route. CU-B.

3200 REED, William B. 1857–1859. His mission as Envoy Extraordinary and Minister Plenipotentiary to the Emperor of China. DLC.

3201 REGAL, Ellen (Mrs. Raymond C. Davis). 1857. Household and school activities of eldest daughter of itinerant minister. MiU.

3202 SAWYER, Alfred Isaac. 1857; 1860–1901. Comments on medical calls, treatment, weather, social affairs, current events, homeopathy. MiU.

3203 SCAMMON, J. Young. 1857–1859. Travels in Europe; spiritual interests; meeting of New Church (some entries in German). ICHi.

3204 SCARBOROUGH, William Harrison. 1857. Kept during tour of Italy. ScU.

3205 SIMPSON, Rev. John H. 1857–1871. Religious; economic; social; agricultural; military. ICMcCHi.

3206 STEPHENS, W. Hudson. 1857–1917. Parties and gaieties of the times; weather; writer's health; his work as lawyer. Room 304, Courthouse, Lowville, N.Y.

3207 STODDARD, Horace H. 1857–1873. Personal; military. CSmH.

3208 STRAWN, J. B. 1857–1859. CNS. OClWHi.

3209 STUART, Granville. 1857; 1866; 1867. Overland journey from Cal. to Malade Creek, Utah; trip from Mont. to Iowa and return; hunting and fishing excursion. CtY. See 3541, 4332, 4466.

3210 TAVENNOR, Jennett A. ca. 1857–1862. CNS. ViU.

3211 WALES, Thomas J. 1857–1858. Pioneer farm life in Dakota Cnty., Minn. MnHi, microfilm.

3212 WALKER, Cyrus H. 1857–1859. CNS. OrHi.

3213 WARD, L. Peirson. 1857–1858. Sea journal; voyage from Boston to Australia and East Indies in the bark *Hollander*. MH.

3214 WILLIAMS, L. White. 1857. Survey of wagon road to the Pacific. PWcHi.

3215 WOOD, Marquis Lafayette. 1857–1885. Personal notes of an M.E. minister; religious conditions in N.C. and in China; early history of Trinity College. NcD.

3216 ANON. 1858–1859. Kept at Muck Farm, Puget Sound Agricultural Company, the Nisqually adjunct. WaU, original; DLC, photostat.

3217 ANON. 1858–1859. Travel diary from Baltimore, Md., to Europe. MdHi.

3218 ANON. 1858. Personal and financial records of the Arnold or Appleton family of Boston or Savannah. NcU. See 1539, etc.

3219 ALCORN, Gov. James L. 1858; 1879. Schedule of property in Miss.; slave record. Nc-Ar. See 4422?

3220 BAKER, J. H. 1858–1918. CNS. Tx.

3221 BEESON, Thomas. 1858; 1861–1863; 1893. Farm work; cider and sugar making; occasional debates and literary society meetings at local schoolhouse; weather. InHi.

3222 BOLLER, Henry. 1858. A trip to the Indian country. NdHi.

3223 BRICE, Albert G. 1858. The culture and accomplishments of the American Negro, Catholic leadership, and educational efforts. OCX.

3224 BRIGGS, Samuel A. 1858–1860. School teaching in De Kalb and Logan counties, Ill.; political campaign of 1858 in Ill. IHi.

3225 BRYAN, J. Edward. 1858. Tour of Europe; sailed from N.Y. for Liverpool on the *Persia*. KyLoF.

3226 [BURGWYN, Capt. W. H. S.]. 1858–1864. Camp life; marches; affairs at his plantation at

Weldon, N.C.; accounts of skirmishes with the enemy and of experiences as a prisoner at Ft. Delaware; a detailed account of the battle near Petersburg. NcHiC. *See* 3588.

3227 CARTER, William A. 1858–1859. A large collection of papers, letters, and other documents including a diary by Mrs. Groshan from letters of 1858–1859; fragmentary original diaries for 1859, 1873, and 1881. CU-B.

3228 CORBETT, Samuel James. 1858–1859; 1862–1865. Voyage from Boston to San Francisco on the ship *Visurgis*; diary of Civil War service in the "California Hundred," volunteers for Mass. quota. CU-B.

3229 COUNTRYMAN, Levi N. 1858–1862. Problems of a frontier farmer and his views on them. MnHi.

3230 DICKEY, William J. 1858–1859; 1879–1880; 1884–1889. Thomas Cnty., Ga. Plantation diary, plowing and planting, sowing and reaping; daily tasks on large plantation in south Ga., before the Civil War, and after Reconstruction. GU.

3231 DRAKE, Samuel Gardner. 1858–1859. Researches in American history in London; offices visited; personalities met; bookshops; London life and places, etc. NhHi.

3232 FLOYD, William P. 1858–1859. Kept by the surgeon of Edward Fitzgerald Beale's wagon road expedition, describing his trip from Va. to Ft. Smith, and thence to the Colorado River. CSmH.

3233 FULGUM, Frederic Clarkson. 1858. Kept by a student at Earlham College. InRE.

3234 GILMER, George Rockingham. 1858. Ga., Va. An account, in rhyme, of a trip to Va., made in 1858 by Gov. George R. Gilmer and his wife. Much about relatives. GU.

3235 GLOVER, Kate E. 1858. CNS. OHi.

3236 GRIFFITH, Dr. Thomas J. 1858; 1859; 1865. Daily occurrences; part as a student in the Medical School of the Univ. of Mich. InU-Li.

3237 HANCOCK, Samuel. 1858–1860. An overland journey to Ore. in 1845, including explorations in Ore. and Wash.; the Cal. Gold Rush; trade and troubles with the Indians along the Northwest coast. CU-B.

3238 HAND, Thomas Jennings. 1858; 1870–1871; 1873; 1899–1901. Weather; stock raising and breeding. NNC.

3239 HILLYER, Carlton. 1858–1859. Washington, D. C. Diary of a schoolboy in Union Academy, Washington, D. C., just before the Civil War. Tells of school activities, lessons, weather, sight-seeing, a visit to the circus, quotes from newspapers. GU.

3240 HOLMES, George Hamilton Moore. 1858–1859. Living with parents and working on their farm. InU. *See* 3916.

3241 HOOKER, Cortez Perry. 1858–1885. Routine daily events; weather; farming. MiU.

3242 HOUGHTON, Chester. 1858. Relative to the invention of the John A. Appleby binding apparatus; agricultural, mechanical. ICMcCHi.

3243 HUBBARD, Almyra. 1858. The experiences of a girl in a Mass. public high school. MoU.

3244 HUME, Fanny Page. 1858; 1860; 1861; 1862. Description of Confederate and Union armies in Orange Cnty., Va. ViU. *See* 3634.

3245 IHRIE, William Muirhead. 1858–1861. Lecture notes and autograph books kept by a Princeton College student. NjR.

3246 INMAN, Myra Adelaide. 1858–1865. People, places, and events as seen by a young girl in Cleveland, Tenn., during Civil War. TC, typescript.

3247 JONES, J. W. 1858–1860. Diary of the purser's clerk on the *Mystic*, which patrolled the African coast to capture slave-trading vessels. NcD.

3248 JONES, Mrs. Julia A. Waystaff. 1858. Stage and drama in U.S.; autobiographical sketch. NN.

3249 KING, [Harriet] Sybil. 1858–1865. Weather and events. NNC.

3250 LEBEY, David A. 1858–1877. Business and personal accounts; wages; recipes. GHi.

3251 LE BLANC, August. 1858–1866. The activities of slaves; plantation accounts. LU.

3252 LEE, William. 1858–1859. Kept by scientific assistant on Capt. J. H. Simpson's expedition to Utah; continued across the Great Basin and return to Washington, D.C. CU-B.

3253 LINES, Charles Burrill. 1858; 1886. CNS. KHi.

3254 LOCEY, Cyrus T. 1858–1859; 1873–1911. Local historical events and Grange affairs. OrU, typescript and photostat.

3255 LONG, Christian L. 1858. Trip to Colorado en route to Pike's Peak. KHi, typescript.

3256 LORING, William W. 1858. A march with a regiment of mounted riflemen from Camp Floyd, Utah, to Ft. Union through southwestern Colo. CU-B.

3257 MACAULEY, Althea. 1858–1869. Daily activities. NCooHi.

3258 MALLORY, Charles. 1858–1876. CNS. Ct-MyMM.

3259 MERRITT, Samuel. 1858–1862. A European tour with Henry S. Low sailing from and returning to Boston; later entries relate to his home in Oakland. CU-B.

3260 MORRISON, James V. 1858. Brief entries, some as late as 1872, giving formulas and receipts and notes relating to his function as justice of the peace. NjR.

3261 NIELSON, Peter C. 1858–1878. Kept by a Mormon convert who emigrated to Utah in 1864; describes Black Hawk war, war in Sanpete and Sevier counties, and life in Juab county. CU-B.

3262 PALMER, Thomas Witherell. 1858–1913. CNS. MiD.

3263 PUFFER, Charles. 1858. CNS. KHi.

3264 ROEDER, Henry. 1858–1877. CNS. WaU. *See* 2715.

3265 RUSSELL, Henry. 1858–1861. Personal affairs; Quaker meeting business; accounts, etc. PHC.

3266 SNOW, Francis Huntington. 1858–1866. CNS. KU.

3267 SOUTHGATE, Rev. William S. 1858–1863; 1870–1878; 1884–1887; 1889–1897. Contains frequent references to baptisms, marriages, and burials; deals mainly with Episcopal church affairs; occasional personal references. MdAA.

3268 SPALDING, Henry Harmon. 1858–? Largely an account of daily meditation. WaWW. *See* 1993.

3269 SPENCE, J. M. 1858–1868. Sea voyages, Liverpool to San Francisco and return; mining in El Dorado. CSmH.

3270 TAYLOR, Rev. Nathan. 1858–1859. Founder of Baker Univ. at Baldwin, Kan., where he lived when diary was written. KHi.

3271 TRACY, Capt. Albert. 1858–1862. With infantry at Camp Scott, Wyo.; march to Salt Lake City; Mormon massacres; army life; travel; appointments in Washington, Me., Mo., etc. NN.

3272 ULMER, Margaret Anne. 1858. Diary of a girl student at Tuskegee Female Academy. NcU.

3273 VAN NEST, Abraham Rynier. 1858–1859; 1872–1873. Journal of a minister of the Reformed Church of America, pastor of the 21st Street Reformed Church, N. Y. city, 1848–1862, American Union Church, Florence, 1866–1875, etc. NjR.

3274 WELCH, R. H. 1858. Personal nature. NcD.

3275 WHITWORTH, James Edwin. 1858–1913. CNS. WaU.

3276 WREN, G. Lovick P. 1858; 1862–1864. Written while he was in the senior class at Emory College; Civil War journal, parts written while he was prisoner at Ft. Delaware. GEU.

3277 YOUNG, Jennie. 1858–1869. Personal; a trip to England, France, and Switzerland. NcD.

3278 ANON. 1859. CNS. OClWHi.

3279 ALBRIGHT, H. C. 1859–1861. 26th Regt., N. C. State Troops. Nc-Ar. *See* next item.

3280 ALLBRIGHT, Henry Clay. 1859–1864. Personal and business affairs; later as a Confederate soldier, gives accounts of marches through Va., Md., and Pa. NcHiC. *See* item above.

3281 ARMSTRONG, Moses K. 1859; 1866. An ox-team trip from Minn. into Dakota Terr. (1859); an Indian Treaty Commission in 1866 to negotiate with the Sioux of the Missouri and Yellowstone rivers. MnHi.

3282 BALES, Eleazer. 1859. Trip to Friends' Meetings in Kan. and Ontario; description of Kan. landscape, Indian houses, and personal ornamentation; impression of Niagara Falls. PSC-Hi, microfilm; InHi, typescript.

3283 BARTHOLOMEW, Mrs. Emily (Ebersole). 1859. Private and travel diary; trip from Ohio to N.Y.; journey by boat from N.Y. to Cal.; life in Forbestown, Cal. InU. *See* 4069.

3284 BARTLEY, Theodore D. 1859; 1860–1900. Operating canal boat *Mary Eva*, from Montreal to N.Y.; moving Adirondacks iron, lumber, etc. to N.Y. and Jersey City. NCooHi.

3285 BOOTH, Dr. John J. 1859–1863. Service in the 36th Regt., Ohio Vol. Inf. in the Civil War, Cincinnati, Ohio, etc. OHi.

3286 BOWKER, Richard Rogers. 1859–? CNS. NN. *See* 1430, 4447.

3287 BROOKS, Alden F. 1859. Grand trip across the plains from Omaha, Neb., to Cal. by way of Salt Lake City. CSmH.

3288 BROWN, George M. 1859; 1861; 1863. Personal affairs; his enlistment; the movements and activities of his regiment; camp life. MiU.

3289 BURT, Franklin. 1859–1872. Weather and the daily routine of farm life in Callaway County. MeU.

3290 BUTLER, Lucy Wood. 1859–1863. The impact of the Civil War on Charlottesville and the university. ViU.

3291 BUTLER, Nathan. 1859–1923. Kept while he was working for several railroads and for the U.S. government. MnHi.

3292 CARNEY, Kate S. 1859–1862. Personal. NcU.

3293 CHEW, Francis Thornton. 1859–1864. Kept from his entrance into the U.S. Naval Academy, included as part of an autobiography. NcU.

3294 CHILLSON, Lorenzo Dow. 1859. Overland journey. CSmH.

3295 COLEMAN, Mrs. Jane Lindsay. 1859. A trip to Europe. ViU.

3296 CRAMER, Thomas J. B. 1859. A journey from Kan. to Cal.; the route; events of the journey; the country; Indians encountered; the conditions in Cal. CtY.

3297 CRAWFORD, Laura Jones. 1859. CNS. DLC.

3298 CRAWFORD, Medorem. 1859–1864; 1869; 1870; 1875. Important overland diaries and political comment. OrU. *See* 3603.

3299 CROSBY, Elisha Oscar. 1859–1860. A voyage from San Francisco to Guatemala. CSmH.

3300 CUMMINGS, Charles J. 1859. A journey from Iowa to Ore., not following the usual route but taking unusual trails and cut-offs. CtY.

3301 CURTIS, Samuel Ryan. 1859–1861; 1862. Record of congressional activities, 1859, to Lincoln's inauguration; Union Pacific railroad legislation; Union army in Ark. and Mo. IHi.

3302 DAMON, John F. 1859. A trip up the Fraser River. CSmH.

3303 DODGE, Henry Nehemiah. 1859–1860. A trip through Europe with Professor Henry Drisler. NNC.

3304 ELLSWORTH, Col. Elmer E. 1859. Drilling of the Chicago Zouaves. MnHi, copy.

3305 EXCELL, Rev. J. 1859–1887. CNS. OHi.

3306 FLAGG, John Foster Brewster. 1859. A trip to Europe. PHi.

3307 FOLSOM, Rev. Willis F. 1859–1863. His activities as missionary among the Indians. OkHi.

3308 FOX, Rev. Louis Rodman. 1859–1872. Sermons; funerals; etc. PPPrHi.

3309 GILPIN, Ann Matilda. 1859–1862. References to secession of state after state, battles; by Civil War nurse. PSC-Hi.

3310 HALL, Francis. 1859–1865. Experiences and observations in Japan. CLU, microfilm.

3311 McALISTER, Daniel. 1859. Military life at Camp Harrison, Columbus, Ohio. OHi.

3312 McCORMIC, R. Laird. 1859–1866 (with gaps). The life of a boy in Clinton Cnty., Pa.; the activities of Saunders Institute, a boys' school in Philadelphia, and of other schools in the state. PHi.

3313 McKINSTRY, George. 1859–1879. CNS. CSdHi. *See* 2295?

3314 McPARLIN, Dr. Thomas Andrew. 1859–1860. Kept while he was stationed in Wash. Terr. as U.S. Army surgeon. MdHi.

3315 MULLIN, Rev. Mark H. 1859–1860. Life of Methodist circuit minister of southern Ind. InHi, microfilm.

3316 NICHOLS, Henry Alonzo. 1859–1860. Trip from western N.Y. to Detroit; comments on weather; personal philosophy; daily activities as schoolboy in Rochester, N.Y. MiU.

3317 OAKLEY, Edward Ellsworth. 1859–1861. Journey from Lecompton, Kan., to Colorado gold mines. KHi.

3318 PARKER, John R. 1859–1911. CNS. ScU.

3319 PARKER, William Foster. 1859–1860. Savannah, Ga. Reproduction. Journal of a businessman, and slave dealer who was also Master of a Masonic Lodge in Savannah, just before the Civil War. GU.

3320 POWELL, John W. 1859. An overland journey from Plattes Mouth, Mo., across the plains to Placerville, Cal. CU-B.

3321 RAVENEL, Henry William. 1859–1887. Private journals, large portions published. ScU.

3322 RICE, William P. 1859–1860. Diary in Alliance, Ohio. OHi.

3323 ROBINSON, George W. 1859. Accounts of weather, temperature, and wind; visits; people are referred to by initials; bills paid. DeHi.

3324 SOWERS, John H. 1859–1860. Travel to San Francisco from Lebanon, Pa., overland; work as printer for San Mateo County *Gazette*, Redwood City, and various San Francisco printing offices. InU.

3325 STEVENSON, Annie and Hannah E. 1859–1902. CNS. MBSpnea.

3326 STEVENSON, Charles C. 1859–1860. An overland journey via Salt Lake; mining at Gold Hill; early efforts to establish a local government; the Paiute war of 1860's; political career. CU-B.

3327 SWAN, James Gilchrist. 1859–1890. Diaries, journals, and meteorological records. WaU. *See* 2613?, 4535.

3328 TAYLOR, Mary. 1859–1860; 1869. Weather; visitors; letters written or received; church services attended and sewing finished for Mississippi City, Miss., in the early years and later for Clinton, La. LU.

3329 THOMPSON, Harlow Chittenden. 1859. Across the continent on foot from Dundee, Ill., to Cal. CSmH.

3330 TYSON, James. 1859–1861. Student days at Haverford College; personal affairs. PHC.

3331 WILKINSON, J. A. 1859. Written on a trip starting at Dowagaic, Mich., and concluded at Cal. CSmH; CSd, copy.

3332 WILSON, John A. 1859–1895. Personal and domestic affairs; accounts of his income and expenses. PHi.

3333 WIMAR, Carl Ferdinand. 1859. Trip from St. Louis to Ft. Benton. CLU-C.

3334 WIRTZ, John B. 1859–1862. Journal of the cruise of the U.S.S. *Lancaster*, flagship of the Pacific Squadron, U.S. Navy, in the north and south Pacific. Photostats, CLU.

3335 WRIGHT, Julius W. 1859–1862. CNS. NcU.

3336 YATES, William 1859–1860. Diary of a participant in the Pike's Peak gold rush; each day's events; distance traveled; buffalo hunting and Indian encounters, but no gold; a second trip to the Cherokee nation to buy mules is also described. MoU, photostat.

3337 ANON. 1860. Trip down the Mississippi from St. Joseph, Mo., to New Orleans, thence to Tex. ICHi.

3338   ANON. 1860–1884. Kept by the Sisters of the United Society of Believers (Shakers); records their work of cleaning, cooking, sewing, weaving, etc.; some events in the colony. KyLoF.

3339   ANON. 1860–1868. CNS. NcU.

3340   ANON. 1860. A voyage to America; a detailed account of the first official Japanese mission to the U.S. written by one of the party; includes descriptions of the voyage, of Hawaii, and Cal., and events in Washington and N.Y. MiU-C.

3341   ANON. 1860? A tour in Ga. NN.

3342   ASH, J. H. 1860–1865. By a Confederate soldier. GEU.

3343   BIERTU, F. 1860–1861. A trip from Los Angeles to Tucson, Ariz. CSmH.

3344   BLACKBURN, Francis Adelbert. 1860–1923. Papers, diaries, travel journals, correspondence, legal papers, sketch books, photographs, family records and memorabilia. CLU.

3345   BRADY, Daniel C. 1860–1865. Economic; agricultural; industrial; social. ICMcCHi.

3346   BREWER, William Henry. 1860–1871. Concerning Western history. CtY.

3347   BURROWS, Mrs. Julius Caesar (Frances Peck). 1860; 1867. A daily journal of two months by student at Prairie Seminary; an account of a trip to Europe. MiU. See 4641.

3348   CALLAN, Nicholas. 1860; 1867–1868. His law practice; state of the weather; politics; the unsettled condition of the country both before and after the Civil War; religion, various government issues. NcD.

3349   CAREY, Henry. 1860–1861. Voyage to San Francisco from N.Y. on the ship Sunshine, and return to Boston; resumé of four other voyages. Ct-MyMM.

3350   CHESTNUT, Mary Boykin Miller (Mrs. James). 1860–1865. One of the best source documents for the Confederacy. NcU.

3351   CLAY, Mary Katherine (Rogers). 1860. Visited "Rockland," "Ellerslie," and "Roseberryland," the home of her grandparents; married Samuel Clay, May 23, 1860, made wedding trip to Washington, D.C., Baltimore, Philadelphia, N.Y., Boston, Quebec, and Montreal; notes on points of interest. KyLoF.

3352   COPE, Sarah Wistar. 1860. Description of Fox House, home of Dr. Arnold in English Lake District, and his wife and daughter. PSC-Hi.

3353   CORNELL, Ezra. 1860–1870. Business affairs; cattle; genealogical tables; personal accounts and notes on Western lands. NIC.

3354   CRANFILL, Isom. 1860; 1863–1877. Includes overland trip, Ill. to Ore., 1847; gives account of affairs of circuit rider in western Ore. OrU.

3355   CRAWFORD, Samuel Wylie. 1860–1861. Kept at Ft. Sumter to the day of the surrender. DLC, copy.

3356   EDMONDSTON, Catherine Ann. 1860–1863. Record of plantation life in eastern N.C.; disturbances preceding the war, various battles, and lists of casualties, and home affairs as the war at first gradually, and then overwhelmingly, affected the plantation. Nc-Ar.

3357   ELLIS, John W. 1860–1861. His official acts as lawyer, judge, gov. of N.C. NcU.

3358   FISH, Lafayette. 1860. Written while he was crossing the plains. CU-B, typescript.

3359   FISH, Mary C. 1860. An overland journey to Cal. CU-B, typescript.

3360   FORT, "Queen." 1860–1866. CNS. TMG.

3361   GARLAND, Kate. 1860–1863. Social life in Va. and Ala. during the Civil War. LU.

3362   GOODFELLOW, Edward. 1860. A tour to Labrador on board the steamer Bibb, by U.S. Coast Survey, the Labrador Eclipse Expedition; hazards of the journey; collisions with icebergs and submerged rocks; fishing industry off Nova Scotia; life of the Eskimos and Indians; magnetic and other scientific observations. PHi.

3363   HALL, Mary. 1860's (?) Kept while she was crossing the plains. CU-B, typescript.

3364   HARRIS, Thomas W. 1860–1870. CNS. MtHi.

3365   HAYDEN, W. W. 1860–1863. His senior year at Williams; his disagreement with Mark Hopkins' views on doctrine; a speech by Elihu Burritt on the extermination of slavery; various college activities. NIC.

3366   JACKSON, Rev. Sheldon. 1860–1881. Diaries by teacher of Choctaw Indians, pastor at Rochester, Minn., Home Missionary, including trips to Alaska. PPPrHi.

3367   JAY, Allen. 1860–? CNS. InRE.

3368   KELLEY, Alfred S. 1860–1864. CNS. OCl-WHi.

3369   LIEBER, Oscar Montgomery. 1860. "A summer excursion to Labrador." ScU.

3370   MANNING, Malvina V. 1860–1862. Includes a record of an overland journey from Tex. to Cal. via Salt Lake. CU-B.

3371   McCARTER, ———. 1860–1866. Includes an account of the burning of Columbia, S.C. DLC, copy.

3372   MEFFERT, William C. 1860–1864. Civil War diaries. WHi.

3373   NAST, Thomas. 1860–1861. Travel diary and daily reminder of his trip abroad. OFH.

3374   OWNER, William. 1860–1867. In Washington, D.C., during the Civil War; gives the extreme Southern viewpoint. DLC.

3375   PARSONS, J. R. 1860–1861. Trips to Cal. NdHi.

3376   PENINGTON, Edward. 1860–1867. CNS. PHi.

3377 PETERSON, Olaf. ca. 1860–1870; 1872–1874. CNS. MnSSb.

3378 PICKERING, J. W. 1860. Diary of incidents in his life as soldier. NElmHi.

3379 PITTS, R. H. 1860–1863. CNS. Nc-Ar. *See* 2712

3380 PRENTISS, George Lewis. 1860. Notes kept in Europe and New York City. NN.

3381 RICHARDSON, Gilbert M. 1860–1861. Lumpkin, Ga. Diary of home life, planting, activities, mentions slaves and their work, picking cotton, etc. GU.

3382 ROUND, W. C. 1860–1862. Personal. NcU.

3383 SAMPSON, Alexander. 1860–1862. CNS. WaU.

3384 SATERLEE, Alfred A. 1860–1861. Brooklyn man's hobby of collecting coins and tokens; political events; Civil War. NN.

3385 SEIDINGER, James D. 1860. CNS. Wv-Ar, typescript.

3386 SMITH, Clement MacDonald. 1860. Personal. MiU.

3387 SOTHERN, Edward Askew. ?–1860. CNS. MH.

3388 SPALDING, Most Rev. Martin J. 1860–1864. CNS. DCU. *See* 3972.

3389 STEDMAN, Edmund Clarence. 1860–1908. CNS. NNC.

3390 TUTTLE, Hyrum S. 1860–1869 (with gaps). Experiences at Columbia, Cal.; corporal in the Cal. Vols., serving chiefly in Utah; return to Cal. and life at Columbia. CU-B.

3391 VOORHEES, Ralph. 1860. Relating to farming, social, and other personal activities. NjR.

3392 WETHERBEE, Nellie M. 1860. Life in N.Y.; marriage; journey to Cal. via Panama; life after arrival in San Francisco. CU-B.

3393 [WOODHOUSE, Commodore Samuel] 1860? A journey from Philadelphia to Liverpool, England. PHi. *See* 1479, 2631.

3394 ANON. 1861. Describes camp life in two eastern Va. locations, one near Aquia; a visit to his home; religious and philosophical meditations. NjR.

3395 ANON. 1861. Diaries of the Cherokee Indian Mission of the Moravian Church. NcWsM.

3396 ANON. 1861. The Confederate camp at Manassas; a trip from Fairfax to Lynchburg; health; skirmishes; life in the Confederate Army, Alexandria, Va.; weather; crop reports; personal accounts. ViU.

3397 ANON. 1861–1862. Kept by a private (?) in an Indiana regt. every day in the Army of Virginia, Gen. Pope's campaign. ICHi.

3398 ANON. 1861–1865. Civil War journal, describing experiences of author as merchant in Fredericksburg, Va., giving account of Union attack on that town; certain details of life behind the lines and in camp. MdHi.

3399 ANON. 1861–1866. Service in Civil War of volunteers of 39th Ohio Volunteer Inf. NN.

3400 ANON. [between 1861 and 1875]. CNS (in Czech). MnHi.

3401 ADAMS, Frank G. 1861–1865. CNS. NNC.

3402 AGER, Edward E. 1861–1918. An overland journey from Harvard, Ill. to Cal. via Salt Lake and the Simpson trail, across Nev.; Civil War experiences; return to Ill. via the Santa Fe trail; includes several subsequent trips to various parts of the West. CU-B.

3403 ARCHER, Fletcher Harris. 1861; 1862. First year of Civil War; references to prayer meetings in the army and everyday events of camp life. NcD.

3404 BAGLEY, Dr. Warren. 1861–1864. Military events in eastern N. C. NcD.

3405 BARHAM, Anna Maria Akehurst. 1861–1871. Athens, Ga., Columbus, Ga. News of war and battles; moves to Columbus and runs a female orphan asylum; prices of commodities, day-to-day life, food, clothing, weather. GU.

3406 BEATTY, Taylor. 1861–1865; 1883–1916 (with gaps). War experience; the management of his sugar plantations in La.; his judicial experience. NcU.

3407 BELL, J. J. 1861. Life at Camp Macon, N.C. NcD.

3408 BELLUNE, J. T. 1861–1862. Farm diary, giving weather conditions, amounts of wood sold, and comments on planting. NcD.

3409 BIRCH, Thomas Stuart. 1861–1862. By a soldier who died while serving in the Civil War. GEU.

3410 BLACKNALL, C. C. [1861–1865]. Civil War diary. NcHiC.

3411 BLACKSHEAR, James Appleton. 1861–1867. A Confederate soldier who after the war taught school, managed a camp of loggers, died while teaching school in La. GEU, copy.

3412 BLOOMER, Samuel. 1861–1863. A trip up the Minnesota to Ft. Ridgely and experiences as color sergeant in the Minn. 1st Vol. Inf. in the Civil War. MnHi.

3413 BONNER, John H. 1861. A journey across the plains to Sacramento, with additional notes of experiences in Cal. CU-B.

3414 BOONE, Thomas. [1861–1864?]. Civil War. PRHi.

3415 BRANSON, W. W. 1861–1862. By a participant in battle of Wilson's Creek, Aug. 10, 1861; day-by-day account of skirmishes with secessionists and other events attendant upon the regt.; trip from Keokuk to Springfield, Mo., via Hannibal, Macon City, and Boonville; rations and living conditions described extensively. MoU.

3416 BROCK, Robert Alonzo. 1861–1862. CNS. CSmH.

3417 BROWN, Stuart M. 1861. CNS. Wv-Ar.

3418 [BRYAN, James A. or James W.] 1861–1864. Ordnance accounts and war diary. NcU.

3419 BUCK, Lucy R. 1861–1862. Civilian reaction to invasion; describes the Federals' occupation and their encampment. ViU, typescript.

3420 BUTLER, James. 1861. With N.Y. Vols. in Civil War at Annapolis, Baltimore, Washington. NN.

3421 CALDER, William. 1861; 1865. Secession in Hillsboro and Raleigh; the final campaign against Sherman's army in N.C. NcD.

3422 CAMERON, Alexander J. 1861–1866. Social and domestic life; considerable detail on Catholic church and lay activity; occasional (remote) references to the war. NjR.

3423 CANANELLO, Charles A. 1861–1864. Confederate diary. FDS.

3424 CANTWEIL, John L. 1861–1864. CNS. Nc-Ar.

3425 CARPENTER, Charles Earl. 1861–1898. Business; political; social; church events. RHi.

3426 CARY, Clarence. 1861–1865. Kept by a midshipman in the Confederate Navy. ViU; DS, copy.

3427 CARY, Wilson. 1861–1864. CNS. ViU. *See* 1813, 3163, 4735.

3428 CHASE, Salmon P. 1861–1863; 1873. Farm diary and calling list. DLC. *See* 3043, 3165.

3429 CLARKE, John Tyler. 1861–1865. Civil War diary. MH.

3430 CLEVELAND, Charles M. 1861; 1864–1866. Weather; current events; daily happenings; the progress of the Civil War. MiU. *See* 2983, 4378.

3431 CLUGSTON, John McNulty. 1861–1864. Civil War Diary in Co. G, 23rd Ohio Vol. Inf. OFH.

3432 COGGESHALL, William Turner. 1861–1867. Kept in Columbus and Springfield, Ohio, and Quito, Ecuador. OHi.

3433 COLEY, Benjamin. 1861. Kept by a lt., begun on Sept. 9 when he left Camden, N.J., and continued through Dec. 31. NjHi.

3434 CONWAY, Edward. 1861–1876. Covering his service with Collins Overland Telegraph Co. and the Western Union's Russian Extension. CU-B.

3435 CORNING, Lizzie M. (Mrs. John White). 1861–1873. A young girl's activities in Concord, N.H., including occasional visits to the army camps, Civil War. NhHi.

3436 CRAWFORD, LeRoy. 1861. Overland trip from N.Y. to Ore. InU-Li.

3437 CREAMER, David. 1861–1862. CNS. DLC.

3438 DENT, Thomas. 1861–1924. Legal affairs; histories of Chicago families; reminiscences of Hennepin, Ill., and Magnolia, Ill.; Chicago Literary Club; Railroad riots of 1876, etc. ICHi.

3439 DICKENSON, Capt. David V. 1861–1863. Civil War diary in the 57th Va. Vols., Pickett's Div., Longstreet's Corps, Army of N. Va.; garrison life; militia recruiting; the *Merrimac*; marches to N.C.; the Peninsular campaign; his resignation. ViU.

3440 DICKINS, Francis A. and Margaret H. 1861–1862. Civil War notes. NcU. *See* 1699.

3441 DOLAN, WILLIAM. 1861–1864. Comings and goings of vessels; sinkings; surrenders; provisioning; Key West as a busy port. ICHi.

3442 DOUGLASS, Garrie. 1861. Notebook and letterbook of life in Maybinton, Newberry Cnty. ScU.

3443 DRENNAN, William A. 1861–1864. Siege of Vicksburg. Ms-Ar.

3444 DURAND, George R. 1861–1865. CNS. NHi.

3445 ELFRETH, Jacob R. 1861–1924. Weather; personal observations; references to Quaker meeting affairs; political events; business matters; fight for local option; prohibition, etc. PHC. *See* 1393.

3446 ELMORE, Grace B. 1861–1872. Personal. NcU.

3447 FAIRCHILD, George. 1861–1864. Civil War. WHi.

3448 FLACK, George W. 1861–1864. Brief entries, kept during his service in Co. M, 8th Pa. Cavalry, attached to the Army of the Potomac. NjR, copy.

3449 FORBES, Stephen Alfred. 1861–1862; 1864–1865. Civil War journals, including his imprisonment in 1862, and subsequent period in an army hospital. IHi.

3450 GALLOWAY, Capt. Joseph D. 1861–1864. With Army of Potomac through campaigns in Va. and Md., and with 3rd Pa. Cavalry in Pa. NN.

3451 GARRETT, Henry A. 1861–1867. Civil War diary and reconstruction in Miss. DLC.

3452 GASKINS, W. B. 1861–1862. Skirmishes with the "rebels," food of soldiers, etc. NcD.

3453 GERE, Thomas P. [1861–1865?] The Civil War period. MnHi.

3454 GILLIS, John A. 1861–1868. Civil War diaries by a member of the 64th Ohio Vol. Inf., Co. K. MnHi.

3455 GORDON, Samuel M. 1861. Kept by a member of Co. H, 25th Regt., Ohio regulars. GEU, copy.

3456 GOVE, Jesse Augustus. 1861. The march of the Utah Expedition from Ft. Bridger to Ft. Leavenworth. CtY.

3457 GOWAN, Lt. W. B. [1861–1865?] Confederate diary. Tx, typescript.

3458 GRACE, Thomas L. 1861. A trip through southern Minn. MnHi, photostat.

3459 GROSS, Oren R. 1861–1862. Life in boarding house in N. Y. city; Civil War excitements. NN.

3460 HAND, George O. 1861–1887. Diary of Civil War period and after; personal experiences and unusual events. AzTP.

3461 HARRISON, John W. 1861. Camp life in Confederate army. NcD.

3462 HARRISON, Dr. Samuel A. 1861–1865. Events in Talbot Cnty., Md., with clippings attached. MdHi.

3463 HART, William T. 1861–1895. Civil War diary in Co. B, 4th Regt. Ohio Vol. Inf.; also views of and notes on Kenyon College, Danville (Knox Cnty.), Ohio, etc. OHi.

3464 HAY, John. 1861–1865. 1865–1870; 1904–1905. Civil War; Paris, Vienna, Madrid. MH.

3465 HAYDON, Charles B. 1861–1864. Experiences in 2nd Mich. Infantry: duties; daily routine; morale; cities and historical sites; Fredericksburg, Ky., and Tenn.; battles of Bull Run; Peninsular Campaign. MiU.

3466 HENLEY, Mary T. 1861–1864. Depredations of Union and Confederate soldiers; desertion of Negroes; burning of property and general lawlessness in Md. NcU.

3467 HILLS, Alfred C. 1861–1862. Army of the Potomac; retreat from Richmond; McClellan's plans; fruitless marches. ICHi.

3468 HOLLOWAY, John Nelson. 1861–1876. The story of his writing and selling *History of Kansas*. KHi.

3469 HOLMES, Emma E. 1861–1862. Detailed account of the Charleston fire in 1861 and of Civil War activities, including local gossip, marriages, purchase of a rapid-fire gun by the city of Charleston, election of officers by the Palmetto Guard, flirtations, etc. NcD.

3470 HOLMES, Henry M. 1861–1865. Activities of a surgeon in Civil War campaigns. ScU.

3471 HOLMES, Philip W. 1861. Military service; camp life in Annapolis and Baltimore; attitude of Marylanders. NN.

3472 HUDGENS, J. F. 1861–1862. Campaigns in Va. and capture at Frederick, Md. MdHi.

3473 INSKEEP, Capt. John D. 1861–1865. Civil War diaries of his service with Co. C, 17th Regt., Ohio Vol. Inf. OHi.

3474 ISAACS, Joseph. 1861–1862. Member N.Y. Vols.: campaigns in N.C.; army dissatisfactions; mutiny. NN.

3475 JENKINS, Walker. 1861. Comments on the outbreak of the Civil War and descriptions of camp life and mercantile transactions. NcD.

3476 JOHNSON, Jesse. 1861–1864. Civil War diary with Co. L, 2nd Regt., W. Va. Vol. Cavalry; fighting at Princeton, Va., and at Lewisburg, Sinking Creek, and Wytheville. PHi.

3477 KEAN, Robert Garlick Hill. 1861–1866. Civil War diary in the 11th Regt., Army of N. Va. as adjutant-general, and as chief of the Confederate Bureau of War; also his later life as an attorney in reconstruction of Lynchburg. ViU.

3478 KELLER, S. B. 1861–1864. Civil War diary. KHi.

3479 KEMPER, Dr. Gen. William Harrison. 1861–1868. Service with the 17th Reg., Ind. Vol., and after. OHi.

3480 KINZER, William T. 1861–1862. In Montgomery Mountain Boys Co. L., 4th Va. Inf. Reg. ViHi. *See* 3122.

3481 LANGBEIN, John Christopher Julius. 1861–1863. Operations of the 9th Reg., N.Y. Vol. Inf., "Hawkins Zouaves." MH.

3482 LEA, A. T. 1861–1863. Army service during the Civil War at various battlefields. NNC.

3483 LEACH, Sarah Gordon. 1861–1872. Diary (and recipe book) describing social and religious life at Hampden-Sydney College; the impact of the Civil War on Southside, Va. ViU.

3484 LE CONTE, Emma Florence. 1861–1865. Burning of Columbia, S. C. Nc-Ar.

3485 LIMLEY, T. H. B. 1861–1863. Civil War diary. Wv-Ar, typescript.

3486 LOCKE, Robert W. 1861–1869. CNS. Ms-Ar.

3487 LURIA, Albert Moses. 1861–1862. War journal, with a description of the battle of Manassas Junction, list of casualties and account of an engagement near Union Mills, Va. Nc-Ar, NcU.

3488 MARSHALL, Rev. M. M. 1861; 1901. Student life at Trinity College and UNC; later, personal. NcU.

3489 MAXWELL, John Anderson. 1861–1865. War experiences; some expense accounts. InHi.

3490 McDOWELL, Sue. 1861. Social activities in Camden. ScU.

3491 McELRATH, John Edgar. 1861. Military in Tenn. TC.

3492 MEANS, Dr. Alexander. 1861; 1873; 1874. CNS. GEU.

3493 MILLER, Alexander R. 1861–1864. Movement of troops; naval maneuvers; encounters with Confederate gunboats; batteries; forts, troops in Ky., Tenn., Ark., Miss., and La. LU, typescript.

3494 MILLIGAN, William. 1861–1862. Experiences in the Union Army as a corporal with Co. A, 85th Pa. Vol. Inf. PWW, typescript.

3495 MITCHELL, Dr. Robert. 1861–1864. Wis. Inf.; movements of the regiments; the wounded; mess accounts. ICHi.

3496 MOORE, Mrs. J. A. 1861–1862. CNS. ScU.

3497 MOORE, James Washington. 1861–1912. War experiences; law practice and legislator. ScU.

3498 MOORE, Robert A. 1861–1863. Military in Tenn., Miss., Ala., Ga., N.C., S.C., and Va. Ms-Ar, typescript.

3499 MORRIS, Robert L. 1861. CNS. MnHi.

3500 NASH, Marie. 1861. Written while she was crossing the plains. CSfC.

3501 NEBLETT, Norman M. 1861; 1867. One kept during the Civil War, the other describing a journey from Va. to Miss., and the life of a cotton planter during Reconstruction. ViU.

3502 NEILSON, James. 1861–1908. Travel to Europe, Canada. PSC-Hi. *See* 3667.

3503 O'BANNON, Lawrence W. 1861–1863. Activities of Catholic priest with Confederate States Army. ScU.

3504 PARKER, Nathan. 1861–1862. Civil War soldier's diary. NcD, microfilm.

3505 PATTON, Charles E. 1861. Events of a buffalo hunt and capture by the Teton Sioux; death of George W. Northrup while with Sibley's expedition of 1863. NdHi.

3506 PHILLIPS, Mrs. ———. 1861–1862 (with gaps). Kept during her imprisonment after her arrest during the Civil War. NcU.

3507 PITCHER, Adolphus R. 1861. Personal experiences and observations by a soldier at Camp Ellis, Raleigh, N.C., and Camp Carolina, Norfolk, Va. Nc-Ar.

3508 PORTER, William. 1861–1885. History of Marion Cnty., Ore, and of local lodge of Good Templars. OrU.

3509 PRESTON, Lt. Col. John T. L. 1861. Diary in Provisional Army, state of Va., on duty at Crany Island. DLC.

3510 REMEY, R. Adm. George Collier. [between 1861 and 1920]. CNS. Ia-HA.

3511 RICKER, Maj. Elbridge G. 1861–1863. His service in the U.S. Army. OCUHi.

3512 RITTER, William L. 1861–1865. Describes various campaigns in the South. MdHi.

3513 ROBINSON, James A. 1861–1863. Civil War diary of Co. H, 120th Regt., Ohio Vol. Inf. OHi.

3514 ROBINSON, William A. 1861–1865. Civil War diary kept by the last commanding officer of the Pa. Inf. 77th Regt. NjR, microfilm.

3515 ROE, Samuel L. 1861–1863. Ga., Tenn., Va. Confederate soldier; brief accounts of battles. Corporal in Co. H., 15th Ga. Regt.; killed at Petersburg, June 20th, 1864. GU, reproduction.

3516 RUSSELL, Rebecca. 1861. Miscellaneous notes and expense accounts. InHi.

3517 SALTONSTALL, Edward H. 1861–1862. Written on the gunboat *Ottawa*. NHi.

3518 SAVAGE, John Nelson. 1861–1862. CNS. WaU.

3519 SCALES, D. Minor. 1861–1863. Daily entries of a sailor aboard the Confederate steamer *Atlanta*, while stationed near Savannah. NcD.

3520 SCOTT, Henry Clay. 1861–1863. Kept by member of 23rd Inf. of N. Y. in Va. NN.

3521 SEARLES, Jasper N. 1861. CNS. MnHi.

3522 SEAY, Gov. Abraham J. 1861–1864. Experiences in the Civil War. OkU.

3523 SEXTON, Capt. Samuel. 1861–1862. Civil War diary of Asst. Surgeon in the 8th Reg., Ohio Vol. Inf. OHi.

3524 SEYMOUR, William J. 1861–1864? Campaigns in Pa. and Va. MiU-C.

3525 SHERLOCK, Eli J. 1861–1865. Account of Civil War experiences; action across South from Vicksburg to Savannah; march to the sea. InHi.

3526 SHOEMAKER, Judge Ferris. 1861–1866. Important people and places; naval activities and ships; Latin American affairs; conditions on the West Coast; relations with Russia; his personal activities and men about him. NIC.

3527 SHOTWELL, Randolph Abbott. 1861–1863. The Confederate Army: battles of Leesburg, Yorktown, Williamsburg, Seven Pines, Seven Days, Second Manassas, Boonesboro, Sharpsburg, Fredericksburg, and Gettysburg. Nc-Ar.

3528 SHREVE, R. C. 1861. Trip from Mount Holly, N.J., to St. Paul, Minn., describing travel by boat and railroad, topography of the country traversed, stopping places, a visit to an Indian reservation on the Minnesota River, events of the Civil War, social and economic conditions. PHi.

3529 SMITH, Benjamin T. 1861–1865. Civil War journal, kept during the period of his service in Co. C, 51st Ill. Regt. NjR, microfilm.

3530 SMITH, Daniel P. [1861–?]? Kept during the campaigns in Ala., Ga., and Tenn., describing army life, his capture, imprisonment, and exchange. ViU.

3531 SOLOMON, Clara Elvina. 1861–1862. Her reactions to thirteen months of the war; describes social conditions and activities in New Orleans. LU.

3532 SPAULDING, Will A. 1861?–? Civil War diaries. MnHi.

3533 SPENCER, Cornelia Phillips. 1861; 1895–1908. Personal. NcU.

3534 STATHEM, David D. 1861–1864. Civil War diaries kept during his service with Co. D, 39th Regt., Ohio Vol. Inf. OHi.

3535 STEBBINS, Jerome K. 1861–1863. Civil War diary by member of Battery C, 1st Reg., Ohio Vol. Light Artillery. OHi, typescript.

3536 STETSON, Sgt. Maj. William Mitchell. 1861–1864. His service with the Northern Army; movements and action of his regt. (chiefly with the 99th N.Y. Vol., U.C.G. Naval Brigade), including an account of the Merrimac-Monitor fight, of which he was an eyewitness. N.

3537 STIARWALT, Andrew. 1861–1864. Civil War diary with 23rd Ohio Vol. Inf. OFH.

3538 STODDARD, Drusilla (Allen). 1861–1862. Four entries only by a teacher and principal of the Ladies' Dept., Central Univ., Pella, Iowa. NjR.

3539 STONE, George G. 1861–1864. Service in Civil War with 16th Mass. Inf.; Baltimore, Washington, Va. campaign; convalescent camp. NN.

3540 STOUT, Charles Bartolette. 1861–1903. Deals with his preparation of school books and magazine articles; Baptist lay activities, visits to Wertsville, N.J. NjR.

3541 STUART, James and Granville. 1861–1866. Life in Montana during the gold rush and the days of the road agents and Vigilantes. CtY. *See* 3209, 4332, 4466.

3542 TAYLOR, Patrick H. and Isaac L. ca. 1861–1865. Kept jointly during Civil War. MnHi.

3543 TERRELL, Henry C. 1861–1862. Men; events; soldier's life in Civil War in Tenn. and Ky. KyHi, typescript.

3544 THOMASON, Matthew D. 1861–1863. First part includes his work as an itinerant Methodist minister; later part, his farming. LU.

3545 THOMPSON, Gilbert. 1861–1864. Military journal in the U.S. Engineer Battalion, Army of the Potomac. DLC.

3546 TICHENOR, G. H. 1861–1863. Activities as 1st Sergeant, Co. B, 2nd Tenn. Cavalry in Ala., Ky., Miss., and Tenn. LU.

3547 TUCKER, Hollis. 1861. CNS. OHi.

3548 TURNURE, David M. 1861–1865. Pertaining to the Civil War. NHi.

3549 VANCE, Zebulon B. 1861–1867; 1878. Diaries on the "Johnston Will Case" with a few entries on economic conditions and political speeches, and on Vance's 1878 campaign for the U.S. Senate. Nc-Ar.

3550 WABRAD, Mrs. Jane Mullen. 1861–1867. Daily events in and about Jacksonville, Ore. OrU, typescript.

3551 WAGENER, J. H. A. 1861–1862. From Manassas to Williamsburg; march from the peninsula below Richmond to Gordonsville, into Farquier Cnty., into Md., and finally to Winchester. ScHi.

3552 WALN, Edward. 1861–1887. The life of a wealthy man interested in politics and country life. PHi.

3553 WARMOTH, Henry Clay. 1861–1931. War experiences; politics; plantation; family; neighborhood and national affairs. NcU. *See* 3125.

3554 WELLS, James L. 1861–1865. Diary of a Confederate soldier and recollections of a Federal prison during the War. ScU.

3555 WHEDON, Helen M. (Mrs. W. W.). 1861–1869. Daily life; few comments on current events of national significance. MiU.

3556 WYATT, Asa J. 1861–1862. Civil War diary with Co. I, 21st Regt. Va. Vol. NcU.

3557 YOUNG, John A. 1861. Confederate War diary while he was at camp in N.C. and Va.; general details of battle of Bull Run; epidemic of measles in camp; nursing service of the ladies of Richmond, Va. Nc-Ar.

3558 ANON. 1862. The voyage and capture by Federal naval forces of a "British Steamship *Emilie* commanded by Captain D. B. Vincent" off Port Royal for blockade running. ScU.

3559 ANON. 1862. Indian uprising. MnMHi.

3560 ANON. 1862–? Civil War diary. Nc-Ar, microfilm.

3561 ANON. 1862–1864. CNS. Nc-Ar.

3562 ANON. 1862–1866. Farm life; Civil War; Lincoln's funeral at Albany; glove making. NCoo-Hi.

3563 ABEEL, Gustavus Neilson. 1862. A trip to Europe and return, describing visits to the British Isles, France, Switzerland, Germany, etc. NjR.

3564 ADAMS, Henry Sylvanus. 1862–1863. Service in 3rd Mass. Cavalry around New Orleans during Civil War. NN.

3565 AINSWORTH, Calvin. 1862–1865. Army life with the 25th Iowa Inf., Vol.: battles, camps, Vicksburg, Lookout Mountain. MiU.

3566 ALEXANDER, Richard H. 1862. Narrative based upon a diary and letters of overland journey from St. Paul to New Westminster, B.C. CU-B.

3567 ANDERSON, Dr. Charles. 1862. Kept on the overland trail from Minn. to Nev.; practice of medicine in Carson City. CU-B, copy.

3568 ANDERSON, Nicholas Longworth. 1862–1864. During the war by a lt. col. of 6th O.V.I., the Guthrie Grays, a Cincinnati regt. OCUHi.

3569 ANTHONY, Henry J. 1862–1863. Military duties and camp life in Co. I, 11th Regt., R.I.; volunteer on duty around Washington and Va.; no combat. RHi.

3570 ARCHER-BURTON, L. J. G. 1862. CNS. MnHi, typescript.

3571 ARDREY, William E. 1862–1907. Civil War service; the weather; home life; family; community life; farming operations and accounts, including a yearly summary; Methodist church; Reconstruction; Negroes; the Grange; fire insurance; local education. NcD.

3572 ARKINS, William. 1862–1863. Civil War diaries. MnHi.

3573 ARMSTRONG, Ezekiel. 1862. The Seven Days Battle at Richmond, Va., and the Maryland campaign; battles; attitude of civilians; sermons preached by chaplains; food purchased. LU, microfilm.

3574 BACHE, Alexander Dallas, Jr. 1862; 1867; 1868–1870. Cruises of the U.S.S. *Hartford* and the U.S.S. *Iroquois*. PPAmS.

3575 BAECHTEL, Luther S. 1862–1865. Combination diary, notebook, and account book; casualties incurred by Burt Rifles in the Battle of Sharpsburg. Ms-Ar.

3576 BAILEY, John Batchelder. 1862–1865. Civil War experiences. NhHi.

3577 BALLANTINE, William H. 1862. Civil War diary of a member of Co. G, 96th Regt., Ohio Vol. Inf., at Newport, Ky. OHi.

3578 BANTA, William H. 1862. A Federal soldier who served in the campaign in eastern N. C.; mention is made of Norfolk, Va., and the *Merrimac*. NcD.

3579 BARD, Isaac N. [1862–1917]. His life as a trader; his early attempts at farming; trips to Omaha with cattle, and to Denver, Chicago, and the World's Fair, to Cal. and Tex.; life on his Chugwater and Little Bear ranches. CtY.

3580 BASSETT, Sgt. George W. 1862–1863. Civil War diary of sgt. of 33rd Regt., N.Y., killed at the battle of Sharpsburg. NIC.

3581 BASSETT, Sgt. Rasmus E. 1862–1863. Civil War diary of sgt. in 126th Regt., N.Y., killed at the battle of Gettysburg. NIC.

3582 BEITH, James. 1862–1888. His life and activities, chiefly in Arcata, Cal.; includes observations on logging, mining, politics, Indians, friends, and associates. CU-B.

3583 BENJAMIN, Judah P. 1862–1864. Events in the Confederacy. DLC.

3584 BENSELL, Royal A. 1862–1864. Life of Co. D, 4th Inf., Cal. Vol., stationed at Ft. Yamhill, Ore. OrU, microfilm.

3585 BOND, Samuel R. 1862. James L. Fisk's expedition, which passed through Minn. on the way from St. Paul to Ft. Abercrombie. MIpHi; MnHi, typescript.

3586 BOSTON, William. 1862–1865. Union soldier of Co. H, 20th Mich. Vol. Inf., 9th Army Corps; army life and battles; campaigns included Fredericksburg, Ky., Miss., Wilderness, Petersburg. MiU, hectograph.

3587 BRADFORD, Augustus W. 1862–1865. Daily actions as gov. of Md. in connection with appointments and pardons. MdHi.

3588 BRANLINGHAM, Henry and W. H. S. Burgwyn. 1862–1864. Routine happenings in camp, with comments on food and other supplies, marches, and news from home. NcHiC.

3589 BRINCKERHOFF, Isaac W. 1862–1863. Experiences and observations as a Freedman's Bureau superintendent of plantations near Beaufort, S.C. NjR.

3590 BROTHERS, Charles. 1862–1865. Kept while he was aboard U.S. sloop *Hartford*, Western Gulf blockading squadron, Adm. Farragut's flagship. InU-Li.

3591 BROWN, W. C. 1862–1865. Military diary by a Confederate soldier recruited in Hamilton Cnty., Tenn., whose battery saw service in Ga., Ala., and Miss. TC.

3592 BULLITT, Thomas W. 1862–1863. Civil War diary of 2nd lt. in Col. Basil W. Duke's regt. of Ky. Cavalry, C.S.A., containing comments on actions engaged in and prison life. NcU.

3593 BURKETT, H. L. 1862. The weather; crops; Union forces; Confederate forces; military operations near the Tennessee River; personal affairs. NcD.

3594 CANRIGHT, Soloman. 1862–1863. Civil War diary. WWauHi.

3595 CARMAN, Ezra A. 1862–1864. His service in the N.J. troops during the Civil War. NjHi.

3596 CARPENTER, Elizabeth. 1862–1863. Kept while at Earlham. InRE.

3597 CHADWICK, Mary Ione (Cook). 1862–1865. Describes Federal raids on and occupation of Huntsville, Ala.; comments on local people and trouble with slaves occasioned by the presence of Federal troops. NcD, typescript.

3598 CHAMBERS, Henry Alexander. 1862–1865. Experiences and observations, first as a private, then as captain on marches through N. C. and Va. NcHiC, typescript. *See* 4338.

3599 CHAPMAN, George H. 1862; 1863. Civil War in Va., with Ind. Regt. during inactivity of peninsular campaign. InHi.

3600 CHILDRESS, George L. 1862–1865. Personal experiences, earnings, and expenditures with the 66th Ill. Vol. Regt. during the Civil War. IU, typescript.

3601 CLARK, John A. 1862; 1867. A trip from St. Anthony, Minn., to Ore. gold mines; entries at Idaho Mines in 1867. MnHi.

3602 CLARK, Nathan. 1862–1863. The weather and the movements of the 6th Mich. Inf. Regt. MiU.

3603 CRAWFORD, Medorem. 1862. A journey by ship from Ore. to N.Y. by way of Panama and return to Ore. by overland trail from Omaha, Neb., conducting a military escort for the protection of emigrants. InU-Li. *See* 3298.

3604 DABNEY, George William. 1862–1865. CNS. ViU.

3605 DEADY, Michael. 1862; 1863. Memoranda in 23rd Ohio Vol. Inf., Co. A. OFH.

3606 DEAN, W. J. 1862–1865. Civil War diary. WOshM.

3607 DIBB, William Denton. 1862–1864. James L. Fisk's expedition from St. Paul to Idaho. MnHi, photostats.

3608 DODD, Mrs. William B. 1862–1863. Visits to hospitals in St. Peter; private affairs; her husband's death during the Sioux outbreak. MnHi.

3609 DOUD, George W. 1862–1864. His service with the 8th Minn. Vol. Inf. in the Sioux War in 1862, guarding the frontier at Ft. Tipley, Princeton, Sunrise City. Ft. Ridgely, and Ft. Snelling, and with the Sibley expedition of 1864. MnHi, typescript.

3610 DOUGLAS, Emily Caroline. 1862–1863. Life in Washington, Miss.; visits to neighbors and to Jefferson College; choir practice; active participation in civilian aid to Confederate soldiers. LU.

3611 DUVALL, W. D. F. 1862. Account of camp life; a march to Culpeper Court House; a camp on Freeman's hill; the burned bridge at Rapidan Station, all in Va. NcD.

3612 EARNHARDT, Peter C. 1862. Memoranda of a Union soldier. NcD.

3613 FISH, Juliette G. 1862. Crossing the plains. CSmH.

3614 FOSTER, Robert Watson. 1862–1864. Establishing a plantation near Apalousas, La.; descriptions of the white and Negro inhabitants; daily work; military activities; life in the Civil War period. RHi.

3615 FREUDENREICH, Baron Frederick de. 1862–1870. His truck and nursery farm near St. Paul; current events. MnHi.

3616 GARDINER, James H. 1862–1863. CNS. NHi.

3617 GAWTHROP, Henry. 1862–1866. Lists officers, movements of troops, weather. DeHi.

3618 GLINES, Henry C. 1862. Union camp life and skirmishing in Ga. and S.C., in the vicinity of Ft. Pulaski and Beaufort. NNC.

3619 GOLDSBOROUGH, R. Adm. Louis M. 1862–? Naval career in the Civil War. PHi.

3620 GRAPLY, D. W. 1862–1863. Civil War diary; naval battles and other experiences off Charleston, S.C. PHi.

3621 GRAYSON, William John. 1862–1863. CNS. ScU.

3622 GREEN, Austin O. 1862; 1864; 1866–1867. Daily activities in Miss., Ala., and Tenn.; the battle for Atlanta; his mustering-out. MoU.

3623 GRIFFITH, Richard H. 1862. His experiences in the Army during the Civil War. PHi. *See* 4385.

3624 GUENGERICH, S. D. 1862–1900. Business; weather; trips. InGoM.

3625 GUION, Lewis. 1862–1863. Siege of Vicksburg and events following its fall. LU.

3626 HANDY, Frank A. 1862–1865. The celebration held in Nashville, Tenn., over the capture of Atlanta; an interview with Gen. W. S. Rosecrans; a trip to Washington; attempts to gain a higher commission; business transactions of the company; social life, customs, and outstanding plantations near Nashville. NcD.

3627 HARPER, Ella A. R. (Mrs. George W. F.). 1862–1865. CNS. NcU.

3628 HASKELL, Sophia Lovell. 1862–1866. Begins with entries at Miss de Choiseul's school in Flat Rock, N.C.; books read; family incidents; poems. ScHi.

3629 HAUSER, Samuel Thomas. 1862. Journey from Sioux City, Iowa, to Ft. Benton, Dakota Terr.; scenery; parley with Indians; trips; events. CLU-C. *See* 4217.

3630 HEPBURN, Hawley S. 1862–1864. Civil War diaries. NNC.

3631 HOCH, John. 1862–1865. Civil War diary in Co. A, 96th Inf. Reg. IHS.

3632 HOFFMAN, William Wellington. 1862–1876. One-line entries; recorded in same volume with scattered farm accounts. NjR.

3633 HOPKINS, Samuel Johnson. 1862–1865. Experiences and observations connected with his military service in Co. H, 7th N.J. Vols., and in 1865 in Co. B, 40th N.J. Vols. NjR.

3634 HUME, Fannie Page. 1862. CNS. ViHi. *See* 3244.

3635 HUMPHRIES, Milton Wylie. 1862–1865. Life in the Confederate Army; capture and release by the Union forces; camp conditions; skirmishes; feelings on hearing the news of Appomattox, etc. ViU.

3636 HYATT, Arthur W. 1862–1864. La. and Fla. companies in the Confederate States Army; day-by-day movements; accounts of battles and skirmishes; conditions on the march and in camp; opinions of superior officers while with the Confederate Army. LU.

3637 JACKSON, William Henry. 1862–1942. Union soldier in Civil War; photographer for Union Pacific Railroad and U.S. Geological Survey in Rockies; world tours; daily life as painter and photographer in old age. NN.

3638 JANZEN, Cornelius. 1862–1913. A yearly record in German of a Minn. immigrant from Russia who settled on a farm near Mountain Lake, Minn. MnHi, microfilm.

3639 JESUP, Rev. Henry G. 1862–1863. His experiences in Minn., where he went to regain his health. NHi.

3640 JILLSON, Daniel A. 1862–1864. Diary with Co. G of the 29th Regt. Mass. Vol. Inf.; camp life and skirmishes in Va. and troop movements. NNC.

3641 JOHNSTON, Capt. George Burgwyn. 1862. Co. G, 28th N.C.V.; prisoner of war on Johnson's Island, Sandusky Bay, Ohio; trip from Ft. Columbus back home. Nc-Ar.

3642 JONES, Ada M. 1862. Kept at the age of 13, while she was crossing the plains to Cal. CU-B.

3643 KING, Cpl. Charles G. 1862–1864. Civil War diary. PPiAcssmh.

3644 KING, W. N. 1862–1865. Confederate diary. Tx.

3645 LAMBERTON, Robert C. 1862–1866. CNS. OClWHi, copy.

3646 LATROBE, Asman. 1862–1865. Describes various Civil War engagements. MdHi.

3647 LAY, Rt. Rev. Henry Champlin. 1862–1885. Confederate history; the post war reunion of the Episcopal Church. NcU. *See* 3931.

3648 LE DUC, Mary C. 1862. CNS. MnHi.

3649 LEMMON, John Gill. 1862–1864. Serving as a hospital orderly at Nashville and with the 4th Mich. Cavalry, through the Atlanta Campaign. CSmH.

3650 LEWIS, Oscar E. 1862–1863. On board the U.S. gunboat *Port Royal*. NHi.

3651 LITTLE, George W. 1862–1863. Military. ICHi.

3652 LITZENBERG, William H. and Charles A. 1862–1878. CNS. PHi.

3653 MARKLEY, John H. 1862–1863. Civil War diary. PHi.

3654 MARVIN, Matthew. 1862–1864. Civil War diary. MnHi.

3655 McCOMAS, Evans S. 1862–1867. Overland journey from Iowa City, Iowa, to Auburn, Ore.; songs and ballads. OrU.

3656 McCREARY, James Bennett. 1862–1863. Observations; people; events of officer of 11th Ky. Cav., C.S.A., who saw action at Hartville and other battles. KyHi. *See* next entry.

3657 McCREARY, James Bennett. 1862–1864. An account of Morgan's raid, north of the Ohio River, and of life in Ky. and Tenn. during the Civil War. NcD.

3658 McCULLOUGH, Samuel Thomas. 1862–1865. Civil War diary in 2nd Md. Inf., Army of N. Va.; battles; lists of casualties; notes on weather. ViU.

3659 McDONALD, Sue S. 1862–1864. Diary of a young girl, commenting on her friends and activities and including copies of poems. NcD.

3660 [MEGIE, Samuel Miller]. 1862. Farm work at Murray Hill, Union Cnty., N.J.; family life; cats. NN.

3661 MERRILEES, John. 1862–1865. Member of Ill. Vol.; good accounts of battles and skirmishes: Vicksburg, Jackson, Nashville, ICHi.

3662 MILLINGTON, Ada. 1862. Written at age of 13, while she was crossing the plains, and elaborated on five years later. CU-B, photostat.

3663 MILLSBAUGH, David. 1862–1865. Civil War experiences of soldier in Co. E, 18th Inf., Mich. Vol., principally as sentry and guard of prisoners of war; life in camps near Lexington and Nashville; arrests; campaign; military occupation. MiU.

3664 MORLEY, James Henry. 1862–1865. Diary from St. Louis to mining in Gold Creek, Bannack, Virginia City, Helena, and Blackfoot City. MtHi.

3665 MORRILL, True. 1862–1863. Military diary by a member of 38th Iowa Vol. Regt., Co. K. (in Graham Shorthand). MnHi.

3666 NASH, Francis H. 1862–1865. Va., Tenn., Miss., Ga., N.C. Private in 42nd Regt. of Ga. Vols., C.S.A., fought all over the South, retreated before Sherman in Ga., surrendered with Gen. Johnston to Sherman on April 26, 1865. GU, typescript.

3667 NEILSON, James. 1862–1866. Farm journal near New Brunswick, N.J. PSC-Hi. *See* 3502.

3668 NELSON, John. 1862–1866. Service in the South and punitive expeditions against the Sioux. MnHi.

3669 NICKERSON, William J. 1862–1865. CNS. NNC.

3670 NICOLS, John. 1862; 1864; 1869. Weather record; household expenses; data on the Methodist Church, the iron trade, University of Minn. MnHi.

3671 NIGHSWANDER. F. M. 1862–1870. Account of trip, via Panama, from Ohio to Cal. in 1862, and removal to Lane Cnty. in 1864; as much reminiscence as diary; some letters supplement the diary. OrU.

3672 NUNNELEE, Lt. L. T. 1862. Many of the major campaigns throughout the Civil War and his furloughs in Pittsylvania Cnty. and Lynchburg. ViU.

3673 OAKLEY, Isaac J. 1862–1902. CNS. NP.

3674 OEHMLER, Capt. H. O. C. 1862–1864. Civil War diary. PPiAcssmh.

3675 OWEN, Mrs. Della (Mann). 1862. Civil War news; personal and local affairs. InU-Li.

3676 PARKHURST, Warner. 1862–1865. Civil War diary of member of Iowa Reg. KHi, typescript.

3677 PARMATER, N. L. 1862–1865. Civil War diaries in Co. E, 29th Ohio Vol. Inf. OHi.

3678 PARSONS, ———. 1862. Diary describing difficulties encountered by a recruiting officer for his regiment and complaining of mismanagement and favoritism. LU, typescript.

3679 PITTS, Florison D. 1862–1864. Personal reactions to the civilian population and impressions of the cities kept by a Federal soldier stationed near New Orleans and at Baton Rouge. LU, microfilm; ICHi, original.

3680 POPE, Col. Albert A. 1862–1865. Describes his Civil War experiences with the 35th Mass. Regt.; campaigns in Va., Tenn., and Miss. ViU, typescript.

3681 RAHM, Louisa Moeller. 1862. Written while she was crossing the plains. CU-B, photostat.

3682 REEDER, William C. 1862–1883. Military in Franklin, Warren Cnty., Ohio, by a member of Co. B, 146th Regt., Ohio Vol. Inf. during the Civil War. OHi.

3683 ROSENDAHL, Paul H. 1862–1863. Kept on the Sibley expedition against the Sioux in 1863 and in various camps in southern Minn. during the preceding winter. MnHi.

3684 RUMLEY, Charles. 1862–1863. Diary of trip, partly on steamer *Emelie*, stops made, Indians encountered; forts. CLU-C.

3685 SCHARF, Albert F. 1862–1915 (with gaps). Boyhood in Peru, Ill.; life in Chicago; scattered entries; trip through Ill. to gather material for Indian maps and mss., 1899–1916. ICHi.

3686 SCOTT, Hamilton. 1862. Interesting account of the Indian massacre which took place below American Falls, Ida., in 1862; additional notes by Alvin Zaring, one of the party. IdHi.

3687 SHANKLAND, William F. 1862. Private journal aboard the U.S. gunboat *Currituck*; begins with the voyage from N.Y. to Hampton Roads as consort to the *Monitor* and later covers a period of duty on the James River. DLC.

3688 SHAW, Charles A. 1862–1866. Personal, introspective diary of a would-be artist, author, and musician. PHi.

3689 SHEEHAN, Timothy J. 1862; 1874; 1885; 1892; 1893; 1896; 1898; 1900; 1908. Kept by deputy U.S. marshal and Indian agent at White Earth Reservation. MnHi.

3690 SHOEMAKER, Franklin. 1862–1867. Short diary of the great rebellion. PHi.

3691 SIBLEY, Henry Hastings. 1862–1863. His campaigns against the Sioux. MnHi.

3692 SKINNER, Rhoads. 1862. Civil War diary during service in the 56th Regt., N.Y. State Vols., and 1st Regt., N.Y. Mounted Rifles. NjR.

3693 SLY, George Eliot. 1862–1864. Service with the 4th Minn. Vol. Inf. in the Civil War. MnHi.

3694 SMITH, Eugene K. 1862–1895. Kept in Graham shorthand by a teacher and minister, Advent Christian Church, Hennepin Cnty., Minn. MnHi.

3695 SNOW, George H. 1862–1863. Civil War journal. NjR, microfilm.

3696 SPAULDING, Oliver Lyman. 1862–1865. Kept by army officer in Civil War; everyday routine; operations in Ky.; weather; fellow officers; freeing of slaves. MiU.

3697 SPENCER, H. H. 1862; 1871–1872. Passage of steamboats on the Minnesota River; news of the Sioux outbreak; farming operations and prices for products. MnHi.

3698 STEVENS, John O. 1862. With company B of the 2nd N.H. Regt. NNC.

3699 STEWART, Isaac Newton. 1862–1864. Civil War diary. WWauHi.

3700 SULLIVAN, W. W. 1862. Crossing the plains. CSmH.

3701 TALLMAN, John. 1862–1864. A record of troop movements supplemented by 52 good letters. ICHi.

3702 TAYLOR, Norman. 1862–1863. Diary of a private in the Vt. Inf., 16th Regt., Co. C; mainly concerns Union camp life in northern Va. NNC.

3703 TAYLOR, Capt. Robert B. 1862. Journal with 32nd Ky. Inf., describing action before and after Perryville, with diagrams and artist's conceptions of the action. KyHi. *See* 3837.

3704 THOMAS, Col. W. H. 1862–1865. CNS. Nc-Ar.

3705 TITCOMB, George. 1862–1865. Soldier in the 9th Kan. Cav., serving in Kan., Ark., and Mo. under generals James G. Blunt, Thomas Ewing, Joseph R. West, and C. C. Andrews successively. CSmH.

3706 VAN VLECK, Arthur L. 1862–1863. Descriptions of camp life by a Union soldier. NcU.

3707 WADDEL, Rev. John Newton. 1862–1864. Kept by president of La Grange College, La Grange, Tenn., and general superintendent of Presbyterian missions in the Western Conference Army. DLC.

3708 WANDLING, Jacob Castner. 1862–1863. His service as a private in Co. B, 31st N.J. Inf., a 9-month regiment engaged chiefly in Va., including Chancellorsville; also a letter which he wrote during the war to a brother serving in the Confederate army. NjR, microfilm.

3709 WHEELER, Delos M. 1862–1885. Farm life; mostly chores done. NCooHi.

3710 WOOD, John Kingsley, 1862–1865. Kept by a member of Co. F of the 6th Minn. Vol. Inf. on Sibley's expeditions against the Sioux Indians, in Minn. frontier forts, and at the Sioux encampment near Ft. Snelling, and in the South during the Civil War. MnHi.

3711 ANON. 1863. Civil War diary. MnRHi.

3712 ANON. 1863. Kept by a member of an Ill. regt.; mentions Danville, Ky., Ft. Donelson, Franklin, Tenn., and 9th Ohio Battery and 40th Regt., Ohio Vol. Inf. OHi.

3713 ANON. 1863. Rebel diary; captured at Resaca, Ga.; events and rumors among the Confederate soldiers besieged at Vicksburg. InU-Li.

3714 ANON. 1863. Kept during Christopher Carson's Navajo campaign in N.M. CSmH.

3715 ANON. 1863–1864. an assistant surgeon of the 60th Regt., Ind. Vol. InU-Li.

3716 ANON. 1863–1866. The British military campaign in the Maori War in New Zealand. PHi.

3717 ANON. 1863–1871. CNS. PHi.

3718 ANON. 1863–1883. CNS. NcU.

3719 ADAMS, Ellen T. 1863. An overland journey from Council Bluffs, Iowa, across the plains to Cal. CU-B.

3720 ALLEN, Littlebury W. 1863–1864. Kept by a prisoner of war at Johnson's Island, Ohio. CSmH.

3721 ALLOWAY, John W. 1863. Civil War diary in Coppers' Battery, Battalion B, 1st Penn. Artillery; eyewitness account of camp life, marches, allocation of troops, and battles at Gettysburg, Rappahannock River, and Williamsford; refers to draft riots in N.Y. PHi.

3722 AREHART, William H. 1863–1865. By a Confederate soldier of Co. H, 12th Regt., Va. Cavalry, describing his war activites and camp life. NcD.

3723 ATWOOD, Darwin. 1863–1865. Kept by a private in the Wis. Heavy Artillery; Madison to Chicago to Pittsburgh and Philadelphia; descriptions of country, rations, conscripts and volunteers. ICHi.

3724 BALFOUR, Miss. 1863. Siege of Vicksburg. Ms-Ar, typescript.

3725 BALLARD, John J. 1863–1864. Civil War diary by Confederate soldier. ICHi.

3726 BELSHAW, George. 1863. Journey from Lake County, Ind., to the Willamette valley in Ore.; daily mileage, condition of the road, description of the camp sites, and prices for food and grain. CtY, typescript; CSmH; WaU.

3727 BENNETT, Peter V. 1863. His service in Union Army, stationed in the South for the greater part of the time. KHi.

3728 BONNEY, Henry M. 1863. Remarks on board the U.S.S. *De Soto*, with lists of prizes taken by the ship. NNC.

3729 BRIGGS, Ellen R. 1863–1872. Life in small Wis. town: church gatherings, music lessons, teaching school. ICHi.

3730 BROWN, Elon Francis. 1863. Kept during Brown's service as a sgt. in Co. H, 2nd Wis. Vols., in Va., etc. NjR, microfilm.

3731 BROYLES, Margaret Taliaferro. 1863–1872. Account book and journal re life in Tenn. ScU.

3732 CARPENTER, Caroline. 1863–1864. Kept at Earlham. InRE.

3733 CLANDENING, William H. 1863–1865. Kept while he was crossing Minn., N.D., and Mont. en route to Mont. gold fields and while on a trip to Philadelphia. NdHi, copy.

3734 CLAPP, George Christopher. 1863. The military expedition against the Sioux Indians. MnHi, typescript.

3735 CLEMENTS, T. W. April 24–July 1, 1863. Va., Md., Gettysburg, Pa. Sgt. in 8th Regt., Ga. Vols.; camp life, forced marches, etc.; diary ends "going into battle July 2, 1863." Clements was "wounded in hip, knee and foot" and died of tetanus July 11, 1863. Original is property of the La Grange Chapter United Daughters of the Confederacy. GU.

3736 CLIFTON, J. B. 1863–1864. Marching, encampments, and weather in Md. and Pa; mentions skirmishes and lists his correspondents. NcHiC.

3737 COLLINS, Loren Warren. 1863. On Sibley's expedition. MnHi.

3738 CONVERSE, John Melvin. 1863–1864. Written by a Confederate prisoner at Andersonville and later at Florence, S.C.; a member of the 39th Ill. Vol. Inf. KHi.

3739 COOKINGHAM, John. 1863; 1868. Chiefly about farming, weather; scattered references to social activity; occasional detached allusions to the war. NjR.

3740 COPPERNOLL, Ferdinando H. 1863–1865; 1884; 1889–1894; 1903–1905; 1918. La. and Tex.; Cayuga County, N.Y. Served in the U. S. Army as cpl., later sgt. in Co. B., 75th Regt. N. Y. State Vols. In 1863–1865 he fought in La. and Tex., was taken prisoner. The diaries for these years concern camp life, battles, prison life. After the war, he returned home to N. Y. state. Diaries from 1884 on are day-by-day accounts of life on a farm at Deposit, near Syracuse, N.Y. GU.

3741 CROSS, Charles H. 1863. CNS. NIC.

3742 CUTTING, A. Howard. 1863. Overland trip from Fidelity, Ill., to Sacramento via Oregon trail and Salt Lake City. CSmH.

3743 DABNEY, Cornelius. 1863–1869. Civil War diary of a Confederate soldier. Nc-Ar.

3744 DARLING, Lucia. 1863. A trip across the plains in the summer of 1863, from Omaha to Bannack, Mont. Terr. MtHi.

3745 DAVENPORT, Phineas F. 1863–1864. Personal; weather; war news. OFH.

3746 DAVENPORT, Seth. 1863–1864. Personal; weather; war news. OFH.

3747 DAVIS, William H. 1863–1864. Serving with the Confederate Army; imprisoned at Rock Island Prison, Ill. GEU, copy.

3748 DOUGHERTY, Daniel. 1863–1864. Civil War diary of a capt. in Co. H, 63rd Regt., Penn. Vol. PHi.

3749 EASTMAN, Enoch N. 1863; 1913–1914. A teamster with Hatches battalion on the Sibley expedition of 1863; four letters, 1913–1914, to state historical society. NdHi.

3750 EDER, Franz. 1863; 1865. Civil War service as private in 119th Regt., N.Y. Vol.; enlistment in N.Y. City. NN.

3751 ELLIS, J. N. and M. H. 1863. CNS. Tx, typescript.

3752 FAHNESTOCK, George Wolff and Anna M. 1863–1867; 1869–1873. CNS. PHi.

3753 FEILDEN, Col. Sir Henry Wemyss. 1863–1890. Includes a description of the attack on Charleston, and of Southern business and finance in this period. ViU.

3754 FERRIS, Rev. Benjamin Franklin. 1863. Includes farm work by a Methodist Episcopal minister and Republican member of Ind. House of Representatives. InHi.

3755 FISK, Wilbur F. 1863–1864. Campaign in Va. and Md. by a private in the 2nd Regt. Vt. Inf. MnHi.

3756 FOX, Sgt. Isaac. 1863–1864. Military: Co. F, 114th Penn. Vol. PHi.

3757 FULKERATH, Abby E. 1863. An overland journey from Iowa, across the plains to Placerville, Cal. CU-Ar.

3758 FULKERATH, William L. 1863. Overland journey with his wife from Iowa to Cal. CU-B, photostat.

3759 GORE, William B. 1863–1866. Autobiographical. NHi.

3760 GRAHAM, Lt. James E. 1863–1865. Service with Co. K, 80th Regt., Ohio Vol. Inf., Vicksburg, Miss., etc., and in Co. G. OHi.

3761 GRANNIS, John U. 1863–1868; 1876–1878 (with gaps). Journey from Colo. to Mont.; life as miner and rancher in Mont. MtHi.

3762 GRATACAD, Louis Pope. 1863. Boyhood on Staten Island; school; church; games; home life. NN. *See* 4315.

3763 GREEN, Dr. J. E. 1863–1872. Co. I, 53rd Regt.: the march through Va., Md., and Pa., and on battlefields of Va., together with notations after the war on a farm near Benson, N.C. Nc-Ar.

3764 GREENLEY, E. M. 1863–1864. A European trip. MiU-C.

3765 GRIFFITH, John W. 1863–1865. Civil War diaries kept during duty with Co. G, 32nd Regt., Ohio Vol. Inf. OHi.

3766 GRIFFITH, Mrs. Martha E. (Hutchings), M.D. 1863; 1866. The excitement at Vernon, Ind., at the time of the Morgan raid; studying obstetrics. InU-Li.

3767 HAIRSTON, Peter W. 1863–? War experiences; a trip to Europe prior to the war. NcU.

3768 HAMILTON, Ellis. 1863–1864. Civil War: Co. E, F, 15th N.J. Vols., with Army of the Potomac. PSC-Hi.

3769 HARDING, Miss Sidney. 1863–1864. Life of a Civil War refugee family fleeing its plantation home for the third time to live in a log house within Confederate lines in Keachie, DeSoto Parish, La., and of its activities in the temporary home. LU.

3770 HARDING, Simeon. 1863–1872. Life at St. Charles, including records of numerous financial transactions, data on agricultural conditions, and accounts of events. MnHi.

3771 HAYES, Mrs. Hiram. 1863–1880. Life of the more prominent pioneer women of early Superior; many of the early Superior residents are mentioned. WSHi.

3772 HEACOCK, J. L. 1863–1868. Civil War diary. PSC-Hi.

3773 HEAZLITT, James B. 1863. Operations of Knap's Independent Battery, "E" Light Art., Pa. Veteran Vol. CSmH.

3774 HEWLINGS, Mrs. Harriet Black. 1863. CNS. OHi.

3775 HICKS, Henry G. 1863. Military: Ill. regts. MnHi.

3776 HILL, William H. 1863. Civil War diaries. Ms-Ar.

3777 HINCKLEY, Oscar B. 1863–1865. Observations on the weather; trip to New Bern, N.C., Camp Currituck canal, and daily army activities. NcD.

3778 HOGE, Rev. Moses Drury. 1863. Trip to England to purchase bibles for the Confederate Army and his return with the bibles through the Union blockade. ViU.

3779 HOPPER, Silas J. 1863. Kept while he was crossing the plains from Nebraska City to Cal. CSmH.

3780 HOSTETTER, Hiram H. 1863–1864. Military in Co. E, 45th Regt., Ohio Vol. Inf. OHi.

3781 HUNTLY, John C. 1863. Eyewitness account of war conditions and operations against the Confederate forces; rumors of battles; troop movements; military and naval affairs; personal notes. PHi.

3782 IRWIN, Lt. Col. John. 1863–1865. Experiences in most of the battles of the Army of the Potomac from Chancellorsville to Petersburg. PHi.

3783 JOHNSON, Charles F. 1863; 1871–1873; 1875; 1876; 1877–1879; 1880–1883; 1884–1886. Military; personal. MnHi.

3784 JOHNSON, Elijah J. 1863. CNS. ViHi.

3785 JONES, Robert Elam. 1863–1864. First lieutenant, Co. K, 36th Regt. of Miss. Inf., C.S.A. Ms-Ar.

3786 KEYS, William Farrand. 1863; 1864. Civil War journal with full and articulate entries; the writer, previously a teacher of Williamsport, Pa., was a private in Co. K, 143rd Penn. Inf. Regt., serving chiefly in Va.; prisoner at Andersonville, Ga.; notes; memos; accounts. NjR, microfilm.

3787 KILLGORE, Gabriel M. 1863. Civil War diary; service with the Claiborne Invincibles. CLU.

3788 LANDER, Edward P. 1863–1864. Co. I, 9th Ill. Cav., seeing action in Tenn. and Miss. IHS, transcript.

3789 LANGFORD, Nathaniel P. 1863; 1870. Trip from St. Paul to Ft. Garry and return in 1870. MnHi.

3790 LARIMER, Robert. 1863–1865? The 62nd Regt., Ohio Vol. Inf., with glimpses of the war on the Carolina coast, especially in Charleston harbor, in the vicinity of Richmond and Appomattox, and in the environs of the capital during the early months of Reconstruction. ViU.

3791 LEVERICH, Charles E. 1863–1864. Visit to parents in Ga. who were Civil War refugees from New Orleans, and record of activities as a staff officer of Gen. S. B. Buckner under Gen. Braxton Bragg, C.S.A.; changes in personnel and retreat to Atlanta. LU.

3792 LINDSEY, John W. 1863–1865. In Co. K, 2nd Ill. Cavalry during the Civil War; the weather; army life and battles. MoU.

3793 LOCKWOOD, Samuel. 1863. Kept by pastor at Keyport, N.J. Reformed Church; bills; receipts. NjR.

3794 LOVERING, Rev. J. F. 1863–1864. Diary and note books of chaplain in 17th Me. Regt. Me. *See* 4038.

3795 MACOMBER, Rev. John H. 1863; 1865; 1866. Kept by a member of the 1st Vt. Heavy Artillery, and as a Methodist pastor at Sauk Centre, Minn. MnHi.

3796 MARSHALL, William Rainey. 1863. Journal of military expedition against Sioux Indians from Camp Pope in the summer of 1863 under command of Brig. Gen. Henry Hastings Sibley. MnHi.

3797 McGLOTHLIN, W. T. 1863. Operations of the 10th and 30th Tenn. Inf., Port Hudson, La., to Jackson, Miss. CSmH.

3798 McGOWN, James Milton. 1863. Diary in Co. A, 76th Regt. of Inf., Pa. Vols.; he was captured at Ft. Wagner, S.C., and died in Libby Prison, Richmond, Va. PHi.

3799 MEHRING, Margaret. 1863. A 13-year-old school girl describes progress of Gettysburg campaign and tells of a railroad accident. MdHi.

3800 MEILE, Frederick. 1863–1864. Diary in German of the Sibley expedition, and the Sully expedition, 1864. MnNuHi, original; NdHi, copy.

3801 MEREDITH, William. 1863–1864. Civil War diary by a Union soldier in Co. C, 1st Ky. Inf., from Chattanooga, Tenn., to Ooltawah, Tenn. OHi.

3802 MILLER, Capt. Joseph W. 1863. Account of the battle of Chickamauga by officer of Co. D, 2nd Ky. Vol. Inf. OMCmm, original; OHi, typescript.

3803 MITCHELL, Joseph H. April, 1863–Dec. 1863. Tenn. and Va. A U.S. soldier's Civil War diary; marches, fights, foraging for supplies; making winter camp in Va.; retreat to Knoxville. GU.

3804 MODIL, George W. 1863–1864. Fighting on the Mississippi River; attack on Port Gibson; battles of Raymond, Jackson, Champion Hills, and Big Black River; siege of Vicksburg; battle of Hull's Hill; burning of Hillsboro; evacuation of Meridian; battle of Atlanta. Ms-Ar.

3805 MONK, John. 1863–1903. Military with 44th Regt., Ohio Vol. Inf. OHi.

3806 MOORE, J. C. 1863–1865. CNS. Tx, typescript.

3807 MOORE, Josephine M. 1863. Commonplace book and journal telling of life of a young girl at home and at Madame Loquet's school, with several allusions to the Civil War and Yankees in New Orleans. NcU.

3808 MOYER, L. R. 1863; 1866; 1869–1870; 1881–1886. CNS. MeMonC.

3809 NEARING, Alicia. 1863–1864. Diaries of her teaching life at Williamsville Inst., Erie Cnty., N.Y. NIC.

3810 OSMUT, John. 1863. Civil War diary. ScU.

3811 PACKARD, Capt. Timothy C. 1863–? A whaling voyage in the bark *Andrews* in the North Atlantic to Hudson's Bay. MH.

3812 PARIS, John. 1863–1865. Daily events of the Civil War. NcU.

3813 PATTERSON, William T. 1863–1864. Civil War diary, while he was on the Staff Co. of the 116th Regt., Ohio Vol. Inf. OHi; Athens College, Ohio; NcU.

3814 PELOUBET, David A. 1863. Civil War journal covering service in the 33rd N.J. Regt. in Tenn. written by a major. NjR, photostat.

3815 PHILLIPS, Horace. 1863–1865. Travels in Ky. and eastern Tenn.; study for teaching; experiences as teacher in small community; scholarly and social activities; religious convictions. MiU.

3816 PHILLIPS, J. W. 1863–1866; 1870–1871; 1873–1876. Including orders and notes on the operation of his business. IHS.

3817 POATES, Mrs. Lemuel. 1863–1865. Describes the devastations of war in terms of the local scene and domestic life in Bolton, Miss. NIC.

3818 POTTER, Alonso B. 1863. Diary with Co. K of the 18th Conn. Regt. NNC.

3819 POWELL, Lt. C. S. 1863–1865. War experiences in Johnston Cnty. Nc-Ar.

3820 PURVIANCE, M. C. 1863. An overland trip from Morristown, Ill. to Cal.; observations on the Mormons; the Indians encountered; the characteristics of the country. CtY.

3821 REED, Seth. 1863. Services to wounded soldiers in Nashville, Tenn., and Stevenson, Ala., and field hospital in Ala. as member of U.S. Christian Commission with the Army of the Cumberland; names of soldiers served; interesting observations on the commission's work, guerrillas, slavery, hospitalization, etc. MiU.

3822 RICHARDSON, Miss Sue. 1863–1865. Kept at Rose Hill, Front Royal, Va. GEU, typescript.

3823 RINKER, Abram, Jr. May 4, 1863–Dec. 1864. N.C., S.C. with Co. B. 52nd. Regt. Pa. Vols., USA, while fighting in N. C. and S. C. 2 small vols. GU.

3824 ROWLAND, Kate Whitehead (Mrs. Charles). 1863–1864; 1877–1878. The activities of a typical upper class Ga. family during the Civil War and postwar period. GEU, copy.

3825 SANDERSON, Lt. George K. 1863–1864. Civil War diary. OHi.

3826 SANDERSON, William F. 1863–1864. A journey from Blanchard Township, Canada, via the Isthmus to Acapulco; from San Francisco to Gold Hill and Virginia City. CU-B, typescript.

3827 SATTERTHWAITE, Joseph C. 1863. Personal. MiU.

3828 SAUTER, C. J. 1863–1864. Ill. Light Artillery; Chattanooga, battle, and surroundings; Christmas in Ala.; winter quarters. ICHi.

3829 SHAFFNER, Dr. J. F. 1863–1864. CNS. Nc-Ar.

3830 SIMONS, Elizabeth A. 1863. CNS. Tx, typescript.

3831 SIMONS, M. K. 1863. CNS. Tx, typescript.

3832 SOULE, Harrison. 1863–1865. Maj. in 6th Mich. Inf. and 6th Mich. Heavy Artillery; daily account of Civil War as waged on the lower Miss. MiU.

3833 STACKHOUSE, William. 1863–1865. Civil War service with Co. B, 119th Pa. Vols. PHi.

3834 STEVENS, William Arnold. 1863–1903 (with gaps). Private diaries; as delegate to the U.S. Christian Commission; as student at the universities of Leipzig and Berlin; and traveling in Germany, Switzerland, France, and England. InU-Li. *See* 2732.

3835 STONE, Cyrus R. 1863. Service with the 16th N.Y. Vol. Inf. in the Civil War. MnHi.

3836 SWEET, Reuben. 1863–1865. Civil War diary, covering Sherman's march to the sea and the drive from Savannah northward. WAnHi.

3837 TAYLOR, Capt. Robert B. 1863. Diary of officer of Co. I, 32nd Ky. Regt. Inf.; appears to be account of the Battle of Perryville. KyHi. *See* 3703.

3838 TAYLOR, Thomas Thomson. 1863–1864. Civil War diary of a Union soldier. GEU, copy; LU, copy.

3839 THOMAS, Abner H. 1863–1865. Expenditures and notes on daily work, the weather, social affairs, and general farm life. NIC, typescript.

3840 TOWER, A. W. 1863. Military activities and hardships; private with 56th Regt., Brooklyn to Philadelphia and Hamburg. NN.

3841 WALDEN, Charles Robert. Sept. 1863 to May, 1864. Va., near Richmond and Petersburg. Civil War diary of an 18-year-old soldier from Talladega, Ala., member of the 1st Co., Washington Artillery, C.S.A. Some fighting, visits to the ladies in Petersburg, expense accounts. Reproduction. GU.

3842 WALL, Oscar Garrett. 1863. Diary of the Sibley expedition. MnHi, typescript.

3843 WARD, Christopher L. 1863. Some entries on state politics in Harrisburg. PHi.

3844 WEBSTER, N. H. 1863. Colo. to Ida. MtHi.

3845 WELLS, L. R. 1863–1864. A Confederate soldier who took part in the invasion of Pa. in 1863. NcD.

3846 WHEELER family. 1863–1892. Diaries and account books kept by various members of the family. NHi.

3847 WHEELER, Oscar N. 1863. Civil War diary kept while he was in Co. K, 31st Ohio Vol. Inf. OHi.

3848 WILBUR, R. P. 1863. Day-to-day doings. CtMyMM.

3849 WILDER, David. 1863–1864. A San Francisco businessman; chiefly social events in his daily life. CU-B.

3850 WILLIAMS, D. E. 1863–1865. Military with Minn. Vol. Inf. NdHi.

3851 WILLSON, Dr. James Caldwell. 1863–1910 (with large gaps). Comments on weather, medical practice, his Civil War service, travels in U.S. and Europe; battle of Spotsylvania. MiU.

3852 WILSON, Gen. William T. 1863–1864. Civil War diary when lt. col. in the 15th Regt. and later in the 123rd Regt. of the Ohio Vol. Inf. OHi.

3853 WOLTERS, Ernst. 1863–1865. Service with 178th Regt., N.Y. Vol. Inf. NN.

3854 WORD, Col. Samuel. 1863. A trip across the plains from St. Joseph, Mo., to Virginia City, Mont. Terr., by way of Salt Lake City. MtHi, typescript.

3855 WRIGHT, Henry C. 1863; 1867. Kept at Earlham and in Germany. InRE. *See* 1775.

3856 YOUNG, John. 1863. Kept by a member of the 4th Minn. Regt. MnHi, microfilm.

3857 ZACKMAN, Daniel. 1863–? Weather; his health; the battles of Fredericksburg and Gettysburg in which he took part; a visit to his camp by Gen. Joseph Hooker and President Lincoln. MoU.

3858 ANON. 1864–1868. European travel of the Arnold or Appleton family of Boston or Savannah (parts written in French and German). NcU. *See* 1539, etc.

3859 ANON. 1864–1886. Kept by a watchman at the [Norfolk] Navy Yard. ViU.

3860 ALLISON, Capt. J. D. 1864–1865. Prison life. KyLoF.

3861 ALTON, Hiram. 1864–1865. An overland journey from Ohio to Cal.; a year's stay in Cal.; return journey by the Isthmus of Panama. CtY.

3862 AMERMAN, Peter S. 1864–1865. Life in camp near Milwaukee; a trip up the Missouri to join Sully's expedition against the Sioux; guard duty in the South. MnHi, microfilm.

3863 [AREY, Henry W.?]. 1864–1865. The maintenance of discipline by an official of Girard College, Philadelphia, Pa. DLC.

3864 ASHTON, Samuel. 1864–1869. Farm life. InHi.

3865 BARLEY, Franklin H. 1864–1865. Military service with Co. E, 4th Mich. Cavalry (in Pitman shorthand). MiU.

3866 BEDFORD, W[imer]. 1864–1865. Covering Sherman's march to the sea. DLC.

3867 BENDER, George A. 1864–1865. Vol. Inf. command at Capitol Hill, Nashville; supplemented by letters (in German). ICHi.

3868 BENEDICT, Gilbert. 1864. An emigrant from Glenn's Falls, N.Y., to Helena, Mont. Terr. MtHi.

3869 BERGH, John J. 1864. A march from the Mississippi River into Tenn. (in Swedish). MnHi, typescript.

3870 BEVERIGE, Henry. 1864. A hospital steward in the 25th Va. Regt., C.S.A.; camp life; executions of deserters; duties of an army surgeon. NcD.

3871 BISBEE, Lewis C. 1864–1865. Kept in Libby Prison and in camp during the Civil War. MnHi.

3872 BLACK, Judge J. C. 1864–1865. Civil War events and Black's career. NcU.

3873 BOYLE, Francis A. 1864–1865. Va., Md., Prison at Point Lookout and Ft. Delaware. Description of prisons and prison life at above Federal prisons during the last 2 years of the Civil War. Boyle was evidently an officer. Reproduction, typescript. Note: Original of this diary is supposed to be in the Southern Historical Collection at NcU. GU.

3874 BRADEN, David R. 1864–1866. Civil War service as priv. and sgt. in the 9th Regt., Kan. Vol. Cavalry. KHi.

3875 BRADLEY, Elmer H. 1864. Civil War diary. WBurHi.

3876 BRECKENRIDGE, Elizabeth E. 1864; 1863–1869. CNS. MnHi.

3877 BROOKE, N. J. 1864. Kept by a cavalryman in the Confederate Army. GEU.

3878 BURDICK, John M. 1864. Kept by a member of 21st N.Y. Cav., while in Andersonville prison. GEU, microfilm.

3879 BURKET, Jacob F. 1864–1882. Carpenter's accounts; clippings. OHi.

3880 CAMPBELL, Sylvester Starling. 1864–1865. Entries made while he was with Co. D, Brackett's batallion, Minn. cav., on Sully's expeditions of 1864 and 1865. NdHi.

3881 CARPENTER, Walter. 1864. A trip to Civil War hospitals and camps from Richmond, Ind., to Murfreesboro, Tenn., and Bridgeport, Ala. OHi.

3882 CHADWICK, Ransom A. 1864. Kept in Andersonville prison by a member of the 85th N.Y. Regt. MnHi.

3883 CLAIBORNE, Capt. Willis H. 1864–1865. Civil War. DLC.

3884 CLEVELAND, Edmund J. [1864–1902?]. CNS. NjHi.

3885 COX, Jabez Thomas. 1864. Civil War diary. InU-Li.

3886 COX, Jacob Dolson. 1864. Military operations in east Tenn.; campaigns of Atlanta, Franklin, Nashville, and in N.C. NcD, microfilm; OO, microfilm.

3887 DALY, Charles P. 1864. Trip along Mohawk trail: scenery, visits. NN. *See* 2769, 4339, 4476, 4920.

3888 DANIELSON, Hans H. 1864. Experiences in the Civil War. MnHi, typescript.

3889 "DEVEREUX." 1864. Diary and list of clothing allowances and descriptive roll of Co. H, 35th Regt., N.C. troops. Nc-Ar.

3890 DOOLITTLE, Theodore Sandford. 1864. His service as a delegate of the U.S. Christian Commission in army camps, hospitals, etc., chiefly in Va. NjR.

3891 DRAKE, Capt. John M. 1864. Military expedition to eastern Ore. in 1st Ore. Cavalry. Or, typescript.

3892 DUNLAP, Katherine. 1864. Detailed account of a journey from Council Bluffs to Bannack City, Mont., with a good description of Bannack and western Mont. CU-B, photostat.

3893 DURKEE, Henry Rogers. 1864–1867. Hunting trips in Pepsin, Wis., trip by raft to Burlington, Iowa. MiU.

3894 DYE, Nathan G. 1864–1865. The life of the common soldiers, especially about food, disease, rumors, and actual engagements, written by a member of Co. I of the 24th Iowa Vol. Inf. NcD.

3895 EAMES, Richard M. 1864; 1872; 1873; 1875. CNS. MnHi.

3896 EDWARDS, Elijah E. 1864. By a chaplain in the 7th Minn. Vol. Inf. MnHi, typescript.

3897 FAIRLEIGH, Lt.-Col. Thomas Brooks. 1864. Military diary; 26th Vol. Inf.; service as member of court-martial for trial of Capt. Black, A.Q.M.; details of army life at Camp Nelson, Lexington, and Louisville; attendance at theater and opera; furloughs at his home in Brandenburg; consolidation of his regiment with the 33rd Ky. Regt.; assumed command of post at Louisville. KyLoF, typescript.

3898 FARLEY, Albert William. 1864–1865. Student life at Univ. of Mich.; weather; professors and their lectures; current affairs; everyday life. MiU, typescript.

3899 FISK, Andrew J., and Robert E. 1864–1870. The Sioux outbreak; an overland expedition from St. Cloud to Mont., led by James L. Fisk in 1866; gold mining in Mont. MnHi, typescript.

3900 FOSTER, W. T. 1864–1865. Merrill's cavalry, in Ark., pursuing Sterling Price, and in Tenn.; includes observations about officers and women. MoU, typescript.

3901 GHORMLEY, James. 1864–1865. Campaigns in the South and the trip home to Mich. MnHi, typescript.

3902 GOODMAN, Rev. Reuben Smith. 1864. His service with the U.S. Christian Commission during the Civil War; his work with patients in the Union Army hospitals in Nashville and Chattanooga, Tenn. MiU-C.

3903 GORMAN, Capt. John C. 1864. Civil War diary. Nc-Ar, typescript.

3904 GRAHAM, William. 1864. The Atlanta campaign with the 53rd Ill. Vol. Inf.; operations following the fall of that city. NcD, typescript.

3905 GRANT, S. Hastings. 1864. War journal. NHi. *See* 3911?

3906 HAINES, William K. 1864. Civil War journal largely about the Army of the Potomac. NjR, microfilm.

3907 HALL, Stanley A. 1864–1865. Army life; battles, etc.; service in Tenn. during most of diary. InHi.

3908 HALLER, Granville Owen. 1864–1865. CNS. WaU. *See* 2125, 2925, 2997, 3055, 3116, 4494.

3909 HANSEN, Eduard. 1864–1865. Activities in Union Army. LU.

3910 HARRISON, William. 1864–1865. Diary of soldier in Co. D, 39th N.J. Vol. NjHi, microfilm.

3911 HASTINGS, S. Grant. 1864. During the Civil War. NHi.

3912 HAYNE, Paul Hamilton. 1864–1885. Notation of letters received and answered, commenting on books Hayne was reading and on his lecturing; comments on the Civil War. NcD.

3913 HEATH, Lt. William McKendree. 1864–1865. Civil War service with the 5th Regt., Ohio Vol. Cavalry. OHi.

3914 HENDERSON, John Wesley. 1864–1865. Civil War diary by member of 16th Penn. Vol. Cavalry. KHi.

3915 HODGSON, William B. Nov. 22, 1864–April 5, 1865. Savannah, Ga. Civil War; events connected with Sherman's capture of Savannah by a citizen of Savannah. GU.

3916 HOLMES, George Hamilton Moore. 1864; 1872–1873. Farm diaries. InU-Li. *See* 3240.

3917 HOPKINS, Aristide. 1864. Reminiscences and descriptions of Civil War camp life. NcU.

3918 HOWE, Edward Robbins. 1864; 1865. CNS. MH.

3919 HOWIE, Neil. 1864–1869. Notes on work, expenses, etc. MtHi.

3920 HULL, Lewis Byram. 1864–1866. Va. campaign in the Civil War by a member of Co. K, 11th Regt., Ohio Vol. Inf. OHi, typescript.

3921 JACKSON, Evelyn Harden. 1864; 1865; 1869–1871; 1875–1887; 1891–1895; 1902–1907; 1909; 1911–1921; 1923–1928. Athens, Ga., Atlanta, Ga. Day-by-day accounts reflect social history of Piedmont section of Ga. GU.

3922 JACKSON, Oscar. 1864–1870. Business school in St. Paul and life in Washington Cnty., Minn. MnHi, microfilm.

3923 JENKINS, David N. 1864. With Co. D, 2nd Minn. Cavalry on Sully's expedition. NdHi.

3924 JOHN, David. 1864–1879. Daily life on farm near Williamsburg. OrU.

3925 JOHNSON, Lewis. 1864–1930. CNS. MnRedHi.

3926 JOHNSON, Ole. 1864. With the 6th Regt. of Iowa Cavalry on Sully's expedition. NdHi.

3927 KELLERS, Edward Henry. 1864–1865. Service as a surgeon in the Confederate States Army. ScU.

3928 KENNEDY, David. 1864. Includes four months spent in Andersonville prison; 9th Ohio Cav. MnHi.

3929 KEPNER, John Price. 1864. Military with Co. I, 6th Penn. Vol. Cavalry, and afterward service as a hospital steward. ViHi, typescript.

3930 LARNED, William L. 1864–1866. The 1864 expedition of James L. Fisk and at Ft. Rice. MnHi, typescript.

3931 LAY, Rt. Rev. Henry Champlin. 1864. Episcopal bishop within the lines of the enemy in Atlanta, Huntsville, Louisville, up the river to Baltimore, and back to Va.; discusses conversations with generals Sherman and Grant. Nc-Ar. *See* 3647.

3932 LEATH, James. 1864–1865. Movements and incidents of the 3rd Brigade, 4th Div., 15th Army Corps during the march from Rome to Savannah. CSmH.

3933 LINVILL, Benjamin A. 1864–1926. CNS. OHi.

3934 LOGAN, Martha. 1864. Journey from Callaway Cnty., Mo., to Sacramento, Cal.; distances traveled and some description of the country. MoU, typescript.

3935 LORD, Theodore Ellery. 1864–1865. Military with 3rd Inf., N.Y. Vols. NCooHi.

3936 MANN, H. 1864. Exploring various parts of the Hawaiian Islands. MiU-C.

3937 MARCHAND, Lizzie. 1864. Kept while she was attending Mrs. Cary's school in Philadelphia. PHi.

3938 MATTOCKS, Brewer. 1864–1865. By an assistant surgeon in the 7th Minn. Vol. Inf. in the Civil War. MnHi.

3939 McCLELLAN, Abram. 1864. Civil War diary with Co. K, 1st Regt., Ohio Vol. Heavy Art. OHi.

3940 McCONNELL, Richard. 1864. A diary of Sully's expedition by a probable member of the 2nd Minn. cavalry. NdHi.

3941 McCROREY, J. L. 1864. Civil War diary. ScU.

3942 McLAREN, Robert N. 1864. Sully's expedition against the Sioux. MnHi.

3943 MERRILL, Julius Caesar. 1864. His trip from Milwaukee, Wis., to Boise, Ida.; descriptions of the country over the Old Oregon Trail, the hardships endured, storms, severe weather, shortages of food and water for their livestock, scarcity of firewood and wild game, difficulties in fording rivers, fear of Indian attack, actual encounters with Indians wanting to trade, and problems of social living in a wagon train. MoU, typescript.

3944 MERRILL, Luke Tuttle. 1864. His journey to Tenn., his work loading army supplies and on a railroad near Bull Run, and his work in a cabinet shop in Horseheads, N.Y. NIC.

3945 MERWIN, James B. 1864. CNS. DLC, typescript.

3946 MILLER, James K. P. 1864–1868. A journey from Chicago to Salt Lake City; a further journey to Virginia City; in Mont.; thence to N.Y. and Europe. CU-B.

3947 MORTON, Capt. John P. 1864–1866. Military in Co. K, 18th Regt. of Miss. Cav.; prisoner of war at Ft. Delaware. Ms-Ar.

3948 MULLAN, Dennis W. 1864–1865. Kept by an ensign on the U.S.S. *Monongahela* off Mobile. NHi.

3949 MURPHEY, V. S. 1864–1865. Kept by prisoner of war at Johnson's Island, Sandusky, Ohio. NcU.

3950 MURRAY, John W. 1864–1873. Kept by a hospital steward near Rolla, Mo., during the Civil War and later a bee-keeper living near Excelsior, Minn. MnHi.

3951 MYERS, Frank. 1864. With Co. B, 6th Iowa Cavalry on Sully's expedition. NdHi.

3952 NEWBURGER, Lt. A. 1864. Diary with the 4th N.Y. Cavalry, 2nd Brigade, 1st Div., Army of the Potomac. DLC.

3953 NICKERSON, John Q. A. 1864–1915. Farming operations and the weather. MnHi.

3954 OBERMIER, Simon Peter. 1864–1865. Diary in 72nd Ohio Vol. Inf., Co. A. OFH.

3955 ORR, James L. 1864. War diary; march through the South; skirmishes. InEm.

3956 OWEN, Richard. 1864. Trip from Omaha to the gold regions of Ida. MtHi, typescript. *See* 4157?

3957 PALMER, S. M. 1864–1865. Brief, irregular entries by a member of the 1st Regt., N.Y. Engineers, serving chiefly in Va.; he was distressed by the rough behavior of his companions; personal accounts. NjR.

3958 POLAND, Samuel M. 1864. Written in Chattanooga, Tenn., Atlanta, Ga., etc., with Co. D, 74th Regt., Ohio Vol. Inf. OHi.

3959 PORTER, Albert Quincy. 1864–1865. CNS. Ms-Ar, typescript.

3960 PRIESTLEY, Thomas. 1864. Kept on Sully's expedition of 1864. MnHi, photostat.

3961 RANDALL, Sewall G. 1864. A Civil War diary of a member of Co. I, 4th Minn. Veteran Vols., who died from wounds received on Oct 5. MnHi.

3962 RAPPALYEA, Lewis C. 1864–1865. Diary of soldier who enlisted at Trenton in Co. I, 1st N.J. Cavalry, Army of the Potomac. NjHi.

3963 RAY, Lavender R. 1864–1865. Activities in Confederate Gen. Alfred Iverson's cavalry division. G-Ar, original; GEU, copy.

3964 RICE, Albert M. 1864. CNS. MnSH, typescript.

3965 RICE, Ebenezer O. 1864. Trip through the Dakotas with Gen. Sully's expedition. MnHi.

3966 ROBERTS, G. W. 1864. Kept while he was stationed at Demopolis, Ala. Ms-Ar.

3967 ROSE, Andrew K. 1864–1865. Military movements of a member of the 124th Ohio Inf., Federal Army in east Tenn.; weather; money, clothes, and rations drawn; routine camp life. NcD.

3968 SAUNDERS, Mrs. Kate. 1864. Some material concerning work at Soldiers Rest. ICHi.

3969 SHOEMAKER, Isaac. 1864. A Northerner who operated a cotton plantation in Miss.; reflecting the trials of a plantation; management after slaves had been freed; information on agriculture. NcD.

3970 SILL, Edward E. 1864–1865. Diary of a lt. during the Civil War, including an account of his captivity by Confederate forces. NjHi.

3971 SNELL, James P. 1864. Diary of Civil War army life; private with the 52nd Regt., Ill. Vol; with military orders, documents, action of courts-martial, hand-drawn maps showing strategic military positions of armies. IHi.

3972 SPALDING, Most Rev. Martin John. 1864–1871. Visitations to monasteries and convents; records of confirmations; some financial accounts of the archdiocese of Baltimore. MdBDio. *See* 3388.

3973 STAPLES, Samuel Chester. 1864–1865. Journey from Washington, D.C., to N.M. and service there; picture of army life and military movements. CFS.

3974 STEENROD, George W. 1864. Civil War diary by member of 85th N.Y. KHi.

3975 STRINGFIELD, William W. 1864–1865. Battle and camp experiences on the Tenn.-Va. line and destruction of his home by the enemy; experiences on the march through N.C. and Tenn. Nc-Ar.

3976 SWIFT, F. W. 1864. Civil War diary with 17th Mich. Vol. Inf. OFH.

3977 THOMAS, Henry Benton. 1864–1865. Co. G, 21st Ohio Regt. in Ga.; military names and events. TC, typescript.

3978 THOMPSON, John Reuben. 1864. Life and conditions in Richmond and England. ViU.

3979 TODD, Lt. Charles D. 1864. Civil War diary with 17th Regt. Mich. Vol, 9th Army Corps. OFH.

3980 TOWNES, A. S. 1864–1865. Confederate soldier in Hampton's Legion; the back of the diary started by a Federal soldier who saw active service in western N.C. and eastern Tenn. NcD.

3981 TURNEY, Maj. Owen T. 1864–1865. Diaries in Cincinnati, New Orleans, St. Louis, etc. OHi.

3982 TYRREL, Truman. 1864. Kept by a private in the Wis. Vol. Inf., 29th Regt. MnHi, microfilm.

3983 VAIL, Rev. John Davis. 1864–1865. Civil War diary, near Nashville, Chattanooga, Atlanta, etc.; includes several speeches and poetry. OHi, typescript.

3984 VINCENT, Lt. John Bell. 1864–1865. 41st Va. Regt., Mahone's Brigade Army, northern Va. ViHi.

3985 WARNER family. 1864. Kept by Mary E. Warner and Mary E. P. Warner on an overland journey to Cal. with their family, under the leadership of Chester H. Warner. CU-B.

3986 WEATHERLY, T. J. 1864–1865. A doctor's Civil War diary. ScU.

3987 WHEELER, Dr. Samuel Jordan. 1864–1876. Family; neighborhood and personal affairs; politics, local and national. NcU. *See* 1842.

3988 WHITAKER, Capt. Carey. 1864. Service in Co. D, 43rd N.C. Regt.; tells of camp life, battles, and hospital experiences. CSmH; NcU.

3989 WHITE, Frank E. 1864–1865. Camp life near City Point, Va., and dwelling in the winter, the flies, drawing of supplies, and trip. NcD.

3990 WHITE, William. 1864. CNS. PWaHi.

3991 WHITNEY, Henry. 1864. Diary in 45th Regt., U.S. Colored troops. NjR. *See* 4274.

3992 WHITTED, Andrew J. 1864. CNS. KHi.

3993 WHITWORTH, Maj. W. H. 1864. War experiences in Miss., Ga., etc.; accounts and miscellaneous notes. InHi.

3994 WILLIAMS, Sgt. James S. 1864. Service with 116th N.Y. Vols. in La.; army hospital and prison life. NN.

3995 WILLIAMSON, Sarah. 1864. Kept by a student at Troy Female Seminary (Emma Willard School), Troy, N.Y. NjR.

3996 WORTLEY, Clark S. 1864–1865. Civil War diary by an officer in the 20th Mich. Inf. Regt. GEU.

3997 WYNN, B. L. 1864. Served in Co. A, 21st Regt. of Miss. Inf., C.S.A., on signal duty in headquarters of Lt. Gen. Thos. J. Jackson. Ms-Ar.

3998 YOUNG, John G. 1864. March through N.C. and Va.; names of battles; casualty lists; names of officers; skirmishes and the good treatment of soldiers in Va. Nc-Ar.

3999 ANON. 1865. The personal experiences of a Confederate surgeon during the retreat of the Army of northern Va. ViU.

4000 ANON. 1865–1868. Concerns family matters, public celebrations, and a storm in Aug. 1867, which is further described by a clipping from the *Sun* (Baltimore). NcD.

4001 ANON. 1865–1869. Personal and financial records of the Arnold or Appleton family of Boston or Savannah. NcU. *See* 1539, etc.

4002 ADAMS, George R. 1865–1867. Kept by a member of Western Union Telegraph Company's expedition for the Russian Extension; includes a separate account of his trading venture to Alaska, 1868. CU-B.

4003 AIKEN, Mary Gayle. 1865. Journal with comments on the Civil War. ScU.

4004 ANDREWS, James (family). 1865–1945. The social life of Hudson, Wis. MnHi.

4005 ARNOLD, Louise Appleton. 1865–1869. CNS. NcU. *See* 1539, etc.

4006 BALL, Levi. 1865; 1866; 1869; 1877. CNS. MnStclHi.

4007 BARTON, Hudson DeCamp. 1865. Written while he was crossing the plains from Wright County, Iowa, to Cal. CSfC.

4008 BAXLEY, Catherine Virginia. 1865. Kept after arrest as blockade runner, written in prison in Washington; women prisoners; psychological effects of imprisonment; war psychosis. NN.

4009 BENNETT, C. 1865. Kept on Sully's expedition from Ft. Rice to Devil's Lake. NdHi.

4010 BENNETT, C. A. 1865. A description of an expedition from Leavenworth into Dakota Terr. MnHi, microfilm.

4011 BIDWELL, John. 1865–1867. Kept by him during sojourn in Washington, D.C. while a member of Congress. CU-B.

4012 BOULWARE, Richard Abraham. 1865. CNS. KHi.

4013 BRADLEY, William Edward. 1865. His capture by Union troops and imprisonment at Petersburg. Nc-Ar.

4014 BROWN, Samuel J. 1865; 1874–1875; 1880; 1891. Memoirs of an inspector of government scouts at Ft. Wadworth, Dakota Terr., teacher in Episcopal mission school at Crow Creek, and member of firm of Brown, Renville & Co. MnHi.

4015 BULKLEY, Charles S. 1865–1867. Kept on the Russo-American Telegraph expedition. CU-B, microfilm.

4016 BURTSELL, Rt. Rev. Msgr. Richard Lalor. 1865–1912. A record of pastoral actions and observations on ecclesiastical affairs in the Archdiocese of N.Y. NYStJDio.

4017 BYRNE, Garrett S. 1865. Detailed Civil War records. NjR.

4018 COHEN, Seixas Eleanor. 1865–1866. Her engagement; separation from her beloved during the Civil War; her family's house and belongings destroyed by fire; hatred for Yankees; resentment of abolition of slavery; her wedding after long months of waiting; move to N.Y.; visit to her parents' home in Charleston, where her first baby was expected. OCAJA.

4019 CRANFILL, Jasper N. 1865–1866. Daily farm life in Linn Cnty., Ore.; some hunting experiences. OrU.

4020 CROOK, George. 1865? CNS. PCarlA.

4021 DAVEE, Ellison B. 1865. Civil War diary in the 16th Ohio Battery camp, New Orleans, La. OHi.

4022 DUNN, Gertrude. 1865. Visit to Washington; witnessing of Lincoln's assassination. NN.

4023 EATON, Amasa M. 1865. A trip to Oil Creek; details of striking oil and gas wells. PSew.

4024 ELDREDGE, Capt. Daniel. 1865–1867. His military history. NhHi.

4025 FERREE, John C. 1865. Civil War diary by a member of Co. D, 29th Ind. infantry while stationed at Chattanooga, Tenn., at Dalton, Ga., and during the process of being discharged. InU-Li.

4026 HAGER, Albert H. 1865. Brief entries dealing with business and financial transactions in horses, scrap iron, and securities. NjR.

4027 HAYES, Hiram. 1865–1880. Life and times in early Superior. WSHi.

4028 HOCKENSMITH, Mrs. M. 1865–1866. Kept by a 23-year-old woman on an overland journey with her family, from Miss. along the southern route to Cal. CU-B.

4029 HOUGHTON, Clarence L. 1865. CNS. NIC.

4030 HUTCHINSON, Abby. 1865. Concert tour in Eastern cities. MnHi, microfilm.

4031 JACKSON, George. 1865. Civil War diary in La., Ala., with Co. K, 114 Regt., Ohio Vol. Inf. OHi.

4032 JATTA, Mary H. 1865. An overland journey from Nebraska City, across the plains to Sacramento, Cal. CU-B.

4033 JAY, Eli. 1865. CNS. InRE.

4034 JOHNSON, N. I. 1865. His experiences along the north Atlantic seaboard as a soldier. MnHi.

4035 KEARNEY, Martin T. 1865–1867; 1870–1871. Mainly his attendance at social affairs in Boston, 1865–1867; his sojourn at the Grand Hotel in San Francisco. CU-B. 1872–1878. His social obligations and small bills living at the Palace Hotel. CU-B. 1881–1886; 1887–1890; 1890–1899; 1899–1903. Trip to Europe; his return trip and extended stay in England and France; return to San Francisco; activities in Europe. CU-B.

4036 KLIPPART, Mrs. John Hancock. 1865. CNS. OHi. *See* 3186 and below.

4037 KLIPPART, Josephine. 1865–1919. CNS. OHi. *See* 3186 and above.

4038 LOVERING, Rev. J. F. 1865. Work as chaplain; location of regt.; reports and rumors relating to the war. InU-Li. *See* 3794.

4039 MALLORY, Charles H. 1865–1890. CNS. CtMyMM.

4040 MAXWELL, J. H. 1865–1919. Personal accounts. MnWoHi.

4041 McCARTNEY, Allen. 1865–1868. Accounts. KHi.

4042 McDONALD, David. 1865. Crossing the plains. WaU.

4043 MONFORT, Charles Junius. 1865. A trip to St. Louis and New Orleans while he was clerk for Maj. Phinney, Paymaster of the Dept. of Dakota. MnHi.

4044 MORRIS, Isaac S. 1865–1868. Kept in New Orleans. OHi.

4045 MOTE, Rhoda. 1865. CNS. InRE.

4046 NORTON, McKendree D. 1865. Soldier in the 9th Ohio Vol. Artillery, Bridgeport, Ala. CSmH.

4047 NYE, James Warren. 1865. Commissioned gov. of Nev. by Lincoln in 1861; U.S. Senator, 1864–1873; contains records of assassination of Lincoln and attempt on life of Seward. NvHi.

4048 OWEN, John. 1865–1871. Diary kept at Fort Owen, Mont.; local life and events; Indians; missions; politics. NN. *See* 2792.

4049 PENNOCK, Isaac B. 1865. Civil War diary by member of 11th Kan. Cavalry. KHi.

4050 PIERCE family. 1865–1874. CNS. NIC.

4051 POST, Lt. John E. H. 1865–1866. Military movements. MdHi.

4052 RAVENEL, Miss. 1865. Living conditions on plantation during war time; experiences with Union troops; Negroes, etc. GHi.

4053 ROGERS, Isaac. 1865. Weather; business; homesickness; arrival of his wife. MoU.

4054 SAMPSON, James P. 1865–1873. Military; farming and construction work. Ms-Ar.

4055 SCHOULER, Rev. William. 1865–? Diaries containing entries relevant to Episcopal clerical duties; books read; everyday activities. MdHi.

4056 SIEWERS, Rev. Jacob. 1865. Journey from Salem, N.C., to West Salem, Ill., via Philadelphia, Pa. NcWsM.

4057 SMITH, John E. 1865. Mainly about Civil War experiences. NNC.

4058 STEPHENS, Alexander Hamilton. 1865. Prison journal at Ft. Warren, Boston Harbor. GEU.

4059 STEVENS, Edward L. 1865. Gen. E. E. Potter's raid from Georgetown to Sumter. ScU.

4060 STONE, Maj. Valentine Hughes. 1865; 1866. Personal journal with 5th Artillery, giving account of the engagements in which the unit took part in 1865, with additional entries through 1866. KyHi.

4061 STRUDWICK, F. N. 1865–1866. CNS. NcU.

4062 SULLIVAN, James. 1865–1918. CNS. MH, typescript.

4063 SUMICHRAST, Frederick Caesar de. 1865–1933 (with gaps). Diaries and summaries. MH.

4064 TILGHMAN, Tench F. 1865. Contains an account of the last days of the Confederacy and flight of the President and his followers. MdAA.

4065 ALEXANDER, Evaline T. 1866–1867. A journey from N.Y. to join husband at Ft. Smith, thence to N.M. and Colo.; describes life at military posts; includes accounts of Indians and a meeting with Kit Carson. CU-B.

4066 ALLYN, Joseph Tyler. 1866. His European tour. ViU.

4067 APPLEGATE, Oliver Cromwell. 1866–1868. Life in and about Klamath Indian reservation. OrU.

4068 BARBEAU, Peter Boisdoré. 1866–1867. Notations of weather and movements of ships through Erie canal. MiMarqHi.

4069 BARTHOLOMEW, Mrs. Emily (Ebersole). 1866. Life in Forbestown, Cal. InU-Li. *See* 3283.

4070 BICKNELL, George A. 1866–1867. A cruise from N.Y. to China aboard U.S.S. *Iroquois*. InU-Li. *See* 1783, 1882.

4071 BRYANT, Julia Sands. 1866–1867. A tour in Europe. NNC. *See* 2318, 3159.

4072 CANFIELD, Sarah. 1866–1867. The wife of an army officer of the 13th Inf. stationed at Camp Cooke, Mont. describes her trip up the Missouri and life at the fort and camp. NdHi, typescript. *See* 4141.

4073 CARTER, James Van Allen. 1866. Kept while he traveled westbound from Nebraska City until arrival at Ft. Bridger. CU-B.

4074 CARTER, John Russell Kelso. 1866–1872. Kept while he was a student and teacher at the Pennsylvania Military Academy, Chester. MdHi.

4075 CHASE, Zina W. 1866–1867. A trip to Colo. from Stillwater, Minn., and back home. MnHi.

4076 CHISMORE, George. 1866–1881. A trip among the Siwash of British Columbia on the way to join, as surgeon, the Western Union's expedition for the Russian Extension; further trips to Alaska. CU-B.

4077 COMER, Laura B. (Mrs. James). 1866–1868; 1872–1873. Two European trips. NcU.

4078 CROTHERS, Rev. S. D. 1866; 1886–1914. CNS. OHi.

4079 CURRY, Dr. Jabez Lamar Monroe. 1866–1902. CNS. DLC.

4080 DeCLOUET, Paul L. 1866–1870; 1880–1888. Plantation operations, politics; the political activities of the freedmen; difficulties with Negro contract labor; levee board meetings; news of local interest. LU.

4081 FELCH, C. J. 1866–1870. Records of a probate judge in Mower Cnty., Minn. MnHi.

4082 FOX, Gustavus Vasa. 1866–1883. Including his 1866 mission to Russia as Assistant Minister of the Navy. NHi.

4083 HACKENSMITH, Mrs. M. S. (Carruth). 1866. Written while she was crossing the plains. CU-B.

4084 HENDERSON, A. B. ("Bart"). 1866–1873. Yellowstone Expedition of 1866; prospecting in the Snake, Wind River, and Yellowstone Country. CtY.

4085 JACKSON, William H. 1866–1874. "Bullwhacking" experiences in the West, including journeys to Salt Lake and Cal.; east to Omaha. CU-B.

4086 JAY, John Clarkson. 1866. Hospital work at Randall's Island, N.Y.; study for M.D. degree; trip to Europe. NN.

4087 KELLY, Jane B. 1866–1898. CNS. WHi.

4088 LIVINGSTON, Dr. Henry Farrand. 1866–1879 (except 1870 and 1872). Life in Dakota Terr.; the duties of an Indian agent; the business transactions and relations with the trade on the reservation; military and Indian affairs; the building of his home in Yanktown, 1879. CtY.

4089 LOVELL, William S. 1866–1887. Plantation diaries. NcU.

4090 LYMAN, Pliny S. 1866–1867. Farming activities; employment records; weather; building a new home; wages paid. MiU.

4091 MALLERY, Bell. 1866–1868. Daily life of female schoolteacher. OrU.

4092 McCOLLAM, Andrew. 1866–1867. A trip to Brazil, chiefly sailing details. NcU. *See* 2130.

4093 McDONALD, Archibald Henderson Spencer. 1866. His printing business in New Orleans. InU-Li.

4094 MORRIS, Prof. George Sylvester. 1866–1867. European trip. MiU. *See* 3131, 4537.

4095 MOULTON, H. M. 1866. Journey from St. Louis, Mo., to Ft. Benton, Mont. OrB.

4096 NEFF, Mrs. Almira (Wright) Beam. 1866. Life in Waterloo, Whidby Island. WaU.

4097 NEILSON, Catharine (Bleecker). 1866–1867. Voyage to England and residence there, social life, excursions, museums. PSC-Hi.

4098 PONZIGLIONE, Paul M., S.J. 1866–1887. Journal by a priest of the Western missions. MoSU.

4099 POPE, Seth Luen. 1866–1902 (with gaps). Daily events; clippings; photographs; trips by steamer and railroad: Lewis River, Cascade Tunnel, Wash. Terr., Portland to Ellensburg, Astoria, Ocean Park, Okanagan, Lewiston. OrHi.

4100 ROBERTS, Thomas S. 1866–1946. Records; trips to various parts of Minn. MnHi.

4101 SMITH, Henry A. 1866; 1867; 1868; 1869; 1870–1880. Records of a journalist of Dodge Cnty., Minn.; description of crops, travels, household details. MnHi.

4102 SPRATLIN, James A. 1866. Oglethorpe Cnty., Ga. Overseer's record of work done by farm hands, corn ground, supplies issued, etc. on a large plantation. GU.

4103 STOCKSLAGER, Storther Madison. 1866–1867. Work as a clerk for the General Court Martial and Military Commission, the Quartermaster's office; as teacher; as a helper on his father's farm and electioneering for the nomination as auditor of Harrison County, Ind.; and as a worker in the auditor's office. InU-Li.

4104 TRAUTWINE, John, II. 1866–1891. Personal. NIC.

4105 WILLIAMS, Edward Barclay. 1866–1888; 1902–1915. Arrival of birds; books read; people; homesteading; establishing a farm in Otego, Ill. RHi.

4106 ANON. 1867. From Collin, Tex., to Southern Cal. near Santa Ana River. CSmH.

4107 ANON. 1867–1870. CNS. PHi.

4108 APPLEGATE, Francis M. 1867–1868. Local affairs in and around Ashland, Ore., and travels to Klamath reservation. OrU.

4109 ATKINSON, Charles H. 1867–1871. Picture of Chicago: business, society, current events, productions in theaters. ICHi.

4110 BAYLEY, Most Rev. James Roosevelt. 1867. A pilgrimage to the Holy Land. MdBDio. *See* 2121, 4279.

4111 BROWN, Franklin Pierce. 1867–1868. Atlanta, Ga. 2 vols., diaries of schoolboy son of Ga. Civil War Gov. Joseph E. Brown; tells of weather and daily activities. GU.

4112 BURTIS, William B. 1867–1870. Cruise on U.S.S. *Delaware* to Asiatic stations and return to N.Y.; ship life, ports, etc. NN.

4113 DOTY, William. 1867–1894. Farm life, profits, expenses; includes account of stringing telegraph wire through town in 1888 and people's reaction. MiU, typescript.

4114 EDWARDS, James F. 1867–1893. Personal. InNd.

4115 EMMONS, George F. 1867. A journal of his command of U.S.S. *Ossipee* conveying U.S. and Russian commissioners to Sitka for Alaska transfer ceremonies. CU-B. *See* 1966?

4116 GREEN, Charles R. 1867–1868. Kept by a member of a surveying party for the Union Pacific Railroad, Kan. to Cal. via N.M. and Ariz. NbU.

4117 HICKS, John. 1867–1917. Early press of Oshkosh and experiences as diplomat; history and events of city included. WOshM.

4118 HUNT, George Lundy. 1867. CNS. CSfC.

4119 HUTCHINSON, Maj. Eben. 1867. CNS. Me.

4120 JACKSON, Preston. 1867–1874. Life in school and surveying trips to Red Lake and White Earth Reservation. MnHi, microfilm.

4121 JEWETT, Sarah Orne. 1867–1868; 1869. CNS. MH.

4122 LANE, Joseph. 1867. Daily activities. InU-Li.

4123 LUEG, Henry. 1867. An overland journey from Minn. to Ore.; describes settlements, camp sites (in German). CtY, original plus typed translation; WaSp.

4124 PECK, S. L. 1867. A trip on the Missouri River from Ft. Benton to St. Louis. MnHi, microfilm.

4125 PHELPS, Pvt. Edward Ashley B. 1867–1868. Army service in Vera Cruz and Mexico City; return to the U.S., and discharge. NN.

4126 RANDALL, Dudley A. 1867–1880. Articles in newspapers and daily weather entries. MdHi.

4127 ROGERS, Joseph Goodwin. 1867. Begun in Madison, Ind., and completed in Cincinnati, Ohio, during the time he was a student in the Medical College of Ohio. InU-Li.

4128 ROODS, John. 1867. From Newark, Ohio, to Wis. Terr.; visits to Wis. towns, and return home. NN.

4129 SCHRIRER, Albert S. 1867. By surgeon in charge of U.S. naval hospital at Norfolk, Va., containing lists of employees, accounts of repairs, copies of letters received and a general record of his activities. NcD.

4130 SMITH, John L. 1867–1916. His career as a businessman, map maker, stock dealer. PHi. *See* 4199?

4131 STOKES, Charles. 1867–1868; 1870. Kept while he was a student at Jersey Shore Boarding School, and while conducting a school at Rancocas, N.J. NjR.

4132 STORY, William C. 1867–1870. Diary of usher at Crosby's opera house and clerk in banking office in Chicago; theater and amusements; public events; politics; public taste. NN.

4133 TATNALL, Josephine. 1867. Weather; breakfast; school; play; knitting; visits; lectures attended; drawings for remodeling Gibbins House in Wilmington. DeHi.

4134 WOODHOUSE, Dr. Samuel W. 1867. A voyage on the ship *William Penn* from N.Y. to Brest, France. PHi.

4135 ANON. ca. 1868. A journey through the Southern states. CSmH.

4136 ANON. 1868. By an inhabitant of Santa Fe, N.M., with enumerations of inhabitants of Taos Cnty., 1866. CSmH.

4137 ANON. 1868–1880. Kept by the ministry of the United Society of Believers (Shakers); names of members; census of members; admission and loss of members by death or otherwise; appointments; arrival of Swedes; voting of members on public measure for the first time; weather reports. KyLoF.

4138 ANON. 1868–1890. By various members of the communal societies of United Society of Believers (Shakers) in Ohio. OHi.

4139 ATWOOD, Edwin H. 1868; 1874; 1875–1877. The Minnesota State Farmers' Alliance and personal matters. MnHi.

4140 BARROW, Clara Elizabeth. 1868; 1875. Athens, Oglethorpe Cnty., Milledgeville, Americus, Camilla, Sapelo Island, Ga. Daily life of a young lady at home and visiting relatives; family life and activities. GU.

4141 CANFIELD, Andrew Nahum. 1868. Kept by an army officer of the 13th Inf. while stationed at Camp Cooke, Montana. NdHi.

4142 CAUTHORN, Mrs. Clothilda M. B. 1868. A wedding trip to Cincinnati from Vincennes, Ind. OHi.

4143 CHASE, George. 1868. A voyage from San Francisco on the steamer *Colorado*; crossing the Isthmus; thence to N.Y. on the steamer *Arizona*. CU-B.

4144 CRAPO, Henry Howland. 1868; 1869. Daily diary of his illness. MiU. *See* 2988.

4145 DAVIDSON, J. F. 1868–1917. Life in Chicago: court cases, politics, recreation, opera, the stage and actors; farming and animal breeding in Mo. and N.D.; references to the St. Louis World's Fair, World War I, and leading politicians. MoU.

4146 FARRAGUT, David G. 1868. His cruise in Europe in the U.S.S. *Franklin*. MdAN. *See* 1445.

4147 FOWLER, Henderson Monroe. 1868–1906. Daily activities, including many details of church activities, births, sickness, and deaths. NcU.

4148 GIBBONS, Cardinal James. 1868–1917. Kept as Catholic Archbishop of Baltimore. MdBDio.

4149 HAGER, Byron G. 1868. Farming and fruit-raising at One Mile Run; weather; operations with father as grading contractor for Newark and Bloomfield Railroad. NjR.

4150 HUNT, Samuel F. 1868. A tour of Egypt, Italy, France, England, and the return voyage. NjR.

4151 INNES, John Henry. 1868–1936. Weather and events, with some commentary. NNC.

4152 JOHNSTON, Gus. 1868–1869. Military trip from Topeka to Indian country. KHi.

4153 KAHN, Feliz. 1868. Emigration from France to Brazil. OCAJA, copy.

4154 LANDIS, Charles K. 1868–1895. CNS. NjViHi.

4155 LIPPINCOTT, William Champlain. 1868. Descriptions of farm life; digging and carting of marl from nearby pits; local amusements and numerous trips to Leonardville, N.J.; Methodist church attendance; notations of expenditures. NjR, microfilm.

4156 MATTSON, Hans. 1868–1889. Kept by secretary of the board of immigration, as a consul-general for India, and for Sweden. MnHi.

4157 OWEN, Richard. 1868–1869; 1882–1885. CNS. IHS, microfilm. *See* 3956?

4158 PATTERSON, John C. 1868–1905. CNS. MiU.

4159 PRINGLE, Elizabeth W. Allston (Mrs. John Julius). 1868–1915. Personal diaries: struggles of a post-bellum woman rice-planter, daily plantation life, family and social life, etc. NcU.

4160 RICE, Mary P. 1868. Written in France. NcU.

4161 SEWARD, William H. 1868. Trip down Potomac. NN. *See* 4198.

4162 SMILEY, Sarah F. 1868–1869. Trip to England on the steamer *Cuba*; details of her philanthropic interests, religious activities, preachings, church meetings, and visits to schools and benevolent institutions. PHi.

4163 STEWART, John Alexander. 1868–1877. Personal; weather; church; student activities at Union School in Ann Arbor; events and people at Univ. of Mich.; teaching school; reading. MiU.

4164 STRENTZEL, Louisiana E. 1868–1882. Record of her personal observations and experiences as a housewife near Benicia, Cal. CU-B.

4165 SULLIVAN, Thomas Russell. 1868–1869. Theatrical journal containing account of plays performed at the Boston Museum and Selwyn's Theater. MH.

4166 THRASHER, Luther A. 1868–1869. CNS. KHi.

4167 THURSBY, Emma Cecilia. 1868–1921. CNS. NHi.

4168 TUNNARD, Fred D. 1868–1870. Personal notes and expenditures, and names of planters visited while he was making various trips through La. selling farming equipment. LU.

4169 WARREN, George. 1868; 1888; 1891. CNS. MnHi.

4170 ANON. 1869. A young girl's voyage across the plains from Collin, Tex., to Cal. CSmH.

4171 ANON. 1869. Trip to south Russia, Holy Land, Egypt, by resident at New Harmony, possibly by a member of Owen family. NN.

4172 ANON. 1869–1870. Wagon-train journey between Tex. and Cal. Mojave Chapter, DAR, Fullerton, Cal.

4173 BOSS, Charles. 1869–1877. CNS. DeU.

4174 BOURKE, John Gregory. 1869–1896. Field-notes; ethnological data; campaign records; day-to-day events; army orders; newspaper clippings; travel data; programs; menus; etc. NWM, original; NmU, photostat.

4175 BRADLEY, George Y. 1869. The first Powell expedition through the Grand Canyon of the Colorado. DLC; NN.

4176 BUELL, Barber G. 1869; 1873. Farm life and weather; occasional listings of costs and comments on agricultural methods. MiU-H.

4177 CARR, Jeanne C. (Smith). 1869. A steamer journey from N.Y. to San Francisco. CSmH.

4178 CORSON, Joseph K. 1869–1873. Experiences as an army surgeon at Ft. Steele and Ft. Bridger. CU-B.

4179 DALY, William. 1869–1900 (with gaps). Personal, local, and weather entries. MiDdHi, typescript.

4180 GORRILL, William H. 1869. A journey on horseback from Walla Walla, Wash. Terr., to San Francisco; the country; its industries; labor conditions; etc. CtY.

4181 HARDENBERGH, Catherine L. 1869–1870. Record of a teen-age girl's social, domestic, and church activities. NjR.

4182 HARKNESS, Edward. 1869–1878. Entries made by a farmer in Fillmore Cnty., Minn. MnHi, typescript.

4183 HIGGINS, Rev. William R. 1869. Life and work of minister in Superior, Wis. MnDuHi, copy; MnHi, typescript.

4184 HOLMAN, Nancy Nash. 1869–1877. Daily life: social life, births, deaths, marriages, recipes, medicines, religion and the vagaries of farm life are faithfully recorded. MoU.

4185 HUGHES, William S. (or L.?) 1869. CNS. KHi.

4186 MARTIN, Edward S. 1869. CNS. OHi.

4187 McKINLEY, Archibald C. 1869–1886. Milledgeville and Sapelo Island, Ga. Reproduction. Day-by-day life on the island and in Milledgeville, during Reconstruction and afterward. An account of the Charleston earthquake. GU.

4188 MEAD, Aaron Benedict. 1869. Personal. ICHi.

4189 NISBET, J. Wingfield. 1869; 1873; 1879–1885. Personal. Southern Hist. Coll., NcU. *See* 4324?

4190 PALMER, Edward. ca. 1869. Description of a journey from Ft. Yuma, Cal., to the coast of Lower Cal. starting from Port Isabella. CLU.

4191 POWDERLY, Terence Vincent. 1869–1890 (with gaps). CNS. DCU.

4192 PUGH, Achilles. 1869. Visit by a Quaker to Indians in Kan. and Indian territory. PHC.

4193 RAWLEY, H. B. 1869–1929. CNS. NIC.

4194 REQUE, Rev. P. S. 1869. Religious activities in Pope Cnty., Minn. MnGlHi.

4195 RICH, John T. 1869–1925. Routine matters of daily life; daily schedule as gov., particularly social events. MiU-H. *See* 4611.

4196 RUTGERS UNIVERSITY, New Brunswick, N.J. College of Agriculture. 1869–1870. Journal of farming operations. PSC-Hi, two mss.

4197 SENCERBOX, Jarvis W. 1869–1870. Record of a tax collector in Scott Cnty., Minn. MnHi.

4198 SEWARD, William H. 1869–1870. Journey across the continent. NN. *See* 4161.

4199 SMITH, (John L.?). 1869. Farming conditions after the Civil War. NIC. *See* 4130?

4200 WHELAN, William. 1869–1872. Daily activities in southern Ariz.; daily log of travelers going through his station. AzTP.

4201 WILLIAMS, Edward. 1869–1874. Includes his distribution of religious literature in a penitentiary. PSC-Hi.

4202 ANON. 1870–1889. By the congregation of the Moravian Church in Kernersville, N.C. NcWsM.

4203 BELWOOD, Mary. 1870–1872. CNS. MoU.

4204 BISHOP, Francis Marion. 1870–1871. Chicago to Salt Lake City, Kanab Cnty., voyage down Green and Colorado rivers. NN.

4205 BROWNE, William M. 1870. Athens, Ga. Diary of his activities on his estate on the outskirts of Athens, gardening, visiting, etc. GU, xerox copy.

4206 BUNN, Sarah Irwin (Mrs. Frank Hatch Jones). 1870. A year in the life of a 14-year old girl; school, parties, family. IHi.

4207 COLE, Martha Knapp. 1870–1900. Events of the day. Mich. Hist. Coll.; MiU.

4208 COOK, Rev. Charles H. 1870. His trip from Mo. to Ariz.; of particular interest is the original list of Pima words; activities as a missionary among the Pimas from 1870 to about 1900. AzTP.

4209 CROFT, Thomas. Early 1870's. Related largely to the founding of Pasadena, Cal. CSmH.

4210 DAVIS, J. C. Bancroft. 1870–1871. Kept while he was Assistant Secretary of State. DLC. *See* 4248.

4211 DAWSON, Henry Barton. 1870. Work as printer; daily activities; weather; etc. NN.

4212 DONALDSON, Thomas. 1870–1893. Letters arranged chronologically. InHi.

4213 DOUGLASS, W. H. 1870–1872. CNS. KHi.

4214 EARLE, Horatio Sawyer. 1870; 1878–1882; 1886; 1890–1934. Selling farm equipment; "good roads" movement; League of American Wheelmen; business affairs; bicycling; Mich. politics. MiU.

4215 FERRIS, William Canby. 1870–1878; 1909–1922. Future dreams of 18-year old boy; introspective; references to spiritualism and World War I. PSC-Hi.

4216 HASSELL, Sylvester. 1870–1898; 1925–1927, intermittently. CNS. NcU.

4217 HAUSER, Samuel Thomas. 1870. Kept as a member of the Washburn-Lanford Expedition to the Yellowstone. CtY. *See* 3629.

4218 HAYES, Webb C. 1870–1909 (with gaps). Personal; travel and soldier's records. OFH.

4219 HOES, Rev. John C. F. 1870. CNS. NHi.

4220 HOPPIN, William Jones. 1870–1875. Journals and letters during European tour. MH. *See* 1900, 4386.

4221 HUDSON, Joshua Hilary. 1870–1877. Diary relating to a law firm. ScU.

4222 JORDAN, E. C. 1870–1871. Kept near the town of Otter Tail during the construction there of the Northern Pacific Railroad. N.P.R.R. Archives, St. Paul, original; MnHi, photostat.

4223 LONGYEAR, J. M. 1870–1922. Experiences of area he traveled in. MiMarqHi.

4224 LOVELL, Vincent Smith. 1870; 1873. Student life at Univ. of Mich.; classroom, social, literary, and musical events; faculty; notes on lecture by Bronson Alcott; travels and visit to ancestral home in Great Britain. MiU.

4225 McCLELLAND, Robert. 1870. Trip abroad. MiU.

4226 MILLER, Halsey D. 1870; 1871; 1872; 1875; 1878. CNS. OClWHi.

4227 SISTER MONICA. 1870. Trip made by seven Roman Catholic nuns who left Carondelet, Mo., for Ariz. to establish a girl's school in Tucson. AzTP.

4228 NEILSON, Mary Putnam (Woodbury). 1870–1913. Travels to Europe; summer trips. PSC-Hi. *See* 4670.

4229 NELSON, N. P. 1870–1898. CNS. MeMonC.

4230 NICHOLSON, William. 1870–1871. Inspection tour of Indian agencies of Kan. and the Indian territory. KHi.

4231 PURDY, Thomas D. 1870. Lists the persons in a wagon train going from Mo. to Colo. in 1870, and tells the distance traveled on most days. MoU, typescript.

4232 READ, John Meredith. 1870–1871. Kept in Paris during the siege. NN.

4233 SCHROEDER, Joseph. 1870–1871. Student reflections: political affairs in Rome (in German). DCU.

4234 SEARLE, Dolson B. 1870. A trip made through Kan. and Minn. in search of land for investment. MnHi.

4235 SHRODE, Maria Christina. 1870. Journey from Hopkins Cnty., Tex., to San Diego Cnty., Cal., following the Butterfield overland mail routes. CSmH.

4236 SUMMERELL, J. H. 1870; 1878. Journal and diary, partially written in Edinburgh. NcU.

4237 THOMAS, H. K. 1870–1871. Train schedules; amount of travel; important people passing through; accidents on the railroad; news of neighboring mines; the weather; the establishment of the local lodge in Laramie, Wyo.; town events. CtY.

4238 TUCKER, Henry Holcombe. 1870; 1877. Penfield, Macon, Athens, Ga. Brief entries re engagements, family life, sermon and lecture notes, trips. President of Mercer Univ. in 1870, Chancellor of the Univ. of Ga. in 1877. GU, reproduction.

4239 TUFTS, Quincy. 1870–1873. CNS. MH.

4240 VAN OSTRAND, Ferdinand A. 1870–1872. Kept by an agent of the Durfee and Peck Company at Ft. Berthold. NdHi.

4241 ANON. 1871. Pertaining to Albemarle Cnty., Va. ViU.

4242 ANDERSON, George C. 1871. The journey of the first locating committee of the Ohio Soldiers Colony to Kan. and Colo. KHi.

4243 BABCOCK, Mrs. George. 1871. Visit to England, Scotland, Belgium, Italy, Germany, Switzerland, and France describing public buildings, churches and church services, historical sites, and processions. LU.

4244 BARTHOLOMEW, Dr. Elam. 1871–1934. An authority on fungi and curator of the Mycological Museum at Fort Hays State College; covers entire residence in Rooks Cnty., Kan. KHi.

4245 BLISS, Eugene Frederick. 1871–1873; 1880–1883; 1916–1918. Personal data of Cincinnati and vicinity, but primarily description of trips to Europe. OCUHi.

4246 BURNET, Jacob. 1871–1872. Law cases; actions; facts and names; dates of entry chronological but many previous dates recorded in entries. OCUHi.

4247 CLARK, Margaret Miller (Davidson). 1871–1872. Voyage from N.Y. to Japan via Panama and San Francisco, and residence at Yokohama with her brother, Sylvanus M. Davidson, agent of the Pacific Mail Steamship Co.; tutoring Japanese children; commonplace-book with verse. NjR.

4248 DAVIS, J. C. Bancroft. 1871–1872. Includes a record of the Geneva Arbitration. DLC. *See* 4210.

4249 DEADY, Matthew P. 1871–1892 (minor gaps). Daily activities; friends, etc. of prominent lawyer, justice, and politician; journey to Atlantic Coast and back to Portland; voyage from Portland to Sitka; trip from Portland to N.Y. to attend General Convention of Episcopal churches. OrHi.

4250 DELLENBAUGH, Frederick Samuel. 1871–1873. 2nd Powell expedition down Green and Colorado rivers. NN. *See* 4340?

4251 DEN BLEYKER, Martha. 1871–1872. Travel. MiU.

4252 DICKSON, Albert Jerome. 1871. Journey through southern Minn., and across northern Iowa to Neb. in search of land; geography and mileage. MnHi, typescript.

4253 DORAN, Mrs. Joseph M. 1871. CNS. PHi.

4254 FRENCH, William Henry. 1871–1873. The people, social happenings, a hanging, lectures and other events in Ithaca, N.Y.; teaching methods; personalities and habits of faculty members; student activities in general. NIC.

4255 HUTCHINSON, Francis McCredy. 1871–1873. Journal while writer in Minn. and Dakota employed on the construction of the Northern Pacific Railroad; vivid picture of places seen and life in the railroad camps. CtY.

4256 JOHNSON, Frank. 1871–1872. Visits to Minn. towns along the line of the Northern Pacific Railroad in search of a position as stationmaster; describes an Indian medicine dance and ball game. MnHi.

4257 JONES, Stephen V. 1871–1872. 2nd Powell expedition down Green and Colorado rivers. NN.

4258 KELLEY, Hermie A. 1871. CNS. OClWHi.

4259 LOOK, John W. 1871–1874. Description of a visit to royalty in Madagascar on the whaler *C. W. Morgan*. CtMyMM.

4260 MARTIN, H.S. and O.E. 1871–1889. CNS. NIC.

4261 MASTERS, Rebecca Kite. 1871–1876; 1889–1892. Her concern regarding her spiritual progress; some mention of her Quaker activities. PSC-Hi.

4262 MATTHEWS, James Brander. 1871–1924. CNS. NNC.

4263 MINOR, William Woolfolk, Jr. 1871–1926. Farm diary. ViU.

4264 PARKMAN, M. R. 1871. Young woman's trip to Egypt and Holy Land: sights, travel conditions. NN.

4265 POWELL, William Clement. 1871. Journey from Ill. to Green River Station; exploration of Green and Colorado rivers. NN.

4266 SILVER, Albert P. 1871. Kept by a student at Lafayette College, Easton, Pa. MdHi.

4267 STEWARD, John Fletcher. 1871. 2nd Powell expedition down Green and Colorado rivers. NN.

4268 THOMPSON, Almon Harris. 1871–1873. 2nd Powell expedition: notes on topography, Indians, and the Mormons. NN.

4269 TOMSON, Albert. 1871. CNS. KHi.

4270 TOWLE, Gardner. 1871. CNS. NhHi.

4271 WASHBURNE, Elihu B. [1871]. The siege of Paris in the Franco-Prussian War. IC. ICHI

4272 WATSON, James Craig. 1871–1875. Journal of trip from Shanghai to Hong Kong and through India: countryside, customs, people, places of interest, etc.; some astronomical observations. MiU.

4273 WATSON, Louis. 1871–1885. Kept by manager of Western Kan. Agricultural Assoc., Ellis Cnty., Kan. KHi.

Chicago Historical Soc⁵ has a 4 p letter- 1871 May 17 — re siege of Paris. Goes into great detail.

4274 WHITNEY, Henry. 1871–1872. Concerns various (factory?) jobs (N.Y., Newark, Jersey City, etc.); personal expenses; a trip to W. Va. NjR. *See* 3991.

4275 WILLIAMS, W. B. 1871. Visit to Italy, particularly Venice; illustrated. MH.

4276 WOOD, Nahum Trask. 1871–1873. Life near San Juan Capistrano, Cal., where he engaged in sheep raising. CSmH; CSd. *See* 4656.

4277 ZAHN, William P. 1871–1907. Black Hills expedition of 1874; scattered entries not in chronological order from Cannon Ball, Standing Rock, Ft. Rice, and Grand River Agency. NdHi, typescript in part.

4278 ANON. 1872. Journey from San Francisco to Liverpool, including train trips across the Continent. CSmH.

4279 BAYLEY, Most Rev. James Roosevelt. 1872–1876. Kept by Archbishop of Baltimore. MdBDio. *See* 2121, 4110.

4280 BROOKS, Abbie M. 1872–1876. Kept by a semi-invalid, concerning travel in Fla., boarding in Ga., and everyday happenings in a small Ga. town. NcD.

4281 BULLOCK, Seth. 1872. A trip to Yellowstone Park. MtHi, typescript.

4282 COLE, Miner T. 1872–1875. Labor accounts. MiU.

4283 CORTHELL, Elmer Lawrence. 1872–1875. Includes autobiographical notes. NN.

4284 EDWARDS, Hugh P. 1872–1909. Diaries for the years 1872–1905; 1909, written at the Edwards' ranch at Crockett, Cal. CU-B.

4285 FIELDE, Adele M. 1872. Personal. WaU.

4286 FISHER, O. A. 1872–1881. CNS. Tx, typescript.

4287 FLETCHER, J. W. 1872. Railroad work; personal and social activities, chiefly church events; a small private business vending N.Y. newspapers. NjR.

4288 FRIEZE, Prof. Henry Simmons. 1872–1873. Historical notes and diary of a European trip. MiU. *See* 2992, 3053.

4289 HARRIS, Frank. 1872–1876. Records of a student, farmer, and naturalist. MnHi, microfilm.

4290 HUDDLESTON, David. 1872–1890. CNS. InRE.

4291 KNAPP, J. G. 1872. Preliminary survey of the Texas Pacific Railroad, by an attaché. WHi.

4292 PARSONS, George M. 1872–1875. CNS. FU.

4293 PORTER, Eugene Hoffman. 1872. 16-year old farm boy: school, farm chores, etc. NCooHi.

4294 REED, Silas. 1872–1874; 1877–1881. Travels to and from Boston and Washington and the West; letters and telegrams received and sent; brief references to business and family affairs. CtY.

4295 ROWE, George Fawcett. 1872; 1877; 1880. CNS. MH.

4296 SISSON, E. A. 1872–1932. CNS. WaU.

4297 SLACK, Hedgeman. 1872. CNS. Wv-Ar.

4298 SNOW, Erastus. 1872. Kept by a Mormon apostle; colonizer of St. George and director of Mormon affairs in southern Utah. CU-B.

4299 STEEVER, Lt. E. Z. 1872. Diary, including a description of the buffalo hunt given for Grand Duke Alexis of Russia. PEL-Kpsm.

4300 STOWE, Lewis. 1872–1908. Records of an Indian agent on the White Earth reservation; describes farming operations. MnHi.

4301 WEBSTER, John McAdam. 1872. CNS. NdHi.

4302 ANON. 1873–1897. Kept by a farmer in Pompey, N.Y. NIC.

4303 ANON. 1873. CNS. MiU.

4304 BANGS, James E. 1873–1874. Personal diaries of the secretary to Archibald Campbell, commissioner, U.S. Northern Boundary Commission. NdHi.

4305 BERNHARDSON, Lars. n.d. [between 1873–1936]. Kept in Clay Cnty., Minn. MnMohCHi.

4306 BOYCE, D. 1873–1874. A blacksmith and wheelwright in Santa Clara, Cal. CU-B.

4307 BRANTLY, William T., Jr. 1873. Kept by law student at the Univ. of Md.; life in Baltimore; reflections on the comtemporary scene; describes visit to W. Va. MdHi.

4308 BROWN, Brig.-Gen. William Carey. 1873–1918. From entrance at West Point through military career to retirement. CoU.

4309 CHRISTENSEN, Andrew. [between 1873–1936]. CNS. MnMohCHi, typescript.

4310 COOKE, Rowena P. 1873–1874. Kept during school days in Harmar, Washington Cnty., Ohio. OHi.

4311 COTTON, Helen. 1873. Social life, presumably in a suburb of Philadelphia; contains personal accounts. MnHi.

4312 DARTT, Edward H. S. 1873; 1875; 1878–1902. Raising fruit; views on prohibition; election returns; fairs; social life. MnHi.

4313 DUNNING, William A. 1873; 1874–1875. CNS. NNC.

4314 ERWIN, William A. [1873–1913?]. CNS. MoU.

4315 GRATACAD, Louis Pope. 1873-1909. Geological observations during holidays in N.Y. state, New England, Canada, Pa., Scotland, etc.; entertainments; current events; art; personal affairs. NN. *See* 3762.

4316 GREGORY, William H. 1873; 1888; 1889; 1891; 1894; 1895; 1898; 1902; 1903. His poor health; the weather; short trips; fishing trips; his attendance at various churches; visiting; etc. NcD.

4317 GROUT, Jane M. 1873. A journey by covered wagon from central Wis. to Luverne, Minn. MnHi, typescript.

4318 HAIGH, Henry A. 1873-1942. Personal life; Dearborn and Mich. history. MiDbHi.

4319 HEACOCK, Jesse. 1873-1878. Weather reports; visits, visitors, deaths. PSC-Hi.

4320 JOY family. 1873. CNS. MeHi.

4321 MACKALL, Benjamin F. 1873-1874. Records temperatures of a winter in Minn. and work with the Episcopal church. MnHi.

4322 McCLELLAN, Sgt. James S. 1873-1874. Indian expeditions and battles in Wyo. etc., by member of 3rd U.S. Cavalry. NN.

4323 MUNSON, Myron Andrews. 1873. Journal including part kept during studies at Harvard, class of 1860. MH. *See* 3192.

4324 NISBET, John W. 1873-1879. Social life at Macon, the Univ. of Ga.; intellectual interests and family connections. NcD. *See* 4189?

4325 NISBET, Ophelia R. 1873-1874. CNS. NcU.

4326 PEARSALL, Mary. 1873. A trip from Philadelphia to Montreal, describing topography, hotel accommodations, and means of travel. PHi.

4327 POLK, Mrs. Leonidas. 1873-1874. Personal. NcU.

4328 RAYMOND, H. H. 1873. Spent the year hunting buffalo southwest of Dodge City, Kan. KHi.

4329 RICHARDSON, Mrs. Ahira. 1873. Records social life and customs in St. Paul, Minn. MnHi.

4330 ROGERS, William King. 1873. Personal; family; Duluth property holdings. OFH.

4331 STODDARD, Ira Joy. 1873; 1876-1877; 1881; 1893; 1894-1895; 1904-1905. Kept by Baptist missionary to Assam, afterward secretary of Central Univ., Pella, Iowa; several stays with children in N.J. NjR.

4332 STUART, Granville. 1873. Trip to the National Park; Yellowstone Expedition of 1873. CtY. *See* 3209, 3541, 4466.

4333 THOMAS, Mary B. 1873. Forsyth, Ga. Diary of a schoolgirl at a boarding school. GU.

4334 THORTVEDT, Levi. [n.d. between 1873 and 1936]. Diary in Clay Cnty., Minn. MnMoh-CHi, typescript.

4335 THRUSTON, Rogers Clark Ballard. 1873; 1920. Travel journal on voyage to Europe and tour of London, Paris, Brussels, Waterloo, Cologne; travel journal from Louisville to Japan, China, and Manila. KyLoF.

4336 WEYMOUTH, James S. 1873-1890. Considerable detail about daily life and the people of Belmont, N.H. NhHi.

4337 BROWN, Joseph Mackay. 1874; 1876. Atlanta, N.Y., Philadelphia, the White Mountains, N. H. Scattered entries for above years; life in Atlanta, trip to Centennial exposition in Philadelphia in 1876, by son of Joseph E. Brown, Ga.'s Civil War gov. GU.

4338 CHAMBERS, Henry Alexander. 1874-1893. Personal and family affairs; many references to legal matters; his law partners. TC. *See* 3598.

4339 DALY, Charles Patrick. 1874. Scenery, sightseeing in Ireland. NN. *See* 2769, 3887, 4476, 4920.

4340 DELLENBAUGH, Frederick. 1874-1922. Trips to Europe: Edinburgh; Iceland; Spitzbergen, Norway; N.Y. AzTP. *See* 4250?

4341 ELLIS, John Stoneacre. 1874-1896. CNS. NHi.

4342 GILLINGHAM, Joseph E. 1874-1879. CNS. PHi.

4343 HAMMOND, Lillie. 1874-1879. A young girl's trip to Europe and Marathon, N.Y., farm life. NCooHi.

4344 HASSELL, Rev. Cushing B. 1874. CNS. NcU.

4345 HEERMAN, Edward Edson. 1874-1876; 1879; 1881; 1883; 1885; 1887; 1892; 1902; 1906; 1926; 1928. Steamboat navigation on the Chippewa and Mississippi rivers, and at Devil's Lake. MnHi.

4346 HORTON, Mrs. James C. 1874. Events in Lawrence, Kan., local and personal. KHi.

4347 JERABEK, John J. 1874. The migration of a group of Czechs to Minn. MnHi.

4348 McINTYRE, Emma Jane. 1874. Life on the Pribilov Islands, with particular attention to flora, fauna, and natives. CU-B.

4349 PETERSON, Edward Pierce. 1874. Kept by a freshman at the Univ. of Minn. MnHi, typescript.

4350 SHAW, Albert. 1874-1922. CNS. NN.

4351 SMITH, Annie Brunson. 1874-1895. CNS. ScU.

4352 TERRELL, Maj. W. G. 1874. Kept in prison in Burlington, Ky., while writer awaited trial. NN.

4353 USHIN, Stephan M. 1874-1894. A clerk in North-Western Trading Co.; chiefly about local affairs and incoming news. CU-B.

4354 WILLIAMS, William A. and his wife, Jane Iredell Meares. 1874. Miscellaneous. NcU.

4355 ANON. 1875; 1881. Includes places and names of performances by a traveling actor. MH.

4356 ANON. c. 1875. Kept probably during a trip to N.M. CSmH.

4357 BECK, Rev. Charles A. 1875–1880. Notations on church affairs and comments on various people. MdHi.

4358 BOYD, Thomas D. 1875–1885. Early years as a member of the faculty of L.S.U.; financial problems of the univ.; political situation; social life in Baton Rouge. LU, typescript.

4359 CARMAN, George Noble. 1875–1880. Kept as student at Univ. of Mich.: courses, personal reflections on life, lists of expenses. MiU.

4360 CRUMPLER, W. J. 1875. Agricultural diary and accounts kept in a notebook prepared by the Patrons of Husbandry; contains some printed matter relative to that organization. NcD.

4361 DUNCAN, Robert D. 1875–1877. Service at Newport barracks, Ky.; journey to Ft. Bridger, Wyo., and service there in the band of the U.S. Inf. InU-Li.

4362 FULLER, John L. 1875–1900. Farm diaries. NIC.

4363 GOOLD, William. 1875–1890. Partly written while he was a senator at Augusta, Me. MeHi.

4364 GREENE, Lt. Francis Vinton. 1875. Trip to Yellowstone Park: scientific observations and descriptions of scenery. NN.

4365 MARTIN, John L. 1875–1892. Weather; crops; current affairs. NbCcHi.

4366 MUTTON, William Watts. 1875–1942. Daily life of self-educated farmer and businessman; personal life; local events; people and organizations; travel in Europe and Near East and U.S.; socialism and socialist leaders. MiU.

4367 RISEDORPH, John E. 1875–1876. Kept at Le Sueur, Minn.; materials on the Younger brothers; local and national politics. MnHi.

4368 STIRLING, John S. 1875. A voyage from Cleveland to Cal. via N.Y. and Panama. DLC.

4369 SUTTER, Rosa Schafer. 1875–1920. Home activities and family affairs. MoU.

4370 TAWNEY, James A. 1875; 1885; 1888; 1891. Scrapbooks and diaries with information on social life near Gettysburg, Pa.; notations about lawsuits in Minn. and a few comments on actions of the Minn. Senate. MnHi.

4371 VOORHEES, David C. 1875. Farming; social and other personal activities. NjR, typescript.

4372 YORK, A. 1875–1880. CNS. NIC.

4373 ANON. 1876–1882. CNS. LU.

4374 ALDRICH, J. Frank. 1876. Trip across the country, Chicago to Cal. CSmH.

4375 BARTLETT, W. T. 1876–1883. In the country near Macon, Fort Valley, Atlanta, Crawford Cnty., Ga. Day-to-day trivia of school days and later life, mostly in middle Ga. GU.

4376 BULLARD, James. 1876–1878. Comments on the weather, game, Indians, ranches, and Mexicans, while he covered the West from the Dakotas to Mexico in search of gold. MoU, typescript.

4377 CALHOUN, J. 1876–1882. Business activities of the Consolidated Association of Planters of La., relative to the protection of property in which the company was interested, work assignments of personnel, and related matters. LU.

4378 CLEVELAND, Charles M. 1876–1893. Current events; market news; personal reflections on life. MiU. See 2983, 3430.

4379 DARCY, Eliza. 1876. Household and social activities. NjR.

4380 ENGLISH, William L. 1876. Field diary in the 7th Inf.; a daily record of the march from Ft. Shaw to join Gen. Terry against the Sioux; camping places, distances, conditions of the roads; news of Custer's defeat; march to the scene and burial of the dead; the rescue of Maj. Reno. CtY.

4381 FERRIS, Matilda. 1876–1902. Record of the ways in which she helped family and friends with cooking, sewing, housecleaning, caring for the sick, etc.; lectures; concerts; boat trips; activities in the Society of Friends. PSC-Hi.

4382 FOSTER, J. H. 1876–1878. CNS. KHi.

4383 FREEMAN, Henry Blanchard. 1876. Journal in the 7th U.S. Inf. in the campaign against the Sioux. CtY.

4384 GORTON, Leander. 1876. Meetings of the Minn. legislature. MnHi.

4385 GRIFFITH, Richard H. 1876–1881. CNS. PHi. See 3623.

4386 HOPPIN, William Jones. 1876–1881. Author's service as first secretary of American Legation, London; separate journal of residence there. MH. See 1900, 4220.

4387 JOHNSON, Mrs. Madison Y. 1876–1877. Household affairs. ICHi. See 4952.

4388 KELLOGG, Mark H. 1876. Correspondence. NdHi, typescript.

4389 LEACH, Josiah Granville. 1876–1920. Business affairs and the social and political life of the period. PHi.

4390 MASON, Rev. James Pleasant. 1876–1893. Cultivation of his farm. NcU.

4391 McVEY, James M. 1876. CNS. NdHi.

4392 MEIGHEN, Thomas. 1876; 1882. Diaries of a storekeeper and political leader. MnHi.

4393 NICHOLS, Charles D. 1876; 1878; 1889; 1907; 1910. 1870's in Columbus, Cherokee Cnty., Kan.; 1889 at National Military Home, Leavenworth, Kan.; 1907–1910 residence in Topeka. KHi.

4394 REYNOLDS, Charles, and Brown, Alexander. 1876. Events leading to and following the Custer fight of June 25, 1876. MnHi.

4395 SHAFFER, J. J. 1876–1879. Plantation events; sugar planting; some personal and family happenings. NcU. *See* 4463.

4396 ANON. 1877–1878; 1908. CNS. LU.

4397 BANCROFT, William. 1877–1880. Personal and political. OFH, copy.

4398 BINNING, James. 1877. CNS. OHi.

4399 CAREY, Nathaniel C. 1877–1887. CNS. CtMyMM.

4400 CLAYTON, Joshua E. 1877–1889. A large collection of papers, letters, and diaries which reflect experiences of a mining engineer in many of the far Western states. CU-B.

4401 COLSON, Mary J. 1877–1880. Kept on board the *George and Susan*, a whaling vessel. CSmH.

4402 HOWELL, Wilson Stout. 1877. Vacation journal of a sailboat trip from New Brunswick down the N.J. coast to the neighborhood of Bayhead; camping, hunting, fishing near Barnegat Bay. NjR.

4403 MITCHELL, Howard. 1877–1880. Travel journal: Denver to Santa Fe, return via El Moro, Trinidad, Denver, Salina, and Colorado Springs. KU.

4404 MOORE, Frank. 1877–1894. CNS. NhHi.

4405 PRICE, William. 1877. From N.J. to the Black Hills. CtY.

4406 TEN EYCK, Tunis. 1877–1893. Concerned with farming, social, and other personal activities. NjR.

4407 ANON. 1878. Kept by a U.S. Army surgeon stationed at Camp Bowie and Thomas in Ariz.; describes scenery, living conditions, and daily activities. NcD.

4408 COFFIN, Alexander Hamilton. 1878–1888. Social calls; politics; Coffin family; clippings. NCooHi. *See* 2763.

4409 COOK, Elizabeth. 1878. Personal. MiU.

4410 CRESSON, Lt. Charles Clement. 1878. Punitive expedition against Indians at Glenn's Ferry, Ida. NN.

4411 FITCH, Dr. C. Wellington. 1878. The campaign against the Bannock Indians. CtY.

4412 FORSE, Lt. A. G. 1878. Sent by government to study terrain of northern Ida. for the purpose of mapping possible route for a road. IdHi.

4413 GRIEVE, Martha Lucy. 1878–1882. Family and personal matters; activity among the poor and sick of N.Y. and Staten Island. NjR.

4414 GRIFFIN, Thomas H. 1878–1883. Weather; dates for planting and other farming operations near Clinton Falls. MnHi.

4415 HUFF, Henry Draper. 1878–1888. World events and Huff's activities in Chicago in connection with his smelting works and hardware business. CtY.

4416 JONES, Charles Joshua Ketcham. 1878; 1879. Trip from N.Y. to San Francisco to Yosemite Valley. NjR.

4417 PETROV, Ivan. 1878. A trip to Alaska in search of information for the Bancroft Library. CU-B.

4418 PURMORT, John E. 1878–1886. Farm life in Anoka Cnty., Minn. MnHi.

4419 PYLE, John Erasmus. 1878. Life in the Indian service; isolation, boredom, illness, red tape; life at Santa Fe and Ft. Wingate. CU-B.

4420 STANTON, Rev. Robert L. 1878–1884. Notes on religious work, writings for magazines, lectures, writings; trip to London. NN.

4421 ANON. 1879. CNS. NcU.

4422 ALCORN, James Lusk. 1879. The weather; farming; sale of produce; social, family, and religious affairs. NcU. *See* 3219?

4423 BALCOM, ———? 1879–1881. Life in Oxford, Chenango Cnty. NIC.

4424 CAMPBELL, J. A. 1879. Kept first time in crossing the ocean aboard the S.S. *Mikado* from Glasgow, Scotland, to N.Y. InU-Li.

4425 COOLEY, Thomas McIntyre. 1879; 1884-1894 (with gaps). His lecture tours and other activities; comments on current events and eminent men; discusses politics and other contemporary topics. MiU. *See* 4561, 4587.

4426 DE LONG, George W. 1879–1881. Daily entries from the time the *Jeannette* expedition left San Francisco until the *Jeannette* was crushed in the ice and abandoned. MdAN.

4427 FREDERICK, Eugene. 1879–1882. Marshallville, Ga. Young man living on a large plantation in middle Ga.; deals with planting and farm work. GU.

4428 GIBBS, M. Alice. 1879. Written by a high school student. OHi.

4429 HALL, Emma Amelia. 1879–1881; 1884. Scattered accounts and remarks on reform school. MiU.

4430 HALL, Sophie C. 1879. Visit to N.Y. city: boarding house, sights, stores. NN.

4431 HOWARD, Lt. Guy. 1879–1880. Field trips to military camps in Ariz.: campaign notes. AzTP.

4432 HUBBARD, Lucius Lee. 1879; 1881; 1882; 1887; 1891; 1893. Geologic explorations of Moosehead Lake region in Me., charts; topography and minute descriptions of territory. MiU.

4433 HUSSEY, Warren. 1879–1886. Describes trips to N.Y., Colo., Cal., Wash., and particularly northern Ida.; active in banking and mining in the West. CU-B.

4434 KANE, Laura B. 1879–1884. Farm household, Lake Cnty., Ill.; trips to Chicago to plays, lectures. ICHi.

4435 KEELER, Lucy Elliot. 1879–1924; 1926–1929. Personal; extensive travel abroad and in the U.S. OFH.

4436 KELLOGG, Elijah. 1879–1899. CNS. Me-Hi.

4437 LYMAN, Plattle De Alton. 1879–1894. Photocopy covering "Hole-in-the-Rock" expedition 1879–1880; continues life and travels in and around southeastern Utah. CU-B.

4438 PARSONS, George Whitewell. 1879–1929. Description and travel in Cal. and Ariz.; resided in Tombstone during the eventful 1880's. AzTP.

4439 ROWE, Peter Trimble. 1879; 1882–1885; 1888; 1894–1923. A record of official activities and some personal notes. PPCHi.

4440 VEBLEN, Andrew A. 1879–1932. CNS. MnHi.

4441 WILBER, Francis Augustus. 1879–1880. Accounts, letters, essays, and diary by a chemistry professor at Rutgers. NjR.

4442 ANON. 1880. Kept during scientific exploration from Ontario to Moose Factory, James Bay, and return. NN.

4443 ANON. 1880; 1881. The activity of steamboats on the Mississippi River at Baton Rouge, La. LU.

4444 ANON. 1880–1890. Ministerial journal kept by members of the United Society of Believers (Shakers), at Pleasant Hill, Ky. KyLoF.

4445 ANGELL, James Burrill. 1880–1881. Concerning his appointment as minister plenipotentiary and envoy extraordinary to China; journey; treaty negotiations; Chinese customs, cities, politics, people. MiU. *See* next item.

4446 ANGELL, Sarah Caswell (Mrs. James B.). 1880–1903 (with gaps). Life in Ann Arbor with her husband, who was president of Univ. of Mich.; trips to Turkey, Greece, Egypt, Palestine, Europe, China; church work. DAR; art and architecture; conditions of countries visited. MiU.

4447 BOWKER, Richard Rogers. 1880–1881. Kept in London by agent for Harper and Brothers: relations with authors, London scene, travel in England, contributions to *Harpers Magazine*. NN. *See* 1430, 3286.

4448 BRISTOL, Sherlock. 1880. Observations and personal experiences on journey from Wis. to the Salmon River mines; Bannock-Shoshoni attacks on emigrant trains, including his own; gold mining experiences in Cal., Ore., and Ida. CU-B.

4449 BROWN, Angeline (Mitchell). 1880–1881. Kept by a schoolteacher on the Ariz. frontier. CSmH.

4450 COFFMAN, J. S. 1880–1895. Trips to Mennonite churches. InGoM.

4451 DINWIDDIE, William. 1880–1886. CNS. ViU.

4452 DONOHUE, Charles. 1880. A trip by train from Jersey City to Cal. and back. CSmH.

4453 ELKINTON, Joseph. 1880–1899. Personal events; spiritual pronouncements. PSC-Hi. *See* 1411, 2382, 3175?

4454 FAVROT, George Kent. 1880–1881. Activity of steamboats on the Mississippi River at Baton Rouge with a few entries concerning progress in the construction of the state capitol building. LU.

4455 GRAFF family. 1880. CNS. PHi.

4456 GRIEVE, Lucia Catherine Graeme. 1880–1937. Life as Wellesley College student and teacher; travel to British Isles, India, Ireland. NjR.

4457 HALLOCK, A. B. 1880–1882. Personal. OrU.

4458 HUBBELL, James Boyd. 1880. Kept during a business trip on the Upper Missouri and in the Black Hills. NdHi, typescript.

4459 KJELAAS, Rev. L. E. 1880. Crossing the Atlantic from Norway to America. MnMAAr.

4460 LONDEN, John Henry. 1880; 1882–1886; 1888; 1891–1892; 1896. Personal; some mention of business transactions; list of accounts. InU-Li.

4461 MELLICK, Andrew D. 1880. A trip to Europe and return, including visits to France, Germany, the Low Countries, England, and Ireland. NjR, typescript.

4462 PORTER, Sarah. 1880–1887. Daily life of farmer's wife. OrU, typescript.

4463 SHAFFER, J. J. and W. L. 1880–1906. Farm and personal affairs. NcU. *See* 4395?

4464 SMITH, William Henry. 1880–1889. Chiefly on political matters. OHi.

4465 SPENCER, Dwight. 1880–1890. Spencer's experiences in establishing the Baptist church in Utah, Ida., Mont., Wyo., and the Dakotas. CU-B.

4466 STUART, Granville. 1880. A trip to the Yellowstone country to look for a cattle range. CtY. *See* 3209, 3541, 4332.

4467 THURSTON, E. B. 1880. Personal. MiU.

4468 WILLCOX, William Goodenow. 1880–1881; 1908. CNS. NNC.

4469 ANON. 1881. Kept by a member of the United Society of Believers (Shakers), at Pleasant Hill, Ky.; includes names of members of the society; weather reports; admission and loss of members by death or otherwise; visit of Harvey Eads of South Union; memorial service for Pres. James A. Garfield. KyLoF.

4470 ANON. 1881–1886. By the congregation of the Moravian Church in Mt. Bethel, Va. NcWsM.

4471 ANON. 1881–1886. By the congregation of the Moravian Church in Providence, N.C. Nc-WsM.

4472 BECKER, John. 1881–1900. Kept by a farmer in the Mennonite community of Mountain Lake, Minn. MnHi, microfilm.

4473 COYNE, Patrick J. 1881–1913. Daily events; notes on distances between towns in Ariz.; weather reports. AzTP.

4474 CROSS, William. 1881–1916. Farming life. MnHi.

4475 DAILY, Henry N. 1881–1890. His work; events in the Shaker colony at Pleasant Hill; weather conditions. KyLoF.

4476 DALY, Charles P. 1881. Trip with wife from N.Y. to Germany. NN. *See* 2769, etc.

4477 DANFORTH, George A. 1881–1882. His life in New Haven Mills, Vt., and later at Sutherland Mills. CtY.

4478 GORE, Prof. J. W. 1881–1883. A European trip. NcU.

4479 HOSMER, Elizabeth S. (Viles). 1881–1923. Tour of Europe; family affairs; notes on the weather; local and world events of headline importance. MoU.

4480 MEADE, Capt. Richard Worsam, 3rd. 1881–1882. Remark book and journal on the U.S.S. *Vandalia*. NHi. *See* 2938.

4481 MORRIS, Henry C. 1881–1890. Grade school; college (Lombard at Galesburg, Ill.); European travel; consul at Ghent. ICHi.

4482 NEWCOMB, Prof. Simon. 1881–1903. Notebooks, diaries, and a journal kept by a scientist. DLC.

4483 PANEBAKER, William A. 1881. Brief entries of farm life in Cass cnty. NdHi.

4484 PAUL, Charles Rodman. 1881. Diary on the Milk River expedition. CtY.

4485 SAWYER, Jennie Toll. 1881–1882. Trip to Europe and Washington, D.C.: museums, important buildings, people encountered, sessions of Congress. MiU.

4486 STEWART, Susan. 1881–1942 (with gaps). Social life of Indianapolis with letters, clippings, etc. pasted in; meetings with prominent people; national and international events; popular thought of the day. InHi.

4487 TILTON, Josephine H. 1881–1882. Description of life at Swarthmore preparatory school and college; description of fire which destroyed main building. PSC-Hi.

4488 WENDOVER, Jessie May. 1881–1953. Life of a middle-class woman from childhood to unmarried old age: household chores, recreation, studies, music, and reading, social life, some limited observations of national and world events. NjR.

4489 ALLEN, George H. 1882; 1883; 1886. CNS. NIC.

4490 BAIRD, Mrs. Sarah G. 1882–1912(?). Kept by housewife on farm near Edina, Minn.; describes meetings of the Grange, trip to Chicago Fair, 1893, and trips to Cal. in 1892 and 1912(?). MnHi.

4491 FARNSWORTH, Mrs. Martha O. (Fred C.). 1882–1922. Life in Topeka. KHi.

4492 GRAFF, Paul. 1882–1893; 1897. CNS. PHi.

4493 GRAUTOFF, Walter. 1882; 1884; 1885. Daily schoolboy life: classes, cello lessons, reading, entertainments; a vacation visit with relatives in Hamburg, Lübeck, and Cuxhaven. NjR, English typescript.

4494 HALLER, Granville Owen. 1882–1889. Cash received and expended in Seattle, Wash. Terr. WaU. *See* 2125, 2925, 2997, 3055, 3116, 3908.

4495 HELME, James W., Jr. 1882; 1886; 1887; 1893. The weather and daily events and monthly account of money, appointments, purchases, and loans. MiU.

4496 SCHIEFFELIN, Edward. 1882–1883. A prospecting trip up the Yukon on a steamboat built in San Francisco. CU-B.

4497 SHIRLEY, John Simpson. 1882–1883. Homesteaded in Russell Cnty., Kan. KHi.

4498 SURGHNOR, Mrs. M. F. 1882; 1886–1890; 1899. Weather; family news; general health conditions; comments on incidents and people in Monroe, La. LU, typescript.

4499 TITSWORTH, Alfred Alexander. 1882. Kept during a survey of boundary between N.Y. and N.J.; personal and informal items, as well as technical details. NjR. *See* 4511.

4500 WILBOUR, Sarah Soule. 1882–1890. History, genealogy, people of Little Compton, R.I., her only son; money. RLcHi.

4501 BROWN, Elijah A. Jan., 1883. Atlanta, Ga. Daily activities for one month of 1883 by son of Joseph E. Brown, Civil War gov. of Ga. GU.

4502 CHASE, Thomas. 1883. Written at Haverford and covering a trip abroad during the summer; several papers of miscellaneous memoranda at the back. PHC.

4503 COLLINS, Bryan. 1883–1887. CNS. OHi.

4504 EAKIN, Benjamin. 1883–1884. CNS. PHi.

4505 EARLE, Prof. Mortimer Lamson. 1883–1905. His student days at Columbia and at Univ. of Berlin; his professional life: his excavations; his academic work at Columbia (in Greek, Latin, German, and English). NNC.

4506 MacRAE, John P. 1883–1916. Personal. NcU.

4507 MASON, Rachel. 1883–1931. Social life in St. Paul, Minn. MnHi.

4508 STODDARD, Charles Warren. 1883–1884. Describing visit to San Francisco. CSfU. *See* 4526, 4627.

4509 STOKES, Helen Louisa. 1883–1884. Household and social life of a wealthy family in N.Y.: servants, yacht, vacation camping trips. NjR, typescript.

4510 SWAN, James Gilchrist. 1883. The cruise to Queen Charlotte Island, B.C., for the Smithsonian Institution. WaU. *See* 3327.

4511 TITSWORTH, Alfred Alexander. 1883; 1884. Kept during periods of reconnaissance for triangulation point in south N.J. (chiefly Atlantic and Cumberland counties) for the N.J. Geological Survey (April–May, 1883), and the U.S. Coast and Geodetic Survey; accounts and detailed descriptions of the various stations. NjR. *See* 4499.

4512 TRIMMER, Edward C. 1883. Daily social and personal activities in Quakertown and other nearby localities of Hunterdon Cnty., N.J. NjR.

4513 WELSH, Herbert. 1883–1928. CNS. PHi. *See* 4679.

4514 AYERS, John. 1884. A march to Cal. and to N.M. with Cal. volunteers; comments on peonage, reform of Catholic clergy, Kit Carson, and mining. CU-B.

4515 CARTER, Henry Hall. 1884–1902. Logbook of yachting cruises. MH.

4516 DAGNE, Harry. 1884–1910. CNS. OHi.

4517 EATON, Arthur Wentworth Hamilton. 1884–1893; 1897–1914. Including journal of trip abroad. MH.

4518 ENZOR, Mary Matilda. 1884–1922. CNS. OHi.

4519 FOULK, George C. 1884. Kept by a Naval attaché to the American legation in Korea; resigned and took up residence in Kyoto; prof. of mathematics at Kyoto; chiefly his experiences in Korea. CU-B.

4520 GNAGI, Elvira M. 1884. Daily entries of a housewife on a vineyard near Saratoga, Cal. CU-B.

4521 GUILDAY, Prof. Peter. 1884–1932. Autobiographical notes. DCU. *See* 4726.

4522 JENSEN, Mae Roberts. 1884–1890. Life on a homestead near Devils Lake. NdHi.

4523 RICH, John A. 1884–1943. His early life as a teacher; experiences of his father; his law practice; politics; travels; business; bank failures and progress made in his community of Salem, Mo.; names of clients appear on the margins. MoU.

4524 SMALLWOOD, Dr. Charles. 1884–1896. CNS. Nc-Ar.

4525 SQUIER, George Owen. 1884–1886 (with gaps); 1897. Daily routine at U.S. Military Academy; studies; professors; trip to Europe; plans for future; poetry; scientific experiments. MiU.

4526 STODDARD, C. W. 1884–1885. Personal. InNd. *See* 4508, 4627.

4527 ANON. 1885–1887. A cruise under the command of Capt. George Dewey on the U.S. steam frigate *Pensacola*, when flagship of R.Adm. S. R. Franklin on the European station. NHi.

4528 ANON. 1885. CNS. MoU.

4529 BLANCHARD, Dr. Hiram Delos. 1885–1886; 1890. Country doctor's professional visits; social life. NCooHi.

4530 BURGESS, Gelette. 1885; 1888; 1917–1951. Kept by a well-known writer, one-time editor in San Francisco of *The Wave*, 1894 and *The Lark*, 1895–1897. CU-B.

4531 BURGWYN, J. A. 1885–1889. Plantation diary. NcU.

4532 CHRISMAN, Comrade Clarence. 1885–1886. Begins at Ft. Wingate during military campaigns and expeditions of 1885–1886; original pencil sketches of camps and routes; a list of recruiting offices and officers in the U.S. Army. AzTP.

4533 HOLLAND, W. B. 1885. Record of his activities. OkU.

4534 JAEGER, ———? 1885–1894. Diary of the wife of a Protestant Episcopal (?) minister, who founded an orphanage at Rustburg, Va., for Negro children. NcD.

4535 McCUISTON, Rev. John Franklin. 1885–1899; 1909–1926. Personal diary of a provincial assistant and minister, mentioning various congregations in Va. and N.C. NcWsM.

4536 McKINLEY, Dan. 1885–1886. A Scotch colonist's difficulties in locating a home; modes of travel in Fla.; weather reports from day-to-day. FSM.

4537 MORRIS, Prof. George Sylvester. 1885. Including extracts from English and German philosophical writings. MiU. *See* 3131, 4094.

4538 PENDERGAST, Warren. 1885–1889. The agricultural experiment station in Grand Rapids, Minn. MnHi, microfilm.

4539 POND, Mr. and Mrs. Gideon H., Jr. 1885–1914. Cashbook and diaries kept at Bloomington; details of prices and raising of farm products; social affairs; weather conditions. MnHi.

4540 SHEPPARD, Anna. 1885. CNS. PHi.

4541 SPRINGER, Viola. 1885–1886. Trip from Princeton, Mo., to Harvey valley, Ore.; includes recipes and receipts. OrU.

4542 VANDERBILT family. Latter part of 19th century. Papers and diaries. NHi.

4543 BRANCH, Mary Cook. 1886. Comments on sermons and a trip to Williamsburg, Va. NcD.

4544 BROOKE, Charlton P. 1886–1887. Student's diary containing several pages of autographs, lists of school faculty and officers, items concerning life at the Bingham School, and comments on the "poor whites" of the region. NcD.

4545 CANNON, W. W. 1886. Daily account of work done. MoU.

4546 CONNOR, Elias H. 1886. His work in installing milling machinery. MnHi.

4547 COOKE, Harriet Ruth. 1886. Distillations of newspaper reports; observations on 1886 N.Y. transport strike. NjR.

4548 DICKEY, John Marcus. 1886–1896; 1908–1909. Books read; quotations; teaching, speeches, and sermons; matters concerning the Rocky Mountain Lyceum of Denver; philosophical observations. InU-Li

4549 ELLIOTT, Charles B. 1886–1891; 1897–1901; 1912. Records of a judge of the municipal court, Minneapolis, a member of the Philippines Commission as Secretary of Commerce and Police. MnHi.

4550 EPPS, J. D. 1886. Local news and weather in Woodruff, Spartanburg Cnty., S.C. NcD.

4551 GRIFFIN, Anthony Jerome. 1886–1930 (with gaps). CNS. NN.

4552 GROSS, John Mason. 1886–1903 (except 1891–1893, 1901). Personal and business affairs. RHi.

4553 HOOKER, John. 1886–1938. Daily routines; costs of farming tools and labor; local events; profits from farming. MiU.

4554 LEITER, Mrs. Mary Theresa (Carter). 1886–1891. Social life in Washington, D.C. ICHi.

4555 MOSHER, LaFayette (?) 1886. Activities as a surveyor. InU-Li.

4556 STEWART, William Rhinelander. 1886–1904 (with gaps). CNS. NN.

4557 TRUEBLOOD, Thomas Clarkson. 1886–1934. Travel in Canada, and the eastern colleges, Great Britain, the Continent, Australia, Tasmania, Africa, South America, Cuba, Mexico, and Cal. MiU.

4558 YOUNG, Hiram H. 1886–1889; 1890–1895. Farming; prices; social life; political activities. InU-Li.

4559 ALEXANDER, Laura. 1887–1892. Miscellaneous. NcU.

4560 COOLEY, Mortimer E. 1887; 1889; 1894; 1899–1935. Appointments and daily schedule by dean of the College of Engineering, Univ. of Mich. MiU.

4561 COOLEY, Thomas McIntyre. 1887–1890. His work on the Interstate Commerce Commission, with some relevant newspaper clippings. MiU. *See* 4425, 4587.

4562 DALE, Samuel Sherman. 1887–1929. Textile tariff; wool-labeling question; weights and measures issue. MH.

4563 GREENE, Samuel. 1887–1910. CNS. WaU.

4564 HANEY, John Lewis. 1887–1959. CNS. PPAmS.

4565 HENDERSON, Moses Young. 1887–1898. Everyday happenings and interests. NcU.

4566 PATTERSON, S. L. (?) 1887–1892. CNS. NcU.

4567 RIDDLE, L. H. 1887–1891. Democratic politics; local events and personal matters in Marion Cnty., Kan. KHi, microfilm.

4568 ROY, Mrs. M. 1887–1888. A trip around the world, leaving England March 13, 1887, on the S.S. *Orizaba* and return to Liverpool, July 10, 1888. CU-B.

4569 TENNEY, Anmon. 1887–1921. Discussion of Joseph Smith and Brigham Young; interesting comments on politics of Mexico; excellent chronology of happenings in Mexico City. AzTP.

4570 CARPENTER, Albert Greene. 1888–1892. Operation of ice cutting on various ponds in R.I. and Mass. RHi.

4571 CLARK, L. S. (family). 1888–1924. Kept by a high school youth and a woman interested in modern literature. MnHi.

4572 CONNETT, Cornelia Ett (Thompson). 1888–1917. Record of household, family, business, and neighborhood activity. NjR.

4573 CROWNER, Mrs. Mary Ward. 1888–1930. CNS. OHi.

4574 FIRKINS, Oscar W. 1888; 1909–1925. CNS. MnHi.

4575 GOULD, J. M. 1888. Routine farm activities and personal matters. LU.

4576 MOSS, Henry L. 1888. Trip through Italy, France, Spain, and England. MnHi.

4577 PAUL, Randolph Casey. 1888. Weather; crops; family affairs; finances; animal breeding. MoU.

4578 SIDDONS, Mrs. Scott. 1888–1890. CNS. PHi.

4579 TARKINGTON, Rev. Joseph. 1888; 1889; 1891. CNS. InHi.

4580 WATSON, H. G. 1888–1894. Pioneer life in Ellis Cnty., Kan. KHi.

4581 ALLEY, J. K. 1889. CNS. Tx, typescript.

4582 BARNES, Mrs. Sudie (McAlester). 1889–1891. Kept while she was away at school. OkU.

4583 BIEDLER, John X. 1889. CNS. MtHi.

4584 BROWN, Ernest L. 1889–1900. Trips into northwestern Minn. by a taxidermist of Warren, Minn. MnHi.

4585 BUTLER, Julia Colt. 1889–1890. Life of a teen-age school girl: social and family visiting, games, interest in sports, including football, church attendance, theater, concerts, a brief trip to Washington, another to relatives in Litchfield, Conn., and Stowe, Vt.; a six-month trip abroad. NjR.

4586 CARROLL, Lew F. 1889–1890. An account of the opening of Okla. Terr. to white settlers by one who made the Run of 1889. OkHi.

4587 COOLEY, Thomas McIntyre. 1889; 1890. Notes of appointments and jottings. MiU. *See* 4425, 4561.

4588 FLORENCE MISSION, New Brunswick, N.J. 1889–1890. Records gospel meetings, conversions, dealings with alcoholics, etc. of a mission (also known as Florence Crittenton Mission) run by Mrs. Anda Kilburn. NjR.

4589 FRANCE family. [1889–1905]. CNS. MoU.

4590 LOWELL, Amy. 1889; 1890. CNS. MH.

4591 MOORE, Charles. 1889–1903. Activities as secretary to senator; reminiscences of architects and artists consulted in committee work; plans to improve Washington; White House renovation; Lincoln Memorial, Mall. MiU.

4592 NIMS, Franklin A. 1889–1890. With Brown-Stanton party exploring the Colorado River. NN.

4593 PALACHE, Charles. 1889. A trip through the southern Sierra Nevadas by the class of '91 of the Univ. of Cal. CU-B.

4594 TAYLOR, Elizabeth. 1889. Trip to Alaska; trip west through Canada to Victoria prior to the voyage. Mr. James Taylor Dunn of NCooHi; to be presented to MnHi.

4595 WHITE, James T. 1889. Written on board the U.S. Revenue steamer *Bear*; Arctic cruise. WaU. *See* 4637.

4596 WHITMAN, Edmund Allen. 1889. Irregular entries by an attorney and author. NjR.

4597 ANON. 1890. Happenings in the Benedictine monastery at St. Leo, Fla. FSlA.

4598 BRAY, John Francis. 1890–1894. CNS. MiU.

4599 COOLEY, Prof. Charles Horton. 1890; 1895–1929. Introspective account of his personality development; ideas on religion, sociology, and democracy; reflections on the individual and his relation to society. MiU.

4600 DONALDSON, Dr. Henry Herbert. 1890–1938. CNS. PPAmS.

4601 GROSS, Edward Tudor. 1890–1948. Business, social, civic, fraternal, and personal life. RHi.

4602 KEEHLN, Mrs. Angelica. 1890. Personal. NcWsM.

4603 LIEBER, Richard. 1890; 1891; 1895; 1909–1944. Personal. InU-Li.

4604 OSBORN, Chase Salmon. 1890; 1895–1915; 1935. Public and private life of newspaper publisher. MiU.

4605 BOONE, Dr. William Judson. 1891–1922. Founding and development of College of Idaho; interesting picture of pioneer life in Boise Valley, IdHi.

4606 FRY, Ann W. 1891. Trip to West coast and back to Philadelphia. PSC-Hi.

4607 LABAW, George W. 1891–1901. CNS. Nj-PatPhi.

4608 LONG, William West. 1891–1892; 1904–1905; 1908–1909; 1911; 1916–1917. CNS (part in Cherokee). PPAmS.

4609 MERCHANT, Stephen L. 1891–1900. Personal and business notes of a Duluth, Minn., real estate and loan man, including reminiscences of Cal. in 1849. MnHi.

4610 PARKERSON, Harriet. 1891–1900. CNS. KHi.

4611 RICH, John T. 1891–1895. Personal and political. MiU. *See* 4195.

4612 RUCKER, William J. 1891–1893. CNS. ViU.

4613 TORRANCE, Eli. 1891; 1892; 1919; 1924; 1925. Business and personal record of a Minneapolis lawyer. MnHi.

4614 VOORHEES, Sarah Rutgers (Neilson). 1891–1892. Social and personal activities with her husband, Willard P. Voorhees; weather; deaths, etc. NjR.

4615 WHITE, Ellen M. 1891–1900; 1902–1909; 1912; 1914–1917. Brief record of social life in Salem, Ore. Or, microfilm.

4616 BUSCH, Wilhelm. 1892–1949. Daily life as bookseller in Mecklenberg, Vienna, and N.Y.: social, political, international affairs, cost of living. NN.

4617 CARITHERS, Elizabeth. 1892. Athens, Ga. Diary of an 18-year old schoolgirl living in Athens, Ga. and attending Lucy Cobb, a private school for girls. GU.

4618 FRIPP, Alice Louisa. 1892–1903. Chiefly family events. ScU.

4619 FRITSCH, Bianca. 1892. Kept during nurse's training. NN.

4620 KNIPP, Rev. L. O. 1892–1904. Notes by pastor of Christian Church. PHi.

4621 LIBBEY, Laura Jean. 1892–1903. Trips through Europe, Egypt, West Indies, Italy, France, Germany, British Isles, etc. NN.

4622 MERRIAM, Ruth M. 1892. Diary of a young girl quarantined because of scarlet fever. NcD.

4623 PATTERSON, Frances Todd. 1892–1894. Domestic and social activities; much on participation in preparation for the Chicago Fair; opening and closing of Fair; important people at Fair. MiU.

4624 RYAN, John A. 1892–1898. Reflections on readings in literature and on problems of the day. DCU.

4625 SCHENCK, Lt. Bard Pendleton. 1892. Horseback journey from Ft. Yates, N.D., to Yellowstone Park and back. NN.

4626 SCOTT, Fred Newton. 1892–1921. Personal; daily work; events and people at Univ. of Mich.; trips taken; comments on reading. MiU.

4627 STODDARD, Charles Warren. 1892–1893; 1895. Private diary of university life. DCU. *See* 4526?

4628 HICKEMEYER, Rudolph. 1893. Describes El Paso, Tex., and Juarez, Chihuahua, Mexico; climate and architecture; people and customs. AzTP.

4629 LAUGHTON, Fred M. 1893. A summer trip to Europe. MeBa.

4630 LYTTON, Legaré Rogers. 1893–1916. N.Y. life; stage and early motion pictures; travels in Europe. NN.

4631 NASH, B. R. 1893–1900. Daily account of travels and expenses of sales agent for the American Tobacco Co. NcD, microfilm.

4632 SIPPI, Charles Augustus. 1893–1897. Mainly covers his work, family, church, and social activities. CU-B.

4633 THOMAS, Charles E. 1893. Trip across the continent made by Gen. Wade Hampton as railroad commissioner. ScU.

4634 COMIN, Rev. John. 1894–1895; 1900–1901; 1919–1920. Student days in Germany; travels in Mich. for church. (Most in Pitman shorthand.) MiU.

4635 COOLEY, Dr. Dennis. 1894. Covering four days on his state of health. MiU.

4636 KING, Pendleton. 1894–1904; 1912; 1913. Work; books read; social engagements. NcU.

4637 WHITE, James T. 1894. Written on the Revenue steamer *Bear*'s Arctic cruise. WaU. *See* 4595.

4638 WILLIAMS, John Fletcher. 1894. CNS. MnHi.

4639 ANON. 1895. A trip from Nashville, Tenn. to N.Y. and a Mediterranean cruise aboard the S.S. *Friesland*; short visits in Holland and other European countries, return from London to N.Y., followed by a stay on a farm (Wis.?) apparently owned by the writer. NjR.

4640 ANON. 1895. By a member of the Dickins or Randolph family. CNS. NcU.

4641 BURROWS, Julius Caesar. 1895–1911. Places visited in Europe, especially England and Germany. MiU. *See* 3347.

4642 CROWNER, Adelbert. 1895. CNS. OHi.

4643 CURTIS, Charles B. 1895. European travels. NN.

4644 DE PUY, Almena R. 1895. CNS. MiU.

4645 NELSON, Mrs. Mary E. 1895. A visit to Spain, Egypt, Italy, Palestine, Greece, Paris, and London. MnHi.

4646 ROOT, George Allen. 1895–1898; 1902–1949. Minute daily account of his life, mostly in Topeka. KHi.

4647 COLEMAN, Evans. 1896–1902. Daily events in his life as a cowboy in Ariz. and N.M. AzTP.

4648 HIDEN, George. 1896–1898. Daily farm operations. ViU.

4649 IJAMS, Elizabeth. 1896. A trip to Europe with descriptions of life and entertainment in London and Paris. ViU.

4650 MANAHAN, James. 1896–1897. Law practice. MnHi.

4651 MERSHON, William Butts. 1896; 1898–1904; 1907; 1912. Hunting and fishing trips: records of each day's haul. MiU.

4652 STEPHENS, Dr. Edwin Lewis. 1896–1897. Activities while he was at NYU, where he was awarded the Helen Gould Scholarship for the study of pedagogy. LU.

4653 STOW, Horace. 1896. Travels from N.H. to Ind.; life in early Ind. InHi, typescript.

4654 WELLING, Richard Ward Greene. 1896–1907. Social and family life in N.Y., Tuxedo, Newport, etc.; law practice; politics; gossip. NN.

4655 WENLEY, Robert Mark. 1896–1925. Personal diary: appointments, travels in U.S. and abroad, social schedule, activities at Univ. of Mich.; some comments on current events. MiU.

4656 WOOD, Nahum Trask. 1896–1903. CNS. CSmH, original; CSd, copy. *See* 4276.

4657 ANON. 1897. A trip to New Orleans. NIC.

4658 BONNAFFON, Edmund W. 1897. Life in Alaska while he was paymaster in U.S. Navy. PHi.

4659 CLARK, J. W. 1897. Teaching school at Owatonna, Minn., and work as a carpenter. MnHi.

4660 HOLLAND, Dr. George Frank. 1897–1899. Diary as apothecary on U.S.S. *Vicksburg*. InU-Li.

4661 MASON, Alfred. 1897. CNS. MnHi.

4662 ANON. 1898. Marine aboard U.S.S. *Massachusetts*: stockade at Santiago, Cuba; visit to Puerto Rico. NN.

4663 ANON. 1898–1901. Vacation travels of young person in Germany and Denmark (in German). NN.

4664 CLARK, Charles Asa. 1898. Trip to the Philippine Islands with the 13th Minn. Vol. Inf. during the Spanish-American War. MnHi.

4665 CURTIS, Asahel. 1898(?) CNS. WaU.

4666 GOSS, John W. 1898–1902. Business transactions. ViU. *See* 4745.

4667 HARTNETT, Maurice A. 1898–1899. Trip to Kotzebue Sound, Alaska. WaU.

4668 KITE, Robert E. Lee. 1898. Problems and daily routine of camp life in the U.S. and Cuba during the Spanish-American War. AzTP.

4669 McKINLEY, William. 1898–1907. Spanish-American War, Philippines Insurrection, Boxer Rebellion. OFH.

4670 NEILSON, Mary Putnam (Woodbury). 1898–1902. Weather; birds; garden; social life. PSC-Hi. *See* 4228.

4671 O'KANE, W. C. 1898–1899. Journal of a sgt. maj. in the Spanish-American War, 10th Regt., Ohio Vol. Inf. OHi.

4672 PECK, Florence C. 1898–1903. Life in high school, in college, and as kindergarten teacher; Rochester and Boston. NN.

4673 PETTIGREW, R. F. 1898. Travel in China. OClWHi.

4674 POWEL, Mary Edith. 1898–1907. CNS. PHi.

4675 RASK, Olaf H. 1898. Diary of an officer in the 15th Minn. Inf., kept mainly in Pa.; mentions a visit to Gettysburg. MnHi.

4676 RIVERS, T. R. 1898. Diary of trip to Santiago de Cuba and the campaign there. OFH, typescript.

4677 RUPPENTHAL, Henry C. 1898. Diary of private, Co. M, 20th Kan. Vol. Inf. KHi.

4678 SELLERS, George Escol. 1898. Diary of last year of his life, in and around Chattanooga, Tenn. PPAmS.

4679 WELSH, Herbert. 1898–1919. CNS. PHi. *See* 4513.

4680 WENDELL, Evert Jansen. 1898. Travels in Europe. MH.

4681 BARRY, E. D. 1899–1900. Service in the Philippines. MnHi.

4682 BECK, Marcus Wayland. 1899–1918; 1934. Griffin, Atlanta, Ga. Personal diaries of Ga. Supreme Court Justice; much comment re WWI. GU.

4683 BENDER, D. H. 1899–1943. Mennonite church affairs. InGoM.

4684 BINGHAM, Emma. 1899–1907. Kept in Cadiz, Ohio, and Washington, D.C. OHi.

4685 BINGHAM, John Armor. 1899–1905. Kept in Washington, D.C., by the Ohio Congressman. OHi.

4686 DEL MAR, Walter. 1899. Tour around the world: scenery, customs, sights, conditions in Japan and Far East. NN. *See* 4737.

4687 DUNNING, Charlotte L. (Mrs. William A.). 1899–1915. CNS. NNC.

4688 GOODHUE, Isaac Newton. 1899–1903. Current political and economic questions; philosophical and literary topics; Emerson and Thoreau as acquaintances. MnHi.

4689 HOLMAN, Robert L. 1899–1918. Personal; business. OHi.

4690 HOWELL, Eliza Dunham. 1899–1906. Stocks and other investments; European trip. PSC-Hi.

4691 HUNTER, Rev. Aaron Burtis. 1899–1926 (with gaps). European trips; vacation travels in America; speaking tours; church attendance; school functions and appointments. Nc-Ar.

4692 HUNTER, Sarah L. 1899–1937. CNS. Nc-Ar.

4693 KEMPER, Willis Miller. 1899–1905; 1907–1913. Legal duties; data on estates, cases, etc.; many prominent Cincinnatians mentioned. OCUHi.

4694 LESLIE, O. 1899–1901. The 40th Regt. during the Philippines Insurrection; describes the army and his own role in fighting the rebels. MoU.

4695 MILLER, Loye H. 1899; 1902; 1903. Univ. of Cal. expedition to the fossil beds of Day River, Ore., and a trip to Hawaii. CU-B.

4696 MORLEY, Fred. 1899–1940. Domestic matters and engineering records. MiU.

4697 PORTER, Joe L. 1899–1900; 1903–1938. Financial matters; politics; personal experiences in Okla. OkU.

4698 RUSSATER, John. 1899. Kept during the Spanish-American War while he served in the Philippines with the N.D. Regt. NdHi.

4699 VILLA, Simeon A. 1899–1901. Flight of Aguinaldo and his capture (translated from Spanish). NN.

4700 WARRINGTON, Immanuel H. 1899–1902. Philippine War diaries by a U.S. infantryman in the Philippines. PHi.

4701 WILDER, Marshall Pinckney. 1899; 1901–1903; 1905–1913. Clippings with manuscript notes; theatrical interests. MH.

4702 ALEXANDER, Edward Porter. 1900. His diplomatic mission to Panama and Nicaragua. NcU.

4703 BARNES, Will C. 1900–1940. Forest service notes; many good stories; notes on the cattle business. AzTP.

4704 HERRICK, Mrs. Myron Timothy. 1900. A cruise in the Mediterranean. OClWHi.

4705 JONES, Ada Alice. 1900–1939. CNS. NN.

4706 KELSEY, Prof. Francis Willey. 1900–1927. Activities and records of correspondence; archaeological expeditions in Europe and Near East; activities of Archaeological Institute of America (president, 1907–1912); Univ. of Mich.; American occupation army in Germany; work of American Relief commissions in Near East. MiU.

4707 NEWMAN, Frederick Bernard. 1900–1904. Service as sailor on board the U.S.S. *Kentucky*: passage from Brooklyn through the Mediterranean and the Suez Canal; fleet duty in the Far East and return. NjR.

4708 PARSONS, William Barclay. 1900–1904. The beginning of work until his resignation as Chief Engineer of Rapid Transit Commission. NNC, typescript.

4709 SETON, Archbishop Robert. Early 20th century. Diaries and notebooks. NHi. *See* 3077?

4710 SMITH, Alice Maude. 1900(?). CNS. WaU.

4711 STEPHENSON, James M., Jr. 1900. Athens, Ga. A few brief entries re lectures, engagements, accounts. Tutor in English at the Univ. of Ga. 1897–1905. GU.

4712 WALTON, Martha. ca. 1900. CNS. WWau-Hi.

4713 WINSTON, Lt. H. T. 1900–1906. Cruises by the U.S.S. *Iowa*. NcU.

4714 WRIGHT, Ellen C. 1900–1909. Kept at Wilmington College, Wilmington, Ohio, where she taught. OHi.

4715 YOUNG, Brigham, Jr. 1900–1902. Personal and family affairs; Mormon activities; Salt Lake City, San Francisco, etc. NN.

4716 ANON. 1901–1905. Diary of Japan; mission of Mormon Church at Salt Lake City en route and in Japan. NN, typescript.

4717 ANON. 1901–1902. A trip through Spain and the Near East. OkU.

4718 BIBBINS, Mrs. Arthur. 1901–1902. Account of visit to Clayden House and the opening of Parliament. MdHi.

4719 McCORKLE, Rev. William P. 1901–1907. Personal. NcU.

4720 MILHOLLAND, John Elmer. 1901–1925. Family; travels, West and to Europe; work; philosophy; religion; activities for various reform measures; experiments with the pneumatic underground tube system. NCooHi.

4721 MULDOON, Most Rev. Peter J. 1901–1918. Activities on assignments while he was a Roman Catholic priest. Chancery Office, Rockford, Ill.

4722 REED, Hugh Daniel. 1901–1906. Account of bird-watching. NIC.

4723 BANTA, I. 1902. Describes prospecting trip from Valdez to Lakima, Alaska. OrU.

4724 COMSTOCK, William Alfred. 1902–1916 (with gaps). Daily account of job as secretary of Rochester and Eastern Railroad Co.; business and politics. MiU.

4725 CULP, Florence M. (Burns). 1902–1903; 1914–1917; 1934; 1937; 1939–1940; 1943–1945. Life led by a clergyman's wife: church services, funerals, choir, Sunday school classes, society, meetings, visits, household and family events, vacation trips. NjR.

4726 GUILDAY, Prof. Peter. 1902–1940; 1945. Personal diary of student, professor, and secretary of American Cath. Hist. Assoc. DCU. *See* 4521.

4727 LEGGETT, Esther G. 1902–1927. Travels, especially in Japan and Alaska. PPh.

4728 LOTTO, Frederick S. 1902. Kept on one of the *Gaze Tours* in Europe; Great Britain. NN. *See* 4853.

4729 OLCOTT, Euphonia M. 1902–1903. Trip to Europe. NN.

4730 REIGHARD, John Jacob. 1902; 1905. Walking trip near Ann Arbor; everyday personal events in life of high school boy. MiU.

4731 ROSENTHAL, Virginia. 1902. Trip through England, France, Italy, Switzerland, Germany, etc.: sights. NN.

4732 THOMPSON, Aaron J. 1902–1906; 1908–1911; 1915; 1917; 1921–1922. Farming; weather; insurance affairs; local events. NjR.

4733 VAN HORTEN, Bertha. 1902. CNS. WaPS.

4734 WARMOTH, Frank. 1902–1911. CNS. NcU.

4735 CARY, Wilson Miles. 1903. CNS. ViU. *See* 1813, 3163, 3427.

4736 CROW, Carl. [between 1903–1945]. Kept on a trip over the Burma Road. MoU.

4737 DEL MAR, Walter. 1903. Trip to Italy. NN. *See* 4686.

4738 ENSIAN, Mary W. 1903–1904. Personal life and missionary work at Mormon Mission in Tokyo. NN.

4739 FURBER, Robert. 1903. Account of a Northfield, Minn., midshipman in the U.S. Naval Academy at Annapolis. MnHi.

4740 MILLS, William Corliss. 1903. CNS. OHi.

4741 STEVENS, William C. 1903–1921. Personal. MiU.

4742 WEDEMEYER, William Walter. 1903. A trip to British Guiana. MiU.

4743 ALLEN, William Charles. 1904–1937. His travels in the Quaker ministry in Africa, Australia, Barbados, China, Denmark, England, France, Germany, Iceland, Japan, New Zealand, Norway, Philippines, Puerto Rico, etc. PHC.

4744 FOSTER, Anna. 1904. Trip by wagon train from Stillwater, Okla., to Brown Lee country of Ida. IdHi.

4745 GOSS, Mrs. John W. 1904–1909. CNS. ViU. *See* 4666.

4746 SPERANZA, Gino. 1904–1926. CNS. NN.

4747 VAN HOUTEN, G. H. 1904. CNS. WaPS.

4748 VAN WINKLE, Edward. 1904–1916. Professional and business operations of engineer and patent attorney. NjR.

4749 ALVORD, Clarence W. 1905. Trip to southern Ill., relating to the discovery of Cahokia and Kaskaskia records. MnHi.

4750 EMERY family. 1905–1907. Diary of Wilhelmina Emery covering first year of her residence in Los Angeles and of her husband recording a trip by train from Boston to Los Angeles. CLU.

4751 HINSDALE, Dr. Wilbert B. 1905. Trip through British Isles: famous places. MiU.

4752 HOBBS, Prof. William Herbert. 1905; 1913; 1921–1923; 1925. Geologic expeditions to Europe, West Indies, and Pacific Islands. MiU.

4753 HOWELL, William Thompson. 1905–1912. Scrapbook and diary; notes on the Hudson highlanders. NN.

4754 HUSSEY, Ethel Fountain (Mrs. William Joseph). 1905–1912. Domestic and social activities of faculty wife; trip to La Plata, Argentina; astronomical events, especially Halley's comet. MiU.

4755 MAGEE, Abbie Eliza. 1905. Domestic and farm chores; visits; family events; sewing (evidently part done professionally); weather. NjR.

4756 MINIS, Louisa Porter. 1905. A European trip; sightseeing; visits with friends. NcU.

4757 MORLEY, Sylvanus Griswold. 1905–1947. CNS. PPAmS.

4758 NILES, Julia. 1905–1907. Personal items of a resident of Topeka. KHi.

4759 NORTH, Harry M. 1905. Diary of a Methodist Episcopal minister, concerning pastoral duties, church meetings, and local events in Elizabeth City, N.C. NcD.

4760 EZELL, John. 1906. CNS. MoU.

4761 FERGUSSON, Harvey. 1906; 1909; 1917; 1922–1953. Diaries of a N.M. novelist. CU-B.

4762 SCHUYLER, Walter Scribner. 1906–1931. Journal; vols. 18–45 on Cal. mining. CSmH.

4763 BATES, Lucy A. 1907; 1909; 1925–1927; Springfield, Ill., Chicago, New York, London, Paris, Montreux, Rossinieres, Venice, Florence, Rome, Boston. Detailed day to day diaries of a young girl at home, on a European trip, and later as a dancer and dancing teacher in New York. GU.

4764 CRANE, Cora. 1907. CNS. NNC.

4765 DU BOIS, Marguerite Delaware. 1907–1908. Social life in N.Y. city; study; theater; trips to Saratoga, Montreal, etc. NN.

4766 HUNN, Lydia Mary (Williamson). 1907–1908. Recounts visits made to various Friends' Meetings in and about Philadelphia by 19-year old girl. PSC-Hi.

4767 MOORE, David and William. 1907–1908. CNS. MoU.

4768 RANKIN, Emma L. 1907–1908. Personal diary covering the last two years of her life. NcU.

4769 VAN HOUTEN, V. V. 1907; 1910. CNS. WaPS.

4770 WILLISTON, W. C. 1907. CNS. MnRedHi.

4771 ANON. 1908. Trip from Cleveland, Ohio, to Brunswick, Ga. InU-Li.

4772 CLEVELAND, James Longstreet. 1908–1937. Life as a boy in an orphanage; trip to Tex. and Colo.; his opinion of the 1914 Mexican situation; stay in a hospital in Boise, Ida.; dedication of the Mo. Univ. Memorial Tower; life in Providence, Mo.; his farm close by; trip to Mexico City in 1931; press conference with Dean Walter Williams; campaigns for U.S. senator. MoU.

4773 HUSSEY, William Joseph. 1908–1911; 1913–1916; 1918–1920; 1922–1926. Daily routine and personal matters; observatory at Univ. of Mich.; faculty members; trips to So. America and to So. Africa; visits to observatories; diamond and gold mines; people; astronomical observations. MiU. *See* 4754, 4783.

4774 MONTGOMERY, A. T. 1908. Plantations; notes. Ms-Ar.

4775 MOSHER, Eliza. 1908. Sightseeing in Europe. MiU.

4776 NELSON, Julius. 1908; 1910–1911; 1912–1915. Routine of academic work at New Brunswick; study and writing; oyster research in the marsh lands adjoining Barnegat Bay, apparently around the village of Barnegat. NjR.

4777 SHOEMAKER, Rev. J. S. 1908–1917. Includes trip around world in 1910. InGoM.

4778 BERRELL, George. 1909. Theater life of a troupe playing in Tucson. AzTP.

4779 CHANEY, Delia E. (Mrs. George Cahoon). 1909. CNS. MnHi.

4780 HOWE, Prof. Herbert Barber. 1909; 1910. Engagements made and kept; brief comments, chiefly personal, of a Columbia Univ. professor and residence hall director. NNC.

4781 CARR, Julian Shakespeare, and Skinner, B. S. 1910–1911. CNS. NcD. *See* 4797.

4782 FINLEY, Prof. John Houston. 1910–1919. Work on *McClure's Magazine* and as professor at Princeton. NN.

4783 HUSSEY, William Joseph. 1910. Travel diary on trips to the Argentine and Barbados. MiU. *See* 4773.

4784 FEININGER, Karl. 1911–1913. Music lessons; concerts; social life; books; writings. NN.

4785 GREENWELL, C. 1911–1913. Cruise to Philippines and China; daily life and work on shipboard; life in Philippines. NN.

4786 HUNTINGTON, Sarah J. 1911–1917. CNS. OHi.

4787 McCANN, R. J. 1911. A trip by launch to Moose Creek, Gilmore Creek, Fox Gulch, and Goldstream. CCP.

4788 WEYL, Walter Edward. 1911–1913; 1915; 1917–1918. Concerned frequently with his writing: ideas, plans, and outlines for books, articles, plays, etc.; observation of usable material; notes of progress; public response to his work; observations during wartime trips in East Prussia and the Orient. NjR.

4789 ANON. 1912–1913. About the West Side Social Center (since 1920 called the Gladden Community House), Columbus, Ohio. OHi.

4790 COLE, Harry E. 1912–1936. CNS. NIC.

4791 GRAHAM, Marion. 1912. Social engagements and life in N.Y. city; travels. NN.

4792 GUTTERSEN, Granville. 1912. Written while he was at the U.S. Army aviation school in Tex. MnHi.

4793 McILVAIN, Hugh. 1912. Mainly accounts of sightseeing. PSC-Hi.

4794 FREY, Samuel Ludlow. 1913–1914. Kept during his visit to John and Helen Beau, Independence, Kan.; mostly concerning the oil fields. NCooHi.

4795 HAYES, Mary Miller. 1913–1914; 1916; 1918; 1921; 1923; 1928. Travel to Europe, Asia, Japan, and So. America; travel in U.S.A.; travel at North Cape; travel in West Indies and So. America. OFH.

4796 SMITH, Judith. 1913–1915. CNS. OHi.

4797 CARR, Julian S. 1914; 1916. Personal life and associations with friends and relatives. NcD. *See* 4781.

4798 EDMUNDS, Albert J. [1914]? Portending events of WWI. PHi.

4799 FAST, Mrs. Herman J. 1914–1920. CNS (in German). MnHi, microfilm.

4800 GAY, Mrs. Walter. 1914. Kept in France. OClWHi, copy.

4801 LEARNED family. 1914. Conditions in Europe. PHi.

4802 MILES, Emma (Bell). 1914–1915. Search for necessary remunerative work; life in a tuberculosis sanitorium and at home on the mountain; love for all nature. TC, typescript.

4803 ROSENAU, William. 1914. Written while he visited Europe; deals with English Jewry; descriptions of Germany at outbreak of WWI; his impressions of the attitude of the German Jews during crucial days; describes services held in Berlin synagogues. OCAJA.

4804 SHIRAS, Mrs. George, III. 1914–1915. Quiet social life. MiMarqHi.

4805 HAPGOOD, Powers. 1915–1925 (with gaps). Activities as student; trip through western U.S. working in iron mines, coal mines, sugar beet factory, and on a railroad; travels in Pa. and W. Va. studying conditions of miners; working in mines and studying mining conditions in U.S. and Europe. InU-Li.

4806 HIGGINS, Vincent Lafayette. 1915. CNS. WaPS.

4807 LILLARD, Dr. Edward N. 1915–1919. Journal of medical officer of the S.S. *Achilles* in Panama and vicinity. ViU.

4808 WHITLOCK, Brand. 1915–1921. WWI diaries. NNC.

4809 BOURNE, Randolph Silliman. 1916. CNS. NNC.

4810 COTTEN, Capt. Lyman Atkinson. [1916–1919?]. Confidential war diary. NcU.

4811 CUSHING, Anne Moreland. 1916; 1917; 1921; 1923. Brief record of family and social events in San Francisco, Cal. Or.

4812 DAVIS, Capt. Chandler. 1916–1919. Service with 6th Engineers in American Exped. Force in WWI. NN.

4813 DILLENBACK, George P. 1916. Voyage from Long Island to Cork and London: incidents of voyage; WWI. NN.

4814 EDDY, George Sherwood. 1916–1917. Preaching engagements and trip to Europe. NN.

4815 STAPLES, Harold H. 1916–1917. Activities of the destroyer U.S.S. *Allen* in WWI off the coasts of France, Ireland, Great Britain, and Spain. LU, typescript.

4816 HELM, Erskine S. 1917–1926; 1928–1934. CNS. Ms-Ar.

4817 HOUSE, Robert Burton. 1917–1918. Camp during WWI. Nc-Ar.

4818 KEISER, Thoburn D. 1917–1918. WWI diary during service in the American Red Cross Transportation Corps. OHi.

4819 LARIMER, M. Winthrop. 1917–1918. Service on the U.S.S. *Cummings*, Destroyer 44. ViU.

4820 PRATT, Joseph Hyde. n.d. [1917–1918?]. CNS. Nc-Ar.

4821 SWANSON, V. 1917–1918. Diary kept by the "Wildman of the Dry Bay," Alaska, whose body was found by trappers. CSmH, typescript.

4822 WESTLEY, Martin D. 1917–1918. Brief record of camps and assignments of a medical officer during WWI, 1914–1918; letters from Ft. Riley, Camp Merritt, France, and England to Mrs. Westley and sons. NdHi.

4823 BABER, Adin. 1918. The Red Cross Transport in France, Germany, and Belgium. ICHi.

4824 CUTLER, Dr. Condict W., Jr. 1918–1919. Record of his war service; entries are factual. NNC.

4825 DYMENT, Prof. Colin. [1918–1919?]. Kept while he was a Red Cross searcher with the 91st Division in WWI. CSt.

4826 EVANS, Mrs. Rosalie Caden. 1918–? Experiences at San Pedro, Coxtocan, Puebla, Mexico, where her British husband had a hacienda, and where she was murdered by the agrarian revolutionists in 1924. ViU.

4827 LONG, George V. Z. 1918. His experiences as YMCA secretary with the 89th Division, A.E.F., in France. PHi.

4828 TOMB, Capt. W. V. [1918?]. WWI diary kept while he commanded the U.S.S. *Maumee* and the U.S.S. *Davis*, consisting chiefly of records of citations, notices of awards, addresses, etc. NcU.

4829 WESTERMANN, William Linn. 1918–1919. Kept at the Paris Peace Conference by staff member of the American Commission to negotiate peace as a specialist on Western Asia. NNC, typescript.

4830 WHITCOMB, David. 1918–1919. CNS. WaU.

4831 YATES, Katherine M. 1918. A 70-day cruise from San Francisco to the Orient on a Panama Mail Steamship Co. vessel. CU-B.

4832 BROWN, Alma McLain Coleman. 1919. North Ga. Housekeeper for Corra Harris, Ga. author; tells of her life at "In the Valley," Mrs. Harris' home at Rydal, Ga., and her opinion of Mrs. Harris. GU.

4833 DERSTINE, William A. 1919–1922. Near East Relief. InGoM.

4834 GRIMES, Mary E. 1919; 1941. Kept while she was in France as a canteen worker and entertainer; also an account of a trip to Ill. and Cal. OkU.

4835 HERTZLER, Silas. 1919–1922. Experiences of a Near East Relief worker. InGoM.

4836 HILL, Frederick Parsell. 1919–1950. Brief entries by a N.Y. architect. NjR.

4837 HYDE, Henry M. 1919–1931. CNS. ViU, typescript.

4838 LANGE, Dietrich. 1919–1920. Trips to Bowstring and Big Fork rivers, to Itasca Cnty. and to Oregon Trail. MnHi.

4839 WARYE, John. 1919–1922. Experiences of a Near East Relief worker. InGoM.

4840 LAMB, George Woodward. 1920; 1944; 1946. Personal. PPCHi.

4841 LONGSTREET, James C. [1920–193?]? Observations on American life in the 1920's and 1930's. MoU.

4842 LOWRY, Alfred. 1920. Travel in Germany and middle European states; description of home at Meidling, Austria, for children who suffered rickets as result of malnutrition during and after WWI. PSC-Hi, typescript.

4843 MILLER, O. O. 1920. Trip into southern Russia in connection with Russian famine relief. InGoM.

4844 MORRIS, William M. 1920–1925. Daily activities; religious affiliations; weather conditions in St. Cloud. MnHi.

4845 CURLEY, Most Rev. Michael J. 1921. Episcopal diary kept by the successive chancellors of the Archdiocese of Baltimore since 1921. MdBDio.

4846 SHELDON, Henry Davidson. 1921–1932. Valuable for history of Univ. of Ore. OrU.

4847 KELLY, John. ca. 1922. Life on a San Diego Cnty. ranch. CSmH.

4848 REDDING, William Foster. 1922–1923; 1937–1939; 1941–1953. A literate daily record showing a relatively broad range of activities and interests typical of a farmer of the period. NjR.

4849 ANON. 1923–1924. Kept at Staplehurst, England; mentions D. H. Lawrence; visits to London; entertainments; concerts. NN.

4850 BROWN, Albert Emerson. 1923–1927. High school days in Detroit; writing, religion, and mission work, comments on articles he wrote for religious magazines. MiU.

4851 HAYES, Mary Sherman. 1923. Personal. OFH.

4852 McCULLY, Newton A. 1923–1924. Correspondence; incidents in the daily life of admiral of the fleet; orders; officers' social calls; promotions; other routine matters. NcU.

4853 LOTTO, Frederick S. 1924. World cruise; sightseeing. NN. *See* 4728.

4854 JONAZ, George and Ann. 1926. Trip from Liverpool to Philadelphia. NN.

4855 RICHMOND, Bessie. 1926. Diary while she was on a West Indies cruise. NcU.

4856 SIBLEY, James L., Jr. Jan.–Aug., 1926. Liberia. Diary kept by Educational Advisor to the Liberian government, re schools, people, customs, outlook in Liberia in 1926. GU.

4857 ANON. 1927. Semi-invalid in N.Y.; Central Park; his health; news of day. NN.

4858 DE FOREST, Henry Pelouze. 1927; 1928; 1931; 1932; 1935. Vacations. NIC.

4859 CUSHING, Stella Marek. 1928–1934. European tour, mostly Slavic countries, collecting folksongs and dances for lectures and concerts in U.S. NN.

4860 JOHNSON, E. B. 1928–1929. Trips to Fla. via Tex. and to Cal. OkU.

4861 VANDENBURG, Mrs. Arthur H. 1928–1948. Covers years spent in Washington, D.C. MiU-C.

4862 ANON. 1929–1937. Social and personal activities in Pa., Tenn., Atlantic City, N.Y., and N.Y. suburbs. NN.

4863 MILLER, Rebecca T. 1929. Train trip to All American Friends Conference, Oskaloosa, Iowa, and return by automobile; includes notes on ideas presented by various speakers at conference. PSC-Hi.

4864 BLAKESLEE, Fred. 1931–1938. World travels collecting material for his books on costumes and uniforms. NN.

4865 CULP, Cordie Jacob. 1932. A European-Mediterranean tour with his wife; short visits in France, Italy, Greece, and the Levant. NjR.

4866 THOMPSON, Rev. Elias Wortman. 1932; 1934; 1944. His pastoral activities as pastor of 1st Reformed Church, Hastings-on-Hudson. NjR.

4867 CONNAWAY, Dr. John W. 1933. His attitude toward political and economic trends. MoU.

4868 RICKARD, Chauncey. 1933–1935. Daily local events and personal memoirs. NSchoOsfm.

4869 SPERANZA, Florence. 1935. Kept in Italy, covers political and social conditions. NN.

4870 BREED, Clara Mona. 1936–1937. Visit to France and England; places; sights; personal. NN. *See* 4876.

4871 KAYE, Colin C. 1937. Visit to Europe: sightseeing. NN.

4872 TURLINGTON, Dr. Marcellus M. 1937 + . CNS. OkU; now in possession of widow.

4873 WOODBRIDGE, Frederick J. E. 1937–1940. Daily happenings, usually very personal. NNC.

4874 CROSS, Prof. Arthur Lyon. 1938–1940. Comments on contemporaneous international situation; trip to England; events at Univ. of Mich.; talk with Kerensky. MiU.

4875 NICHOLS, Marjorie. 1938–1939. Childhood in New Rochelle, N.Y.; home, school, amusements. NN.

4876 BREED, Clara Mona. 1939. Kept in England: ocean trip to N.Y., outbreak of WWII. NN. *See* 4870.

4877 ZOETE, Beryl de. 1939–1940. Observations, events, and experiences in London at the outbreak of WWII by a friend of orientalist Arthur D. Waley and member of a circle which included many authors and other noted individuals. NjR. *See* 4889.

4878 BROWN, Ralph Minthorne. 1941. Trip along both coasts of So. America prior to outbreak of WWII; ornithological notes; description; personalities in Cristobal, Panama Canal, Salinas, Callao, Arica, Tocopella, Valparaiso, Viña del Mar, Santiago, Antofagasta. ViU.

4879 JOHNSTON, R. Wickliffe P., Jr. 1941–1942. On duty in the Western Desert with the British 8th Army, in American Field Service. ViU.

4880 SIMPSON, Lt. Carter Berkeley. 1941–1944. Experience during the Bataan and Corregidor campaigns and as a Japanese prisoner. ViU.

4881 MORLEY, John Coffinberry. 1942–1944. Letters and journal describing activities before surrender of Bataan to Japanese. CLU, typescript.

4882 OLIVER, Capt. William P. 1942–1944. Life in Japanese prisoner-of-war camp in Philippines. MiU, typescript.

4883 SMITH, Philip G. 1942–1943. Diary of military service: troop ship from Honolulu to Australia, air battles with Japanese, bombing New Guinea shipping, air raids in Australia, Australian soldiers and civilians. MiU.

4884 SVIHRA, Lt. Col. Albert. 1942–1944. Siege of Corregidor and his experiences as a prisoner-of-war of the Japanese. ViU.

4885 WEEKS, Marian E. 1942–1944. Experiences as air raid warden in N.Y. city. NN.

4886 ASPINWALL, Francis H. 1943. Log of a journey by train from Rome, N.Y., to Dawson Creek, Canada; thence by automobile to Whitehorse. CU-B.

4887 MARVIN, William Richard. 1944. Missions against the Japanese. ViU.

4888 LANCEY, Thomas Crosby. ca. 1946. Cruise of the *Dale*. Original, CLU.

4889 ZOETE, Beryl de. 1954. Voyage from England to Brazil, via Portugal. NjR. *See* 4877.

4890 ANON. Extract of a journal of the King's ship *Triumphant*, commanded by M. Le Ms. de Vaudreil, chef d'escadre and commander of the royal and military order of St. Louis. DLC, facsimile.

4891 ANON. CNS. MnManHi.

4892 ANON. CNS. C.H. McCormick Family Papers. ICMcCHi.

4893 ANON. Journal of the original surveys of the Ohio Co. OMC.

4894 ANON. Prices and character of goods, names of customers, and methods of doing business, with occasional weather records and personal diaries. WHi.

4895 ANON. Journal of the United Society, an organization of Methodist ministers at Chillicothe, Ohio. WHi.

4896 ANON. (several persons). About Ohio, especially the Miami region. WHi.

4897 ANON. Voyage from Western Islands to Cape Verde Islands in ship *Atlas*. MH.

4898 ANON. Account of the first journey of the first company of Single Brethren traveling to N.C. Nc-Ar.

4899 ANON. (but evidently before 1780). Travel from Salem, N.C., to Lititz, Pa. NcWsM.

4900 ANON. Relating especially to the period of the American Revolution, the late 18th century, and the early 19th century. MiU-C.

4901 ALLEN, George T. Written between Ft. Vancouver and Ft. Factory. WaSp.

4902 ARCHULETA, Don Juan Andres. CNS. Tx.

4903 ATKINS, Q. F. Kept while he was among the Wyandot Indians. OClWHi.

4904 BEAUREGARD, G. K. Mexican war journal. MoSHs.

4905 BIXBY, Jotham. The early development of the city of Long Beach, Cal. CSmH.

4906 BLAKE, William. 18??–1910. Experiences and incidents in Ariz. mines, trips to Baja Cal., missions in Ariz. and Cal., vegetation, etc. AzTP.

4907 BRUFF, Capt. J. Goldsborough. CNS. CU-B, typescript. *See* 2459.

4908 BRUNSON, Rev. Alfred. Journals and letter books of a pioneer Methodist rider and Indian agent. WHi.

4909 BURROWES, Rev. George. CNS. CSaT.

4910 BYNUM, William Preston. CNS. NcU.

4911 CAIGNY, Don Mayeul de. By former abbot of Bahía, Brazil; written during his retirement at St. Leo Abbey, Fla., and containing family records, pictures, documents and letters (in French). FSIA.

4912 CALL, Gen. (Richard Keith?). A portion of his journal. FJHi.

4913 CARPENTER, Orlando E. Civil War diary of soldier with Co. E, 4th Mich. Cav. Army life, foraging parties, battles, morale, and capture of Jefferson Davis. MiU-H.

4914 CARY, Archibald, CNS. ViU.

4915 CARY, Sidney Carr. CNS. ViU.

4916 CHANNING, William Ellery. Notebooks, journals, with poems and prose writings. MH.

4917 CHOUTEAU, Auguste. Describing the founding and settlement of St. Louis (in French). PPM.

4918 CLARK, William Adolphus. Personal. MH. *See* 3168.

4919 COSTANSO, Miguel. Trips to Cal. (in Spanish). MH.

4920 DALY, Charles Patrick. Trip from Paris to London and travels in British Isles. NN. *See* 2769, etc.

4921 DAVIS, Washington. CNS. Tx.

4922 DENNY, Ebenezer. CNS. WHi.

4923 DERING, Thomas. Sea Trade. Custom House, N.Y. city.

4924 DUERST, Mathias. CNS. WHi.

4925 DUNBAR, William. CNS. PPAmS.

4926 DUNCAN, Joseph. CNS. IHS.

4927 EDWARDS, M. B. Journal of the Mexican War. MoSHs.

4928 EELLS, Jeremiah. Imprisonment in N.Y. city. NN.

4929 ELY, Edward. CNS. MnHi.

4930 FAIRFIELD, George. CNS. WHi.

4931 FILSON, John. Two voyages from the falls of Ohio to Post St. Vincent on Wabash River. WHi. *See* 878?

4932 FITCH, John. CNS. CtY. *See* 854?

4933 FRANCL, Joseph. Personal. CU-B.

4934 FRAZER, Rev. Thomas. CNS. CSaT.

4935 FROST, D. M. Journals of Mexican War. MoSHs.

4936 GARDNER, A. V. Record of attempts to get Minnesotans to ship grain to N.Y. MnHi.

4937 GIDDINGE, Andrew R. CNS. MeHi.

4938 GIDDINGS, David. CNS. WHi.

4939 GILISON, G. R. Mexican War. MoSHs.

4940 HALL, Maggie. Crossing the plains (Southern route) when she was about nine years old. CU-B.

4941 HALLIDIE, Andrew Smith. CNS. CHi.

4942 HARVEY, Alexander. CNS. VtHi.

4943 HAWXHURST, James. Events of author's farms in N.Y., Long Island, and Flushing. Includes accounts. NN.

4944 HEART, Capt. Jonathan. Journal at Revolutionary army headquarters. OClWHi.

4945 HODGE, Orlando. CNS. OClWHi.

4946 HOUGH, Franklin B. CNS. N.

4947 HUBARD, Edwin W. Diaries and account books. NcU.

4948 HUNT, Mrs. Memucan. CNS. Tx.

4949 HUNT, Rev. Timothy Dwight. CNS. CSaT. *See* 2163.

4950 HUNTER, R. H. CNS. Tx, typescript.

4951 IMOBDEN, Frank H. Diary of a capt., Co. H, 18th Va. Cavalry, C.S.A. Wr-Ar, typed copy.

4952 JOHNSON, Madison Y. Civil War prison diary. ICHi. *See* 4387.

4953 JOHNSON, Rev. Neil. CNS. OrHi.

4954 JOHNSON, P.K. CNS. MnManHi.

4955 JOHNSTON, John. Journals with data on Tecumseh and a brief Shawnee vocabulary. WHi. *See* 1268.

4956 JONES, Carlton. The trip west from Great Salt Lake to Ringgold, Cal. MoU.

4957 KEARNY, Ravaud. Farm notes, receipts, and prescriptions; mentions various wagers laid upon the success of the British army. NN.

4958 KELPIUS, ———? CNS. PPG. *See* 29?

4959 KENNAN, W. H. Trip from Mexico, Mo., to Charleston, W. Va. MoU.

4960 KILMER, Joyce. CNS. Joyce Kilmer Memorial Library, Campion Jesuit High School, Prairie du Chien, Wis.

4961 KIMBALL, Frank A. CNS. CSdHi.

4962 LAW, Samuel A. Lumbering, farming, and sheep-raising projects; community, civic, and cultural enterprises; and local, state, and national politics. N.

4963 LAWLER, Davis B. CNS. OCUHi. *See* 2067.

4964 LAWTON, Alexander Robert. CNS. NcU.

4965 LOGAN, Charles L. CNS. MnRHi.

4966 MARSH, Rev. Cutting. Journals and letter books. WHi.

4967 MARSH, John. CNS. MnManHi.

4968 MARSHALL, Christopher (?). Personal, business. Nc-Ar.

4969 MARSTON, Otis. CNS. CSmH.

4970 McCOLLAM, Ellen E. (Mrs. Andrew). CNS. NcU. *See* 2130.

4971 McFEELY, G. Soldier; military, war of 1812. NHi.

4972 MENZIES, John. Trip from Philadelphia to Scotland. PHi.

4973 MERRILL, Isaac Watts. CNS. MHa.

4974 MOORE, William G. Libby Prison during the Civil War. Copies in WaPS.

4975 MORSE, Samuel F. B. CNS. DLC.

4976 NARVAEZ, José Maria. Diary of the second pilot of the armada sent to explore the coast of Cal. to 61 degree latitude. CLU-C.

4977 NOLAND, William. Diaries and account books kept by Commissioner of Public Buildings, Washington, D.C. ViU.

4978 OWENS, Isaac. CNS. CU. *See* 2707.

4979 PADEN, Thomas. Diary of a Presbyterian minister. CSaT.

4980 PAIGE, Harriet Bower. Stories of old Schenectady families and diagrams of Schenectady streets, lots, and houses. NSchHi.

4981 PARSONS, Rev. William. Almanac jottings; sermons book. NN.

4982 PEASE, Seth. CNS. OClWHi, transcripts.

4983 PHILLIPS, Elmira. Diary of a Methodist missionary in Ore. OrSaW.

4984 PIERSON, Edward A. U.S. Navy surgeon killed in line of duty. NjHi.

4985 POILLETT, (Victor E. or Louis). CNS. PWbWhgs.

4986 PRAY, Otis A. CNS. MnHi.

4987 PRESTON, Leander A. Overland trip from Strawberry Point, Iowa, to Yuba City, Cal. CSmH.

4988 PUTNAM, Gen. Rufus. CNS. OMC.

4989 RANEY, Ann. CNS. Tx.

4990 READING, Pierson B. CNS. C. *See* 2169.

4991 ROGERS, Robert. CNS. PPAmS.

4992 ROWE, Judith. Notebook used in teaching school, containing a list of her pupils, attendance, notes, quotations, and diary. MeHi.

4993 SAVAGE, C. R. Kept by the official photographer of the driving of the Golden Spike at Promontory, Utah. Photostat in NbOUpm.

4994 SEYMOUR, Isaac Gurdon. Civil War. MiU-C.

4995 SMITH, David Eugene. CNS. NNC.

4996 SOULE, A. C. CNS. MnManHi.

4997 SPATES, Samuel. Diary about a trip from Sandy Lake, Minn., to La Pointe, Wis. and back. MnHi.

4998 STEPHENS, James. Raising funds and volunteers for Fenian movement; John Mitchell and other Fenians in U.S.A. NN.

4999 STERNE, Adolphus. CNS. Tx.

5000 STEVENSON, Rev. Robert. Diary of pioneer Presbyterian minister. CSaT.

5001 STILLMAN, James. CNS. NNC.

5002 SUMNER, Charles Pinckney. CNS. MH.

5003 TAYLOR, William. CNS. CBPac. *See* 1994.

5004 THOMAS, W. K. Journey across plains over Bridger Trail to Mont. MtHi.

5005 THOMPKINS, Edward A. Expedition to Cal. via Salt Lake and Fremont's South Pass. CSmH.

5006 THOREAU, Henry David. CNS. CSmH.

5007 TOMPSON, Joseph. Includes copies of poems by his brother. MH.

5008 TOWNSEND, John. CNS. NjCmHi.

5009 TRUEHEART, James Lawrence. Diary of a member of the Mier expedition. TxGR.

5010 TYLER, J. B. History of an old wagon road and railroad. CSbCL.

5011 VAN METER, ———. Motor trip from Mo. to Cal. and back. MoU.

5012 WALDEN, Edward H. CNS. WWauHi.

5013 WARD, Samuel. Travel in France and Germany, especially Paris and Frankfurt. NN.

5014 WARNER, William. Operations in Louisiana; Red River Expedition. CSmH.

5015 WASHBURN, Gov. Cadwallader C. CNS. WHi.

5016 WEIDENSALL, Robert. CNS. ICGw.

5017 WHITE, Orland Emile, Journal of the Mulford expedition to the Amazon. ViU.

5018 WHITTAKER, William. CNS. Wv-Ar.

5019 WILLIAMS, Stephen. His captivity in Canada. MDeeP.

5020 WILSON, W. E. Diary of service in the Confederate Army. ScU.

5021 WISWALL, Rev. John. Diary and letters. MeHi.

5022 WYLIE, Rev. Richard. CNS. CSaT.